CAMBRIDGE LATIN AMERICAN STUDIES

GENERAL EDITOR
MALCOLM DEAS

ADVISORY COMMITTEE
WERNER BAER   MARVIN BERNSTEIN
AL STEPAN   BRYAN ROBERTS

36

COFFEE IN COLOMBIA, 1850–1970
An economic, social, and political history

To my mother
To the memory of my father

Coffee in Colombia, 1850–1970

An economic, social, and political history

MARCO PALACIOS
Centro de Estudios Internacionales,
El Colegio de México, Mexico City

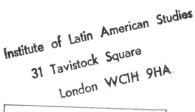

CAMBRIDGE UNIVERSITY PRESS

Cambridge
London   New York   New Rochelle
Melbourne   Sydney

Published by the Press Syndicate of the University of Cambridge
The Pitt Building, Trumpington Street, Cambridge CB2 1RP
32 East 57th Street, New York, NY 10022, USA
296 Beaconsfield Parade, Middle Park, Melbourne 3206, Australia

First published 1980

Printed in Great Britain
at the University Press, Cambridge

Library of Congress Cataloguing in Publication Data
Palacios, Marco.
Coffee in Colombia, 1850–1970.
(Cambridge Latin American studies; 36)
Bibliography: p.
Includes index.
1. Coffee trade – Colombia – History. 2. Colombia –
Economic conditions. 3. Colombia – Social conditions.
4. Colombia – History. I. Title.
HD9199.C62P34   338.1'7'37109861   78-73251
ISBN 0 521 22204 4

Contents

Tables

Figures

Maps

Preface

The aim of this book is to describe and explain the conditions under which
Colombia, by becoming an important mono-exporting country of a product
characteristic of tropical agriculture, coffee, managed to link its economy
solidly with the world market. At the same time the book attempts to
show the full effects of such an integration on the structure of contemporary
Colombia.

My purpose is a study of the changes which the diffusion of coffee
cultivation in Colombia and its hegemonic role in Colombian exports brought
about in production, and in the class structure, in the balance of regional
forces and in parts of the machinery of state.

In undertaking this task I have found particularly appropriate the advice
of Karl Marx to those seeking to understand the situation in Spain during
the middle of the last century: reject the fallacious belief that national
life can be followed in the 'almanacs of the Court', in 'the activities of
that which we are accustomed to call the state'; instead 'discover the resources and the strength of such countries in their provincial and local
organization'.

Great importance is given in this book to the links between the world
market and the rhythm and direction of regional and local changes. It is
argued that such links were maintained and even strengthened without the
presence and involvement of the *central* state. The first five chapters show
how coffee renewed the vitality of the regional picture, with its demographic
and ethnic idiosyncrasies and peculiarities, with the blessings and curses
inflicted on the inhabitants by the particular environment. It also shows
the success or failure of the different regions in adapting and assimilating,
with the least cost, the minor changes or major transformations brought
by external trade.

The detailed study of the hacienda system serves to emphasize – paradoxically – the stability of this society and of its traditional peasant
economies. If these did not succumb in the face of the 'thrust' of the
haciendas, they were ultimately controlled and exploited economically
by the large export traders, a control more evident and also more necessary
in the areas without haciendas in the west of the country. The power and
importance of the monopsonists is described in chapter 7.

The revisions which I propose in chapters 8 and 9 concerning the sociopolitical aspects of the economic occupation and private appropriation of uncultivated lands during the *antioqueño* avalanche that rolled over the vast uninhabited and isolated spaces of the central cordillera indicate the urgent need to go beyond economic analysis narrowly defined. In effect this revision is not only of the sources and some of the legends derived from the biassed use of these sources, but a wholly new look at the processes involved and the resulting society. I find that elements such as municipal patriotism, *gamonalismo* (bossism) and legal chicanery, all associated with an endemic violence and the insecurities peculiar to frontier societies (insecurity of title to property, for example), are phenomena that must be integrated with purely economic analyses of the market.

If it is true that agrarian society manifested a dynamism of its own which has not yet been fully recognized, and which is expressed in an authentic regional and local autonomy, the advice of Marx cannot be taken too far. From President Núñez in 1880 up until the Liberal reforms of the 1930s, an ideology surfaced intermittently which called for a central state, for a macroeconomic policy with well-defined rules of the game, for that 'scientific peace' that might at least check the further impoverishment of a poor country and check the fiscal haemorrhages of a miserable and perpetually indebted state.

Five chapters are devoted to the description of the trajectory and vicissitudes of this centralizing project. In the sixth I re-examine the links between the exporting bourgeoisie and political power, through a brief study of inflation, monetary policy, and export taxation between 1880 and 1903. In the seventh I examine the period which I call a return to *'laissez-faire'*, which culminated *politically* although not *economically* in 1930. The last two chapters, the tenth and eleventh, are written in a perspective which illustrates the interactions between the spontaneity and stability of the peasant economy and the requirements of economic growth, urbanization, and the industrialization process. Finally, I analyse the 'modernization' of Colombian coffee cultivation and its relations with the world market in coffee. The scope of the analysis of agrarian problems has to be widened to include a better evaluation of the role of peasant economies and societies, and the functions of state policy. The analysis of the penetration of capitalism into the countryside can only then be made more realistic. It does not seem to me that peasant societies tend to disappear as automatically as is supposed, or that state policy in the agrarian sector is a rational and coherent whole which brings about this destruction in order to ensure the capitalist development of the country in question.

In the pages which I devote to the Federación Nacional de Cafeteros de Colombia I do not intend to formulate any general explanation of the nature or the role of the Colombian state. I believe that an analysis of state power that concentrates on economic policy only explains one area of the relations between the state and the groups and classes who explicitly demand certain orientations and decisions. Even more, coffee policy is only one of the elements – not always the most important, as is believed – in general economic policy. I wish to call the reader's attention to these obvious limitations in my description.

I believe that this book demonstrates the immense wealth of unexplored sources on which we can draw to write with greater understanding about Colombian history. There is no reason to suppose that the same abundance of local, private, or even national sources does not exist for other potential areas of research.

I have consciously avoided a systematic quantitative treatment, not so much because of my own ignorance of quantitative methods – an ignorance easily corrected in this age of computers – but because of the incongruence and the slight reliability offered by all Colombian statistical publications at all times. That which for an economist is a 'strong' statistical treatment of a series that proves the truth of a model, can for an historian often be a monstrous falsification. The reader must recognize from the start the weakness of all the statistics in this book, including those based on recent publications. They all have nevertheless some indicative value. The tables elaborated on the basis of hacienda accounts must be used with caution when making generalizations. Even so I defend their relative value: I am convinced of their internal consistency, and they agree with other, qualitative sources, often much more trustworthy.

Acknowledgements

For the last six years I have been able to dedicate myself exclusively to the study of my country's history, and to carrying out the research necessary to write this book. This was primarily made possible by the organizations which supported me. A grant from St Antony's College allowed me to spend three years enjoying and, I hope, profiting from Oxonian peace. The two years of research in Colombia were made possible by financial aid for this project from the Ford Foundation, the Universidad de los Andes, Bogotá, and the Corporación para el Fomento de la Investigatión (CORP). Within these organizations, the late John Farrell, Fernando Cepeda, and Miguel Urrutia showed a special interest in my work. The last year of my stay in England was made possible by the Latin American Research Fellowship 1977–8, awarded me by the Institute of Latin American Studies, University of London. I am grateful for its cordial and studious atmosphere, presided over by Professor John Lynch.

If a history is its sources, some of the most valuable in this book were only made available for my use by the generosity of those in Bogotá and Medellín who gave me access to their family archives: Sra Maria Carrizoza de Umaña and Alberto Umaña Carrizoza in Bogotá, and in Medellín the late Don Luis Ospina Vásquez, Juan Manuel Ospina, Miguel Robin, and Dr Fernando Díaz.

The presence of a stranger in public offices, especially when this lasts for some weeks, is rightly regarded as an intrusion. This was not so in my case and I owe a debt of gratitude to the patience and collaboration of Sr Eduardo Herrera, Registrar of the Oficina de la Mesa, and to his secretaries, as well as to the staffs of the Oficina de Registro de Fredonia and of the Hacienda Jonás, Fredonia. The Directors of the following libraries: the Biblioteca Nacional, Biblioteca Luis Angel Arango del Banco de la República, Biblioteca de la Federación Nacional de Cafeteros, and the Library of the International Coffee Organization, London, namely Sra Pilar Moreno de Angel, Dr Jaime Duarte French, Sra Clemencia Fajardo and Mr C. P. R. Dubois respectively, and the staff of the Archivo Nacional de Colombia, also facilitated my research. Dr Eutiquio Martínez and Dr Jorge Quintero helped me to obtain access to the archives of the Ministerio de Trabajo and of the Caja Agraria. In the Fundación Antioqueña para los Estudios Sociales (FAES) Clemencia Ocampo and Constanza Toro, with their knowledge of the Ospina Archive, helped to lighten immensely a task which, without them, would have been much more prolonged and arduous.

Sr Benigno Galindo helped to give me a greater understanding of the world of the Viotá peasant and Señores Dolcey Garcés Molina and Miguel de Narváez Vargas, owners of coffee haciendas in Cundinamarca and Tolima, were generous and patient enough to explain to me their opinions about the system and the life of the hacienda.

My biggest debt is to Don Luis Ospina Vásquez for his hospitality in Medellín and on his coffee hacienda in Venecia. During the two months spent researching in Antioquia I enjoyed a steady dialogue with Don Luis on many of the themes which appear in this book. To him I owe a good deal, for stimulating me to proceed with my research, for granting me access to his own archives, and for introducing me to others.

This book is based on my doctoral thesis presented in 1977 at the University of Oxford. Mr Lawrence Whitehead, political scientist of Nuffield College, Oxford, one of my examiners, considered it both unnecessary and difficult to accept my arguments in chapter 11 of this book. As this was not the opinion of other specialists, I have decided to introduce the same arguments here with some formal modifications designed to clarify doubts that might arise for the English-speaking reader. Dr Christopher Abel and Dr Alan Gilbert of the University of London also made valuable comments on the thesis; Professor Maria Isaura Pereira de Queiroz of the University of São Paulo and Professor Gabriel Tortella Cáceres of the University of Madrid made certain observations which prompted me to dare to insert some more general questions which help, perhaps, to establish comparisons of the case I present, with others.

Mrs Rosemary Thorp of the Institute of Economics and Statistics, Oxford, made pertinent suggestions to me, in particular concerning the economic arguments.

This English version has been the result of the patient work of Paul Cammack, Mike McKinley, Graham Sharp, and Malcolm Deas, who also corrected and revised the completed version. To Malcolm Deas I owe a special debt for his abiding intellectual stimulus, which allowed me to concentrate for so long on one subject, as well as making it possible for me to write a book, and not just a thesis. During these six years, he has been more than a supervisor: a friend. Both in Colombia and in Oxford I received the support and understanding of my wife Alicia Puyana de Palacios. I hope that, on handing this manuscript over to the publishers, she will be liberated, as much as I, from 'coffee'. There is no single argument in this book that we have not discussed together.

M.P.

1. The Colombian export economy in the second half of the nineteenth century

The way towards 'civilization'

Judging from its limited participation in international trade, Colombia during the nineteenth century was one of the poorest countries of Latin America, with a backward and stagnating economy. Nevertheless, the size of Colombia's exports has never really given an indication of the extent of economic activity in the country. Historically, a large section of the economy has been relatively isolated from the international trade and its accompanying cycles of booms and busts. For example, the sharp fall in gold exports between 1600 and 1650 did not lead to a similar depression of the internal market. The latter, on the contrary, showed signs of dynamism.[1] Again, in 1884 during a marked contraction in the export market, Salvador Camacho Roldán (one of the most distinguished economists of the time) calculated that the value of the agricultural produce sold for internal consumption — excluding subsistence agriculture — was 120 million pesos, over twelve times the value of agricultural exports, which then amounted to 10 million pesos.[2] Even adding the figures for gold exports, the coefficient of total Colombian exports was rarely over 10 per cent.[3] The one period which seems to have been an exception to the rule was the first half of the 1870s, when the export economy began to expand.

The low export coefficient was certainly the result of the Colombian economy's isolation from the flow of capital, manpower, and technology from Europe to the temperate zones of the world.

A straightforward quantitative history of Colombia's exports is still not possible. Nevertheless, Camacho's crude calculations should be accepted, not least because Camacho's overall observations correspond with other nineteenth-century views of economic growth. Classical and neo-classical economists, and even Marx and Engels, shared the view that exclusion from the international stream impeded economic growth. With the benefit of hindsight, one can see that the imperialist epoch and its philosophy of trade did not lead to untrammelled growth, and although no one would suggest that Colombia could have achieved higher rates of growth if it had followed an autarkic model of development, the precise role of trade as an agent of growth is now much more disputed.[4] The influence exerted by the theory of comparative advantage on the ideologies, value systems, and

1

economic thinking that lay behind the free-trade reforms carried out in nearly all the Latin American countries is well known, as are social and political conflicts.[5]

The expected benefits of participation in the international market offered the nascent and struggling commercial bourgeoisie of the Granadine Confederation an incentive that both corresponded with old ideals of the Independence period and provided a means of its surviving as the ruling class of a developing nation. Crudely stated, a country had either to export or sink into barbarism. No word was used as often or as emphatically as 'civilization', that century's synonym for 'economic development'. 'Civilization' meant free trade and free trade became a science with which to analyse reality. It was seen as the only means of doing away with the archaic stigma of colonialism. Colombians aspired to overcome what they saw as their semi-barbarous state by joining the international system there in the making.

Although the Liberals dominated the free-trade period (1847–86), not all Liberals were free-traders nor all free-traders Liberals. During the reform era of 1847–54, the Liberal faction led by General Jose María Obando (an old *santanderista*), defended what was popularly referred to as *la protección* (protectionism). Towards the end of the free-trade period, Rafael Núñez, himself a statesman of Liberal origins, undertook the most formidable and systematic nineteenth-century attack on free-trade ideology, all in the name of a more modern Liberalism.[6]

In the Conservative camp Julio Arboleda, Mariano Ospina Rodríguez, and José Eusebio Caro were all partisans of free trade.[7] Nevertheless, Liberals and Conservatives put different political interpretations on the role of free trade in society. For the free-trade Liberals (known as *gólgotas*), the principles of free trade were inseparable from the political postulates associated with the democratic radicalism of the European revolutions of 1848. The Conservatives in turn, as first represented by Arboleda, Ospina, and Caro, saw free trade as compatible with a hierarchical political and social structure in the Spanish tradition, capable of republican expression.

It is important to note that there were limitations to *gólgota* domination during the free-trade period. Their political hegemony lasted only the ten years from the coup of 1867 (with its subsequent state trial of General Mosquera) to the end of the civil war of 1876, when the *independiente* Liberal faction led by Núñez began its ascent. Furthermore, during the lifetime of the Federation, the support for the *gólgotas* was never more than regional, heavily concentrated in Cundinamarca.[8] The two sovereign states of Antioquia and Tolima, centres of Conservative resistance during these years, openly rejected the ultra-liberal tenets of the national constitution of 1863 in the drafting of their own local constitutions.[9]

Coinciding with the mid-century reforms, there began a succession of agricultural export cycles of short- and medium-term duration. These proved beyond doubt that there existed a certain internal mobility of resources within the Colombian economy. These movements are dealt with in more detail in chapters 2, 3, and 7, but it is useful to mention a few cases now. For example, the capital accumulated by the mining and commercialization of *antioqueño* gold made its way to the centre of the country, and during the 1850s played an important role in the investments made in Ambalema, the main tobacco-producing region. At the end of the century, *antioqueño* capital was helping to develop coffee production in the south-western part of the department, as well as cattle in the Lower Cauca region and on the Atlantic coast.

The inter-regional migration of labour was more restricted. Nevertheless, in each of the three regions which developed coffee production at the end of the century, that is the north-east (Santanderes), the centre and south-east (Boyacá–Cundinamarca–Tolima), and the west (Antioquia), the labour supply remained elastic except during times of armed conflict. One last point: the distribution of land responded adequately to the needs of the export economy. The process was carried out by land sales (in which mortgages were very much in evidence) and by the concessions in and sales of public lands.

Indeed, the very ability of the internal productive structure to respond to the demands and fluctuations of the external market was a clear indication of the capitalist development which was getting under way. After all, in the thirty years after 1847 there were three distinct shifts in investment, first to tobacco, then to indigo and quinine, and finally to coffee, each of which demanded the mobilization of capital and the organization of land and labour on a scale which was by no means inconsiderable for a country whose economic resources were modest even by Latin American standards.

The relative, and even surprising, mobility of capital described above occurred in a very restricted environment. Colombia was essentially an agrarian society. The techniques of production were still so primitive that savings generated by the most important sector of the economy were very scant. In these conditions the opportunities for productive investment were limited, both in size and in possible direction.

The transport bottleneck

From the middle of the century the allocation of available resources depended on comparative international advantage. But the geographical location of the centres of production still required social capital investments (for example in transport) before their products could become competitive. The problem was that the capital was not available locally. Partial solutions to this problem were found, in that Colombia's isolation from foreign capital was not absolute. In the mid 1850s the rise in tobacco exports attracted a small group of foreign investors, most of them small businessmen in their country of origin, although some had the backing of grander speculators. Some of these managed to establish themselves in Colombia, and later to form association with local capitalists (particularly the Santa Marta group) without difficulty. This foreign investment was quite different in scale and in nature from that made by the British in the River Plate. The positive impact these enterprises had on the development of steam navigation on the Magdalena river is nevertheless undeniable.[10]

During the ascendancy of tobacco no less than fifteen steamers travelled the river. The boats must have represented a net investment of 800,000 pesos gold, a sum which would have been impossible to extract exclusively from internal savings for such a high-risk venture. Local commercial capital preferred surer speculations and shorter-term investments, patterns that can be seen in the operations of *bogotano* banks of the 1870s, funded with local capital. The dominant Colombian firm of the 1850s, Montoya y Sáenz, itself functioned in the same manner.[11]

Towards the end of the 1880s twenty steamboats were running on the lower Magdalena, most of them between Barranquilla and Yeguas, some few kilometres below Honda. On the upper Magdalena there were two small steamers which occasionally reached Neiva. There were also small steamers on the Lebrija river, which connected the region of Bucaramanga with the Magdalena, as well as a steamer on the river Cauca between Cartago and Cali. The steamer of the lower Magdalena had a capacity of 40,000 *cargas* in each round trip, enough to satisfy demand.[12]

Nevertheless, the lack of capital prevented the development of an adequate system of transportation, and this lack continued to be one of the major bottlenecks of the Colombian economy during the period. A system did evolve whereby in theory local roads were built and maintained by the *servicio personal subsidiario* (personal-service subsidy) which the poor paid annually in work and the rich in cash. The system functioned to some extent in all the federal states, a corvée which aroused the ire of many Radical Liberals.[13] Federal roads and bridges were a different matter. During the Liberal epochs, contracts were given to private firms which undertook to construct and maintain roads and bridges in return for concessions in public lands and the right to levy tolls. However, this system was generally a failure and the states soon had to allocate sums directly from their budgets for the construction and administration of their trans-

port systems. In addition, the era of contract building led to many conflicts, and even to political problems over state boundaries.[14]

The history of the railroads is also complicated by the political and
regional interests involved, as well as by much debate on their economic
consequences. In general, the federal states of 1863—85 and thereafter,
though to a lesser degree the departments and the central government,
took on the cost of building and administering the railroads. There were
exceptions, such as La Dorada railway and the United Fruit Company
railroad, but they were few in number. The various state organs tried to
meet the costs through a wide variety of financial expedients. In spite of
the railroad fever which gripped the country in the 1870s, a number of
politicians remained lukewarm to the idea of basing the country's transport
system on railroads. Camacho Roldán convincingly upheld an unpopular
viewpoint, shared by a few others. He pointed out that the costs of railroad construction were too high, taking into account the country's low
population base, difficult topographical conditions, the lack of national or
foreign investment capital, and the inability of the state to guarantee debts
incurred in building the system or to administer it once built. He referred
to eight projects of which four had collapsed, and he considered it a miracle
that more had not failed.[15] By 1883, 150 kilometres of track had been
laid and put to partial use. By 1888 the length of the lines had been extended to 240 kilometres. Eight lines were involved, of which four serviced
the maritime ports of Barranquilla, Cartagena, Santa Marta, and Buenaventura and a part of the frontier with Venezuela. The La Dorada railway,
which was completed in 1888, joined the upper and lower Magdalena.[16]
The other lines took a long time to complete: the Girardot line was not
finished until 1910, and the *antioqueño* (Puerto Berrío—Medellín) line
not until 1929. After 1888 five more lines were opened, making a total of
thirteen by 1915, with a combined length of 1,120 kilometres.[17] In that
year, the coffee centres of south-western Antioquia and the *caldense* region
had yet to be connected with the Pacific system. Nor had the Manizales
region been connected with Mariquita near the Magdalena river. Although
the second, and most important, cycle of coffee expansion was beginning,
mules continued to be the main means of getting the coffee from the
fincas to the principal market centres or to the river ports.

The differential impact of the cycle on the state and on the regions

A very well-known trait of the Latin American export economies, which has
manifested itself down to the present day, is the heavy dependence of

government finances on the external trade cycle. Any unforeseen or drastic rise or fall in the income earned from exports affects (after a time-lag) imports and Treasury receipts, upsetting the state budget. This in turn creates political tensions which have nearly always led to crises, contributing to the general atmosphere of instability.[18] But the Colombian peculiarity is that the cycle does not affect as markedly the social and economic structures of the country. This situation is the result of the low export co-efficient which has already been referred to. Nevertheless, some sort of wider explanation is required. Historically, the ties between the state and the agrarian society were weak, indeed well-nigh non-existent, from Inde-pendence until well into the twentieth century. The state—peasant relation-ship in Colombia is the exact opposite of the classic case of Imperial and Kuomintang China, where the state was able both to exploit economically the rural population through an elaborate system of taxes, and to keep the vast majority of the population under political control.[19] For example, a Colombian official, faced with a large budget deficit, can implement any measure to solve the crisis, except one which would involve the imposition of an exceptional tax on the bulk of the agricultural population and their production. Such an act is inconceivable, not least because the bureaucracy and organizations to implement it do not exist. Of course a prolonged export crisis can dislocate everyday life and even alter the social basis of a region dependent on the external market. The latter happened in some of the tobacco-, cotton- and banana-producing regions. But the population and the areas affected by decline were insignificant at any given time in relation to the majority of the population, which did not feel any *direct* effects of the depression. This generalization remains true for the coffee-producing regions, at least during the period that is the main subject of this chapter.

The well-known history of tobacco production offers a good example of what has been said above. For the purposes of analysis we can take the mean production figures for land and labour which predominated in the Ambalema region during the 1850s, before the fertility of the land was exhausted.[20] One hectare, on average, contained 10,000 tobacco plants which produced 150 *arrobas* per year, of which 100 came from the main harvest, and 50 from the secondary. One efficient *cosechero*, or tobacco tenant, could take care of 5,000 plants or half a hectare. If we extrapolate these proportions to national production we get the result in table 1. This sketchy example shows how the fall in the level of employment and area under cultivation were so marginal that it cannot be compared with the political consequences of the crisis in tobacco production: namely, the fall of Liberalism. Even in a major tobacco-growing region like Girón, the export

Table 1. *Tobacco production: area under cultivation and work force, 1840–75*

Years	Hectares	Harvesters
1840–5	1,310	2,620
1850	2,650	5,300
1858	7,500	15,000
1865	8,000	16,000
1875	5,100	10,200

crisis went unnoticed owing to the marginal role of tobacco in the agri-cultural sector.[21] The decline of Ambalema as a producing region opened the way for the rise of Carmen de Bolívar, which from then on took the lead in tobacco production for local consumption.

The dynamism of the local economies contrasts with the cyclical nature of the export economy. The case of cotton production and its effects on the Santander economy helps illustrate this. Once again, extrapolations help make the point clearer. It is assumed that the mean national pro-ductivity level was that of Santander in 1880: 400 kilos per hectare. The export statistics confirm the familiar pattern: exports rose during the American Civil War, only to fall when it ended. Coincidentally, the pessi-mism of the elite set in. Taking the productivity figure as given above, and arbitrarily accepting that all production was exported (which was not the case), the following statistics on land under cotton cultivation emerge: 3,800 hectares in 1866–70, 2,500 in 1870–5, and 1,600 in 1876–9.[22] In any case the figures highlight the infinitesimal amount of land actually under cotton cultivation. A different picture is given by the Commissary for National Agriculture, who in 1880 wrote to B. Koppel, the United States Consul in Bogotá, describing cotton production in Santander as follows:

'there are 5,000 hectares of cotton under cultivation, with a production of 2 million kilos, of which 872,000 kgs. are exported to Boyacá and Cundinamarca at a price of 12½ cents per kilo. The rest, 1.1 million kgs., is used in Santander to produce more than 500,000 kgs. of thread worth 60 cents per kilo. An additional 100,000 kgs. of English thread valued at 2.42 pesos per kg. or 1.1 pesos per English pound, are used to manufacture 25,000 units of 51 metres each of common and fine coloured cotton shirting, which is sold from 12 to 21 dollars per piece, and for these were used 300,000 kgs. of thread of both kinds amounting in value to 350,000 pesos; 830,000 mts. of linen in which are used

100,000 kgs. of domestic thread, which being sold at 15 cents per metre gives the sum of 125,000 pesos; 100,000 bed-spreads and hammocks valued at 200,000 and in these have been used 250,000 kgs. of domestic thread together with a small quantity of English thread. The remaining 13,800 kgs. of thread are used in making caps and heels for hempen shoes. Some of these items, valued at 365,000 pesos, are exported to Venezuela and other Colombian states. Santander buys 200,000 metres of linen for internal consumption valued at 40,000 pesos.[23]

In 1880 these artisan manufactures of Santander were continuing to swim against the economic current, favoured by their close links with local agriculture. Looking at the case more closely, it can be seen that the mini-boom in cotton production only affected a few localities in Bolívar in northern Colombia. The experience of cotton production in fact seems to confirm the observation made by a student of Santander in the nineteenth century: local prosperity owed more to its isolation from international trade than to integration with it.[24] Not many contemporaries in Bogotá would have felt in sympathy with such a line of analysis.

The commercial bourgeoisie, which was caught up and directly engaged in the uncertainties of the cycle of coffee, learned one major lesson from the pre-coffee export cycles: the need to diversify as a means of protection against the trough. This will be discussed in more detail in chapter 2. It must be noted that the merchants lived in the era when the gold standard (in Colombia, a gold and silver standard) was strictly adhered to, and that consequently fluctuations in international prices were reflected immediately and automatically on the balance-sheets of the commercial enterprises involved in the export–import economy. Bankruptcies of commercial firms, such as Montoya y Sáenz, and the less well-known cases of the *trabajadores de la tierra caliente* involved in quinine and indigo production reinforced the above awareness.[25] The repercussions of bankruptcies were so immediate and direct on the local commercial economy that they led to wild fluctuations in interest rates, and when combined with an export crisis to fluctuations in the exchange rate. In such an unsettled climate, merchants preferred to buy bonds of the internal debt, to invest in short-term commercial loans to import–export firms, and to maintain liquidity in gold (bills of exchange on London), or even to export their capital. Investment in land or urban property was, in any case, a very speculative affair, especially after the mid 1870s when the inflation rate began to accelerate.[26] Investment was not determined by calculating the profitability of agriculture in relation to the interest rate; it was conditioned more by the dividends resulting from the monopolization of land and of well-situated urban property in a time of marked inflation and of a crisis in the agricultural export cycle. The coefficient of the year-to-year variation of prices for tobacco was 30 per cent between 1846 and 1880.[27]

Political instability

Another important characteristic of these merchant families was their participation in party politics. This participation was nearly always active. The close and systematic relationship between parties and families is analysed in detail in chapter 2. Party loyalties, regional loyalties, ideologies, values, and norms all seem to have depended on the export curve. Nevertheless, when the latter turned downwards in a particularly marked and rapid decline after 1875, the so-called transition from *laissez-faire* to 'positivism' was not produced automatically. Nor was the transition process as clear as it may have been in other Latin American latitudes.

From 1885 the *Regeneración*, or Regeneration period (1886–9), represents a break with the Liberal era in many ways, but it was more difficult to maintain political hegemony at that time than previously. The inability of any social group or class to control the state apparatus becomes more apparent, now that functions the state should normally fulfil are so clearly thwarted by the lack of an integrated economy. The formula implied in the Unitary Republic was diametrically opposed to the local particularism of the Federal period; yet it had to work within a loosely centralized power structure. The regional oligarchies were ill disposed to pay the fiscal price of political centralization, and at the same time the export economy entered one of the most deficient periods of its history.

It is in this context that the formulation of the economic policy of those years, and the response of the merchants involved in the export trade, should be analysed. The area of greatest interest seems to lie in the political and ideological arena, but that falls outside the scope of this book. Nevertheless, this aspect should be stressed here: in Colombia the central and secular state, with its 'progressive' or 'developmentalist' ideology, only partially achieved its aims. The Liberal bourgeoisie, alienated from political power, organized their opposition in terms of a return to the free-trade governments of the past, in spite of their continued accumulation of capital and riches in the subsequent period of the Regeneration. A 'positivist' elite did not materialize, and in accord with the logic of party alliances, Núñez had to accept Conservative support, and make pacts with the Church, returning to it prerogatives and privileges it had lost. As a result, he weakened the very state he was trying to strengthen.[28] The Conservative leaders and *caciques*, and their dependent forces, the proponents of a traditional hispanist ideology and the Church, all allied themselves to Núñez's national vision, which in its most skeletal terms expressed plans for industrialization, material progress, and the centralization of political power and authority. Thus it is not surprising that the ideology of free trade and the romantic Liberalism of the mid century should have continued to capture the imagination of youth and to retain the loyalty of the merchant bourgeoisie at least until the end of the nineteenth century, and even beyond. The legitimacy of the national bank and the paper money the government forced as currency on the economy were questioned as part of a wider conceptual attack shared and politically defended by an important faction of the enlightened bourgeoisie located primarily in the centre and east of the country.

The economic collapse of the 1870s highlighted three major problems of Colombian politics and economics, which the Regeneration tried to solve. Colombia was an overwhelmingly agricultural country, crippled by topographical conditions and the huge distances which fragmented it, and by the political instability which manifested itself in violence, electoral feud, and civil war. Turning Colombia into a country industrialized on a national and integrated scale, and one governed by stable and democratic institutions, seemed to require a major change in the political process. It seemed absolutely necessary to establish political peace via a strong presidential system which would curb the anarchistic tendencies of federalism.

Political stability was not seen as an end in itself: it was viewed as the means to expand and develop both transport and productive investment, which in turn were seen as more than functions of the external market. The diagnosis of, and the solutions to, the problems offered no new insights; and the obstacles facing their implementation were formidable. During the last thirty years of the nineteenth century, a curious and contradictory development was taking place. The technological advances being made, the increasing economic integration of the world, the social change produced by urbanization in the United States and Europe were accompanied by the political retreat of the Liberals and constitutionalists, who dominated these developments, and the ascendancy of Conservatives on the right, and socialist movements in a few countries on the left. It was a time when the executive was gaining ground against the legislature. In England, the Liberals fell in 1885, giving way to twenty years of Conservative rule. In the United States the Republican party came into its own, as did the republicans in France, where Opportunists and conservatives held power between 1880 and 1898.[29] The Colombian elite could not be immune to these developments.

Colombian political parties took sides depending on their reaction to the following contradictions, to which no peaceful resolution seemed possible: centralism versus federalism; clericalism versus secularism; institutionalism versus *caudillismo*; strong executive versus weak legislature or vice versa. In the politics of the municipalities these contradictions mixed with local interests and aspirations. From the above set of alternatives the politicians of the Regeneration chose centralism, clericalism, and an institutionalism which consisted in eliminating *caudillismo* and *caciquismo*, which were seen as deriving their existence from the 'abuse' made of universal suffrage and the weakness of the central government. It can be argued that the civil wars of the second half of the nineteenth century were fought to resolve these contradictions, one way or another. The problem was, however, that these wars never reached their logical conclusion, the total destruction of the vanquished. This last observation throws into relief the high level of direct participation of all elements of the local oligarchy in the wars. In such social conditions, victories were bound to be ephemeral. It was only after the Three Years' War (1889–1902), and during the five-year term of office of General Rafael Reyes (1904–9), that the oligarchy finally achieved some consensus which permitted the continuity of the Conservative Republic and the formulation of plans for economic development based on the Porfirio Díaz model.[30]

Continuities in 'export-led development'

During the decade of the 1870s, many Latin American countries, especially those of the River Plate region, were incorporated into the international economy with unprecedented rapidity and completeness. This development can be interpreted as yet another sign of the transition from the era of competitive capitalism to that of imperialism.[31] In Latin America the period from 1870 to the world crisis of 1930 is generally known as the period of *desarrollo hacia afuera*, export-led and outward-looking development, and it is assumed that the agricultural–mining–export sector was the leading sector of the economy. Applying these generalizations to the Colombian experience is a dangerous exercise: 'export-led development' does not really occur in Colombia until after 1910. It is true that coffee exports grew rapidly between 1870 and 1897, after which they stagnated until 1910–12, but coffee exports by themselves could not in those nineteenth-century years recapture the level of exports set in 1845–75. The year 1870 was not the symbolic date in Colombian history which signified the social and economic transformation of the country, as it was elsewhere in Latin America. Nevertheless, by 1870 coffee was spreading away from the Santander redoubt it had held since the 1850s. The decade of the 1870s represents one of the great watersheds in Colombian history: in one sense they are the years when Liberalism was at its political and ideological height, and when the export economy reached its nineteenth-century peak. In another sense, however, the decade represents decline: by the late 1870s the catastrophic fall in tobacco exports made inevitable the demise of the political and economic system based, optimistically, on the axiom of free trade.

In spite of all that has been said earlier, there were important elements of continuity between the pre-coffee export economy and the first cycle of coffee expansion (1870–1910). In spite of the sketchy nature of the periods as set up, and the differences between the two which have been discussed, together the periods represent the civilizing blueprint of the free-traders. Frank Safford is right when he states that the 1870s mark the transformation of an economy based on gold, mules, and tobacco to one dominated by coffee, railroads, and banks.[32]

The transformation was certainly less clear-cut than his phrase suggests. The commercial banks were a product of the end of the tobacco era and the banking capital of Antioquia came from mining and trading in gold. The mule as a form of transport was even more important for coffee than for tobacco: the geographical location of the centres of coffee production meant that mules remained an essential form of transport during the first and even second cycle of coffee expansion. In addition, the steady and continued export of gold in the second half of the nineteenth century helped sustain coffee. The total value of gold exports (including minted gold coins) was surpassed by the value of coffee exports only in the 1890s.

Before beginning an introduction to the first coffee cycle, two more general points should be made about the continuity the advent of coffee represented for Colombia's economy and society.

Coffee introduced greater variety to the agricultural structure. It was grown in the temperate zones — heights between 1,000 and 1,800 metres above sea-level — alongside traditional crops, whose production had evolved considerably since colonial times. The most important of these crops was sugar-cane, which was crudely processed in rustic *trapiches* which extracted the *miel* to make *guarapo* and *aguardiente* (fermented drinks), and fabricated *panela* (loaves of unrefined sugar). These products were often sold in distant towns and isolated mining centres. Coffee coexisted with sugar-cane, maize, yuca, *arracacha* (a root vegetable: *Arracacia xanthorriza Bancroft*), and, in some regions, with livestock production after the introduction of certain varieties of grass.

Coffee has a natural cycle of both weeding and harvesting. Both activities are very labour-intensive, and thus coffee accommodates itself to another basic institution of traditional Colombian agriculture: the peasant family

from the *altiplano*. These peasant families were the basic cell for the repro-
duction and geographical diffusion of coffee, either via their own plots of
land, or in the new haciendas, which as social units were quite weak and
transitory except perhaps in Antioquia. The coffee plantations, which were
brought into production so that Colombia would not deviate from the
path towards civilization, were created by borrowing from the systems
of organization and remuneration existent in the colonial and post-colonial
past. The verbal contracts of *arrendamiento* (land rental), of share-cropping,
and of tenant farming all attest to the strength of traditions. The enlightened
hacendados thus had to develop capitalism with methods which, during
the later peasant revolts of Cundinamarca, were thought of as feudal by
all who considered themselves even moderately liberal. It was not for lack
of modernizing ambitions or imagination that this state of affairs existed.
The causes were more concrete: primitive technology, geographical isolation,
and the prevalence of subsistence farming all limited the possibilities of
consolidating the internal market.

The spread of coffee cultivation in western Colombia ran parallel with
the prosperity of areas colonized primarily by *antioqueños*, even though
settlers from Cauca, Boyacá, and Tolima played an important part in the
opening of Quindío, northern Valle, and the north-western Tolima. The
internal migration is part of the process of continuity referred to earlier,
but here taking a more complex form. Continuity not only affected the
agricultural structure but the ideology and politics of local power as well.
In the western part of the country the validity of the Liberal ideologies,
which originated with the Spanish Enlightenment and with the Independence
struggle, was put to the test. The *oidor* Mory Velande is the man usually
associated with these developments.[33] Legislators, lawyers, and ideologues
seemed obsessed with principles proclaiming the importance of the small
property-owner and cultivator for the economic and social development of
the country. Arguments based on the social function of property, the
juridical claims deriving from the economic use made of land, the role of
small property-owners as a foundation for democracy, were given weight
and momentum by the demographic pressure on public lands. The discussion of these issues (debated again during the drawing up of the agrarian
reform of the 1960s) emphasizes the ideological importance of an agricultural institution (the small property-owner) which sometimes con-
flicted with the necessity of raising the level of agricultural productivity.
This will be seen more clearly in chapter 11. The fascinating part of the
above process is how the 'left' and the 'right' adapted the principles to
their arguments, and how there existed wide divergencies between written
law and social practice. In chapters 8 and 9 I explain some of the impli-

cations of the issues by studying their legislative evolution. This may be
the best means available to analyse concepts, intentions, and expectations
about man, land, and property and how they were entertained by different
social classes and groups. The study of their practical effects reveals precisely
to what extent law is mere ideology or legalism. It is important to point
out the continuities here, which the Liberals of the 1930s Revolución en
Marcha (Revolution on the March) characterized as a rupture. It will be
seen that what was new in the circumstances of the 1930s was not the
juridical ideology represented in the radical project for agrarian reform
presented during the government of Olaya Herrera (1930–4); nor even
the timid and casuistic law finally approved by the government of López
Pumarejo (1934–8). Rather, it was the existence of a social situation with
few antecedents, the product of a chance meeting of circumstances. There
must be sought the key to the contradictions and the vulnerability of the
coffee haciendas of the central regions of the country. Let us see how the
story begins.

The beginning of the coffee era: the Santander redoubt

Like rubber, tea, cacao, and bananas, coffee is only produced in the tropics,
unlike cotton, leather, wood products, and sugar, which can be produced in
temperate zones. This fact explains the flexibility of international commercial policies as regards coffee during the last century. There were no
'protectionist' groups in the importing countries and, except for short
periods at the end of the century, Colombian coffee always had tariff-
free access to the main market: the United States. Coffee production has
never been threatened by competition from consumer countries.

Coffee became a popular beverage in the West three centuries ago, but
not until the nineteenth century did its consumption become truly universal,
following the fall in maritime transportation costs and the growth in employment and incomes in the United States and Europe which accompanied
industrial development and urbanization. England, where coffee consumption
was overshadowed by that of tea, remained something of an exception.
After the eighteenth century, the geography of coffee production came to be
intimately linked with Western colonial and neo-colonial expansion. Coffee
is not a vital foodstuff, and its cultivation is limited to tropical climates.
These two factors go some way towards explaining both the speculative
nature of the coffee trade and the geographical shifts in production over the
centuries. Coffee was, and in some degree continues to be, a *produit
colonial* and is largely cultivated in parts of the world geographically
removed from the centres of greatest consumption.

In the eighteenth century Dutch colonial expansion provided momentum
for the spread of coffee; cultivation extended first to the Indian Ocean,
and later further east to Java and Sumatra, while the French were responsible
for its introduction to the Caribbean. 'At that time, Santo Domingo (Haiti)
occupied the position now held by São Paulo, since the production of
coffee in the Far East was most certainly of a secondary nature.'[34]

The French Revolution, the abolitionist measures adopted in the Convention which led to the uprising in Haiti, and the Napoleonic wars, all
contributed to disrupt the commercial and productive supremacy of France
and her Antilles. Their places were taken by Holland and Java, respectively.
Amsterdam continued to be the centre of world coffee trade until the
middle of the nineteenth century, when it was succeeded as a major centre
by New York, and in Europe by Le Havre and then Hamburg. The coffee
tree had also reached Surinam at the beginning of the eighteenth century
(1714) and from there spread slowly westwards through the Guianas to
Venezuela. To the south it entered Brazil through Palheta. By the middle
of the century it had gained ground in the provinces of Caracas and Cumaná
and exports were shipped from La Guaira.[35] Around the same time disease
ruined the coffee plantations of Ceylon and the Dutch Indies. The centre
of world production passed to Latin America. Brazil, Venezuela, and Costa
Rica were already important producers in 1850. Guatemala, El Salvador,
and Mexico began their first coffee cycles some ten years later.[36]

In 1828 the cultivation of coffee earned the scepticism of Bolívar,[37]
but by that time the coffee tree had become firmly established in the
Venezuelan Andes, in Táchira and El Zulia, and in the bordering Colombian
provinces of Cúcuta and Salazar, which were also geographic dependencies
of Lake Maracaibo. At the end of the eighteenth century the colonial
authorities of Santa Marta and Cartagena made a proposal to the Crown
that in accordance with current colonial policies aimed at promoting the
export of tropical agricultural goods, the cultivation of coffee should
become a priority in the poor and backward areas of the kingdom as a
remedy for poverty. The idea was to imitate the successes experienced by
Cuba, Puerto Rico, and Venezuela,[38] The establishment of a coffee economy
was accomplished only in the era of the Unitary Republic.

The cultivation of coffee in Santander spread to those regions which had
formed the basis of slave agriculture since the middle of the eighteenth
century. Cocoa was produced in the valleys of San José de Cúcuta and El
Rosario and Salazar de las Palmas, and was exported via Maracaibo or was
traded in the central highlands. Cotton was also cultivated in Girón and
Rionegro, having followed a route along the Sogamoso river into Magdalena,
and from there it advanced to Mompós and Cartagena. Towards the middle

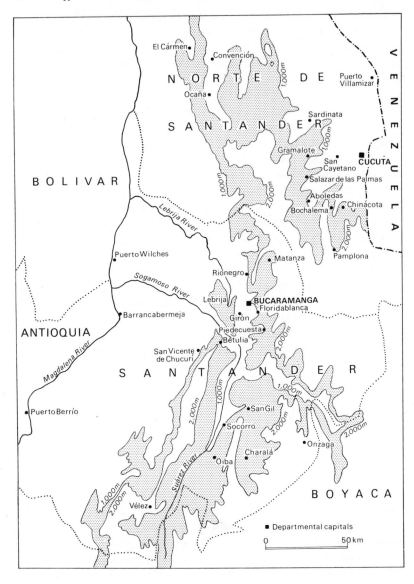

Map 1. The Santander coffee zones.

of the nineteenth century the Comisión Corográfica reported that from San José de Cúcuta, Rosario, and Salazar alone, 50,000 bags of coffee per year were sent to Puerto de los Cachos on their way to Maracaibo. Following the pattern of the established colonial trade routes, coffee was marketed through Santa Marta and Cartagena 'and even availed itself of the great trade fairs held in Mompós'.[39] Slave haciendas had already disappeared from the scene in Cúcuta and El Rosario; new agricultural ventures created on the lines of the *latifundista* holdings operated with free labour; the social structure of the labour force in general assumed the sharecropper pattern, and this was to become a characteristic feature in Santander's coffee haciendas until the middle of the twentieth century. However, while the large estates continued to dominate the coffee scene, a growing number of small family farms were gradually coming into the picture. The unanimous impression of visitors was that 'Santander has the advantage that its territorial property is greatly divided . . . and that the excess of capital is as rare as the existence of poverty.'[40] The cultivation of coffee continued to expand across the eastern Andean range towards the centre of the country and reached regions where high transport costs made coffee production barely an economic proposition: this was the case of the areas on the eastern mountain slopes far from the river Magdalena.[41]

The growth of coffee exports, 1853–1909

When first the Bogotá merchants in the 1870s, followed by those of the Medellín ten years later, began to participate actively in 'coffee speculation' (this was the term used at the time), nobody doubted their business acumen, or their status as men of progress, true patriots.

The large estate exporter emerged as the main driving force behind the setting up of the complex network of commercial and banking facilities. He was closely identified with the structures of patronage, political ties, and the representation of well-defined provincial interests. The merchant of the time was, or genuinely aspired to be, an enlightened man. He was susceptible not only to the political ideologies which predominated in England, France, and the United States, but also to the pragmatic doctrines deriving from the realities of the world of business, and he had access to manuals of tropical agriculture published in London and Paris.[42]

Moreover, tobacco had been a school of commerce, and had multiplied contacts between the merchants of Bogotá and Antioquia and the rest of the world. The merchants had already recognized the importance of a basic knowledge of markets, prices, transport costs, routes, competitors, and the various idiosyncrasies of the buyer. Similar skills had already been acquired by *antioqueño* merchants by the end of the Bourbon period through experiences gained in either the legal or the contraband trade with Jamaica.[43] Primitive but firmly established merchant firms began to appear, generally confined to the family business model, with meticulous though rudimentary book-keeping methods, and their appearance marks the undeniable advance of commercial capitalism. The few representatives of foreign firms followed this development closely, and were particularly sensitive to any changes in demand for imports in taste and fashion or shifts in the relative importance of each commercial enterprise in Bogotá, Cúcuta, Medellín, or Bucaramanga.

The merchant played a singularly decisive role in establishing the Colombian coffee economy. Consular reports despatched after the 1870s must also have had a positive influence. For example, 1871 reports from Rafael Núñez (Liverpool) or Juan de Dios Restrepo (New York) accurately described the prevailing situation in the country of their post; they wrote on the possibilities open to Colombian coffee, and assessed the idiosyncrasies of the buyers.[44]

Between 1870 and 1885 the country was probably producing in the region of 125,000 60-kilo bags of green coffee, of which at least 100,000 were exported. Seventy per cent of these were shipped via Maracaibo.[45] Colombia's emergence as a coffee-producing nation was relatively late in Latin America. Colombian coffee exports at the beginning of the twentieth century barely reached the modest level of 1.5 per cent of total world exports, although her exports accounted for 10 per cent of the so-called *café suave* (mild coffee).[46] However, coffee proved to be the nearest thing to salvation for the trade balance in the latter part of the nineteenth century. In the 1870s, when the decline in tobacco had become fully apparent, coffee accounted for 17 per cent of total export value. By the end of the century and despite the price crisis which occurred in 1897, the contribution of coffee as a proportion of total export value rose to 40 per cent. This was, in fact, the take-off period for the product. Coffee production increased fivefold from 1870 to 1897. Accompanying activities such as cattle-raising and the growing of sugar-cane, plantain, yuca, and maize also increased, but to a lesser extent.

We are dealing with tentative data, as can be seen from table 2. What stands out is the incompatibility of the two sources, although both indicate a period of rapid expansion in the 1890s. The scattered figures available on exports from Cúcuta and the size of production and exports from Cundinamarca and Antioquia nearly always diverge from the estimates shown in Table 3. Take, for example, Santander, the main producer of coffee

Table 2. *Colombian coffee exports, 1853–1909 (60-kg bags)*

	I Annual average, 3 years		II Annual average, 5 years
1853–5	1,186	1854/55–1858/59	42,750
1856–8	5,412		
1859–61	12,462	1859/60–1863/64	–
1862–4	14,654		
1865–7	36,553	1864/65–1868/69	64,383
1868–70	49,900		
		1869/70–1873/74	109,816
1871–3	75,403		
1874–6	87,000	1874/75–1878/79	65,083
1877–9	100,744		
1880–2	101,996	1879/80–1883/84	81,666
1883–5	96,000		
1886–8	127,000	1884/85–1889	99,533
1889–91	195,000		
		1890–4	142,116
1892–4	326,000		
1895–7	266,000	1895–9	442,333
1898–1900	273,000		
1901–3	333,000		
1904–6	600,000	1906–9	629,533[a]
1907–9	400,000		

a Annual average, 4 years.

Sources: (I) Data from 1853 to 1882 based on C. F. Van Delden Laërne, *Brazil and Java* (London, 1885), p. 413. The author concludes that his data are 'tolerably correct' in that a great part of Colombian coffee is exported through Venezuela. Data from 1883 to 1909 based on *El Café* (El Salvador, January 1938), derived from the New York Coffee Exchange. The latter figures are adjusted according to recommendations in H. Roth, *Die Ubererzeugung in der Welthandelsware Kaffee im Zeitraum von 1700– 1929* (Jena, 1929), pp. 131–3.

(II) Armando Samper, *Importancia del café en el comercio exterior de Colombia* (Bogotá, 1948), pp. 87–8, cited by Miguel Urrutia, 'El sector externo y la distribución de ingresos en Colombia en el siglo XIX', in *Revista del Banco de la República*, November 1972, p. 13.

H. Arboleda in *Estadística general de la República de Colombia* (Bogotá, 1905), pp. 174–5, gives the following figures on coffee exports (in 60-kg bags): 1894, 466,350; 1895, 480,830; 1896, 627,166; 1897, 566,683; 1898, 627,750. All the figures in the table refer to exports. It is probable that internal consumption, usually of lower-grade coffee, amounted on average to 10% of what was exported. Using European or North American import statistics would not resolve the question of the size of Colombian exports, since Colombian coffee was classified as 'Maracaibo'-type coffee.

during the nineteenth century: according to the already cited calculations by Codazzi, Santander's exports via Cúcuta during the 1850s were approximately 50,000 bags;[47] the reports by the Colombian Consul in Maracaibo estimated the same exports to be 100,000 bags in 1860. In 1887 the United States Consul in Bogotá estimated Santander's production to be 91,000 bags; at the same time, the British Consul reported that 110,000 bags were exported through Cúcuta alone that year, and 135,000 more in 1888. The above sources contradict the figures given by the Cúcuta customs house, according to which the export figures were the following: 150,000 bags in 1887, 181,000 in 1888, and 131,000 up to 1 September 1889. For the 1890s, the accepted estimates accord Santander exports of 270,000 bags.[48] The above glimpse at the available statistics highlights two points: (a) the difficulty of estimating the amount of land under cultivation, the size of the workforce, and the importance of coffee production in the different regions; and (b) the underestimation of Santander's exports and, given the importance of these, the underestimation of Colombia's total exports.

In general, nearly all the estimates for the 1890s coincide, especially for figures after 1892/3. Exports grew rapidly, which meant that coffee-growers were responding to the rising price of coffee. It went from 10 U.S. cents per pound in 1886 to 17 cents in 1887, to 25 cents in 1889, with further rises up to 1894, with the exception of two short drops in 1889 and 1892.[49]

Regional trends in coffee-growing

Taking into account the unreliability and diversity of the statistical sources available, it is worth outlining the general tendencies of production in the three most important coffee centres of the nineteenth century. Table 3 refers to different export estimates. Total production was probably greater by roughly 10 per cent. No significant coffee stocks were kept.

A glance at the statistics confirms the known facts: Santander's stagnation after 1913, and the giddy rise of Antioquia. It is useful to remember that the greatest year-to-year increases in exports during the nineteenth century occurred between 1888 and 1895–1900. The very high rates for Cundinamarca (21.6 per cent) and Antioquia (20.4 per cent) contrast with the moderate increase of Santander's production (5 per cent). The rates confirm one of the observations of this book: the impulse to economic growth was different between Santander and the newer regions of production. In Santander (excepting Rionegro), an ordered response to demand from an economy with a peasant base and where cultivation had a certain tradition

Table 3. *Export estimates for Santander,[a] Cundinamarca, and Antioquia, 1870–1932 (60-kg bags) (1895–1900 = 100)*

Year	Santander		Cundinamarca		Antioquia	
1860	110,000[b]	41	ND		ND	
1870	ND		3,000	2	ND	
1872	92,000[d]	34	ND		ND	
1888	181,000[e]	67	38,000	25	5,200[g]	12
1895–1900	270,000[h]	100	150,000[i]	100	43,805[j]	100
1913	328,000[i]	121	200,000[i]	133	161,000[g] (185,000[i])	368
1922	372,000[k]	138	226,000[k]	151	472,000[k]	1,077
1932	381,000[l]	141	452,000[l]	301	630,000[l]	1,438

a Figures include both departments, created in 1886. As the figures are based on exports through Cúcuta (except for 1895), it is probable that the estimates do not include exports from the districts of Bucaramanga–Rionegro and Ocaña.

Sources: b ANC, Consulados: Correspondencia consular: Maracaibo, vol. 4, pp. 584–616. c Based on *Mensaje del Gobernador de Cundinamarca* (Bogotá, 1870), pp. 17–18, 85–8. d *Informe del Presidente del Estado de Santander, 1874* (Socorro, n.d.), pp. 23–5. e Based on 'Datos de la Aduana de Cúcuta', *Gaceta de Santander*, 8 June 1890, p. 4. f Based on J. G. Walker to the Secretary of State, Bogotá, December 1887, U.S. National Archives (microfilms), T.116. g A. López and J. Rodríguez, *Estadísticas de Antioquia* (Medellín, 1914), p. 150. h S. Dickson, *Report on the Present State of Coffee Trade in Colombia*, P.P., vol. 96 (1904), p. 763. i Based on my own calculations on material used in the following chapters. j P. L. Bell, 'Coffee, the Mainstay of Colombia', *Tea and Coffee Trade Journal*, no. 42 (February 1922), pp. 165–74. k J. Ancízar, 'La industria del café en Colombia', *R.N.A.*, nos. 239–40 (May–June 1924), p. 292. l FNCC, *Boletín de Información y Estadística*, 1, 7 (August 1933), p. 1.

served to limit possibilities. In the other regions entrepreneurs appeared who quickly converted themselves into 'coffee speculators' as they were referred to then, who exploited to the full the potential of their areas. This development becomes obvious when the dates of the foundation of the great haciendas in the most economically active areas are taken into account. Another aspect of growth which the statistics shed light on is the beginning of a renaissance in Cundinamarca coffee production during the 1920s, which contrasted with the relatively slower growth of Antioquia during those years. Analysing the peasant disturbances in the Cundinamarca region, this backdrop must be kept in mind: renewed productivity with its necessary and rapid reallocation of land and labour resources in a changing political environment.

It should also be remembered that Santander's production cycle is much older and longer than those of the other regions. In about 1808, 100 bags (60 kilos each) were already being exported from the district of Cúcuta. In the 1820s some rich merchants from Bucaramanga tried to encourage coffee cultivation via the *aparcería* (share-cropping) system, but apparently they failed to find tenants interested in taking up the land they were offering.[50] According to the Comisión Corográfica (Chorographical Commission), which studied the region at mid century, the following cantons were exporting coffee: Vélez, Chiquinquirá ('the supreme Muzo'), the three cantons of the province of Soto, the three cantons of Santander – Cúcuta, Rosario, and Salazar. Ancízar stated that already in Chinácota the local 'capitalists' were beginning to grow coffee, and cultivation was spreading. In the province of Ocaña, 'coffee is the base for commerce'.[51]

There are other factors which may have influenced Santander's slow growth towards the end of the century. The intermittent closing of the international boundary considerably increased the uncertainties for cultivators and merchants. Furthermore, the general political instability of the second half of the nineteenth century profoundly affected life in the region. A traveller from Brazil noted the physical destruction of coffee trees and processing machinery caused by the war of 1899–1902.[52] The diversity of currencies in Santander's monetary system also played a part in slowing growth. The merchants of Cúcuta never accepted paper money, and the government was powerless to enforce its circulation.[53] They always negotiated with silver coins of 0.835 weight (the legal standard of quality). These had the advantage of devaluing at a slower rate against the dollar than paper money. This situation may in fact have been beneficial, but a provincial official complained in 1878 that 'thanks to the negligence of the police force anarchy reigns in this important matter . . . Each individual imposes his own will when receiving the pay of some sum, and discrepancy [in exchange rates and currency] is all the more notable from locality to locality. Coins accepted in Socorro do not circulate in Simacota or in Oiba; the latter's common currency is different from that of Suaita, and to go to Gámbita one must take special coins. It is not unusual (in fact it is quite common) that a coin in free circulation in one town will not be valid currency one kilometre outside the town.'[54]

It is doubtful that the above factors on their own explain the obvious stagnation in Santander's coffee production between the 1890s and the world crisis. Other factors such as the low fertility of the soil compared with that of the soils of the central regions, the relatively high costs of transport, and the low international prices for a brand considered inferior to Medellín, Manizales, or Bogotá, all influenced Santander's decline.

Santander in 1900 was still producing 60 per cent of Colombia's coffee. Nevertheless, it is the relative stagnation of the region's agriculture and commerce which has concerned us here. In 1884 'more than 30,000 Colombians have left for the frontier towns of Venezuela, and have enriched them, cultivating coffee, contributing to the formation of large fortunes, which of course are not ours'.[55]

After 1870 coffee production was characterized by a very rapid territorial expansion, passing from the west of Cundinamarca into Tolima and the regions of Sumapaz, Chaparral and El Líbano and into south-west Antioquia.[56] The rapidly spreading coffee frontier made the implementation of some railway projects finally possible. It also increased the value of hillside land, stimulated economic activity along the Magdalena river, and created a network of financial and mercantile institutions which would form the basis for the development of the new socioeconomic, entrepreneurial elite which was to consolidate itself in the first three decades of the twentieth century.

In the forty years between 1870 and 1910 the Colombian coffee economy established and consolidated itself. It was not a period of continual expansion, and at the end of the depression in coffee production between 1897 and 1910 most observers were convinced that the coffee era had passed, to be replaced by bananas and rubber.[57] By 1910, however, the more difficult stages of the settlement of the western part of the country were over. The area contained the most fertile and ecologically most propitious conditions for the cultivation of coffee, perhaps of anywhere in Latin America.

In the next chapters I give a brief description of the initial process which led merchants to invest in land, to plant coffee, and to become *hacendados* and exporters. I then consider some of the problems of administration during the phase of establishment of the coffee hacienda, particularly those created by absentee owners. I shall go on to show how this group acquired a series of specific interests, and how it was affected by the economic policies dominant in the period, especially by the introduction of compulsory paper money.

Chapter 2 describes the degree of fluidity between these groups, and the relative lack of differentiation in the early years among growers, merchants, and bankers, at least among those groups directly linked with foreign trade; this does not apply to the traditional landowners of the *altiplano*, nor would it apply to the small and medium traders dependent upon importers. It is very probable that with time some degree of differentiation took place in the original groups, resulting in instances in which the immediate economic interests of individuals engaged in banking and importing may have clashed with those of *hacendados* involved in the export business. Nevertheless, given the prevailing political conditions, the atmosphere of chronic instability and the recurrent civil wars, these conflicts were never translated into political antagonisms, and may have been so insignificant that the individuals involved did not themselves become aware of them. Furthermore, despite such differentiation, many commercial and family associations were engaged in exporting and importing, as well as in the production of coffee, and it is likely that these groups tended to work to reduce the impact of any possible conflicts. This seems to have occurred, for example with the crucial problems related to inflation and devaluation. Their political unity was, however, cemented and consolidated by the incoherence of the monetary policies adopted during the period, and by the attempt to tax exports which had previously been free of tax; by the nineties they had emerged clearly as a bourgeoisie dependent upon coffee.

2. The making of an oligarchy

About 80 per cent of the investment in opening new coffee haciendas took place between 1880 and 1895 in Cundinamarca, and between 1890 and 1900 in Antioquia. Although there were coffee-producing peasants, who responded favourably to the opportunities opened by organized buying, the merchants were in the forefront of development, and their participation was decisive for the future of coffee.

Two central aspects that turned the merchant into large-scale coffee-grower and -exporter are analysed in this chapter. In the first part, the social environment and political ties of the merchant families of Bogotá and Medellín are discussed in general terms. There is also an analysis of their tendency to diversify assets, given their fear of excessive specialization.

In the second part of the chapter, the incentives and obstacles facing the merchant-turned-planter are examined. The advantages offered by investment in coffee can be summarized as follows: the high profitability of coffee production when it was linked to exports; the relative security of this investment in an inflationary period; access to external credit with interest rates 50 per cent lower than any available in Bogotá or Medellín; and, finally, the abundance of good lands and the availability of labour. The obstacles to profit must also be recorded: the necessity to invest considerable sums of capital; the slow initial rate of return on investment; the risks of expropriation and disruption of production in periods of political instability; the risk of contracting debts in gold when the rate of devaluation was increasing; and the fact of being subject to an uncontrollable cycle of international prices. Transport costs enter both sides of the ledger. On the one hand, the maritime charges for freight dropped considerably all over the world after 1880, to the benefit of exporters of primary products with lower specific value. On the other hand, the costs of mule transport, steamers, warehouse storage, packing, and insurance rose sharply inside Colombia during these same years.

In the face of the above realities, a certain type of entrepreneurial mentality was necessary for survival: one which could resist the temptation during boom conditions to overspecialize. In 1900, when the disruption caused by the War of the Thousand Days was accompanied by an international depression in coffee prices, many of the more specialized producers went out of business. Before describing the dangers of the mortgage in the

25

final part of the chapter, a case study is made of Roberto Herrera Restrepo, an entrepreneur who did not specialize. His hacienda and his book-keeping account are a rarity, and have been analysed in pioneer works by Darío Bustamente and Malcolm Deas. Miguel Urrutia, using Bustamente's work, came to conclusions about the political economy of the Núñez era, con-clusions which will be discussed in chapter 6 and which I do not share.[1] On the other hand, my disagreement with Bustamente does not stem from his interpretation but from his data. The data I found were different from the ones he used, and therefore my own conclusions must be different. There is still a lack of usable accounts and other sources. Nevertheless, I think that Roberto Herrera and his coffee hacienda fit the general pattern of development in Cundinamarca during the period in question. His production curves and profits square well with the cycle of optimism which lasted until 1897, and with the years of frustration and pessimism of the last civil war and its aftermath. Until new data appear, Herrera's figures and what they represent will have to serve as our guide to the realities of Cundinamarca haciendas in our period.

Merchants and politics

The decade of the seventies saw the settling in the capital of the Republic — a city of 40,000 inhabitants — of a compact group of families, 'a new class',[2] led by 'those strong sons of second-generation peasants'[3] who had been inspired in the middle years of the century by the *gólgotas*. These were men new to the capital, coming mostly from modest homes and localities in the provinces, and achieving social and economic mobility through politics and commerce. Aquileo Parra, Manuel Murillo Toro, Santiago Pérez and the Camacho Roldán and Samper families all formed part of this group and were the most notable standard-bearers in society itself of the new historical epoch opened up by the triumph of free trade.[4]

There can be no doubt that the ideology of Radicalism played a legit-imizing role in the social ascent of the new middle strata. Samper himself declared that 'many of those called rich here because they have accumulated sufficient capital to live distant from their labours have before been tireless workers, who have imposed upon themselves the harshest of privations, beginning their careers as lay brothers, carters and muleteers.'[5]

These 'fanatics of progress' were also fanatics on occasion about equality of opportunity. Nothing makes this point more clearly than Santiago Pérez's presidential inauguration speech: 'Our institutions must in truth be effective when the steps to the Presidential Chair can reach down to the most humble levels [of society], from which I have myself ascended, and come now to give thanks to the Republic.'[6] Their rapid rise to eminence provoked the resentment of such traditionalists as José Manuel Marroquín, Rafael Pombo, or the writer José María Cordovez Moure, who, a little at odds with the tide of the times, wrote with bitter scorn and wit of this new class which was introducing into the peaceful rural life of Bogotá habits and ways of life of showy ostentation and doubtful refinement. However, they carried their protest no further than the pages of their books, while other men of letters, such as the poet José Asunción Silva, and more significantly such leading Conservative politicians as Julio Arboleda and Mariano Ospina Rodríguez, themselves adopted the economic principles of free trade.[7] The economic aspects of the mid-century reforms produced relatively little disagreement among political leaders, while the issues of the constitutional organization of the Republic, and of relations between Church and state, provoked the most passionate discord.[8]

Between 1847 and 1875 this commercial bourgeoisie began to take a share of power, although it never attained absolute hegemony. As it rose to prominence it had to engage in a protracted political struggle on three fronts: against groups of artisans who favoured protectionism, against the 'liberators', as the Samper brothers ironically called the men associated with the Independence movement, and against the political power enjoyed by the Church. The first of these struggles took on open class connotations in Bogotá, Gran Cauca, and Santander. In the latter region the latent class struggle burst to the surface and reached its climax in September 1879 with the street riots which took place in Bucaramanga, events which were coloured by the nationalistic feeling of the artisans and some of the smaller merchants against the Germans who controlled the larger trading concers.[9]

Nevertheless, in the important artisan centres of Santander such as Socorro, San Gil, Pamplona, and Girón, there were no artisan movements comparable to those of Bogotá or the Cauca valley. Popular violence, the so-called *retozos democráticos* which surfaced in the Cauca valley and particularly in Cali in 1850–1, was not strictly artisan-based. On the contrary, the lack of a middle-class artisan group made inevitable 'the clash of interests between the Conservative economic elite and the populace mobilized by the few frock-coated Liberals of Cali'.[10] On the other hand, the real or apparent danger posed by militarism was eventually dispelled only after a tortuous process involving parliamentary, electoral, and conspiratorial activity. In this respect, the judgements obtained against Generals Obando in 1855 and Mosquera in 1867 in political trials brought before Congress by Liberal politicians can be seen as signs of victory on this front.[11]

But constitutional and legal triumph over the radicalized artisans and against militarism and clericalism was not sufficient to assure the commercial class of political hegemony, for although there were the beginnings of the creation of a nation state and of an explicit programme of development based on the export of agricultural products, which would principally benefit the merchants, this social class was split by deep internal ideological divisions, and was forced to share power with other 'traditional' groups. In 1867 Miguel Samper bemoaned some aspects of life in Bogotá which he saw as evidence of an irritating continuity of the 'colonial' order: 'An excess of employees, of recipients of pensions, of clerics and of graduates, all investing their capital in bonds issued to cover the public debt; these were the factors which made of Bogotá a city dedicated to the production of salaries, pensions, rents, fiscal profits, and fees.'[12]

But at this time, access to the resources of power was often decisive, whether in obtaining essential means of production such as the land, or for the survival of financial institutions. Only during the brief period from 1867 to 1877 did the Bogotá merchants achieve, through the Liberal party, anything approaching class hegemony: even then it was confined to the sovereign state of Cundinamarca. Many commercial banks were founded during those years, and official protection and encouragement were given unconditionally to the Banco de Bogotá, the Banco de Colombia and the Compañía Colombiana de Seguros. These banks were lauded in the official press as community projects created for the common good.[13] The exceptionally favourable terms offered to the banks by the government of the state of Cundinamarca during the war of 1876 were well rewarded. Here one can consult the recently republished articles of Miguel A. Caro, who wrote in 1887: 'In my mind the Banco de Bogotá remains sadly linked with the memory of the Radical domination of 1876.' Recalling the expropiations to which he and his brother had been subject in the war of 1876, and the role which had been played by the manager of the Banco de Bogotá, he wrote: 'The Banco de Bogotá was Koppel, and Koppel was the founder and soul of the bank. Koppel was a personage to whom the government paid much attention, for the bank had taken special care to *serve the government with special deference*, saving it in 1875, and making considerable and timely loans in 1876. The government authorized the bank to suspend exchange of its bills, to the great detriment of the general public, and prevented creditors from taking action against the bank while allowing the bank to pursue its debtors, or to increase interest rates due to delay in repayment, in the middle of the war' (emphasis in the original).[14]

It should not be forgotten that in those same years the situation in Antioqu was entirely different, and that there the majority of the mercantile bourgoisie was both Catholic and Conservative: Tomás Rengifo's 'villainous government' ('*gobierno abellacado*' is the expression used by L. Ospina Vásquez) terrified the bankers and merchants of Medellín. A strange irony lay behind the aphorism that 'bankers live off peace': the Banco de Bogotá, and presumably the Banco de Colombia too, made loans to enable Radical-dominated central government to establish control of Antioquia, whose own bankers were among the first victims of this action.[15] Bankers survive by power. A theoretical neutrality on the part of the state hid much actual favouritism, and political power and the accumulation of wealth often went together. Liberal merchants and politicians found their bourgeois status increasingly less compatible with the social and political romanticism which had inspired them in their youth. By the end of the century they were almost to a man, examples of sobriety and moderation, and models of civic virtue; if, like Santiago Pérez, they were persecuted, this was due more to the ferocious ultramontanism sometimes displayed by the Regeneration, and to the blind fear on the part of its ideologues of the phantoms of the past, than to the radicalism of the old Radicals of the 1849 generation.[16]

From the 1860s, the market for urban and rural lands in Cundinamarca was quite an active one. The Liberal merchants participated enthusiastically in the auction of Church lands, and in addition, they bought lands in the valleys of the *altiplano* and the hot country. Fatstock raising increased in importance; on the lists of the share-holders and directors of the new banks, ranchers, urban and rural landowners, and importers appear side by side. The lists of the pioneer coffee-planters generally coincide with the lists of main urban property-owners, merchants, cattlemen, recipients of public lands, and importers.[17] During the 1890s, coffee was the centre of many entrepreneurs' wealth and influence; nevertheless, they took care to maintain their interests in other fields: many coffee-growers could still be found securely placed behind their shop counters in the *calle real*.

It would be an error to attribute too much wealth or political control to this group from Bogotá, at least in comparison with the landowners and merchants of Mexico or Peru, the cattle ranchers of the River Plate, or the coffee magnates of the Paraíba valley and, in due course, of São Paulo. They were men of modest wealth even in comparison with the mine-owners and merchants of Antioquia. If, for example, we consider the importance of the extensive kinship links of the merchant groups, it is clear that coffee, in common with any other expanding activity, offered employment and opportunities for advancement to the poorer sons of good families. It is not surprising that the police force of Bogotá, founded at a time when the export economy was in crisis, and commercial activity was depressed, should have attracted this kind of recruit particularly. But once the establishment of coffee haciendas began and commerce began to pick up as a consequence, the police force was deprived of these recruits, much to the regret of the Chief of the force.[18]

Ospina Hermanos of Medellín

One characteristic of the merchant class was the low degree of differentiation between its diverse activities. Although the Vargas, Samper, Liévano, Camacho Roldán, and Tamayo families, for example, sought to specialize in the import trade and in banking and insurance operations,[19] it was more common to seek to diversify one's assets, and the degree of diversification was greater where capital was abundant and where there was a variety of opportunities for investment.

The history of the Ospina family of Medellín demonstrates some of the basic characteristics we have discussed – diversification of assets and the way ties between the commercial bourgeoisie and the government could guarantee the success of economic enterprises. The voluminous commercial correspondence of Ospina Hermanos highlights both the above points.

Between 1885 and 1905 Ospina Hermanos were managing an average of ten different businesses at any one time, reaching the number of eighteen on more than one occasion. The assets of the Ospina group included coffee and banking interests in Guatemala, the mining and smelting of gold, the importing of manufactured goods and their distribution throughout Antioquia by means of various systems of credit extended to municipal merchants, financial intermediation through banks in Bogotá, the exporting of gold, railway contracts, speculation in urban real estate and public-land bonds, and the sale of rights to farm taxes on liquor in different departments of the country; during the eighties the Ospinas, in partnership with the Vásquez family, established in the municipalities of Amagá and Fredonia a dozen large haciendas dedicated to sugar-cane, cattle, and coffee, and by the end of the century they were exporting coffee and planning to set up sizeable factories for the production of dynamite and footwear. To give an example of the degree of 'economic rationality' of the Medellín oligarchy, it is sufficient to cite a letter from Ospina Hermanos directed to one of their agents in the capital regarding the arguments that he should put forward to back a request for the concession of the exclusive privilege to build a dynamite factory in Medellín to supply the market of miners in Antioquia: (*a*) saving of foreign currency, (*b*) use of national raw materials, (*c*) a low price to the consumer, (*d*) the creation of employment.[20] They had also tried to produce beer, and in 1892 they planned investment in a chocolate factory which 'can give good results here, as much because the product is consumed here in great quantities, as because the city does not have a single factory . . . In this business we would come straight into contact with the indescribable tyranny of crisis which plagues Antioquia.'[21]

Existing legislation, or privileges which could be extracted from the central government, determined the birth and evolution of a majority of these activities. The conclusion one draws from the correspondence is that the fall of Liberalism transformed the *antioqueño* bourgeoisie from victim of official discrimination into beneficiary. Many economic activities — mining, railroad concessions, the sale of liquor — require individual studies on their respective relations with local and national government. The Ospina archive is a good starting point for such studies. Projects of industrial development were likewise dependent on networks of political and personal relations. Thus Santiago wrote to his brother Tulio Ospina about a proposed dynamite factory in the following terms: 'Cuervo [Minister of War at the time] is committed by his interest in this speculation to help directly. We think it an impossibility that they will deny a concession to him, Arboleda, and you together, a concession which will hurt no one.'[22] Influence at a similarly high level was required to carry through a project to supply foot-wear and Colt carbines to the Colombian army. To gain concessions of mines, political influence was crucial.[23] 'From a very detailed study of the tax books done by Tulio, it seems that there are many important mines which have been abandoned, and among them *all* of those we thought could be sold in Europe; but they cannot be claimed until the Council decides what interpretation to give article 345 of the "Mining Code". We are making unheard-of efforts to obtain a favourable resolution which could be worth hundreds of thousands to us.'[24]

The same occurred with railroad concessions. Despite their political and economic risks, these concessions let loose a chain reaction leading to new businesses and investments. For example, this was the case with the coal mines of Amagá: 'if the railroad becomes a fact, then they are worth a lot, and will be worth more'. Such a reaction is seen too in urban land speculation: in the commercial centre of Medellín the value of plots depended on the location of the railroad station, a decision which, according to the concession, belonged to Ospina Hermanos.[25]

The study of the auction of the *aguardiente*'s taxes would be yet another important source for research into the provincial power structure, and the relationship between elections, departmental *caciques*, and auctioneers. The Ospinas were closely linked to the above operations in Cauca, Tolima, Cundinamarca, and Antioquia, and in all these departments fought real political—economic battles or formed transitory alliances with their main competitor, Pepe Sierra.[26]

The overall view above should be rounded out by mentioning two points. First, each one of the enterprises referred to required a detailed knowledge of economic factors. For example, there are numerous studies of feasibility in the correspondence. For investment in the liquor business, calculations were made of potential demand, comparative costs of producing the sugar-cane or buying it, costs of processing, transport, different kinds of stills (French stills were preferred), administration, storage, etc. Such calculations would have been unthinkable without the practical bent and technical education valued so much by important sectors of the Colombian elite.[27]

On the other hand, politics continued to be unstable, and business uncertain. The Ospinas sold their Guatemalan hacienda, Cerro-Redondo, in 1888. The political and economic climate seemed to close off the possibility of 'transferring to another country . . . depreciation of the currency is ruining us slowly'. To this observation was added 'the conviction that this country will never settle down'. In February, they blamed the instability on the policy of 'liberalization' begun by Vice-President Payán. Six months later, in August 1888, they saw the two enemies of the country as being 'a government that cannot organize its fiscal branch, and the triumph of Radicalism in Venezuela'.[28]

As will be seen later, the political economy of the time caused them the same uncertainties it caused the Liberal merchants of Bogotá. Both for investment in cattle and coffee production (undertaken on a grand scale in the 1890s) and for dealings in the foreign-exchange market, the risks continued to be very high: 'letters of exchange rise here [Medellín] from day to day, as a 50-centavo piece is worth only 1 French franc, and it is very convenient to have assets outside the country'.[29]

The Ospina archive is helpful in one last respect: if one wants to know more about the climate and protagonists of the civil war, the codes used by Ospina Hermanos in their telegraphic correspondence are useful reading.[30]

Indiscriminate expansion can present problems of management to a family firm. By 1893 there were so many problems associated with the sale of liquor that Santiago Ospina wrote to Tulio, apparently the most enterprising of the family: 'For now it is necessary that we think of making life more tranquil and tolerable, to suppress unsettling ambitions, to limit ourselves to businesses we can administer calmly, in conjunction or separately. Speaking for myself, every day I feel more strongly the desire to lead a tranquil life in which I can consider at leisure how to educate the children properly. In the present pressure of business and its conflicts, this is almost impossible, because it takes up nearly all my time.'[31]

To their functions as merchants the Ospinas had to add their functions as public men. Sons as they were of an ex-President, their active participation was demanded by their Conservative co-partisans. Together with business went politics, and in this generation Pedro Nel Ospina made a political career. Thus influence in social and political life had its inescapable duties. This rich tapestry of economic, political, and cultural inter-relation, which guaranteed the hegemony of the Antioquia bourgeoisie as a class, led Luis Ospina Vázquez to state in his classic work that writing about the economic history of Colombia required something of the skills of a novelist.[32]

Every merchant was or wished to be like Santiago Eder, the 'founder': 'A lawyer by profession, he preferred to devote himself to trade; he undertook the production of sugar, but also acted as agent for other growers; he sought out markets for industrial products, and dealt in rural properties when the occasion presented itself; he invested in river transport and in mining, and finally became the first to plant, cultivate, and export coffee from the bountiful lands of Palmira, finding foreign markets at the same time for the high-grade tobacco he grew and cured there. Like all Colombians, he had a finger in every pie.'[33]

In Santander too, the largest and most modern haciendas were established by merchants from Bucaramanga, San Gil, and Cúcuta with capital accumulated from the export of tobacco and cotton, quinine and coffee, and the importing of food, fine cloths, porcelain, glassware, and pianos – all of which, according to the chronicler of life in Bucaramanga, wrought a revolution in the customs and social life of that remote township.[34]

Underlying this whole process was the fact that free trade, which favoured the export of agricultural products, necessarily led the merchant to become an owner of land himself.

Investment in coffee production, 1870–99

Contrasting with the pessimism that came with the general decline of exports after 1875 were the islands of optimism that appeared in isolated corners of Colombia, sustained by the possibility of expanding coffee cultivation. The response to a survey drawn up in 1878 by the new Commissioner for National Agriculture, Juan de Dios Carrasquilla, was strong and enthusiastic. From Chaparral a group led by the Rocha brothers reported the opening of four haciendas with 300,000 trees planted with scientific methods. Their motto was 'few trees well kept are better than badly tended plantations'. What stands out also is their jealousy in keeping secret their modern methods of production. They had little success, since neighbouring farms could 'spy'. More important, the differences between current costs of production and transport (1 peso = 1 *arroba* of *pergamino*) and the prices offered in the Chaparral market (2.40 pesos = 1 *arroba*) created such a favourable situation 'that even ignorant peasants have recognized it as such' and had planted small plots of trees.[35]

Conditions in Chaparral were apparently excellent: fertile and abundant land; cheap transport via the Saldaña river (if we accept Rocha's calculations that it was cheaper to get their coffee to Honda than it was for producers in Sasaima); 'and a locality which encourages emigration from localities where there is a lack of cultivable lands'.[36] Reports in the same vein, often with much exaggeration about yields, came from Fusagasugá, Viotá, Nilo, La Mesa, Villavicencio, Gachalá, Palmira, Yarumal, and La Florida in Santander.[37] In many of these places, extensive plantations were owned by prominent individuals. In Nilo, for example, Francisco Groot, Antonio Ricaurte, and Daniel Junguito had 480,000 trees in production. Near Milo, in La Mesa, the traditional division of land between the sugar-cane of the proprietors and the maize of *colono* labour was complicated by the appearance of coffee, even though small producers could not pay the high transport costs.[38] Information from Medellín stated that the only obstacle to coffee was the lack of cheap transport.[39] Private efforts were sometimes aided by official stimulus. A bonus of 50 pesos for every 500 trees planted was offered in Cauca that year.[40] In 1874 a law was approved declaring the machinery required for processing coffee free of import charges.[41]

In 1880, former President Mariano Ospina Rodríguez's pamphlet *The Cultivation of Coffee* was published. The very high prices since 1860 were what attracted entrepreneurs most. The average price for a pound of coffee in New York had been: 1860–5, 24.5 U.S. cents; 1866–70, 17.7 cents; 1871–5, 19.2 cents; 1876–80, 16.3 cents.[42] The fall in international transport costs had not yet had an effect, but it is possible to estimate that the c.i.f. (cost, insurance, freight) price was around 8 U.S. cents per pound. Furthermore, in May 1872 the United States, which was one of the main markets for Colombian coffee, removed the import tax of 3 U.S. cents per pound.[43]

Had Carrasquilla repeated his survey in 1882–6, the picture would have been much darker. Between 1881 and 1885, the price of coffee in New York fell to 11 cents per pound, to recover to 13.1 cents in the late 1880s. Between 1891 and 1895, the price rose to 17.1 cents, only to collapse again: in 1896 to 15.7 cents; in 1897 to 13.5 cents; in 1898 to 11.5 cents; in 1899 to 8.6 cents; and in 1900 to 7 cents.[44]

Between 1880 and 1888 growers in many regions seem to have converted their coffee lands into pastures, a process which would be repeated in later crises. In 1886 the government was alarmed enough by the crisis to decree a premium of 4 per cent for exporters. The dire financial straits of the country, however, led to the suspension of the measure less than a year after its implementation.[45] Good prices after 1888 finally gave the stimulus needed for recovery. The effects of the monetary policies implemented after 1880 will be discussed later.

Let us look more closely now at factors which affected the process of investment in its period of growth between 1888 and 1896. The *bogotano* merchants who set up plantations in the south-west of the department serve as a general case study. Later, I take a specific case. Some general points about problems of finance and investment in Antioquia will also be discussed.

In the Tequendama and Sumapaz regions some 35,000 hectares were brought under cultivation, mainly through the setting up of haciendas between 1870 and 1898. The taking up of lands for coffee proceeded most rapidly between 1885 and 1896, for Camacho Roldán estimated that 80 per cent of the direct investment in coffee took place in those years, and the register of land transactions confirms his statement.[46] Coffee-growing was accompanied by the cultivation of sugar-cane, maize, yuca, and bananas, and the maintenance of pastures to provide forage for mules and other beasts of burden and to fatten cattle for sale. In all, the area occupied by coffee plantations in these areas can be calculated at around 10,000 hectares. These 10,000 hectares can be seen as the heart and *raison d'etre* of the 35,000 hectares brought under cultivation, for the 25,000 hectares devoted to other purposes were, so to speak, a function of the 10,000 hectares devoted to coffee.

The investment required to set up a coffee hacienda was of a particular nature. The process took five years from the first clearing operations to the production of the first commercial harvest, and the monetary cost of the various factors of production can be broken down proportionately as in the accompanying table. The price of land rose much more quickly than prices for machinery, animals, seeds, or wages. Evidently inflation played a significant part in this rise. It is difficult to draw reliable conclusions about land prices, since there was no established land-market structure and prices were influenced by a number of very local or accidental circumstances. However, it is perhaps possible to detect a trend in the price of uncultivated land in the *municipios* of Viotá and El Colegio in Cundinamarca and Fredonia and Amagá in Antioquia as shown in table 4.

But the more important factors in this process of appreciation appear to have been the suitability of the soils in the area for growing coffee and a process of general improvement, if only of the roads, which, like all roads in the Republic, were 'mud in winter, dust in summer'. Profiteering and speculation accompanied the rise in land prices: 'Until a year ago there was

	1879–84	1892–6
Purchase of land	23%	37%
Purchase of machinery and tools, construction of buildings	10%	10%
Seeds and animals	12%	9%
Payment of labour force	55%	44%
Total	100%	100%

Sources: J. de D. Carrasquilla, *Segundo Informe Anual que presenta el Comisario de la Agricultura Nacional al Poder Ejecutivo para conocimiento del Congreso: año 1880* (Bogotá, 1880), pp. 60–2. N. Sáenz, 'Memoria sobre el cultivo del cafeto', *El Agricultor*, no. 11 (May 1892). The two calculations do not agree on the kind of machinery which should be used for processing. The 1879–84 calculation assumes an annual 10% interest rate on annual expenditure; for 1892–6, I have calculated an interest rate of 12%, which was the prevalent rate in merchant transactions in Bogotá, and I have applied it to all annual expenditures.

I have also made my own calculations of the price of land, which according to Sáenz was between 1 and 50 pesos per *fanegada*. I chose the price of uncultivated land in the Tequendama region, which in those years (1892–6) was 34.50 pesos silver per hectare.

vigorous and enthusiastic support for activities related to coffee. But the fall in prices on the European market, and more important, the excessive rise in the value of rural coffee-producing estates even before production has begun' acted as disincentives, wrote Carlos Abondano to the Agricultural *comisario* at the end of 1879.[47] In spite of the attractions offered by investment in land in a period of inflation, in these circumstances the hazards were a common trait, and the return on capital was slow. Taken year by year, the costs involved were approximately as follows:

First year	48%	Purchase of land and tools, clearing, planting of coffee and shade trees, establishment of pastures, etc.
Second year	16%	Maintenance of the coffee plantation and pastures, sowing of cane
Third year	10%	As second year
Fourth year	8%	As second year, plus first harvest of *pepeos*
Fifth year	18%	Purchase and installation of machinery and first commercial harvest

Sources: See table above.

Table 4. *Price per hectare of uncultivated land in four municipalities of the coffee zones, 1865–91*

Year	Viotá–El Colegio		Fredonia–Amagá	
	Pesos silver (8/10)	£	Pesos silver (8/10)	£
1865	5.35	1.06	–	–
1875	8.40	1.66	7.65	1.51
1879	17.37	3.56	18.54	3.80
1886	26.03	4.01	31.60	4.87
1891	31.40	4.97	36.20	5.73

Source: Based on the archives of transactions of land sales of the Oficianas de Registro de Instrumentos Publicos y Privados of La Mesa, Cundinamarca, and of Fredonia, Antioquia. It must be mentioned that silver was devalued in relation to gold in 1873, so that part of the increase in the price of land between 1875 and 1879 should be attributed to this factor.

According to the estimates made by a Viotá *hacendado*, Carlos Abondano, it cost 10,000 pesos in paper money to set up a 100-hectare hacienda between 1880 and 1884. In this case 40 hectares were planted with coffee, the remaining 60 being divided between pastures, cane-fields, tenant holdings, and woodland.[48] A similar calculation made by Nicolas Sáenz ten years later gives a clear impression of the effects of inflation.[49] These estimates tally well with the accounts of Roberto Herrera.[50] If we take a simple average from the figures given by Abondano and Sáenz, it appears that the opening up of one hectare in a typical coffee hacienda in Cundinamarca between 1880 and 1894 was 140 pesos in paper money. For a rough estimate such as we are making here it is sufficient to apply to this figure the average rate of devaluation during the period to convert it into terms of gold;[51] this gives us a sum of 83 pesos gold. Multiplying our original 35,000 hectares by 83 we reach a figure of 2,905,000 pesos gold, and we can conclude that the establishment of the one hundred coffee haciendas in Tequendama and El Sumapaz during the last thirty years of the nineteenth century demanded of the Bogotá merchants an investment of approximately 3,000,000 pesos gold. Where did this money come from? The question is a crucial one if we take into account the constant complaints of a 'dearth of capital' and of the high cost of money for investments of this kind.

The production of coffee was an uncertain business, with capital tied up for a considerable period. Once the commitment to the initial investment had been made, involving as we saw 48 per cent of the cost in the first year, the enterprise continued to demand considerable and regular expenditure. In these conditions, the cost of the capital invested in establishing a hacienda must have been high compared, for example, with speculative operations with bonds issued against the internal or external debt, or with imports financed as was customary through the internal or external banking systems, each offering a rapid return on invested capital. As a result of this situation (which calls for a quantitative analysis to establish with greater clarity the initial conditions surrounding capitalist development in Colombia) the new *hacendados* were forced to seek mortgages and to enter into agreements with foreign coffee-dealers.

At the present time, it is difficult to know the total amount of loans given out by foreign agents, but there is no doubt that the credit given by them was crucial. The conditions they offered made investment more attractive: 6 per cent interest a year and a two-year repayment period. The debt was paid with coffee at the existing price at the time of sale. The foreign firms here charged their clients a middleman's commission of between 1.5 and 2 per cent.[52]

It is very difficult, as well, to quantify even approximately the specific origin of the funds invested in the creation of coffee haciendas. Despite the proliferation of laws and decrees creating mortgage banks, and references in official literature to the importance of credit for agriculture for medium- and long-term loans at low rates of interest. The merchants-turned-coffee-planters found two main sources of credit: the first was through mortgage, generally granted by the landowners who sold them the land, the second through the advance sale of crops to agents abroad.[53]

Practically no land transaction was made which did not begin with a mortgage; in Cundinamarca the most common method of purchase was by instalments, generally falling due every two years, with interest running at between 10 and 12 per cent per annum. The buyers formed civil or commercial companies, with membership usually limited to their immediate families. These companies had recourse to various forms of finance, and their creditors were the former owners of the land or the import houses of Paris, London, and New York. The former gave them convenient terms for the purchase of the land and the latter made them advances for the purchase of machinery and the payment of wages to the workforce.

The aim of these companies was to produce and export coffee. 'There are very few in this district who do not send their coffee for export', wrote a contemporary observer,[54] and the same could be said of the *hacendados* of Cundinamarca, Tolima, Santander, and Antioquia during the period. To a certain extent the growers were obliged to sell directly to foreign agents.

If mortgage was the principal method of finance in the period in which the coffee hacienda was being established, coffee as an international com-

Table 5. *Commercial companies investing in haciendas*

Company	Date founded	Nominal capital	Hacienda
Antonio Samper & Co.	1878	630,000 francs[a]	Golconda
Sáenz Hermanos	1881	6,513 paper pesos	Liberia, Misiones, Ingenio San Antonio[b]
De La Guardia & Co.	1881	22,000 paper pesos	Costa Rica
R. & C. Williamson	1881		Los Olivos
Camacho Roldán & Tamayo	1882	914,000[c] paper pesos	Costa Rica
Tovar Hermanos	1892	45,000 paper pesos	Java
Iregui Hermanos	1892	44,000 paper pesos	La Argentina—California
Ortiz & Sayer	1894	50,000 paper pesos	Los Olivos—La Magdalena
De Mier & Umaña	1896		La Africana
Gómez U. & Co.	1900		La Rambla
Abondano & Uribe	1901		Arabia, Delicias, La Carolina

a The nominal capital is that declared at the time of its reconstitution as Samper Uribe & Cía in 1897. *b* The Ingenio San Antonio as such was formed only in the 1920s, but the hacienda was acquired by Sáenz Hermanos at the end of the nineteenth century, and worked from that time onwards. *c* This sum is that relating to the sale of the estate of Salvador Camacho Roldán, partner in the enterprise in 1900.
All the other figures for nominal capital are given at the time the companies were founded; where no figure is given, it was assumed that the hacienda itself constituted the capital base of the company.
Source: Oficina de Registro de Instrumentos Públicos y Privados, La Mesa; ANC, Notarías de Bogotá.

modity was the basis of a system of external credit which expanded without restraint in periods of optimism and high prices. Not only in Cundinamarca, but throughout the coffee zone, the agents of the foreign commercial houses appeared on the scene very early on, and to a certain extent tied the hands of the *hacendados*.

In July 1899 Jose I. Márquez Vásquez, the owner of La Amalia, the largest coffee hacienda in Antioquia, wrote to C. Ponthier, the representative of the interests of Amsinck of New York, requesting a credit of U.S. $16,000 at 6 per cent per annum, and offering to pay off the loan with half of each coffee harvest, calculated at a total of 800 bags. In his written request Márquez gave a brief description of La Amalia; it had 400 *cuadras* (256 hectares) of the best land, with 120,000 coffee bushes in perfect condition. 16,000 of them 'older stock' (all of seven years old!), 70,000 in full production, and the rest coming into full production with the next harvest. The hacienda also boasted modern installations for processing the crop, and 70 *cuadras* (44.8 hectares) of sugar-cane, with its own sugar mill. The property was valued by experts at 140,000 paper pesos; nevertheless, the most interesting observation came at the end; three years before, in 1896, Fould & Cie of Paris had advanced £3,500 on the property, 'a sum almost wholly invested in the improvements described'.[55]

It appears that the proposed loan was not negotiated, for in December 1899, after the start of the War of the Thousand Days, Márquez wrote to Fould apologizing for the delay in the despatching of coffee, a result of the disturbances brought about by the war. By May 1901 Fould & Cie were planning to wind up their activities in Medellín, and asked Márquez to make his own arrangements to export his coffee, and to repay his debt with cash. At this point, Márquez turned again to Amsinck.[56]

Events in Cundinamarca turned out even worse, for the war was a complete disaster for the great planters. Around 1907 a new ritual formula made its appearance in the deeds which formalized the contracts between the Bogotá merchants and their agents; the mortgage would be converted into an *anticresis* contract 'should disturbances in the public order of the Republic of Colombia prevent the debtor from meeting his obligations'.[57]

Pedro Alejo Forero has given a typical summary of the merchant's attitude toward investment in coffee: 'To set yourself up in a plantation requires eight to ten years of labour, considerable capital, a great deal of patience, and no small degree of sacrifice . . . When I hear people talk of the prosperity which the cultivation of coffee is bound to bring to our country, I rejoice . . . but I think of the distance we are from the sea, the oppressive nature of the government, the scarcity of labour, the idleness of the hands we have, the cost of money and of tools, the insecurity in which we live — for when we are not suffering a revolution we are expecting one — the backwardness of our mechanical arts . . .'[58] Some elements of this gloomy vision are entirely justified, especially the emphasis upon the negative effects on investment of the chronic civil wars and political instability. During the period of the coffee take-off, there were four major civil wars in succession, which discouraged further investment. For example, 1876 was a year of insecurity in the area of Tequendama, with Conservative guerrilla fighters constantly making incursions, particularly into the La Masa region to kidnap Liberal *hacendados* and to obtain ransoms for their return.[59]

Among the *antioqueños* the shift into coffee was also viewed with apprehension, and it was undertaken cautiously.

Later we will discuss in more detail why the relationship between the monetary policy of the Regeneration and coffee expansion was not as simple as is thought. Here it is sufficient for our purposes to study one important example: the opening of coffee haciendas in the south-west of Antioquia by a family group closely linked to the highest levels of the Conservative government.

In Antioquia coffee-growing took off in the 1890s, and it is during these years that we see most clearly the favourable effects of inflation and devaluation. Nevertheless, in August 1897 Ospina Hermanos wrote the following letter to Enrique Cortés & Co.:

'We had hopes of being able to process the coffee of this harvest in the machinery we are building for this purpose, but we have decided to send at least a part of the said harvest in párchment, in order to cover the amount we owe you on our overdraft. We wish to know your opinion on the outlook of coffee, stated in a more explicit manner than in your magazines. We have great extensions of land given over to the cultivation of coffee in Amagá and Fredonia, the best districts of Antioquia in terms of soil fertility, and we also have numerous healthy nurseries of small trees which we have been preparing since last year. Do you really think it is worth while to plant coffee in Colombia in spite of the high price of exchange? Will English production [sic] be as great as they promise?'[60]

That same year they had a total of 240,000 trees on two plantations (El Porvenir and El Amaro) in Amagá and Fredonia, and they had taken care to use the same shade methods as Asian plantations. At the end of the same year, 1893, the governmental prohibition on the circulation of cheques had an automatic repercussion on the exchange rate, forcing it downwards. The effects were analysed by the Ospinas in the following terms: 'what will happen will be that, without a way of meeting expenditure, the exploitation of mines and plantations will diminish, and scarcities in gold and coffee will occur'.[61] In January 1894, 'the situation here [Medellín] is more difficult each day: it is impossible to get money even at the highest interest rates; the banks are reduced to even more complete inaction than before because of the order to recover the cheques'.[62] Thus the same perception of the phenomenon can be seen in Antioquia which will be shown in later pages actually operating in Cundinamarca: inflation raised the cost of production too high and devaluation did not compensate exporters for this rise.

Investment based on low interest advances from Amsinck, and the high level of diversification of their haciendas (sugar-cane and cattle as well as coffee) allowed the Ospinas to ride out temporary losses occasioned by the fragility of the money market. Nevertheless, their opposition to such government measures, at least in private correspondence, was as dramatic as that of the *bogotanos*: 'with the suspension of the circulation of cheques . . . the crisis will reach the highest levels, and businesses and industries will stop functioning, leaving thousands of people subject to unemployment and hunger'.[63]

Bernardo Herrera Restrepo and his Hacienda Santa Bárbara

Before closing this chapter, it is worth while sketching the case of a typical *bogotano* merchant who converted himself into an *hacendado* and coffee-exporter.[64] In the middle of 1879 Bernardo Herrera Restrepo and Nepomuceno Santamaría formed a family commercial society, for 'speculation in coffee'. With 12,000 pesos silver (8/10)[65] they bought a farm of 128 hectares in Sasaima, which was still at the centre of coffee cultivation in Cundinamarca. They took advantage of good hillside lands near a route which since colonial times had joined Santa Fé de Bogotá with Honda on the Magdalena river. In March 1883, the society was dissolved and Herrera remained as the sole proprietor of the hacienda, which by now had been paid for. The large initial expenditures give an idea of the abandoned state of coffee plantations, their processing equipment and other buildings. In 1880 Herrera invested 6,173 pesos, and in 1881 another 5,644 pesos or almost as much as the land was worth. He used the money to prepare the land for cultivation, to buy draught animals, for buildings, and to import machinery. A large share of the wages were paid towards the construction of water-works, buildings, washing-tanks, and drying-stoves. The initial production of coffee was very modest: in 1880, 92 bags were exported to London; in 1881, only 63. Between 1882 and 1895 Herrera tried to export coffee to New York, but finally settled for London when

Steibel Brothers offered him their services as agents and advanced him some credit. During the brief history of Santa Bárbara hacienda production after 1885, all exports went to London.

From the production curve and Herrera's activities three clearly defined periods emerge:

(A) From 1880 to 1887 Herrera improved on existing crops, extended coffee cultivation, introduced cattle, and established the lines of internal organization. He contracted an administrator who was to stay with him until at least 1903; and he instituted the system of service tenure, *arrendamiento*, for the resident population. The hacienda seems to have made sure of a seasonal labour supply from the *altiplano*, the Bogota–Boyacá *sabana*, and in some cases from among small cultivators from the municipality of Sasaima. In 1887 the production of coffee was 311 bags of 60 kilos each. The hacienda, as was then the custom, had among its installations processing machines which peeled and 'polished' the grain, so that except when the machine broke down, the hacienda exported peeled or green coffee. The advantage of exporting green coffee was obvious: it weighed 20 per cent less than parchment and was worth 15–20 per cent more on the market. In 1887 Herrera bought an adjacent property, San Bernardo, also of 128 hectares, worth 10,000 pesos silver. It was immediately integrated into the Santa Bárbara system.

(B) At this point the second phase, that of expansion, begins. From 1892 sizeable returns begin to flow in, a year when 426 bags were produced. In 1894 nearly 700 bags were exported. Herrera built what was by local standards a commodious country house. A greater part of wages between 1892 and 1895 were paid out towards the new building. The production figures continued to rise, with some drops in 1895 and 1899, caused perhaps by climatic factors.

(C) The third and last phase began in 1902, when production fell from 1,200 bags to 320. From 1900 little was exported as a result of the civil war, and stocks were piled up in poor conditions. By 1900 it was almost impossible for peasants and farm labourers to travel the roads without danger of falling into the hands of recruiting patrols. Although nominal salaries rose, the price of foodstuffs like meat and *miel*, after a temporary local decline shot up. It became impossible to find harvesters.[66] Santa Bárbara never recovered to its pre-war production figures. In 1909, in a sworn declaration made to the municipality of Facatativa, the administrator of the property stated that the hacienda was reduced to 'a third of what it was', and that its value was 25,000 pesos gold.[67] As a last attempt to put the hacienda on its feet, Herrera made a final investment in weeding the property, and in 'Nitro-Bactarine' patent fertilizer. It was probably too late:

in the next two years production was only an average 480 bags a year.
Herrera then decided to sell the property for 60,000 pesos gold (1 peso
gold = U.S. $1) but there were no buyers. Herrera died in 1912. In 1930
the hacienda was divided into summer properties for holidaying *bogotanos.*[68]

Santa Bárbara's fate after 1910 was not typical of Cundinamarca haciendas,
as will be seen later. Its rise in the 1880s, and its decline during the international depression and the civil war were, however, typical experiences of
coffee cultivation throughout the country, except in Antioquia.

Now we can answer questions about the profitability of Santa Bárbara
and the measures Herrera undertook to raise the profit margin. Profitability
is one of the central themes in economic history. Herrera's accounts are a
good point for further research into the field. No attempt is made here to
use the case study to calculate the rate of return on investment in coffee
in Colombia as a whole.

The calculations of profitability that have been elaborated for plan-
tation-owners in the southern United States show the complexity of theory
and historical method that has to be brought to bear. They serve as a good
example for the historian interested in this type of analysis.[69] There are
two explicit studies of the historical profitability of coffee cultivation in
Colombia. Darío Bustamante did a calculation of accounting profitability
based on the Herrera archive.[70] William McGreevey, working within the
theoretical context of the 'new economic history', worked out a projection
of economic profitability (as opposed to accounting profitability).[71]

According to the accounting profitability posited by Bustamante,
Santa Bárbara gave a return of 34 per cent per year between 1886 and 1900,
and an even more surprising 50 per cent in the price-depression years of
1896–1900. According to McGreevey, 'an investment in coffee cultivation
in 1893 would have brought a real rate of return over the next 20 years of
over 35% to the investor'.[72]

Bustamante's conclusion is the easier of the two to reject, because it is
based on an incorrect reading of Herrera's accounting. Bustamante took as
100 per cent of the capital just one of its components, the rather subjective
value Herrera gave to the hacienda. He did not include stocks or other
assets of the enterprise. Two additional points must be made. First, the
commercial value of a coffee harvest could be greater than the commercial
value of the hacienda. Furthermore, there is a time-lag factor: the commercial realization of a harvest took in those days an average of six months.
Also, Herrera was a planter who exported and was likely to have at any one
time stocks in the hacienda or on the way to London or in the hands of
his London agents. In table 6 one can see the trend in account profitability

Table 6. *Hacienda Santa Bárbara account profitability, 1889–1900*

Year	Capital (A) Paper pesos	Profits		Account profitability (B/A × 100) %
		Paper pesos (B)	£	
1889	76,632	10,839	1,116	14.1
1890	77,336	10,301	1,059	13.3
1891	83,761	11,949	1,172	14.3
1892	100,537	13,310	1,366	13.2
1893	110,146	13,002	1,128	11.8
1894	119,648	23,511	1,749	19.7
1895	165,006	46,547	3,905	28.2
1896	216,400	57,722	4,810	26.7
1897	205,500	37,879[a]	3,049[a]	18.4
1898	165,102	14,435	991	8.7
1899	141,339	15,955	908	11.3
1900	136,418	27,141	474	19.9[b]

a The profit that year was 43,450 pesos, but he discounted 20% because of the 'lifeless market for coffee in Europe'. *b* The profit in 1900 is a hypothetical calculation as in the account books there were no shipments to London.
Source: Archivo Herrera, Libros de Contabilidad.

calculated in paper pesos and English pounds sterling, which in this case would be the equivalent of profits in 1889 pesos.

We are fortunate in that Herrera calculated the commercial value of his stocks, thus simplifying a problem which would otherwise be immense. In table 7, I present the hacienda's trend in account profitability, which should be closer to real profit rates, and adjust more easily to the price curve. The calculations resolve the contradiction that in a time of an international depression of coffee prices, profits should sharply rise. As will be seen in chapter 5, monetary policy was also unfavourable to the profitability of coffee during this period.

McGreevey's conclusion is also difficult to discuss at a strictly empirical level because he does not formulate what the real rate of profit was. Rather, he projects the expected profits of 1893, a year of good prices, to 1913. Furthermore, the comparison he makes between coffee and railway investments is very debatable, because in the railway business there existed barriers to entry which permitted super-normal profits for extended periods of time, whereas in coffee, on the supply side there was an increase in competitors, and on the demand side an uncontrollable price cycle. In addition, the railway companies imposed monopolistic tariffs which maintained extraordinary benefits.

Table 7. *Santa Bárbara: trends in account profitability, 1889–1900*
(1889 = 100)

Year	Profits (pesos)	Profits (£)	Account profitability
1889	100	100	100
1890	95	95	94
1891	110	105	101
1892	122	122	93
1893	120	101	83
1894	217	157	139
1895	429	350	200
1896	532	431	189
1897	349	273	130
1898	133	89	61
1899	147	81	80
1900	250	41	—

Source: See table 6.

It would not be surprising to find in the history of Latin American haciendas rises in profitability which do not correspond to rises in productivity, but which instead originate from harsh exploitation of the workforce in the context of a static production function. Later we will discuss the problem of 'efficiency'; but accepting that Herrera, like other entrepreneurs, tried to make his workers produce more for less, he still had to take into account ecological, technical, and economic factors affecting at the same time both labour and land productivity. In other words, he could exploit labour better if he exploited his land more efficiently. The latter proposition is valid only when used to discuss the system of the central plantation worked by *arrendatarios* which reigned on Santa Bárbara and the haciendas of Cundinamarca. It is probable that the share-cropping system prevalent in Santander and the Brazilian *colono* system had different implications for the relationship between profitability and productivity.

We assume that Santa Bárbara kept up the density of 1,600–1,700 trees per hectare common among the plantations of Cundinamarca. Its average yearly yield between 1897 and 1901 was 950 kilos per hectare of green coffee or 1,187 kilos per hectare of parchment coffee. The latter figures represent one of the highest levels of productivity possible under the so-called traditional system of cultivation.[73]

Using table 8, it would be possible to calculate the rate of return using the capital—value formula. The uncertainties, however, are very many.[74] On the one hand, we know little about the prevalent effective rate of interest, or the rate of profit in the other activities all Bogotá merchants had access to. Furthermore, the period was one of great monetary instability, during which assets do not depreciate but constantly appreciate in money terms. In addition there is the problem of deciding which currency to make calculations in. Initial investment and running costs (excluding maritime transport, insurance, storage, commissions to foreign agents) were paid in paper money, while income was received in pounds sterling. Herrera, on occasion, had to calculate the value of his property in pounds sterling. Nevertheless, for my merely descriptive aim of establishing the structure of the running costs of a coffee hacienda, the table still has value.

The only sure conclusion is that economic profitability was high, although perhaps not as high as McGreevey suggests. It was probably near the account-profitability figures in table 6. Even so, the history of Santa Bárbara underlines the risks accompanying these enterprises.

In concluding tentatively with the Herrera case, we accept the following two propositions. First, the nominal rate of interest prevalent in the transactions of the Bogotá merchants at the end of the century (10—12 per cent) was more or less equivalent to the normal rate of profit on capital. Second, Herrera's account profitability of 16.4 per cent, as shown in table 6, is equivalent to the normal rate of profit of coffee investment. One last point about profits: Herrera never took the equivalent of a salary, as manager of his enterprise, from the profits. It is thus not too difficult to accept that the difference in return was paying for his entrepreneurship and for the higher risk of this investment.

After 1910 coffee prices recovered considerably. McGreevey's projections become more untenable if we consider that after 1910 no massive transfer of capital to coffee investment took place in spite of the price increases. It is true that between 1910 and 1930 the majority of the haciendas recovered. Nevertheless, massive investment on the scale of that which took place between 1880 and 1895 never occurred again. The experience of a rate of profit which did not compensate for the risk of investment, coupled with the possibility of alternative activities involving less effort and risk, probably accounts for the relative decline in coffee investment.

To summarize, in the process of consolidation of the coffee economy urban merchant groups became coffee-cultivators; the commercial capital accumulated in the tobacco cycle was placed in the financial sector, and went to finance foreign trade, transport systems, and the public debt, or

Table 8. *Santa Bárbara: production costs and prices of coffee*

	Capital		Wages			Administration
Year	Capital (paper money)	Value of hacienda (paper money)	Day-wages of *arren-datarios*	Picker's day-wages	*Miel*	Salary of administrator
1880	–	–	657.0	–	–	1,065.0
1881	–	–	2,475.0	–	–	507.0
1882	–	–	–	–	–	–
1883	–	–	–	–	–	–
1884	–	–	–	–	–	–
1885	36,703	–	–	–	–	–
1886	–	34,000	2,408.6	841.9	–	536.0
1887	–	45,156	2,648.01	572.02	–	634.0
1888	–	48,000	2,408.61	992.98	–	940.0
1889	76,632	51,100	5,463.62	1,052.97	–	1,200.0
1890	77,336	54,500	5,622.41	956.33	–	1,200.0
1891	83,761	57,811	5,455.29	1,050.15	–	720.0
1892	100,537	62,613	7,150.70	1,207.97	166.98	960.0
1893	110,146	68,000	7,800.45	1,243.62	690.0	960.0
1894	119,648	70,000	8,678.9	2,899.78	857.27	600.0
1895	165.006	70,000	8,367.07	4,610.4	760.12	600.0
1896	216,400	80,000	7,369.68	6,704.24	1,372.10	840.0
1897	205,500	78,205	9,075.93	8,156.73	1,678.15	900.0
1898	165,112	80,000	8,347.08	5,497.5	1,136.50	900.0
1899	141,339	80,000	7,383.89	3,806.88	1,406.25	900.0
1900	136,418	–	5,084.14	7,813.61	1,086.0	900.0
1901	–	–	8,397.32	9,468.63	3,621.0	2,400.0
1902	–	–	11,748.70	4,946.30	7,592.0	2,400.0

a Shillings and pence converted to decimals.
Note: Using this table it would be possible to arrive at a different estimate of account profitability. By multiplying the number of bags by the peso price per bag one gets the total gross income, from which by subtracting total costs one arrives at profit.

into lands and cattle, giving rise to the modern cattle ranching latifundia, and to coffee thereafter; the foreign commercial houses in London, Paris, and New York, which specialized in importing coffee, soon penetrated into the Colombian market, and performed a role as providers of cheap credit which under other conditions might have been reserved for the native banks. The initial immobilization of capital, its high opportunity cost, and the uncertainty of any return all tended to restrict the size of investments. The coffee-growers organized commercial companies on a family basis whose fortunes were linked to the conditions of the external market and to the degree of political stability or instability.

Administration

Wage of *mayordomo*	Others	Transport, insurance, commission	Total costs	Production (60-kilo bag of green)	Prices (annual average) £ per bag[a]	$ per bag
–	1,837.0	2,614.0	617.3	92	–	–
–	2,003.0	659.0	564.4	33	–	–
–	–	–	–	–	–	–
–	–	–	–	–	–	–
–	–	–	–	364	–	–
223.15	1,032.0	1,508.51	6,550.2	315	4.17	29.19
234.50	922.0	675.8	5,686.3	433	5.44	41.60
210.80	3,515.0	2,279.5	10,346.9	442	5.35	53.50
218.00	1,552.0	1,845.0	11,331.6	452	5.82	57.52
228.20	1,473.0	1,592.72	11,072.6	473	6.11	59.26
256.0	1,130.0	1,967.07	10,578.5	491	5.30	49.29
246.0	2,288.0	2,379.4	14,399.1	462	5.63	53.51
260.0	2,000.1	2,474.57	15,428.7	384	5.56	64.21
691.30	2,618.0	3,458.9	19,804.2	694	5.64	74.73
683.80	3,267.0	14,141.02	32,428	1,236	5.25	67.20
653.90	4,897.0	8,420.10	30,525	1,002	4.84	60.50
799.55	6,289.0	10,753.45	37,652.8	1,709	4.44	57.72
633.00	5,958.0	12,458.4	34,930.5	1,087	2.79	40.73
715.40	3,838.0	4,032.35	22,082.8	802	2.62	64.95
727.00	2,639.0	738.92	18,988.7	1,300	–	–
830.40	3,346.0	–	28,062.9	1,200	–	–
470.00	12,549.0	–	40,706.0	320	–	–

But an economic analysis is much more difficult. It would be necessary to calculate also the cost of capital, the opportunity cost of land given over to the *arrendatarios*, and the benefit obtained from this arrangement in terms of permanent availability of labour and the lower requirement of working capital.
Source: Archivo Herrera.

The dangers of mortgage

It is important to point out the tremendous limitations imposed by mortgages. In a study of forty important haciendas of Tequendama, producing between 1870 and 1940, I found that 70 per cent had mortgage burdens 80 per cent of the time. In periods of crisis these debts forced them to the verge of bankruptcy.[75] Mortgages seriously affected profits, strategies of production, and employment and wage policies. Chronic mortgage indebtedness was harsher for *hacendados* who did not diversify their activities, but who left off varied enterprise for the uncertain pose of the rentier landlord.

Debts incurred through mortgages had become a significant problem by the beginning of the twentieth century, with the appearance of two unexpected hazards, the economic and financial ruin suffered by the estates as a result of the War of the Thousand Days and the dramatic fall in coffee prices on the world market. Many estates changed hands. This period also saw the deaths of the majority of the generation of estate founders, and properties which were passed on within the family rather than being handed over to their creditors ran the risk of being divided up. Problems of administration were increased when it was realized that the division of a coffee estate was an uneconomical measure, since economies of scale were lost at the only stage of coffee production where they existed at all, in the processing plant itself. At that time, various kinds of civil and commercial associations were formed among the inheritors. These were clearly designed to prevent the property leaving the family and to avoid exceptionally high overheads. We may consider the case of the Ceilán estate, which is quite typical of the debt-ridden enterprises of the time.[76] The setting up and later development of this estate had been based principally on credit. When Eustacio de la Torre Narváez purchased the property from Jorge Crane it was already heavily mortgaged. An outstanding mortgage debt had existed since 1865 between Crane and Baron Goury de Roslan, former French Minister in Colombia, landowner and well-known moneylender in Bogotá. Thus de la Torre inherited Crane's outstanding debt to the Baron. By 1877, only two years after the transaction had taken place, de la Torre had completely cleared all of the estate's outstanding financial obligations. However, in 1878, he incurred a new mortgage of 15,400 pesos gold in order to import machinery. By the nineties the estate had been made one of the most modern in the country, and provided a fine example for both *bogotanos* and *antioqueños*. In order to finance the considerable expansion which took place in the eighties, reaching a peak towards the middle nineties when the estate boasted half a million coffee trees, de la Torre incurred further debts. A loan to the value of 12,500 pesos gold was made by another estate owner, Vincente Duran, and a further loan was made by Alfredo Merizalde some years later. In the early nineties, Rafael Uribe Uribe was the administrator of the Ceilán estate. De la Torre was as active in Liberal politics as his administrator, and gained a certain political notoriety as one of the leaders of the abortive uprising of Facatativá at the beginning of 1895, and as one of the most vigorous supporters of the Liberal wing which opposed the pacifism of Aquileo Parra and his Liberal merchant friends in Bogotá. De la Torre, when not engaged in such political activities, led a far from frugal existence, if we are to judge from his will. In 1897 he recognized publicly a debt due to his agent in London, the well-established firm of Cotesworth & Powell,[77] which had been trading in Colombia from the beginning of the tobacco boom. The debt amounted to £8,000 sterling and consisted of loans and advance payments on harvests. De la Torre left a large part of his Java estate to the London firm as an *anticresis*.

During the civil war of 1899–1902, de la Torre contracted another substantial debt in the presence of the Second Notary in Bogota, this time with Fould & Cie, perhaps the largest and most prestigious of the firms which dealt in coffee in Colombia before 1910. A similar procedure was followed in the case of this loan and de la Torre agreed to leave his Ceilán estate in bond to the Parisian firm. That such a situation was allowed to occur is, perhaps, a reflection of de la Torre's high living and careless administration, as well as of falling prices and the prevailing political situation. But in the Cundinamarca of the time many of the big coffee *hacendados* behaved as he did. In 1907 the total outstanding debt with interest amounted to £25,000 and 360,000 gold francs. De la Torre Sánchez, who had just inherited the estate from his father, began negotiations with Enrique de Narváez, a reputable Conservative politician of the Regeneration, and representative for a number of French financial interests. According to the terms agreed, de Narváez acquired the right to exploit the estate directly in settlement of the debt. De la Torre meanwhile stayed on to administer the property.

Twenty-two years later, on 30 January 1931, de la Torre succeeded in paying off the last of his debts. However, the matter did not end there. Only three weeks later, on 23 February, another loan was negotiated comprising, as before, a mortgage and an *anticresis* contract. The creditor on this occasion was the Banco Francés e Italiano and the sum in question was £16,000. On 15 May of the same year de la Torre obtained a further loan from the Banco de Bogotá amounting to 25,000 pesos, leaving in pledge '3,000 62.5-kilo bags of first-class parchment coffee, duly packed and marked "BB", to be delivered to Giradot' which 'the Bank will export or sell if necessary to recover the debt'. Thus the transactions carried out in the first half of 1931 consisted of an agreed transfer between debtor and creditors.

The enormous size of the debt of 1907, scarcely redeemable in practical terms, was at all events a disincentive to reinvestment in the estate. Consequently, we are left with the impression that the property was in a state of considerable disrepair by the thirties. De la Torre died in 1931 leaving to his heirs a dilapidated estate with assets only barely outweighing liabilities at a time when prices were experiencing a severe crisis on the international market. The end came in 1936. On 1 October of that year, the Ceilán estate, valued at 214,420 pesos by a civil *juzgado* (local court) in Bogotá, was put up for public auction at a starting price of 70 per cent of this value. Within the statutory sale period of one hour only one buyer appeared and the property thus passed to Mauricio Stanich, assistant manager of the Banco Francés e Italiano, at the bare starting price. This transaction thus ended the first phase of the property's history, 'one of the first properties in the Republic's history'.[78]

Between 1905 and 1907 old debts were being renegotiated, as is shown by the list of haciendas with serious financial problems in table 9. Many of these companies went bankrupt or were dissolved before 1900; others were caught up in disputes which threatened the domestic peace of the families concerned when suits were brought over the estates of the founders. But

Table 9. *Sample of hacendado debtors in Cundinamarca, 1905–7*

Creditor	Debtor	Hacienda mortgaged
Fould & Cie, Paris	E. de la Torre N.	Ceilán (Viotá)
	Mariano Tanco	Calandaima (Tibacuy)
		Escuelas de Tibacuy (improvements)
		La Cajita (Tibacuy)
		La Concepción (Nilo)
		Batavia (Tibacuy)
	Manuel M. Aya	El Reposo (Tibacuy)
	Maximiliano Aya	San Isidro (Tibacuy)
	Alvaro Uribe	Balaúnda (Nilo)
	Núñez & Cía	Subia (El Colegio)
Schwann & Co., London	Tovar Hermanos	Java (Viotá)
	Ramon Umaña Rivas	La Viña (Viotá)
	Ricardo Umaña	Cocunche (Nimaima)
Acpli & Co., Hamburg	Jorge D. Ortíz	Los Olivos (Viotá)
Perkins van Bergen, London	Abondano & Uribe	Arabia (Viotá)
Cotesworth & Powell, London	E. de la Torre N.	Ceilán–Java (Viotá)
Stiebel Bros., London	Iregui Hermanos	La Argentina (Viotá)
Banco de Colombia	Samper U. & Cía	Golconda (El Colegio–Anapoima)
Schloss Bros., N.Y.; Colombian Northern Railway Company, N.Y.; Isaac Brandon Bros., N.Y.	Nicolás Sáenz	Misiones (El Colegio)

Sources: La Mesa, Oficina de Registro de Instrumentos Publicos y Privados, and ANC, Notarías de Bogotá.

the predominant tendency, particularly after the lawsuits of 1903–10, was for the consolidation of the haciendas through the creation of commercial companies by the heirs to the properties. A dominant role was played in many of these companies by the husbands of heiresses, as a result of the doctrine of *capitis diminutio*, which regulated the woman's position in civil law; in Bogotá at least the period is one of which cries out for a social history of the second generation of the coffee families, epitomized by widows and prodigal sons living in Europe and following no recognized profession, while their administrators enjoyed greater autonomy than they had known in the days of the founders.[79] The story is one of decline and premature decadence; the case of Hacienda Ceilán discussed earlier is an eloquent example of the shifts and chances of circumstance to which the pioneers were subject.

Other risks

The histories of these companies and the biographies of their protagonists are closely linked; the careers of Nicolás and Francisco Sáenz may be taken as typical. In 1881 Nicolás and Francisco, from Rionegro (Antioquia), formed the joint company Sáenz Hermanos with capital of 6,513 pesos in gold. Francisco contributed a stretch of land which he had accumulated in Viotá during the seventies. Each partner made an equal contribution and would receive an equal share of the profits. Decisions would be taken by mutual agreement and neither could extend credits beyond 1,000 pesos or stand as guarantor for any third party. The offices of this commercial and agricultural enterprise were in Viotá and Bogotá. After going through a number of reconstitutions, it was finally dissolved in July 1898. By then its net capital was 759,157 pesos in paper money, or 253,000 pesos gold. During those seventeen years the assets of the company increased fortyfold, and at the end of each year the partners distributed growing dividends. Let us examine their assets in 1898:

(1) Coffee haciendas
        Sebastopol (Melgar) – coffee
        Calcuta (Melgar) – coffee
        Liberia (Viotá) – coffee and cattle
        San Miguel de Amanta (Viotá, share only) – coffee
        Icononzo (Melgar) – coffee and sugar-cane
(2) Other haciendas and farms
        San Antonio (Viotá–Anapoima) – sugar-cane, cocoa, pastures
        Birmania (Fusagasugá) – pastures
        La Ficha (Guachetá) – cattle
        Las Mercedes (Barrío de las Nieves, Bogotá, 25.6 hectares)
        Empresa de Tocaima (Tocaima) – cattle and pasture

(3) Other assets comprised minor holdings in the Compañía Colombiana de Seguros and in El Puente del Protillo, a part share in the company José M. Sáenz P., credits with the national government for forced loans, etc. All these together made up 10 per cent of the total assets.

The liquidation of the company coincided with the end of the period of high profits for Nicolás Sáenz. Among the properties which belonged wholly to him were Sebastopol, Calcuta, and the Empresa de Tocaima.[80] At this time Sáenz was organizing the Banco de Exportadores, an enterprise aimed at the financing of coffee-export operations and at providing funds for shipment and commission charges. It had offices in Bogotá and New York.[81] In 1900 he bought the hacienda Misiones.

The violent fall in the exchange rate during the War of the Thousand Days destroyed the favourable prospects of the Banco de Exportadores. The debts in gold contracted in New York on behalf of their clients at 300 per cent had to be paid at 10,000 per cent, and Sáenz, as the manager and one of the leading shareholders, received a severe blow. Furthermore, buying a coffee hacienda in Cundinamarca in 1900 was a rash and highly dangerous thing to do. When Sáenz died in New York at the age of 52 in 1909 the discovery in his estate inventory of liens on his mortgaged property of Misiones revealed the errors he had made in 1898–1900; and as late as 1918–20 his heirs were fighting desperately to pay off old mortgage debts which had fallen into the hands of the Bank of England.[82] These developments in the coffee business, by no means unusual or extraordinary, reveal the insecurity and degree of risk which it entailed. There was a great deal of manipulation, risk, and adventure involved, especially in the financial sphere, but there were few other possible foundations for a career of wealth and power. Among the leading merchants nobody doubted the strategic position of the bankers. In 1888 the Ospinas were faced with the necessity of closing down their banking and coffee interests in Guatemala and investing in Colombia, 'either setting up a small bank with the modest name of a mining agency, of buying for ourselves one of the best *fincas*: the bank would be an excellent investment, and would assure us of a certain status here [in Medellín], while investing in coffee is still a risky business, and it is imprudent to put all one's resources into one enterprise'.[83]

3. Land and society in central Colombia in the second half of the nineteenth century

The coffee hacienda was the result of the entry of urban merchants into rural society. On a yet more general plane, it was the product of emphasis on agricultural exporting, of the urge and the need to form links with the world market and 'bring to the country the civilization that is overflowing in Europe'.[1] Investment in coffee did not penetrate the rural world in order to create new types of social or productive relations. By the end of the century, for all its dynamism, commercial capital had only scratched the rude surface of the older social formations. The traditions, habits, and customs of the little worlds of a few square kilometres in which most lived out their lives showed a persistent rigour, despite the expectation that the old patterns would dissolve in contact with the new economy which the coffee entrepreneur wished to impose. In part it was a problem of quantity: coffee investment was heavily concentrated in relatively few areas. Even there, the phenomenon of specialization that occurred with tobacco in Ambalema was not repeated. Within the old haciendas of colonial origin there was a peasant stratum accustomed to the degree of independence that came from producing its own food. The coffee hacienda of Santander, Cundinamarca, Tolima, and Antioquia was founded within an existing social structure, to which it had to adapt itself, while at the same time it introduced new elements of the monetary economy which, simple and weak at first, would produce effects that disturbed the old order. In Cundinamarca, for example, the coffee *municipios* were old centres of colonial production and commerce. Guaduas, La Mesa, and Fusagasugá already had a life of their own before the arrival of the new hacienda. The difficulties of moving men and merchandise favoured routine, and so did some of the particularities of coffee as a crop.

But the towns did change. Their populations grew, the markets became more lively, money was used more widely lower down the social scale. How deep were these changes? How rigorous was the continuity? What was the social expression of the meeting between the coffee 'speculator' and these seemingly stagnant societies? The demographic and social structures of these distant *veredas* in the centre of the country were strongly influenced by the gradual opening of Colombia to the world market. New methods and new motives for getting land changed the established social heirarchy and created a new one, more heterogeneous and complex. The diffusion of

55

cultivation by the *bogotanos* had immediate effects. It isolated and pushed aside many traditional landowners who had not the capital to clear land and open plantations. It lifted up others who were more active and enterprising, and it created on the fringe of the system a network of small peasant cultivators, increasingly numerous but dispersed and left out of account, whose forebears had inhabited these regions since colonial times.

But at the summit of the heirarchy was the *bogotanos*. At the start of the process they enjoyed an additional monopoly, the processing of the harvest.[2] It cannot be said that the arrival of the *bogotanos* displaced the peasantry, expelling them from their parcels of land and throwing them onto the labour market. In some districts the new haciendas were a source of supplementary employment, an additional source of subsistence. Lands became more valuable, roads gained a new importance. The small towns, with their resident population of storekeepers, *caciques*, dealers in cattle, and the lands, hot, cold, and temperate, prospered with coffee. According to Salvador Camacho Roldán, the value of transactions in La Mesa doubled between 1864 and 1890.[3] To have an idea of the relative importance of this commerce, it is enough to know that in 1864 the value of the business of La Mesa was as much as 25 per cent of the total value of Colombia's exports. That the volume of commercial transactions thus doubled in an area where the large haciendas exported their coffee directly, without local intermediaries, shows that a good part of this prosperity derived from the mass of local cultivators entering this new economy. The agrarian policies of the mid-century governments had hardly any effect on the structure of land-holding in these regions. In western Cundinamarca the appropriation of land did not originate with the break-up of the *resguardos* or the *desamortización*, nor were these haciendas formed from *baldíos* (public lands). The vast colonial latifundio was broken up by sale and purchase, as it was on the *sabana* of Bogotá. This was what created smaller and more manageable units for the enterprise of coffee. Let us examine this process in more detail.

Liberal land policies

The three basic elements of Liberal land policies in the middle of the last century in a number of countries of Latin America may be summarized as follows:

(*a*) The expropriation of Church lands,

(*b*) The sale of communal Indian lands (*resguardos*) and that owned by the *municipios* (*ejidos*), and

(*c*) Policies aimed at developing a cash-crop export sector through the concession of *baldíos* to settlers.

It was hoped that, in this way, new settlers would be attracted from Europe and that investment in the sector by native and foreign capital would also be encouraged.

Only the last policy had positive effects on Colombia's coffee development, although it was largely confined in practice to the areas of colonization in Antioquia, and had not been originally intended to promote coffee-growing. However, the favourable effects which resulted from the policy were not felt before the early years of the twentieth century. There is clear evidence that in the middle of the nineteenth century many merchants in Bogotá had received concessions of public lands situated on the hill-sides of the Sumapaz massif and of the El Subia cordillera. The object of these concessions was to stimulate the exploitation of quinine.[4] Much of this land was then abandoned by its original owners, who only began to revive their interest in their property at the end of the nineteenth century. Conflicting claims were in part responsible for the social conflict which was to reach its culmination in the 1930s. The areas of Cunday, Icononzo, Pasca, and Fusagasugá became the chief centres of such conflict after the 1890s, and it was the cultivation of coffee, with its influence on migration and the rise in land values, which was mainly responsible.[5]

Despite the lack of authoritative investigations on the subject of the 'expropriation' of *resguardos*, it is in general very difficult to confirm Ospina Vásquez's thesis that the principal source of the so-called 'Republican latifundia' was the purchase of reservation lands. The cattle-raising *latifundia* on the Bogotá *sabana*, a prosperous area in the 1870s, sometimes occupied the land which twenty years previously had been *resguardo*. However, we should also note the transition from communal to private property as defined by the Código Civil, which appears to indicate that the process was relatively slow and that it occurred in two separate phases. Once the laws abolishing the *resguardos* had been approved, the *vecinos* gradually bought up plots of land from the 'Indians'. In practice, the distinction between *vecino* and *indio* was tenuous, to say the least, since both categories contained *mestizos*. Secondly, the merchants and traditional estate-owners in Bogotá bought land from the *vecinos*, although some of the latter group achieved the step upwards to join the class of well-established *latifundistas*.[6]

But the 'assault on Indian lands', as the process has been called, was not directly related to the development of coffee. Most *resguardos* were in *tierra fría*, the highlands. Those situated in areas suitable for coffee-growing, such as Pasca and Tibacuy, had disappeared altogether by the eighteenth century.[7]

The effect of the decrees of church-land expropriation on agricultural and financial matters appears to have been negligible. The extent of Church land has undoubtedly been exaggerated in the past, and little of what there was in coffee country. The major part of ecclesiastical property was situated in urban Bogotá, Popayán, and Pasto. Bogotá alone accounted for 40 per cent by value of total expropriated land in the country. According to a table drawn up by M. Samper, the expropriated area in Bogotá, Boyacá, and Cauca amounted to 64 per cent of the total value.[8]

Some latifundia holdings in the region of Tequendama had been tied in various ways. Several monasteries and *colegios* in Bogotá (El Rosario for instance) and in Boyacá received rent from *censos* in La Mesa, Tocaima, El Colegio, and Viotá. Thus, to take a few examples, Pastor González, owner of the Doima estate in La Mesa, had a mortgage arrangement of 960 pesos with the Monasterio del Carmen in Leyva, on which he paid interest of 5 per cent annually;[9] Guillermo Lindig, owner of the Calandaima estate in Viotá (famous for the 1926–36 peasant movements, along with the Florencia estate, which was the centre of Communist party organization and agitation), was found to have paid a similar interest rate to the same establishment on a debt of 800 pesos contracted in 1853.[10] The La Junca estate in El Colegio, leased by Francisco Barriga, paid ground rent to the Convento de la Enseñanza in Bogotá after 1841, and the Hato San Vivente estate in San Juan de Rioseco, paid ground rent to the Convento de Predicadores in Bogotá after 1837. In 1819, the Convento de la Concepción in Santa Fé placed an embargo on the Tena estate after the disappearance of Clemento Alguacil, who was the owner at the time.[11]

By 1862, one year after the decree expropriating Church lands, thirteen *censos* from La Mesa and one 'family *capellanía*' from Viotá had been fully redeemed from the Tesoro Nacional. Many of the names which appear on the register of exempted *censatarios* were later prominent in the chronicles of the coffee pioneers: Pedro Alejo Forero, Leandro Caicedo, Enrique Umaña, Pastor González, Rafael Rivas, Anacleto Millán, Marcelino Pradilla, etc.[12]

No tied properties remained by 1862 and, indeed, in the district of La Mesa, no land is recorded as having been auctioned in accordance with the decree. Meanwhile, the Church in the region played a strictly secondary role, while in the Catholic and Conservative region of Antioquia its influence as landowner or financier was virtually nil. In Amagá and Fredonia in the south-west of Antioquia, no reference appears to have been made either to *censos* or *capellanías.*[13]

Table 10 shows the secondary importance of *censos* in the Tequendrama region. Nor would this region figure as one where *desamortización* would gain in respectability by increasing the number of proprietors, which, accordir to Camacho Roldán, 'would give property more defenders'.[14]

Table 10. *Censos redeemed in La Mesa, 1864*

Municipality	No. of censos	Value (pesos)	Average (pesos)
La Mesa	13	24,638	1,895
San Antonio	4	7,760	1,940
Viotá	1	2,400	2,400
Tocaima	13	5,345	411
Anolaima	9	12,666	1,407
Anapoima	4	8,292	2,073
El Colegio	2	1,440	720
Quipile	1	40	40
Nilo	2	800	400
Total	49	63,381	1,291

Source: ANC, Bienes desamortizados: Cundinamarca, vol. 19, ff. 482 et seq.

At the time of Independence, Amagá in Antioquia was fast becoming the centre from which efforts were made to push the agricultural frontier out towards Fredonia and the fertile valleys along the Cauca river. These were to become the most important areas for producing coffee and sugar-cane and for cattle-raising (for hides and beef) towards the end of the century.[15]

The cultivation of the western slopes in Cundinamarca occurred at an earlier date than in the south-west of Antioquia. Estates established in the areas bordering the main highways, such as Tena, El Colegio, and Tocaima, reared livestock for beef and grew sugar-cane for producing *panela, miel* and *aguardiente*. These estates had links with the uplands and with the cattle-raising latifundia of the Tolima plains. They appear to have been run mainly on slave labour; poor transport, long distances, and low productivity, coupled with static markets, combined to discourage immigration of free labour into the area, at least until the advent of coffee. Some of them were in fact vast latifundia which were notable for their very extensive use of land and their very vaguely defined boundaries. The abolition of slavery appears to have been a hard blow for them, although little is known about the true importance of the part played by slavery in these regions, or about the relative significance of the smallholders, both poor whites and mestizos, who grew sugar-cane and owned small *trapiches*.

The social landscape in western Cundinamarca, c. 1860

The future centres of coffee production were still in 1859 scattered and

Map 2. Cundinamarca pioneering areas and *boyacense* emigration.
(*Source:* Instituto Geográfico Agustín Codazzi, *Diccionario geográfico de Colombia*
(2 vols. (Bogotá, 1968), vol. 1, p. 401.)

isolated family settlements, hemmed in by rugged landscape and dense
growth, hours from the nearest village. Except for Fusagasugá, which had
something of a town centre, the rest were only insignificant hamlets. In
1867 there were only thirty-five houses in Viotá; in 1879 there were forty-
nine, though of these a good number were hacienda warehouses.[16]

This panorama did not change fundamentally in the north-east of Cundinamarca, especially in the *municipios* most dedicated to producing cane
juice with rudimentary techniques, which left the small *trapichero* only a
wretched income. The progressive merchants of the capital thought that
coffee would be a salvation for these too.[17]

Coffee was not the first agrarian investment made by the merchants.
'One buys land', wrote Medardo Rivas, 'only as a means of securing capital
against the hussars of liberty and the *guerrilleros* of religion.'[18] Samper
had written that capital would not be forthcoming for tailors' shops, shoe-
making, or leather-working enterprises, but would be attracted to agricultural

Table 11. *Tequendama: population census, 1859*

Profession	El Colegio	Fusagasugá	San Antonio	Tibacuy	Viotá	Total
Children	463	1,520	618	299	150	3,050
Agriculturalists	926	1,192	872	257	278	3,525
Artisans	12	417	64	73	14	580
Students	5	66	3	1	0	75
Servants	150	359	135	43	0	687
Merchants	8	18	0	0	0	26
Domestic servants	95	583	381	92	18	1,169
Others[a]	10	43	8	10	1	72
Total	1,669	4,198	2,081	775	461	9,184

a Here 'Others' means the following: muleteers, vagabonds, officials, soldiers, priests, doctors, and lawyers. In the five municipalities only two 'capitalists' and eleven 'proprietors' are recorded, in Fusagasugá. In the whole Tequendama region there were only five 'proprietors' recorded in El Colegio. Of the artisans 70% were in Fusagasugá, and 75% of these were women; it is possible that this refers to domestic cottage industry. Among the 'agriculturalists' 30% were women, which is a much more realistic proportion than the indices of female participation in agricultural work given in more recent studies.
Source: ANC, Fondo E. Ortega Ricaurte, box 38.

exports. In 1880 he considered that 'society [*el cuerpo social*] has chosen coffee as the product most adequate for filling the gap left by the two previous products' – tobacco and *quina*.[19] 'Society' was enthusiastic about the new enterprise. As early as 1858 Codazzi had foreseen the development of coffee in the western slopes of Cundinamarca and on the hills stretching down to the llanos in the east.[20] Coffee caught on in both areas in the seventies, though in the latter high transport cost restricted its spread. It brought some important shifts in Cundinamarca's regional development, and in the relocation of capital and labour.

Towards 1870 Cundinamarca still maintained much of its old colonial structure. Table 12 shows the pre-eminence of Facatativá, with the colonial foundations of Guaduas, Sasaima, and Villeta, in the number of *trapiches* and in distilling. The *municipios* of the highlands hold most of the population and the cattle. Tequendama, similar in geographical configuration to Facatativá, is marked out by its indigo-tanks, to be the ruin of their owners. It can be seen too that coffee begins in Facatativá. The 'scientific' plantations set up by Tyrrel Moore with a group of *antioqueños* in the region of Guaduas (Chimbe and Sasaima) date from the same time as the collapse of the indigo enterprises established in Nilo, Tibacuy, and Tocaima. Speculative

Table 12. *Population and principal economic activities of the regions of Cundinamarca, 1870 (percentages)*

Region	Cattle	Sheep and goats	Horses and mules	Pigs	Corn mills[a]	Sugar mills (*trapiches*)[b]	Tan- neries
Bogotá	22.4	11.6	18.8	18.4	11.3	9.1	20.2
Ubaté	20.2	41.1	12.1	14.2	36.0	5.0	59.4
Facatativá	15.3	6.3	32.7	37.0	11.3	53.1	1.3
Tequendama	17.6	3.2	18.5	19.0	7.2	13.6	–
Zipaquirá	24.3	37.6	17.8	11.2	34.0	19.0	19.0
Total (%)	100	100	100	100	100	100	100
Total (000)	59.1	136.9	71.5	53.5	0.096	3.4	0.74

a Only one steam-driven mill in Bogotá. *b* 17 water-driven *trapiches*, the rest animal-driven. *c* The neighbouring *municipios* of Guaduas (25.8%), Sasaima (11.8%) and Villeta (8.18%) in the Facatativá region had 46% of the coffee. Gachalá in the Zipaquirá region had 15%.

plantings spread down towards the Magdalena river along the western edge of Cundinamarca, and between 1870 and 1885 the centre of the coffee zone shifted from the north-west to the south-west of Cundinamarca.

There was also some movement of capital into cattle-ranching in the *sabana* of Bogotá and in the highland valleys. In the seventies many Bogotá merchants became major cattle-ranchers, buying up the land of the abolished *resguardos* from the local farmers and *gamonales* who had acquired it during the previous decade. The period thus saw the emergence of 'those vast deserts known as haciendas', and the change from the specialized and intensive cultivation of cereals, fruits, and vegetables which had been practised in the *resguardos* to extensive ranching which depopulated the *sabana*, changed the landscape, and forced up the price of foodstuffs in Bogotá, depriving the landless peasants of the possibility of finding work in the area.[21] After 1875 it is difficult to find in the *sabana* of Bogotá a hacienda similar to that described by Eugenio Díaz in his novel *El rejo de enlazar*. With the exception of the completely unproductive latifundia in the Tequendama and Sumapaz regions, and a few mediocre sugar-cane haciendas along the banks of the Bogotá river and the Río Negro, the cattle latifundio was the only kind which, in Cundinamarca at least, merited the denomination 'republican'.

A comparison of the names of the 13 per cent of owners who had 78 per cent of the total number of cattle registered and a list of the richest merchants

Distil-lation	Indigo-tanks	Coffee trees[c]	Popu-lation	Tiled dwell-ings	Straw dwell-ings	Urban prop-erties (no.)	Rural prop-erties (no.)	Churches
9.6	1.3	9.6	27.1	75.6	21.4	70.3	27.8	35.1
8.3	2.6	0.8	17.3	5.1	25.9	2.3	25.0	13.2
64.7	12.0	52.0	25.4	6.8	22.4	10.0	16.6	24.2
17.0	82.6	20.3	10.9	3.1	8.7	10.7	5.6	11.5
0.2	1.3	17.2	19.2	9.4	21.5	6.7	25.0	16.0
100	100	100	100	100	100	100	100	100
0.406	0.075	1.821	409.6	4.8	65.1	7.8	18.0	0.182

Sources: Based on *Mensaje del Gobernador de Cundinamarca a la Asamblea Lejislativa,
1870* (Bogotá, 1870), pp. 17–18, 85–8. Population figures based on *Anuario Estadístico
de Colombia, 1876* (Bogotá, n.d.), p. 119.

in Bogotá reveals that many of the families involved are the same, and it is
from those same families that the pioneers of coffee cultivation in Cundinamarca and Tolima later emerged.

The degree of speculation in lands in the *sabana* during those years was
very high, if we are to judge from the volume and rate of transactions in
the municipalities with the greatest latifundia and hence the greatest social
prestige, such as Mosquera, Serrezuela (Madrid), Funza, and Facatativá.[22]

The establishment of the coffee hacienda did not take place at the
expense of communal lands and the minifundia holdings, as had been the
case in other parts of Latin America, where commercial agriculture had
come into sharp conflict with peasants and local communities. Colombian
coffee-growers were able to claim, perhaps justifiably, that the consequences
of their activities had been to further the advance of civilization in a wild
and hostile environment.

In such circumstances as these, coffee cultivation in the pioneering zones
of Cundinamarca, Tolima, and Antioquia took place on private property
and on lands whose titles could be traced back to the sixteenth and seventeenth
centuries. Thus, the coffee latifundia were established firmly on the foundations of the traditional latifundia. This process was most evident in the
municipios where land concentration was greatest, such as El Colegio and
Viotá; and four latifundia, Neptuno, Calandaima, San Miguel de Amanta,
and Mesa de Yeguas,[23] were in fact divided to form ten coffee estates.

Table 13. *Survey of cattle latifundia in Cundinamarca, 1876*

Head of cattle	Owners		Haciendas		Total head of cattle	
Less than 200	577	86.8%	645	80.7%	19,010	21.7%
201–500	57	8.6%	82	10.2%	28,110	32.1%
501–1,000	20	3.0%	43	5.3%	21,039	24.1%
1,000–2,000	8	1.2%	25	3.1%	11,400	13.0%
More than 2,000	3	0.4%	4	0.5%	7,769	8.9%
Total	665	100.0%	799	99.8%	87,328	99.8%

Source: Calculated from the Censo de Ganado Vacuno in the *Registro del Estado: Organo Oficial del Gobierno de Cundinamarca*, edns of 18, 21, and 25 October, 4, 17, and 24 November, and 2 and 20 December 1876.

Five of the latter were subdivided further in the twentieth century to form nine more.

A similar trend occurred in Antioquia. The Jonás, San Pedro, La Granja, Gualanday, and Cerrotusa estates and others were not additions of small or medium holdings, but rather resulted from the division of old latifundia.[24] In practice the estate boundaries became finally fixed only after long periods in which frequent land transactions continued to take place on a small scale as the owners negotiated their respective boundaries according to the contours of the terrain and the location of the properties in relation to rural highways.

Old landowners and new: the case of Viotá

As has been stated, the expansion of coffee cultivation dislocated the social hierarchies of the isolated municipalities where it penetrated. In some cases, the local landowners managed to adapt, survive, even prosper. In La Mesa and Anolaima, and in the much-referred-to list of Medardo Rivas such examples abound. For some, coffee was the means of social ascent, as it was for 'Manuel Aya, a poor youth, but one who through his great energy, tenacious love of work, total honesty, supreme thrift, and great intelligence, succeeded in becoming the richest man of the whole province of Sumapaz'.[25] But the accounts do not speak of the failures. A glance at the documents of sales carried out from 1860 to the end of the century in these regions brings to light this aspect, forgotten and submerged. Let us look at a typical example from the most typical coffee-hacienda municipality of Cundinamarca, Viotá.

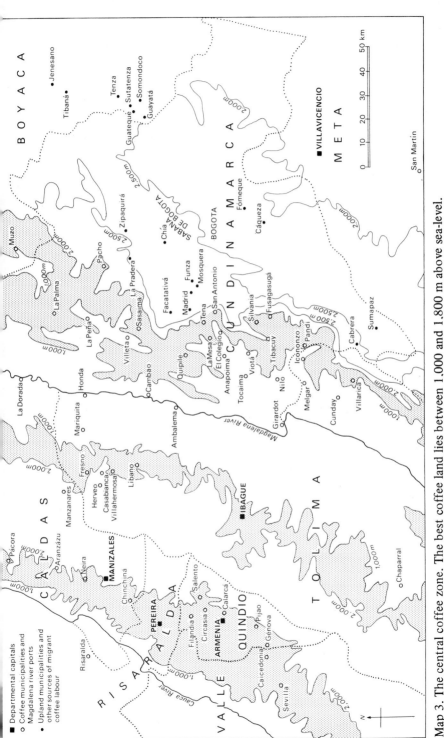

Map 3. The central coffee zone. The best coffee land lies between 1.000 and 1.800 m above sea-level.

Table 14. *The fragmentation of colonial latifundia and the origins and collapse of the coffee haciendas, 1860–1956*

Latifundia before 1860	First division	Second division	Third division
1. Neptuno	1. Los Olivos, 1888	1. Los Olivos, 1894	Parcelaciones[a] begun in 1954
		2. Magdalena, 1894	Parcelaciones begun in 1954
		3. Costa Rica, 1891	Parcelaciones begun in 1954
		4. Africana, 1898	Parcelaciones begun in 1954
		5. Buenos Aires, 1898	Parcelaciones begun in 1936
	2. Java, 1888	(6. Java)	1. Java
	3. Argentina, 1888	7. Argentina, 1915	Parcelaciones begun in 1936
		8. California, 1915	Parcelaciones begun in 1955
	4. Argelia, 1891	(9. Argelia)	Parcelaciones begun in 1955
2. Calandaima	5. Ceilán, 1870	10. Ceilán-Java, 1927	Parcelaciones begun in 1956
	6. Calandaima, 1865	11. Calandaima, 1931	Parcelaciones begun in 1954
		12. Buenavista, 1931	Parcelaciones begun in 1939
3. San Miguel de Amanta	7. Liberia, 1884	(13. Liberia)	Parcelaciones begun in 1934
	8. Florencia, 1869	14. Brasil, 1936	Parcelaciones begun in 1946
		15. Florencia, 1936	Parcelaciones begun in 1936
4. Mesa de Yeguas	9. Golconda, 1892–4	16. Golconda, 1905	2. Golconda / Parcelaciones begun in 1954
		17. Sevilla, 1912	Parcelaciones begun in 1954
		18. Cataima, 1912	Parcelaciones begun in 1955
	10. Misiones, 1892–3	(19. Misiones)	3. Misiones / Parcelaciones begun in 1946

a *Parcelaciones* refers to subdivision into medium and small holdings, carried out by the landowner directly or through a private commercial company, or through some official or semi-official organization. In many cases the core of the hacienda, the house and land round about, remained in the possession of the proprietor. I do not know what happened to the processing machinery, but seeing that there was no collective organization of production and processing, it is probable that it was sold off by the *hacendado* to buyers from outside the region.
Source: La Mesa, Oficina de Registro de Instrumentos Públicos y Privados; Libros de Compraventas (1862–1955); Hipotecas (1873–1955); Sucesiones (1890–1955); and ANC, Notarías de Bogotá (1860–1930).

The owners of the San Miguel de Amanta estate represent a distinct social type of the time, namely that of the local landowning family which, while enjoying high status, held land of little commercial value, and was as isolated and poor as its neighbours. An owner of this type, who was the product of a society with little internal class differentiation with respect to wealth, was usually unable to take full advantage of the appreciation in land values and improvements in communications. Despite his family's status there, he remained completely cut off from the merchants in Bogotá.

Families such as the Bazurtos, Azas, and Montillas in Viotá and Tocaima provide us with examples of this phenomenon: in the course of a single generation they were completely absorbed by estates which were undergoing vigorous expansion, and once their land had been sold off, they took employment in local public posts or ran small businesses or small, insignificant estates. Some even went to work as foremen in the estates in the area or beyond the mountain ranges which had enclosed their little traditional world.

San Miguel de Amanta was the name given to some 2,000 hectares of fertile land situated against the western flank of the El Subia range. Its southern boundaries reached Viotá and in the west it extended to the very edge of the cordillera. It was officially designated a *comunidad*, a term almost unknown today but in frequent use at that period. In the legislation of the time it was defined as a *cuasicontrato*; that is to say, each *comunero* had a *proindiviso* right to an unspecified share of the property, but not a right to the whole or to any specific part. This right was held on the understanding that no member of the *comunidad* should have previously entered into partnership with another. Such a situation might occur where a property was inherited by the husband or wife and family of the deceased owner and where no clear statement as to the exact allocation of the property among his heirs had been provided in the owner's will. The property would thus remain a *cuasicontrato* pending a court decision as to its due division among the heirs.

San Miguel was the *comunidad* of the Bazurto family.[26] Its history can be traced back to 1781 when Matías Bazurto and Isidora Patiño married and made their home in Viotá, then a remote area which had not yet acquired the status of a parish. Their last child, Mariquita, was baptized in 1801. In 1808, in partnership with his brother, Matías bought a large tract of uncultivated land from Camilo and Joaquín Díaz. They divided the land between themselves, each one acquiring sole ownership of his own share. Matías retained what was later to become the Comunidad de San Miguel de Amanta. In 1837, Matías donated a piece of land, the future site of Viotá, reserving plots for the church and the cemetery. Evidently his financial situation was sufficiently strong for him to manage adequately without the land. He died a year later leaving five children, Fernando, Josefa, Vicente, Teresa, and Mariquita. It was at that point that the *comunidad* was born, shared by these five heirs.

Fernando had five children. All agreed to sell their share to Fernando Martínez, with the result that he acquired one-fifth of the *comunidad*. Josefa then sold her one-fifth share to the same Fernando Martínez in 1857. Vicente's four children also sold out to Martínez, who therefore now owned three-fifths of the *comunidad*. However, the situation became rather more involved in the cases of Teresa and Mariquita. Teresa married three times and had six children by her three husbands. If we convert these figures to a common denominator of 30, we can conclude that since five of the children sold a 5/30 share to Martínez, while the sixth sold his 1/30 share to Pedro Alejo Forero, then Martínez owned a 23/30 share, Forero 1/30, and Mariquita Bazurto the remaining 6/30.

There were additional complications in the case of Mariquita's six children, who, following her death in 1886, began selling their shares separately. A 1/30 share passed through a number of hands until 1892 when it was purchased by Carlos Zamora and the Sáenz brothers. Fernando Martínez purchased a further 2/30 and then sold all of his rights (i.e. 25/30) to the well-known *latifundista* Anacleto Millán, who in turn sold out to Pedro Alejo Forero.

In 1897, then, the situation stood thus: Pedro A. Forero owned 25/30; Zamora and the Sáenz brothers owned 1/30; and Dolores Vejarano, daughter of Mariquita Bazurto, owned the remaining 3/30. The formal legal division of the property into separate units between these several owners took place in 1914, and Florencia, the new estate belonging to Pedro A. Forero, was one of the largest in Viotá.

The crisis of *minifundista* communities in the highlands

The circumstances of the peasantry in the highland areas of Cundinamarca, Boyacá, and Antioquia were also changing. Past studies have tended to dwell on the importance of the latifundia and the estates situated in the more economically advanced regions that enjoyed well-established links with urban markets or international trade. Such studies have rarely paid any significant attention to the existence of large centres of peasant smallholders. On the other hand, studies of minifundia societies have concentrated their attentions on areas where the minifundio and its owner have been subjected to various types of social oppression, economic exploitation, and political manipulation at the hands of the large estates.[27] Nevertheless, those regions in which land had been subdivided into family holdings, both geographically isolated and without close links with the latifundia, were also of some significance.[28] It is undeniable that in these areas the land had not been equitably distributed in terms of size and quality and, as a result, considerable differences in economic and social levels existed between neighbouring families. The influence of the wealthiest of these was, however, in no way comparable to that exerted by the large estate-owners and, in spite of the large differences in wealth, they all shared a level of poverty in comparison with the *latifundistas*.

These communities (*veredas*) were largely concentrated in the centre of Boyacá, the Valle de Tenza, and further north in *municipios* such as Guayatá and Jenesano. In Antioquia they were confined to the high-lying areas to the west of the Aburrá valley. Eastern Cundinamarca is also a typical case. Recent studies have shed considerable light on these communities, although several gaps still exist in our knowledge of the specific conditions prevailing during the second half of the nineteenth century. The evidence available appears to confirm the thesis that further fragmentation of property tended to follow the break-up of the *resguardo*.[29] The general thesis regarding diminishing marginal productivity, as a result of the technical and productive limitations encountered by the small unit of exploitation in a situation of rapid population growth, also seems to be amply corroborated. It is well known that this situation has led to unemployment or under-employment. The exhaustion of all available cultivable land resulted in a surplus of labour and falling real incomes, the impact of which was felt in the income differentials of the various families. Of these families, those with the largest labour surpluses (as defined in relation to their holding of cultivable land) were obliged to find other employment for some of their family members, usually on nearby holdings able to absorb outside labour.

Peasant societies had undergone considerable change by the latter half of the nineteenth century. In Boyacá certain *corregimientos* composed of minifundia were already displaying characteristics evident in areas with a latifundio—minifundio structure: they contained groups whose ties with land-ownership had already been broken and who were thus transformed into a floating labour force in search of work, and who made up the categories of tenant farmers, sharecroppers, and *concertados*. It is difficult ⏤ to trace chronologically the development of this process, but it seems reasonable to assume that by the 1880s the situation in central Boyacá had reached the point where the limit of the land's capacity to support the expanding population had been overtaken. This explains the emergence at that time of groups of landless peasants, and a subsequent migratory move-

ment from the Valle de Tenza region towards the temperate areas of El
Tequendama. The labourers in Sumapaz appear to have originated from the
minifundio *municipios* of the eastern regions, principally from Cáqueza and
Fómeque. The Valle de Tenza region of Boyacá and those of La Ceja, Rionegro, and El Retiro in Antioquia soon became the principal sources of
labour for the estates to the south-west of Cundinamarca and Antioquia
respectively. All public and private documentation found in Cundinamarca
points to the importance of *boyacense* labour, both in the early cycle in
Guaduas–Sasaima and in the later development in El Tequendama and
Sumapaz.[30] The population of these areas grew commensurately with
the spread of coffee cultivation. In 1879 labour was apparently still in
short supply there. According to Forero, 'there is a notable lack of manpower and the situation would get far worse if it were not for the fact
that the large population, low salaries, and poverty in Boyacá encourage
seasonal migration to our lands for harvesting in April and May, September
and November'.[31] While the population of the areas of Boyacá in which
demographic pressure was very strong declined or remained static in the
second half of the nineteenth century,[32] in the coffee municipalities the
percentage variation of the population increased at very rapid rates, much
higher than the national variation, as can be seen in table 15.

However, not all of the peasants who arrived at the large estates were in
the same situation. To some extent it could be said that a whole minifundia structure, and not merely a part, had migrated. The systems used by
the estate-owners required more than the employment of day-labourers. The
first stages of the work such as *rozas* (burning) and, in some cases, certain
duties related to the upkeep of the coffee plantations and pasture land
were contracted out. But who were the *contratistas*? They were individuals
with a certain capacity to save and with sufficient capital to enable them to
employ *jornaleros*. They needed some knowledge of the 'labour market'
and some influence within it. They were usually small landowners who had
risked leaving their properties in order to try their hand as contractors and
rental agents. They took with them workers and labourers to carry out the
work for their civil contracts. But this social stratification was related to
family ties and to existing patterns of kinship and, in some cases, was
weakened by such structures.

Both a seasonal and permanent labour force emerged from Boyacá. However, the actual mechanism of the migratory movement is still not generally
understood and even if we are able to relate with confidence the process of
population 'expulsion' to conditions in the minifundia, and that of 'attraction'
to the work opportunities offered by the large estates, the actual operation
of the migratory process remains largely a matter for conjecture. The

Table 15. *Population and percentage variation of the population of six typical coffee municipalities, 1859–1912*

	Population			
	1859[a]	1870[b]	1905[c]	1912[d]
Fredonia (Ant.)	4,049	7,540	21,260	26,430
Viotá (Cund.)	461	1,284	6,557	7,197
El Colegio (Cund.)	1,669	3,229	5,556	6,336
Fusagasugá (Cund.)	4,198	–	4,097	13,443
Chaparral (Tol.)	6,421	7,266	11,787	15,486
Salazar (N. de Sant.)	4,631	7,775	11,074	9,210
	Percentage variation		
	1859–70	1870–1905	1905–12
Fredonia	86.2	181.9	21.8
Viotá	178.5	410.6	9.7
El Colegio	93.4	72.0	14.4
Fusagasugá	–	–	228.1
Chaparral	13.1	62.2	31.3
Salazar	67.9	42.4	– 16.8
Colombia	30.7	49.3	16.4

Notes: Venecia was separated from Fredonia in 1905, forming a separate municipality. For the year 1912 I have added the populations of the two (Fredonia, 18,700; Venecia, 7,730).

The rate of growth between censuses is not arrived at by the simple division of the percentage variation by the number of years between each census. The percentage variation is arrived at by the simple formula $(p_1 - p)/p$.

Sources: a ANC, Fondo E. Ortega Ricaurte, box 38; Censo de Población, 1859, except for Salazar: *Censo de la Problación del Estado Soberano de Santander, 1864* (Socorro, 1868). *b Anuario General de Estadística*, 1876 (Bogotá, 1876). *c* and *d Censos Nacionales de Población* (see bibliography).

enganchadores in these estates certainly played an important role in the early stages of the process, and we can speculate that the families that settled permanently on the estates in the region may have encouraged their former neighbours and distant relatives to take the first steps in descending to the temperate zones at harvest time. Local chronicles lead us to believe that many of these seasonal workers chose to remain on the estates or in surrounding areas and to bring their families to settle there. The *enganchadores* continued to function until well into the twentieth century; this mechanism was common to Cundinamarca, Tolima, and Antioquia.[33]

Social Darwinism

It is still hard to explain adequately why the *hacendados* were unable to draw their workers from the native population, or from the underemployed peasantry which inhabited the Magdalena plains. It is known, however, that these *jornaleros* had become the object of scorn and mistrust; during the tobacco development of Ambalema all imaginable kinds of vices were attributed to them. The inhabitants of the hot and temperate zones were seen by the bogotanos as 'an ugly, colourless race which works little and grubs around amidst lush vegetation'.[34] Social Darwinism among the merchant classes appears to have been more marked in Liberals, who were strongly inclined to regard the labourers in racial rather than class terms. Enrique Cortés, known as one of the great Liberal educationalists of the nineteenth century wrote in the following terms: 'If we take a Magdalena boatman or an Indian from Cundinamarca and compare him with an educated Bostonian, we will have before us both our starting point and our goal.'[35] When choosing between the 'boatman' and the 'Indian', the *bogotano* merchants undoubtedly felt more at home with the latter. The view that workers made jobless following the decline in the tobacco industry made their way to the coffee zones appears to be totally unfounded. Moreover, migration to the tobacco areas along the Magdalena river was halted at an early stage towards the end of the fifties, according to a study made by Luis F. Sierra.[36] Migration to Sumapaz and El Tequendama became significant only after 1880. The fate of redundant tobacco workers must be found elsewhere. There are, on the other hand, clear signs of a cultural link between the inhabitants of El Tequendama and the Valle de Tenza, particularly in their musical folklore. It could also be suggested that the *arrendamiento* system used by the estates for paying their workforce was better suited to the peculiar characteristics of the *boyacense* peasant than the systems adopted in tobacco cultivation. The coffee estates adopted a rental system based on that of the small sugar-cane plantations of western Cundinamarca, similar in many ways to that in use in the highland areas.

The image of the *boyacense* peasant continued to suffer from the old colonial prejudices rooted in the racial discrimination of the 'caste' hierarchy. A man of science (if we can call him that) like Vergara y Velasco reiterated in his 1901 geography the traditional arguments of *criollo* society concerning the nature of the *boyacense*. It is worth quoting him in full:

'The *Indio* of Boyacá and Cundimarca, whose purity is still untarnished in some districts, especially in Boyacá, is small, melancholic, resigned and moderate in his customs, except on non-working days when he likes to get drunk. He is hard-working and tireless, submissive and worthy, but he is also obtuse, stubborn, sly, distrustful, and apathetic even in war. He is a machine, for he serves all causes with equal passiveness and duty. In other words he obeys the bidding of the whites whom he claims to bear considerable ill-will, and whom he both fears and respects. He is impervious to change, and will always lower his eyes, even when he holds a position of rank. The Indian women love the white men with true passion, causing extreme jealousy in their menfolk.'[37]

For the coffee estate-owner, the *boyacense* worker seemed to confirm his belief that three centuries of *encomienda*, Catholicism, *resguardos*, and poverty must necessarily find their expression in a servile personality. Indeed, the first generation of peasant settlers appeared resigned not only to the prevailing working conditions but also to the heavy demographic toll imposed by their move to a hostile environment. They suffered from 'tropical diseases' to which their bodies had no resistance, and which society lacked the technical skills to prevent. Anaemia, maleria, and alcoholism were part and parcel of the establishment and consolidation of the large estates, as were high rates of infant mortality and shorter life-expectancy.

Illness

Illness and diseases such as uncinariasis (*tun-tun, imborera o jipatera*) affected coffee-workers on a wide scale. Poor hygiene and living conditions, backward medicine, and a generally indifferent attitude towards the health of the workers doubtless contributed greatly to a 'demographic catastrophe' in the earlier generations of *peons* and *jornaleros*, though the gravity of the situation was largely disguised by the continued migration to the coffee zones from the highlands.[38] In 1915 Luis Cuervo Márquez wrote, 'Endemic disease is so extensive in regions such as Fusagasugá, Sasaima, Viotá, and Pandi, among workers employed in coffee picking, that more than 50% have *uncinaria*.'[39] This phenomenon was not confined to the estates and was equally apparent in *antioqueño* coffee plantations, in the mines, and on the cacao plantations.

The study of epidemics and diseases endemic in coffee climates attracted the attention of many Colombian doctors between the turn of the century and 1930. A good proportion of the theses in the Bogotá Faculty of Medicine were based on empirical investigations of these phenomena.[40] One of these gives an account of the mechanisms and modes of dissemination from the endemic centres of the disease. In the Santander regions the epidemics of *caquexia paladica* were severe; since 1880 in San Cayetano 'maleria has prevailed in all its forms and in 1884 yellow fever arrived, and has hardly spared a single inhabitant. Today

[1897] no cases are reported, thanks to the immunity conferred by the first epidemic.' The epidemic had arrived from Cúcuta, which it reached in 1893, apparently from Maracaibo. The railway was the principal transmitter. The fever also affected Sardinata and Gramalote, Salazar and Arboledas. The author of this thesis describes two phases: 'the epidemic, 1883–4, and then an endemo-epidemic phase during which the fever attacks the natives benignly, but very strongly affects those who came from *tierra fría* or who suffered badly in the first phase'. The rest acquired immunity. A second epidemic cycle occurred in 1890–4.[41] Another doctor documented his thesis on tropical anaemia with sixty-nine cases attended in a Bogotá hospital, cases which fully confirm the migration referred to above. Seventy per cent were peasants coming from Boyacá who had worked as *cosecheros* in the coffee plantations of the Tequendama region.[42]

Although there is magnificent material available for the study of these themes, a proper historical account of disease as a specific manifestation of social structure has yet to be carried out. Perhaps, as Louis Chevelier has indicated,[43] it is not a matter of phenomena that should be analysed as just pathology. These epidemic and endemic diseases indicate the unequal chances run by the different social classes engaged in the process which is the subject of this analysis. Those who suffered them were the *jornaleros*, *arrendatarios* and *agregados*, *minifundistas* forced out by the limitations of highland production inherent in the structure that prevailed in Cundinamarca and Boyacá. They descended from *tierra fría* to hotter climates and there, with insufficient diet, lived in ways and in hygienic conditions very propitious to the spread of these diseases. (There are also many references to the role of disease in *antioqueño* colonization.)

Social complexities in the new coffee municipalities

Although in the 1889 report already cited, Sasaima's principal resource was still coffee 'cultivated in extensive and beautiful haciendas', the centre of gravity of the industry in Cundinamarca had shifted towards the south-east. It was also gathering strength on the slopes of the *cordillera* of Sumapaz, a region of *baldíos* and quinine, populated from colonial times with some scattered peasants. In Tequendama, where there were already around a hundred coffee estates, according to the local authorities the population was made up as follows: sugar-millers, wheat-harvesters, coffee-growers — 'beside the commercial enterprises, there prosper as well those who on a smaller scale plant out their trees to sell the fruits to the principal producers' — maize-, yuca-, rice-, and *arracacha*-growers, 'who keep their operations to the level our markets and their resources permit'. There were also some hat-makers, blacksmiths, and carpenters. The cattle latifundio was expanding in the flat hot-lands on former tobacco and indigo land. The consumption of meat was rising, and in per capita terms was greater than that of the *sabana* of Bogotá, where the *jornaleros*, from 1880 until the end of the century, were suffering 'frightening wretchedness' (*'una miseria aterradora'*).[44]

The social patterns surrounding the estates grew more complex with the interaction between the resident population, the independent peasants, and the settler communities. The natural surroundings also had undergone something of a transformation. A traveller in the 1870s would have seen small patches scattered among the thickly forested slopes at levels between 1,000 and 2,000 metres. These were crops, mainly sugar-cane, maize, and grass for animal fodder. On the eve of the War of the Thousand Days, which converted the region around El Tequendema into a Liberal bastion (Viotá, 'wet-nurse of revolution'), the countryside had become crowded with cane plantations and pasture land which had spread considerably all over low-lying flatlands, while a new type of forest – the dark expanses of coffee trees and their shade trees – covered the higher slopes. Old *municipios* like La Mesa were to take on a new lease of life; the merchants, large and small, money lenders, shopkeepers and innkeepers had by now prepared on a trade in *mieles* and *panela* which independent smallholders and peasants on the large estates in the temperate zones supplied to the market.[45] Coffee was transported to Girardot, where it was received and shipped on by local agencies. There existed a certain degree of mutual dependence between peasant and shopkeeper. Later, when the tenant farmers fought against the large estate-owners, many businessmen and middlemen in these villages would offer them their support, not out of a sentiment of class solidarity but because these groups stood to gain from dealing with the peasant market, which in times of crisis the estate owners would attempt to close.[46] This group of small-scale merchants, from which the political *caciques* came, had always been the object of the contempt of the merchant class in Bogotá (and also, apparently, Medellín). Money-grabbers, *mercachifles*, and *chucheros* were the kindest words Medardo Rivas found for them, although Camacho Roldán, writing in a better humour, called them 'a well-off, moral, and hard-working population'. A similar opinion, at least in the case of La Mesa, was held by the colonial authorities at the end of the eighteenth century.[47] In a later chapter I will return to analyse in some greater detail the social structure of the regions which in the twentieth century would be the 'traditional' coffee cultivators of the country.

In summary, we can say that the minifundio in the *altiplano* reached the limits of its productive capacity: the population increased and became fragmented. Minifundio society, which produced foodstuffs with traditional and rudimentary tools such as the simple wooden plough and the metal (or wooden) ploughshare, was caught in the trap of diminishing returns with no further possibility of expanding its agricultural frontiers, and culturally restricted to the *vereda–municipio* habitat. Demographic growth resulted in increased unemployment and underemployment, 'idiocy and thieving'.[48] Most of these conditions worked in favour of the estate-owners, who found an abundant labour supply to satisfy their requirements. The need for a permanent workforce on the estates gave impetus to a migratory movement which quickly led to the settlement of El Tequendama, Sumapaz, and some regions of Tolima, thus satisfying the basic needs of the estates and giving rise to a new type of minifundio society in the late nineteenth and early twentieth centuries.

Having outlined the problems relating to the appropriation of land on the one hand, and having on the other described the social context which brought about a migratory movement from the minifundio zones to the new coffee regions, we may now pass to a brief examination of the difficulties faced by both the owners and the workers in the period of settlement in new ecological and geographical surroundings, where patterns of discipline, work organization, and land distribution, although not entirely unfamiliar, still differed significantly from those prevailing in the old minifundio areas of the highlands.

4. The internal structure of the coffee haciendas, 1870–1930

The *hacendado* is a man of progress, which for him is synonymous with unrestricted access to a 'free' labour supply, better roads, cheap railways, and free exports. He is Europe-centric. His desire is to impose civilization in the hollows of the Andes, through growing coffee. He was once a capitalist entrepreneur, but he became an 'oligarch' – in the Colombian social meaning, not the wider political meaning of the term. He got land and credit, and did business on the bases of trust and honour, business in which family and social relationships and political contacts were often all-important. The family, the politico-social connection, sends out its pioneers. Once the haciendas are founded, the commission agents of foreign houses appear and offer funds at low interest and secure market for the product. If he is a Liberal, he emphasizes his faith in the common cause of international capitalism, rebaptizing his properties with names like Java, Ceilán, Costa Rica, Brasil, Liberia, Arabia, remote countries which had also ascended, or were ascending, through coffee in the scale of a universal civilization.

But the internal structure of the hacienda was far from capitalist. It rested on colonial origins. The coffee hacienda as an economic and social construct, as the concrete expression of relations between the *hacendado* – urban in his origins and vocation – and the peasant, is the subject of this chapter. The background is a country which at the same time is developing two defining characteristics: it is gradually becoming a mono-exporting economy, and outside the coffee sector the latifundio – in cattle, sugar, and bananas – is expanding and consolidating. It is necessary to make clear why it was that the hacienda in coffee development is not so much the base as the precursor. It does not come to dominate the whole system. Its development is atrophied; in Cundinamarca and Tolima its economic, entrepreneurial, and social contradictions bring it to a dramatic collapse in the 1930s.

Between 1870 and 1930 the Colombian coffee hacienda differed more from one region to another than it changed over time. In these circumstances the classification called for is a regional one.

I shall first present a general picture of the different regional systems, before describing the internal organization of the hacienda, its rules and hierarchies. Later I shall indicate the different problems originating in the (inevitable) absenteeism of the owner, and relating to the implanting of labour discipline, weakened by the impact of civil wars and politics on the daily life of the hacienda. A brief description of the typical conflicts over the allocation of resources within the hacienda leads to an analysis on another level of the use of land, the techniques of cultivation, and the labour needs imposed by the botanic cycle of the coffee tree. This leads on to a more detailed description of the hierarchy of different sorts of worker, and the systems of payment that prevailed. In the next chapter I shall illustrate very rapidly the trend of money wages, level of employment, and family income in a large *antioqueño* hacienda in the quarter century after 1896. I end with some tentative conclusions on the internal contradictions of these structures which help to explain later developments.

A regional classification of estates

From what we have seen so far, it will be clear that in a country like Colombia geographic diversity and the relative isolation of the various regions give rise to distinct characteristics peculiar to the individual locality. For this reason any system of classification of Colombian coffee estates must necessarily be organized on a regional basis. If we take into account six basic features relating to the social and economic structure of the estates, we are immediately aware of the diversity present in the three large geographical areas in which the first steps of coffee expansion were taken: the Santander region, Cundinamarca–Tolima, and Antioquia. We can see from table 16 that in all three regions the estate-owners came from the merchant classes based in Cúcuta, San Gil, Bucaramanga, Bogotá, and Medellín respectively. Their social and economic rise was made possible by exports which preceded the advent of coffee, namely tobacco, quinine, and indigo, and in Antioquia, gold. The number of 'traditional' *latifundistas* becoming owners of large coffee estates was very small. In fact, the general tendency in the three regions was that of the town merchant's conversion into *latifundista* and estate-owner. But here any similarity of a general nature ends and each region becomes characterized by its own peculiar system.

The features chosen to illustrate this should not be considered as isolated or unrelated. For example, the systems of work were certainly in some way related to the class and 'race' factors, as were the patterns of settlement within the estates. Moreover, the particular features of regional history relating to the land-tenure system which preceded the coffee era no doubt had a direct and decisive effect on the systems of work. Santander displayed a most varied social structure in colonial times, unlike that prevailing in the

Table 16. *The coffee haciendas: regional systems*

	Cundinamarca–Tolima	Antioquia	Santander
Social origin of owner	Merchant	Merchant	Merchant and *vecino rico*
Diversification of owner's assets	Low	High	ND
Land tenure in the coffee zones	(a) Mainly *latifundismo* (b) *Latifundismo* and peasant holdings	*Latifundismo* and peasant holdings	*Latifundismo* and peasant holdings
Class and 'race' factor	Owner and worker 'racially' dissimilar	Owner and worker 'racially' homogeneous	(a) Like Antioquia (b) Like Cundinamarca
System of work	Pre-capitalist *arriendo*	*Agregado* contract	Share-cropping
Pattern of settlement inside the hacienda	Scattered holdings	Concentrated settlements	Scattered holdings

highlands of Cundinamarca and Boyacá . The *encomienda* and *resguardo* were
weak in Santander, through the lack of an indigenous population of any
appreciable size, and the region was settled by white and *mestizo* families
which established a prosperous manufacturing and commercial economy
intimately linked to an agriculture based more on small and medium
independent land-holdings than on large estates or *latifundia*. Slavery
was introduced there to provide manpower on some plantations. This
also occurred in the Cauca valley and in the *antioqueño* mining regions, but
demographically it constituted a somewhat peripheral feature of *santandereano* society. The share-holding system can be seen as based on a type of
contract in which economic disparities were often very great but where
such differences did not necessarily imply very great social distances.
Thus status depended almost entirely on the individual's degree of wealth.

The system was one of 'mutual contract', *contrato de compañía*, which
gradually acquired very diverse characteristics.[1] But it continued to be
one in which the estate-owner and share-cropper were related only at the
economic level; they agreed to share the proceeds of the harvest according
to a form of contractual arrangement which governed the sharing of resource
and assets, land and work and, on occasion, the sharing of expenses when
money was required to finance an operation. The obligations of both
parties cease here, and nowhere is there any case of personal subjection of
the sharecropper to the estate-owner. The former enjoyed full independence
in directing his efforts to the benefit of his own crop. If, as a result of the
size of the coffee plantation under contract, he was obliged to take on any
extra hands from outside his family, the share-cropper was unable to be
overexigent in the conditions of employment, since he was not a landowner
and his contract was for a fixed period and not automatically renewable.
In general the agreed period tended to be short rather than long. No form
of life-long share-cropping tenancy existed. The day-workers who went to
work for the share-cropper never had any direct contact with the landowner.

Share-cropping constituted a contract which typified a society differentia**
by the wealth of its members. As a result of prevailing patterns of cultural
and racial homogeneity, of traditional patterns of coexistence and, perhaps,
of existing ties of co-operation and solidarity (e.g. with regard to the coffee
price) between different agricultural units, big and small, it was impossible
to impose a servile or semi-servile work system.

A succinct description of the system was given by Francisco Zapata, a
share-cropper on one of Ramón González Valencia's estates, in a letter sent
from Chinácota in July 1897:

'The *finca*, which as I believe I mentioned to you in Bogotá, produces 80 *cargas* per year and belongs to the hacienda which I administered for Ramón González Valencia. It was contracted to me half and half, or in other words, I agreed to pick and dry all of the coffee produced, pay all expenses, and give half of the production to Don Ramón. The estate produces 2,000 *cargas* of coffee a year, and he has everything shared and divided up 50–50 as this system has a lot of advantages for the owner, without taking away the satisfaction of supporting all the poor people who have nowhere else to work.'[2]

At the other extreme we find the type of estate which prevailed in Cundinamarca and Tolima. For example, in the region of Chaparral–Ataco, which was isolated both geographically and politically from any significant urban centre, the estate-owners were able to establish semi-servile systems of work. They had monopolized the best land in the region by appropriating *baldíos*, and the region also came to be inhabited by Indians forced from their lands in Cauca whose position *vis-á-vis* the *hacendados* was particularly weak. We have already noted that these regions were characterized by considerable disparity, both cultural and ethnic, between the landowners ('whites') and the day-workers and peasant labourers ('*indios*'), and this tended to reinforce racialist attitudes and ideologies among the owners and their administrators. The workers were looked on as inferiors, a kind of ugly and degenerate 'proletariat race' rather than as a social class. In the Cundinamarca region, where migration from Boyacá and some *municipios* of the eastern *minifundia*, such as Fómeque and Cáqueza, provided the most important source of permanent and seasonal workers for the coffee estates, the peasants quickly became identified as *indios*.

The *arrendamiento* which developed in the area consisted of a type of contract which could only be applied in conditions where a labour force was freely available and composed of large numbers of poverty-stricken workers with an inbred servility resulting from three centuries of *encomienda*, *resguardo*, and domination by traditional Catholicism.

Nonetheless, the diffuse pattern of settlement within the Cundinamarca–Tolima haciendas led gradually to a degree of personal and economic autonomy on the part of the *arrendatario* in relation to the estate; this resulted in a marked dichotomy within the hacienda, namely the economy based on the *estancia* of the *arrendatarios* and the economy of the hacienda proper. With the passing of the generations and with the advent in the twenties of socialist preaching, the dual nature of the hacienda economy became largely unworkable. Tension rose between the two parties concerned: the estate-owners attempted to bend the *arrendatarios* to their will and to try to block

Institute of Latin American Studies

31 Tavistock Square

London WC1H 9HA.

their outlets to local markets, and the *arrendatarios* strove to break down the institutional restrictions which weighed heavily on their work and food production. They now wished to become landowners in their own right.

The merchants did not in all cases succeed in diversifying their activities and assets. In Cundinamarca the pioneer generation tended to specialize in coffee, abandoning other entrepreneurial activities. Very soon many of these *hacendados*, especially those of the south-west, ended up living on their coffee income, reinvesting little and confidently running into debt. In any event these *hacendados* had very few economic options. Thus, an abrupt fall in the international price of coffee forced them to attempt to reduce money wages, which from the 1920s led to social conflict. Their other alternative was to abandon coffee-picking, but since they were usually heavily in debt they were obliged to maintain their haciendas in running order to pay up.

In the case of the *antioqueño* estates, their owners had been more closely involved in mining and mercantile activities in the nineteenth century, and in developing industries in the twentieth. Consequently, they were better placed to sit out a period of depression in the coffee market. In Antioquia there came into being a system midway between that of the other two regions. There the *agregado* can be considered as occupying a social position immediately below that of the traditional *aparcero*. The *antioqueño* estate-owners made efforts to separate the *agregado*'s dwelling place from his plot of land, his *trabajadero*. This prevented the process of consolidation of the *agregado* family economy occurring as it occurred in Cundinamarca; at least, it reduced the *agregado*'s expectations of independence from the hacienda.

It is not therefore surprising that in an area like south-western Cundinamarca, characterized by marked social polarization (i.e. latifundio–minifundio complex), a low level of diversification of landowner assets, and a scattered resident population, in a situation of political mobilization on a national scale, the degree of social conflict became quite intense. In many places the haciendas were obliged to yield to the demands of the *arrendatario* and in others they were completely absorbed by the latter.

Bearing in mind these specific regional characteristics and the way in which the different elements were determined or were mutually influential, we can study in more depth the systems and forms of organization which shaped the labour force working on the haciendas, and examine the nature of the links which existed within the resident population. Unfortunately, time did not permit me to investigate all three geographical areas mentioned above, and the following pages are accordingly devoted to a description of the situation of the coffee estates in the Cundinamarca and Antioquia regions

However, in view of Cundinamarca's geographical position and the considerable importance of the part played by the *bogotano* oligarchy during
the period in which violent social conflict came to the surface (1920–40),
these factors quickly outgrew their local character and acquired importance
at the national level, as we shall see later.

Organization and hierarchies

The merchants who were transformed into *hacendados* became 'absentee'
owners through the very nature of the coffee trade. Men without rural
ties or traditions, their aspirations tended towards a city life and civilization.
The poor conditions of the roads further aggravated the degree of absenteeism.
At this period the question of road improvement became an obsession, as
it had during the Bourbon era. In practice few appreciable improvements
were made. The winter rains, the movement of cattle, and the lack of
adequate funds left the roads in a very sorry state.[3] Once the plantations
had been firmly established, there were few possibilities of innovation. The
administration became characterized by caution and habit. There was
virtually no room for new techniques or for fresh entrepreneurial organization.

The merchant–*hacendado* stood at the apex of the social system: he
enjoyed the highest social status, and his wealth was considered to be the
foundation of national wealth. On occasion, although not always, he succeeded in establishing close relations in high political circles at the regional
or national level.[4] His more important business functions were carried on
outside the coffee estate, where his presence was infrequent and brief. The
owner made decisions concerning the use of land not given to coffee
cultivation, the type of shade trees to be used, and the degree of care to be
given to the plantation, which would depend on the movement of wages
and the coffee price. He also decided replanting times and the number of
trees to be used in this process (this represented the minimum amortization
on capital invested in the plantation) and determined the location of internal
mule paths and so forth. These duties rapidly became routine. In view of
his absence from the estate, the traditional friendly and 'paternal' relationship between boss and worker was never firmly established. In general he
involved himself little in the day-to-day conflicts which arose within the
resident population, and his participation in matters of local government
was, contrary to popular belief, sporadic and discrete. In his heart of hearts
he probably despised rural life with its local public administration, 'money-
grubbers', and petty *caciques*, although he was always careful not to show
it.[5] He delegated authority to an administrator: manager or foreman,
depending on the size of the estate. The administrator would normally

assume the functions of general work inspector, accountant, and 'judge' in the conflicts arising between the estate and the workers, or simply among the latter.

The *administrador* was a fundamental figure on the coffee estate. He had to be able to act on the owner's behalf in all spheres of activity within the estate itself and in dealing with neighbouring estates and with the *municipio.* He also needed to interpret correctly orders relating to production and wages received from the owner, and put these into effect. But the true link between the estate and the working population, permanent or temporary, was the *mayordomo*, who differed from the *administrador* in being almost always of rural origin. He was selected for the post for his loyalty, his knowledge of psychological and social factors inherent in the local working population, and on some occasions for the advantages to be derived from his local background, although on many estates, particularly in Antioquia, it was thought preferable to recruit foremen from other regions. His principal role was to act as a link for the orders given by the administrator with regard to assigning and organizing working groups for specific jobs and supervising the work and the conduct of the workers. The *mayordomo* was also responsible for conveying upwards, somewhat less formally, the complaints and requests of the workers, and for reporting on their state of morale and their reactions to changes in their working instructions or in their access to certain facilities within the estate. Besides receiving a substantially higher wage than the other workers (although far lower than that of the administrator) he often enjoyed certain privileges of a personal and flexible nature. For example it was common for a *mayordomo* to have free grazing rights for two cows or mules, etc. This was a typical feature of the administrative systems in use on the large estates of Cundinamarca and Tolima. In Antioquia it appears to have been common to appoint an *encargado* in an intermediate position between *administrador* and *mayordom*

Between the *mayordomo* and the workforce there were still some other rungs in the ladder: supervisors and foremen, *capataces*; overseers of harvest *mayordomos de coscheros*; the heads of work-gangs, the *antioqueño asistent de corte*, the Cundinamarca–Tolima *jefes de cuadrilla*. Under the direct orders of the administrator or of the *mayordomo* there were the machine-minders and those in charge of the processing plant and the *trapiche*, the muleteers and cattlemen, as well as the house servants, mostly women employed in the kitchen, who at harvest time went out into the plantation to cook for the workers. The proportion of seasonal and permanent resident labour varied with the crop cycle. There were evident social and economic differences between the two groups, but there were also very important gradations within them. As time went on the differences between one resident family and its neighbour could become substantial. These differences had their origins in such factors as the different consumer–worker ratio of the families,[7] the size and quality of their *estancias* or *trabajaderos*, and the unequal distribution of entrepreneurial talent. The differences in income among the seasonal workers were also marked, and they were employed by the hacienda in a variety of ways. Thus for example in 1905 the following categories of workers were to be found on the Jonás estate:

(*a*) Daily *peons* (i.e. workers paid at a fixed *jornal* rate)

(*b*) Peons with token (i.e. pickers who were paid piece-rates)

(*c*) Contract peons (workers who dealt with the hacienda solely through the contractor)

(*d*) *Almuderos* or piece-work *cosecheros*, differing from the peons of group (*b*) in that they were contracted in return for a fixed quantity of *almudes* at a fixed price

Otherwise, workers directly related with the hacienda could be divided into:

(*a*) Peons receiving food rations or

(*b*) Peons without such rations.[8]

Finally, the most striking fact is the degree of disparity between the different cash incomes of the workers. Thus a machine-operator or a *mayordomo* received ten times more than the average *jornal* of a *chapolera*. But between the *jornaleros* and *chapoleros* differences were also relatively large. In 1897, for example, the most common range on the Jonás estate was from 0.25 to 0.50 paper pesos daily. In 1899 we find accounts like the following: '58 coffee-pickers in two sections . . . including the *cesteros* and *gariteros* in 186 *jornales*, paid at 0.10 to 0.55'.[9]

Problems of absenteeism

To the *hacendado* the *administrador* and *mayordomo* were key figures. The loyalty expected of a delegate of this kind could be recognized from his personal history or in certain characteristics: 'he is not a great drinker of *aguardiente* but he is a bachelor' would represent one favourable and one unfavourable point for the Bogotá estate-owner.[10] But naturally enough, marriage did not provide a remedy for the heavy drinker:

'Answer the next question as an honourable man should and with the same sincerity with which it is asked: Will you give your word of honour to administer the estate properly at all times, to abstain from drinking alcohol, and to avoid bad company?' wrote Tulio Ospina to his *encargado* in Fredonia.[11]

During the period of expansion, the administrator of the Santa Bárbara estate was obliged to explain his behaviour to his employer by letter, which was couched in a somewhat papal style:

'Last year we attended several gatherings which took place on our days of rest, and we danced, but it appears to us (and I am quite certain on this point) that the persons who were present were all of the highest class in Sasaima, and that in these little gatherings we committed no impropriety whatsoever, either in the eyes of society, or with respect to our duties, and the *mayordomos* and the labourers here will gladly speak out if on any work day they have witnessed us deserting our post.'[12]

The *administrador*, the *encargado*, and *mayordomo* on the coffee estates did not have at their backs the weight of tradition of *tierra fría*. To use for a moment the language of the *sabana* of Bogotá, one could say that the temperate coffee-growing zones were societies without *orejones* and it was therefore necessary to create them.[13] Disloyalty, or the fear of disloyalty, was a price paid by the absentee landlord in these areas. During periods of social and political strife, the absentee owner ran the risk of losing his property, as indeed occurred later during the *violencia* in Quindío where the *cofradías de mayordomos* carried out a campaign of terror against the owners.[14] At the end of the nineteenth century, even during the War of the Thousand Days, the situation did not reach such extremes, but headaches always remained: 'You are a witness. You found the estate in a complete mess with everyone doing as they liked in it, running private business transactions often at my expense, and they cared little, or at all, if I had gone to the devil'.[15] wrote the owner of La Amalia to the new *encargado* who had just been put in charge.

An absentee owner not only needed to ensure the loyalty of his employee but also a great degree of solidarity in some rather less obvious duties. In some cases, for example, a certain amount of complicity was required in activities which did not altogether conform to expected levels of commercial or labour ethics. For example, an *encargado* might receive instruction thus: 'having consulted several exporters on the subject, I think it is not advisable to mix second-class with first-class coffee to be sold as first class'.[16]

Politics and wars

At times when the communication of information was very restricted and spread very slowly, news such as the events occurring in the civil war, or the latest coffee prices, was kept jealously secret by those receiving it. But inevitably an administrator would be up to date and would be given the following instructions in confidence: 'War has broken out and all work should cease with the exception of the following: pick the coffee; depulp, wash, dry, and put it in the lofts where you can grind as much as possible so that, together with our *panela* sales, we can keep the firm in business. Be especially careful with the mules and take them to a safe place particularly at night.'[17]

On other occasions, loyalties could arise out of the ups and downs of political fortunes. Ramón González Valencia recommended a candidate to Roberto Herrera: 'He came to me just after the war [of 1895] and helped me during my short campaign at that time and thereafter I employed him as administrator of a coffee estate.'[18] González Valencia, who was later to become briefly President of the Republic (1909–10), was a Conservative, a pro-clerical and ultramontane politician. Herrera, in spite of his family ties with the Archbishop Primate of Colombia, was a Liberal, an opponent of the Regeneration, and an enemy of civil wars and military men. Evidently, in this particular case, common party membership does not appear to have been the most important factor in establishing a degree of trust in one's agent. Nevertheless, *copartidismo* doubtless helped cement good relations between the owner and his administrators. In time, their letters became inevitably tinged with politics.

The correspondence between owner and his administrator also reflected the pendulum swings of war and peace occurring in the Republic, not only in the sense that such events directly affected the rhythm of life on the estates, but also because in times of crisis one could expect a greater degree of trust and a common view of events. When conflicts were not divided clearly along monolithic party lines, or when the parties were divided internally, the owner and administrator assumed similar factional stances. It is not difficult to imagine who took the initiative in these matters. In October 1898, Rubio, an administrator on the Santa Bárbara estate, wrote to his employer in the following terms: 'I only hope that we shall have peace at last and that it will work out well for us [i.e. the Liberals]. It wouldn't surprise me if the diehard and hot-headed politics of the Dr Rudas camp came to be reconciled with Dr Parra's line, now that Samper is carpeting for nomination: it seems that they want nothing less than the leadership of the Liberal Party.'[19] Rubio, in common with most of the *bogotano* Liberal 'oligarchy', thus unequivocally sided with the supporters of legalism and pacifism in the Samper–Parra camp, in opposition to those factions within the Liberal movement who, like Rudas, considered a rising to be the only means of overthrowing the dictatorship of the Regeneration.[20] Meanwhile, there is evidence of similar solidarities in *antioqueño* correspondence. Estate-owner Marquez Vásquez wrote the following to his *encargado* at the height of the civil war: 'Dr Vélez took over as Governor yesterday, or if you prefer, as civil and military leader of Antioquia. The Nationalists are finished, probably for good. I hope to God that they are.'[21]

Labour discipline and resource allocation

The rulers of the estates hoped always to find a community whose inhabitant had grown accustomed to obedience and hierarchy. At first they tried to isolate them from contact with better-established and more wordly citizens.

'I believe that we should most certainly take steps to ensure order on the estate. You should arrange with the Mayor to take two good, strong, trustworthy lads to Fredonia to act as police. That way we know all will be safe and we can put an end to the gambling that is going on on the estates. As you know, there are certain wicked and corrupt individuals who go to the estates, usually on Saturdays and Sundays, and rob the hands of their week's wages through gambling. We have to get rid of these rogues, and we'll have to do the same with those that go to sell drink.'[22]

Poor roads and sheer distance between the estates and the nearest villages contributed to preserve 'decent' customs and manners. Perhaps as a further measure for avoiding contact with the outside world and perhaps also as a demonstration of the estate's autocratic strength in a hermetic, self-sufficient world, some large estates set up their own shops and stores which took care to avoid extending credit to their clients. Not surprisingly, such an aim was far from realistic. The landowner—merchants were hardly aware of the complexity of rural society and they understood it still less in this new environment, they did not foresee the transformations which would occur as a consequence of the various wage systems being introduced. Feelings of mistrust and fear towards the resident population were very much in evidence. This in the first place took the form of an incurable obsession with robbery. Any relaxation of discipline, such as might result from drinking, was thought to lead to theft. Contact between the resident population and the seasonal coffee-pickers was very much resented: 'When you leave Fredonia on Sunday afternoon, if you see any drunks causing trouble or making a noise, do all you can to make them calm down and give them the sack on Monday morning.'[23]

Thieves and robbers always formed part of the owner—merchant's picture of his estate. 'Many *cafeteros* have told me how much robbery now takes place on the estates', wrote the worried Márquez from Medellín. Rubio reported to Herrera: 'We're finding that there is a lot of robbery round here', and he claimed that in the neighbouring Las Mercedes estate three farm-hands had stolen a calf and had eaten it.[24] When the coffee price soared, then it was said that 'coffee is like gold dust'; the oft-repeated refrain was: 'We must now be on the lookout for thieves as, on every pound of coffee stolen, they can make a fortune. Take care, keep a lookout at all times.'[25] This feeling of mistrust was directed at all the working sectors of the estate until, finally, the whole community was thought to be affected by 'corruption'. Around 1911 Mariano Ospina Vásquez gave clear instructions to his *encargado* on Jonás: 'Nail up the wire fence hard and at regular intervals round the processing plant and keep an eye open for any sign of tampering. Do your best to see that only the engineer sleeps there, and one other trustworthy man, preferably not a friend of his.'[26]

The estates resorted to a number of devices to ensure an adequate supply of labour during the crucial picking season. The importance of the part played by established labouring families in attracting workers should not be underrated. However, the large scale of the work to be accomplished led the estate owners to improve their organization in this respect. 'Commissions' were sent from Fredonia to Itagüí, Amagá, and Piedraguda; from Sasaima, Viotá, or El Colegio men experienced in the job of recruiting were sent up to Boyacá. In 1906, it was reported in the *Revista Nacional de Agricultura* that in several cases these *enganchadores* had 'taken off with the money' received from the Sociedad de Agricultures de Colombia (SAC) in the name of the coffee-growers for the purpose of facilitating necessary recruitment: everywhere 'corruption'![27]

When a coffee estate found that some of its share-croppers were engaged in the cultivation of another crop, such as sugar-cane, there was conflict on a minor scale. The owners resented the degree of independence this might give the share-cropper. When *panela* prices rose, and cane was ground in the *trapiche*, problems arose over the shifts which were necessary to deal with this extra activity. Comments made about the 'sugar-cane *compañeros*' are pregnant with resentment: 'they are opportunists'; they don't co-operate when the estate needs their help and so 'such people shouldn't be allowed to get away with it'.[28]

In their first years of existence, the estates also encountered a number of difficulties with the families who had come to work and settle. Relations between the estates and these families were undoubtedly awkward and complicated notwithstanding the estate's apparent firmness and confidence in dealing with them, and in spite of the positive response to the estate's demands on the part of the *agregados* and tenant farmers of the earlier generations. On occasion orders were given to dismiss those '*agregados* caught stealing plantains'. Often the owner was given to fits of uncontrolled anger: 'I am determined not to allow layabouts there, and when they least expect it, I'll have the *agregados*' houses knocked down so that their bamboo

wood and straw can be used for the oven.'[29] However, it was no easy
matter to evict an *agregado* in Antioquia. Generally, his contract stipulated
that kidney beans and maize were cultivated on *trabajaderos* on a share-
holding basis (one-third and one-half respectively) and the legal status of
the plots of land was left largely undefined, particularly where changes
made could be interpreted as '*mejoras*' (improvements) according to
civil law. Both the owner and worker preferred to avoid legal conflict on
this point: 'It has come to my attention that Toño is becoming a trouble-
maker on the estate and is therefore providing a very bad example. Please
inform him of my concern and tell him that if he doesn't mend his ways
I'll have him and all his family removed from my land whether the estate
buys his share of the *trabajaderos* or whether we find a worthwhile person
to buy it. I would rather be alone here than have bad, immoral people on
the land.'[30]

It seems likely that the estates had the opportunity to rethink their
values with regard to good or bad people and that they acted, in fact, with
a great degree of flexibility, particularly in the periods of seasonal shortage
of labour or in times of war. During the wars the estates frequently assumed
an attitude of paternalistic responsibility. 'Recruitment round here has
been appalling; only Braulio Garzón has been taken from here and I had
to persuade the *comandante* to set him free', reported Rubio from Sasaima,
referring to the effects of the '*bochinche*' in 1895.[31] In spite of the military
isolation of Antioquia during the War of the Thousand Days, recruitment
there was no less intense. The correspondence between Márquez and his
encargado testifies to the high-level political manoeuvres necessary to gain
a guarantee from the Governor or from the military chiefs that his estate
'should remain untouched': 'kindly persuade the workers on the estate
that they are absolutely safe with the guarantee of safe-conduct which
you obtained last Sunday. The Government has made no order to apprehend
any individual, least of all the farm-hands working on the estates. We
estate-owners have received promises that we shall be allowed to work
without the least interference.'[32] In Sasaima the estates chose to pay for the
tax-exemption of their workers from military service; even so, this was
not necessarily a guarantee that a recruitment commission would not take
off the young single men or a few mules or slaughter a few head of cattle:
'We might as well be in the middle of a war. Recruitment is carried out
brutally and the commissions commit the usual outrages and abuses . . .
we have reason to fear that our crop will remain unpicked as the people
are terrified by this horrific persecution and no one dares to work for fear
of being taken. We all feel a true sense of outrage at these events.'[33]

In Fredonia it was impossible in 1899–1900 to persuade the coffee-pickers to sleep in their quarters (*cuarteles*) on the estates. And at the same time it was difficult to impose regular working hours on the resident populace. The estates were obliged to find new methods by trial and error. The problem rapidly crystallized into the question of which jobs should be paid at *destajo* (piece-rates) and which should be paid at *jornal*. In both cases special and costly measures would be necessary to control the workers or the quality of work carried out. 'Allocate one *asistente* (overseer) for every fifteen workers' was an order heard in Antioquia. But the main problem encountered with *agregados* and *arrendatarios* was their reluctance to work on the estate plantations; they preferred to concentrate on their own land or on *trabajaderos* and *estancias*. An order like the following was difficult to put into practice: 'You must come to some agreement with the sugar-cane workers in case we're short of men for cutting and carrying etc. so that they can lend a hand. The price of sugar is going to shoot right up and it will be worse for them if there aren't enough hands to grind the cane. Put the women and youngsters to work so we don't lose coffee. All the men not busy grinding cane should also go and pick coffee.'[34]

The response was equally pragmatic. Where an institutional obligation made it necessary to work for the estate on certain days of the week, an *estanciero* had the right to send a replacement to fulfil this obligation. In Antioquia, where no such institutional arrangement existed, the obligation was implicit in the relationship between the *agregado* and the estate, and here the only means of enforcement lay in the exertion of pressure and threats of eviction: 'I am determined to put a stop to these *agregados* because it is obvious that they contribute little to the estate and want everything for themselves. When I get the chance, I shall make them all, without exception, work for the estate for two or three days a week. I have come to realize that these people work on Amalia only for their own ends and they really are not concerned if the estate goes to rack and ruin as long as they are making money for themselves.'[35]

Use of land and techniques of cultivation

On the traditional *haciendas* the only type of coffee under cultivation was the common *arabigo* (*Coffea arabica typica*), known as *nacional* or *pajarito* coffee.[36] Other varieties of *arabigo*, such as the *borbon* (*Coffea arabica* L. var. Bourbon) and the *Maragogipe* (*Coffea arabica* L. var. Maragogipe) were also introduced. Other species of coffee (e.g. *Coffea liberica*) or *robusta* types such as the *Coffea canephora* were tried unsuccessfully in the Sierra Nevada.[37] The *arabigo* species flourishes in temperate zones

(17 to 24°C), which in Colombia are to be found generally between 1,200 and 1,800 metres in altitude. The Andean slopes of Colombia also offer other conditions which favour the growth of this coffee tree, such as deep, soft soils rich in organic deposits, and regular rainfall patterns (amounting to 1,000–2,500 mm annually). The western slopes of the central cordillera are particularly well endowed with such conditions, although long wet winters and heavy downpours occurring during the plant's flowering stage occasionally have the effect of reducing the size of the final crop. However, such meteorological disasters in Colombia are in no way comparable to the sharp frosts which devastate the Brazilian coffee regions of São Paulo and Paraná and adversely affect the 'biennial cycle' of coffee production. Indeed, this particular cycle can hardly be said to exist in Columbia. The tree normally enjoys an average productive life of thirty years, and is at its productive prime between the seventh and fifteenth year, after which it gradually declines. Commercial production begins in the fifth and sixth years.

The early coffee plantations were established on the sites of subtropical forests cleared by burning, the cheapest and simplest method available to the coffee pioneer. Once the original vegetation had been burned down, the next step was to sow the reclaimed land with the basic crops necessary to feed the workers: maize, yuca, kidney beans, and plantains, while cultivated grasses and sugar-cane were planted to provide fodder for the mules and oxen essential for transport. The main nursery was then established and here the seedling coffee trees were tended for six or seven months before being planted out on a permanent site. The young trees were planted alongside shade trees in soil which had already yielded one or two harvests of other crops. After a few years, the shade trees would form a secondary forest, protecting the top soil and the coffee plant, and maintaining even levels of humidity and temperature. This new vegetation produced what experts call the 'coffee-tree microclimate'.

In almost all the coffee regions in the country, with the exception of the older coffee areas of Santander and Cauca, the coffee tree was always accompanied by shade trees. The controversies concerning the advantages and disadvantages of the use of shade trees made picturesque, though interminable, reading, but it is possible to discern beneath the surface of 'technical' arguments a preoccupation with pruning costs. Several varieties of *guamo* tree (*Ingas*) and trees such as the *cámbulo* and *chocho* (*Erythrina*) and the *gualanday* (*Jacaranda*) as well as the plantain have all been used to provide shade for coffee. It was widely agreed among the producers that, although the use of the shade tree might lead to a reduction in total annual production, it prolonged the life of the coffee plant and prevented soil erosion

The coffee plantations were compact and evenly cultivated but divided into somewhat arbitrary sections, known in Antioquia as *tongas* and in Cundinamarca and Tolima as *tablones*. A coffee grove expanded in terms of *tongas* or *tablones*, depending on the system in use. Each section contained trees of roughly the same age and consequently required reasonably uniform upkeep. Its productivity level was also relatively stable. The shape of the coffee plantations was largely determined by the contours of the terrain and by altitude, but in all cases the processing plant would be located as nearly as possible at a point equidistant from the plantation boundaries.

The haciendas were not monocultures. On the contrary, they displayed a marked tendency to diversify production in two ways: foodstuffs, sugar-cane, and beef were produced for both resident and seasonal workers in order to guard against rises in market prices, and to supply local and urban markets and thus to obtain the cash income necessary for financing the running costs of the estate; this income also served as a buffer against the cyclical fall of coffee prices. In this way the estates were able to make the best use of their land and to create additional employment. This should not be taken to mean, however, that the haciendas attempted to exploit their land at maximum productive capacity, but rather that the process of diversification was clearly the most sensible and 'rational' choice in the circumstances.

The geographic location of the haciendas also had some bearing on the way in which land could be put to use. An hacienda situated some distance from a railway or river port required a large mule herd for transport and had to devote additional land to grazing. The development of railways and roads made it possible for the haciendas to reduce the area of land given to mule-grazing and to increase their stocks of cattle.

A coffee hacienda had to have at its disposal an area of mountain above the 1,800-metre line. This provided wood, the fuel for the drying stoves and *guardiolas*. The high mountain was also the source of the springs whose waters were harnessed to drive with Pelton-wheels the machinery used in the processing plant. Those estates larger than 300 hectares conformed to the 'optimum' model shown in fig. 1. The main crop complementing coffee was sugar-cane. It had different planting and harvesting times from coffee and created extra jobs for resident families, thus ensuring that the hacienda would have at least a minimum of workers for the busy coffee-picking season. Sugar-cane also served as food for the workers and as fodder for beasts of burden. *Dulce* or *panela* often formed a part of the food rations given by the hacienda to the workers in Antioquia, Cundinamarca, and Tolima. In the latter case *miel* rations were also given for making *guarapo*. Any surplus was sold on the urban markets.

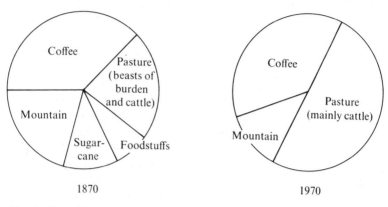

1870   1970

Fig. 1. Use of land on the haciendas.

Corn, another complementary crop, though of secondary importance, was more common in Antioquia. The privileged position occupied by cattle was partly due to the small investment required after the land had been taken over and cleared. The hacienda tended to be self-sufficient in food and paid part of the total salary for the harvesting in food rations. In the case of permanent workers, the hacienda conceded them the right to produce crops for their own profit, and to sell them either on the estate or elsewhere.

It would be difficult to make even a tentative estimate of the area occupied by the resident population on the *estancias* or *trabajaderos*. On the large estates of Viotá, this figure probably fell somewhere between 10 and 15 per cent of the estate's total land area. In a number of cases the *estancias* were strategically placed in order to protect the estate boundary in remote areas or in places where the ownership of the property was in doubt, but in general the *estancias* and *trabajaderos* were grouped around the coffee plantations. However, the majority of the Colombian haciendas were of medium size and the availability of land for complementary and functional purpose was strictly limited. Under these circumstances the hacienda offered to its *arrendatarios* or *agregados* a meagre plot of land for the cultivation of subsistence crops, and consequently there tended to be a high turnover rate.[38]

Permanent and seasonal workers and systems of payment

Coffee is a very labour-intensive crop, which does not present any economies of scale in the plantation. Topography defies mechanization. These factors explain the fundamental strategy of the haciendas in relation to their workforces. As there are no labour-saving techniques available, the hacienda tries to impose forms of work organization which economize on wages and monetary costs. The diffusion of coffee culture, processing apart, did not bring any technical advance to Colombian agriculture. There was no new technique of neater control, soil management, fertilizing, pest-control, or intense cultivation. The tools were still the heavy hoe (*azadón*) and the *machete*.

The haciendas obtained a greater productivity per unit of land in coffee than the small producers, but one has to make two qualifications: they had to dedicate from two-thirds to three-quarters of their total land to other uses, and for the most part their coffee land was exclusively planted to coffee and shade, except in its first three or four years of life. The small producers, on the other hand, planted food crops amongst their coffee trees.

The opening up of new lands to coffee was particularly irksome. The climate, terrain, vegetation, and distances made this an exhausting endeavour. The sequence of land usage was classic: (1) *rocería*, (2) sowing of corn and grasses, (3) harvesting of corn, (4) replanting of coffee trees and of the shade trees planted previously in the nurseries, and (5) the shift to another part of the property where the cycle was repeated.

At the time the plantation was being established the haciendas handed over areas of around three hectares to each family, to be cleared and planted with food crops and coffee. In general they did not make *contratos de formaçao* on the São Paulo pattern, although there are traces of such an experiment in some of the haciendas of Sumapaz.[39] Once the population was established, the intensity of work depended on the botanic cycle of the plant, but also on the social conditions prevailing, of which the most important was the availability of labour. In clear contrast with Brazil – which suffered from scarcity of labour before the abolition of slavery in 1888 – in Colombia and in Central America the harvest accounts for 60 per cent of the total annual labour input. In these countries the coffee is picked berry by berry, as each ripens. In Brazil the labour input of the harvest, including the preliminary tasks, never reaches 40 per cent. In Brazil, Colombia, and Central America these proportions have remained fairly constant over the last century.

Given the seasonal nature of the harvest, a hacienda could not rely only on its resident population and had to rely on the *enganche*, the recruitment of seasonal labourers. The graph (fig. 2) illustrates clearly the seasonal variation of the labour force in a coffee hacienda. I chose Santa Bárbara because it also shows the period of the formation of the hacienda. Only

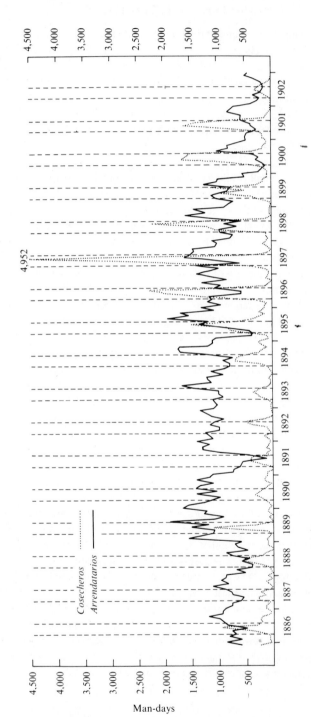

Fig. 2. Santa Bárbara: labour input, 1886–1902.

after 1895 does the temporary workers' labour input overtake that of the resident *arrendatarios* in harvest time. As we saw in chapter 2, developments in Santa Bárbara followed very closely the trough of international prices, and they were directly affected by civil war. In more normal conditions the curves of labour input would have followed those of the years 1896–1900. In the four months from April to June over 80 per cent of the crop was picked. This hacienda, like many others, had only a small minor harvest, or *mitaca*, which could be picked by the *arrendatarios* without additional labour.

The *cosecheros* were paid according to a piece-rate system and only in extreme cases of labour shortage did the *administradores* consent to pay the day-rate (*jornal*). The piece-rate system held clear advantages for the haciendas. Since it is possible to calculate the production of parchment coffee according to the weight of the harvested coffee berries (4.4–5.0 kg of berries = 1.0 kg of parchment),[40] it was more reasonable to fix the rate according to weight (i.e. fix the wage-rate according to a given piece-rate). In order to avoid a fall in quality due to the *cosechero*'s attempts to maximize the overall weight, the hacienda was obliged to run to the additional cost of employing supervisors (one *jornal* extra for every 15–25 harvest workers) and to impose a minimum picking limit in exchange for meals. This was the most frequent system for this type of labour: 'If the *chapoleras* bring in less than 9 *tarros*, these should be paid at 2 to 2.50 pesos without meal rights, according to the circumstances. Thus we have the following figures: meals at 10 pesos plus 8 pesos for picking equals 18 pesos (at 1 peso per *tarro* plus meals) so that each *tarro* works out at 2.25 pesos. It is better to pay 2 pesos without rations especially when they pick four or five *tarros* as occurs during the *graneos*.'[41] On the basis of the piece-rates the hacienda could, therefore, calculate the approximate total cost of the harvest and increase production by giving an incentive to the coffee-picker.

The pickers generally shared a common social background and the same geographical origin with the permanent workers: they were largely *minifundistas* who were obliged by circumstances to take on casual work, since their own land did not require work for a large part of the year, and they had to eke out a subsistence income. Others were simply landless day-workers. Beyer gives the example of an estate-owner in North Santander who decided to buy up the land of his coffee-pickers in Boyacá in order to tie them to his estate, thus putting a stop to the migratory movement.[42] This somewhat exceptional situation illustrates, nevertheless, the problems inherent in the mobility of the workforce which in certain *municipios* led on occasion to an acute labour shortage.

The contractual relationship between the estates and the resident population was by no means uniform. Taking into account the money costs and the necessity to 'save labour' the specialists tended to come out in favour of the *contratista* system described above. But many *haciendas* in Cundinamarca–Tolima attempted to tie their labour force from the beginning and to make a verbal agreement which came to be known as *arrendamientos*.[43] These took on a number of variations, but in formal terms an *arrendamiento* was a bilateral legal agreement in which the *arrendatario* rented an *estancia* where he could construct a basic dwelling, *choza*, and cultivate any crop with the exception of 'root crops' (*mata raizal*), such as coffee. In payment of his rent he accepted an obligation to work on the estate at a salary and for a time commensurate with the size and quality of the land of his *estancia*. When the *arrendatario* fulfilled his obligation he received about 50 per cent of the cash wage paid to '*peones voluntarios*'. During the early stages the language was less obscure in describing these relationships and these workers were not called *arrendatarios* but *peones de asiento*, *peones de obligación*, or simply *obligacioneros*. The hacienda attempted to implement a system of exchange which would be both profitable and workable: work in exchange for land, thus guaranteeing itself a permanently available workforce, while the *arrendatario* was assured of a no less permanent income. The basic elements in this exchange were, then, land and work. If, as it has been suggested, monetary penury was a contributing factor in the establishment of the pre-capitalist rent system in the seventies and early eighties,[44] other factors were also highly influential, as we have seen.

The *arrendatarios*, *agregados*, and *vivientes* were not the poorest members of society, though they were in some ways the most dependent. They formed a permanent nucleus of workers for the routine duties of the coffee plantations and a reserve labour force for the picking season. It appears undeniable that they enjoyed higher incomes, greater job stability, and more opportunity to save than the peons and *jornaleros* '*voluntarios*'. Taking on casual work (*jornalear*) for debt-repayment was quite unknown on the coffee estates. Selling goods to the workforce on credit in the shops and stores of the hacienda, making advances on *jornales*, and similar practices were apparently so unusual that they rarely formed the subject of debate between the *administradores* and their employers. In general their policy was clearly to refuse to give credit to anyone. This rule, which applied in both Cundinamarca and Antioquia, was broken only in exceptional circumstances. Indeed there seems more reason to believe that the haciendas were more likely to owe cash debts to their workers.

Meanwhile, we should add two more elements common to the *arrend-*

amiento system which, as we shall see, contributed to aggravate social tensions on the estates. First there was the employment of substitutes. As in the traditional *arrendamiento* system of the *altiplano*, the *arrendatario* was under no personal obligation and he was soon able to '*sacar recibo*'. In other words, he was able to send another worker or family member to work in his place in order to meet his agreed obligations. Another form of paying off such an obligation was by 'killing time': in order to fulfil, for example, an obligation of six days' work the *arrendatario* could engage six hands for a day, three hands for two days, or two for three days. Secondly, in most cases the *arrendatario* had full rights over his harvests of plantain, yuca, maize, and other crops, or to the pigs which he might have on his *estancia*. The *arrendatarios* soon found themselves important suppliers to local markets. It seems likely that this independent activity would have provided a greater income than that received by a *jornalero*.

5. Living conditions and internal contradictions in the hacienda structure

Types of worker and forms of payment

Before going on to the final analysis it is convenient to have a clear idea of the relative magnitudes of the permanent and seasonal workforce. The calculations here given as an example are from the hacienda Jonás, 1912–17 and from Santa Bárbara, 1894–1900, and information obtained at the hacienda Valparaiso, Tolima, in April 1975. These results have been compared with those in two other recent studies.[1] Given the technical limitations outlined above, it is not surprising that both labour input per hectare and the proportions of permanent and seasonal labour have varied very little in these eighty years. These examples can then be taken as typical.

A coffee hacienda of 100 hectares of adult trees, with a density of 1,110 trees per hectare and a production of 10.4 bags of parchment coffee per hectare requires the following labour input per year:

Weeding and pruning	2,814 9- to 12-hour days	42%
Harvest, principal	2,700 9- to 12-hour days	40%
Harvest, *mitaca*	1,186 9- to 12-hour days	18%
Total	6,700 9- to 12-hour days	100%

Weeding and pruning are carried on throughout the year. As the resident population had to work 150 days a year, the minimum number of permanent workers can be arrived at by dividing the total number of days of obligatory work required: $2,814 \div 150 = 19$ workers. The same procedure can be applied to the harvest, but one must take into account that the principal harvest is spread on average over 70 days and the *mitaca* over 50. On carrying out the same sum of dividing the number of worker-days required by the number of days, the results are 39 workers and 24 workers for the principal harvest and the *mitaca* respectively. One can assume that the permanent workers' families and some of them themselves can provide 20 workers a day at the time of the principal harvest, so the hacienda must therefore recruit 19 more each day, a quantity roughly equal to the permanent workers so employed. In this example I have not considered some relevant factors, such as the concentration of 60 per cent of the picking in the space of three or four weeks. But the hacienda must contract an average number of temporary workers equal to its permanent labour-force.

To understand the internal hierarchy of the hacienda, its relations with the workforce, and the relations between the different components of this, we can therefore divide the work into two main categories, maintenance and harvesting, and the workforce into two main groups, permanent and seasonal. Let us examine this schema more closely.

Fig. 3 sets out the forms of payment that prevailed in the three main regions, the preferences of the workers and their families, and the potential areas of conflict, both between the hacienda and the workers and between different categories of worker. Equally, it helps to establish the lines of stratification in the workforce, and its lines of aspiration in social ascent.

The upper group is made up of the *aparceros*, share-croppers, who have access to the resources of the hacienda and who share with it, usually getting 50 per cent, the proceeds of the sale of the product. In Antioquia and Cundinamarca the share-croppers on coffee haciendas were engaged in producing *panela* and *miel*. The lowest level of the resident population in the Cundinamarca haciendas is made up of the *obligacioneros*, who exchange their labour for a plot and who do not receive any cash wages at all. The intermediate stratum is that of the *arrendatarios*, who exchange labour for land but who are also partly paid in cash. As can be seen, the most important area of conflict between these two groups of workers and the hacienda is that relating to the form of payment for harvest labour. In general, with these workers the hacienda allotted them a fixed quota of coffee to pick, or assigned them to other tasks, such as weeding or pruning, thus preventing them from taking part in the harvest. This placed them at an obvious disadvantage in comparison with the temporary harvester, paid at piece-rates. In the principal harvest an able *cosechero* could, working on piece-rates, earn two or three times the customary day-wage. There was thus frequently resentment felt by the permanent workers towards the temporary. As for the heaviest tasks such as weeding, the haciendas also imposed on the permanent workers a minimum annual area for them to clear, while the workers wanted a fixed daily wage for this work.

The neo-classical dictum on the inefficiency of share-cropping is well known:[2] The share-cropper will exert a minimum effort to obtain a crop that he will have to halve, calculating when the half will cover his basic necessities. Perhaps the assumption behind this argument is that the share-cropper is the one who determines how much land he will take on, and not the proprietor. In fact it was the proprietor who did the determining; in

Harvesting (58% of total labour input)

Region	Resident workers	Food rations	Money wages — Fixed	Money wages — Piece-rates	Land	Per cent of product
Antioquia	Compañeros (caña)	A B			B	X
	Agregados		A	B	A B	
Cundinamarca–Tolima	Aparceros (caña)			B	B	X
	Arrendatarios	A	A	B	A	
	Obligacioneros	B		B	A B	
Santander	Vivientes				B	X

Care (42% of total labour input)

Region	Resident workers	Food rations	Money wages — Fixed	Money wages — Piece-rates	Land	Per cent of product
Antioquia	Compañeros (caña)	A B			B	X
	Agregados		B	A	A B	
Cundinamarca–Tolima	Aparceros (caña)			A	B	X
	Arrendatarios	A	B	A	A	
	Obligacioneros	B	B		A B	
Santander	Vivientes				B	X

Seasonal workers

Region	Seasonal workers	Food rations	Money wages — Fixed	Money wages — Piece-rates
Antioquia	Chapoleros (-as)	X[a] B		A B
Cundinamarca–Tolima	Voluntarios (-as)	X[a] B		A B
Santander	Cosecheros (-as)	X[a] B		A B

[a] In this case the minimum quota that entitles the harvester to rations must be remembered

Fig. 3. Components in the remuneration of labour on Colombian coffee haciendas. A = usual form of payment established; B = form of payment preferred by the worker; X = established form of payment burdensome or risky to the worker.

order to make the share-cropper work more intensively the hacienda reduced the size of his parcel to the size that proved best for its purposes. A similar method of getting the maximum benefit from the work of the *jornalero* can be seen in payment on the piece-rate systems. Such payment is also subject to minimum quotas which are burdensome to the worker. Seeing that the productivity of the *cosechero* does not depend only on his own effort in the picking, but on the state of the crop – 'good', 'bad', 'average' – by imposing a minimum amount of coffee to be picked the hacienda makes the pickers pay for falls in production attributable to natural factors. In these cases the pickers would organize themselves to demand a fixed daily wage and food, not a piece-rate and food only for those who picked a determined amount.

Where A and B coincide in the same box in fig. 3 this does not mean that there is no potential for conflict. On the contrary, in these cases the demands of the workers are directed at higher cash wages, better-quality rations, and more or better-quality land for their own plots. It is logical to suppose that the interest of the hacienda was to give parcels of smaller size than the optimum for family cultivation, so that there would always be labour available from the resident family.

All this goes some way to explain why, when in the 1920s and 1930s the hacienda's legitimacy as a social and productive organization came to be questioned, there existed many obstacles in the way of united action on the part of the different social strata in the hacienda. But it also explains the administrative difficulties with which the haciendas were faced when they wished to impose work systems and forms of payment that were at the same time acceptable to the peasants and profitable for the hacienda. These would be designed to get the peasants to work their families harder. It would have been possible to obtain such higher levels of work if the *hacendados* had possessed an effective monopoly of cultivable land over large stretches of the country. But, as was shown above, this was only the case in a very few of the pioneer municipalities. Just as the central plantation in a coffee hacienda contained a number of small family plots worked by the resident labour, the haciendas themselves were only islands in a sea of small and medium holdings of independent peasants. The *latifundismo* that expanded in Colombia was not on the slopes of the Andes, but in flat land suitable for cattle, sugar-cane, or bananas. On the slopes, besieged without and sometimes within[3] by the *minifundio*, the hacienda appears a fragile construction. Using the language of a certain school of historians, one would conclude that while the peasant small-holder belongs to the 'long duration' (truly millennial – he has survived all the known modes of production), this type of hacienda belongs only to the 'medium duration' category, and to that only as a result of much striving.

Employment, wages, and family income on the haciendas, 1880–1930

Salary scales and salary series may be constructed, but these leave out certain fundamental aspects of the relationship between the worker and the hacienda. For a full understanding of this, two factors should be taken into account: (*a*) that the permanent worker's total income is made up of three elements, cash, food rations (although by no means always), and access to a plot of land for growing foodstuffs; (*b*) that it is unrealistic to isolate the individual from his family when trying to calculate his personal income.

The historical study of wages is not very far advanced in Colombia, although there has recently been some important progress.[4] From what has gone before, it can easily be understood that coffee wages are not the expression of a pure capitalist relationship, and that *enganche* and the conditions of labour prevailing are not signs of a labour market in the full capitalist meaning of the term. We still do not have all the elements needed to know what determined the agricultural wage at this time, that is, the minimum for which the *jornalero* would sell his labour. There was some mobility of labour within each region, which made for uniform regional wages, the variations not always determined by differences in the skill of the worker. Thus in the area dominated by Bogotá a *cosechero* in the coffee zone earned double the wage of a labourer on the *sabana*, lodging and food included in both cases. A labourer who had moved to Bogotá could gain almost double the wage of the coffee zone. In these three cases the daily wages were respectively 15 centavos, 30 centavos, and 50 centavos in 1886.[5] All these workers earned much less, from four to ten times less, than the intermediate group of skilled but dependent artisans: upholsterers, carpenters, shoemakers, and blacksmiths earned an average of 2 pesos a day. Watchmakers earned 4 pesos a day; saddlers, printers, painters, and bakers 1 peso.[6] In Antioquia a similar ranking can be seen among agricultural workers, and it is skill rather than necessarily the occupation itself that determines the wage. If one compares the wage of an agricultural labourer of the Medellín district with that of a worker in the mines — each working a twelve-hour day — in 1884, we find the first earning 40 centavos and the second 60 centavos, both receiving food and lodging.[7] The difference probably derives from the greater intensity, effort, and risk of mining.

Using the weekly series of wages of the Jonás hacienda, I made two correlations: one with the prevailing coffee price abroad (converted to pesos), and the other with the level of employment of permanent labour within the same hacienda. The first was made for the period 1910–33, that is, when the coffee economy was well established in south-east Antioquia, so that it is reasonable to conclude that there the agricultural wage was determined by the coffee sector. The results of both attempts are conclusive: no correlations exist. (The results were for the first $r^2 = 0.53$; for the second $r^2 = 0.25$.) Leaving aside the question of what determines the minimum wage in an agrarian society such as this in conditions of elasticity in the supply of labour, the Jonás accounts enable us clarify some other aspects of the role of wages in the economies of the hacienda and of the workers. Given the duality prevailing at the turn of the century in the money market, it seems clear that for a *hacendado* who calculated in pounds sterling, costs in devalued pesos represented an additional source of profit. In chapter 6 I try to show that this theory simplifies and distorts what actually occurred. Leaving aside this element and assuming that the hacienda calculates in pesos, let us examine the impact of the price of food. The money wage can be analysed from various points of view. For the hacienda the sum of wages, plus the costs of food purchased for rations, makes up the most important item of costs. For the resident worker it is an important element in his total income, although in the case of the *arrendatario* who sells his produce in the local markets and hires peons to fulfil his work obligation to the hacienda, it may be of secondary importance. If the price of the basic foods that the hacienda must buy for rations remains constant, its effect is 'neutral' on the running costs of the hacienda, and the purchasing power of the workers' money-wage changes only through movements in the prices of other goods, such as textiles and tobacco, that he must buy in the market.

What can be seen in the series of prices for basic foodstuffs bought by the hacienda Jonás on the spot are violent weekly and monthly fluctuations, especially in maize, beans, and *panela*. The weekly and monthly fluctuations of all these products are surprisingly alike. Equally surprising is that the compound price of the typical ration does not change, as rises in one price are compensated for by falls in another. I do not have an adequate explanation for these variations. Assuming that the demand, from haciendas and peasants, is constant, then these oscillations must be the result of variations in supply characteristic of primitive agrarian economies where climate and pests (locusts) and disease determine the volume of production. To this must be added the fact that demand itself is not constant but seasonal. In harvest time the local money supply increases, and it is logical to think that the *cosecheros*, even though they receive their rations on the hacienda, stock up with more food as well. By all accounts, for the hacienda the management of this aspect of costs, the purchase of rations, was much more troublesome than fixing the nominal wage.

In rural society quantity and quality of the food rations reflected a person's rank in the social hierarchy. Not every worker received the same food. In July 1901 Amalia's owner wrote to his *encargado* on the matter of some carpenters who were to carry out some work on the estate, 'They should not receive the same food as the peons but they should not have the same as our administrators either. You should not go to too much trouble and they should have meat only at lunchtime. Mariano [i.e. Mariano Ospina Vásquez] and I told them in fact that they would be fed as *peones*.'[8]

On occasion the hacienda preferred to reduce the ration and pay more to the *jornalero* in cash. Between 1901 and 1902 Ignacio de Márquez attempted to cut down on the size of the *arepas* and reduce the amount of meat which the Amalia estate gave in rations. In 1903 he decided that he ought to give something in return and when in that year, in anticipation of a rise in the price of maize which occurred after a plague of locusts, he eliminated *arepas* from lunch and dinner, he made the following remark: 'I think that to do this, we should raise the *jornal* by one peso [1 centavo gold] for the peons, and by 50 cents [½ centavo gold] for the *chapoleras* so that the loss of the *arepa* will not be so sorely felt.'[9] The following instruction of 3 April 1901 is typical: 'I met Ramon Molina in Itagüí yesterday and he told me there were many people who were ready to go with him [to pick coffee]. It seems to me at the moment that we should stop giving *arepas*, lunch and supper, to the *chapoleros* and peons as I'm quite sure that the other *fincas* like La Rita, El Amparo, San Pedro and lots more like them only give *arepas* to their workers for breakfast or as a snack. Tell the cooks to cut down on the *arepas*. I think you should try to do the same with meat so try and save a pound of meat for every 4 peons and a pound for every 5 *chapoleros*. As I think we're likely to be having a lot of people you'd better weed me out all those women with lots of kids and put them on a *jornal* of 30 centavos.' By 12 April 1901 he appears to have been satisfied with arrangements: 'Thank God you managed to get rid of all those lazy, child-bearing women. You'd better see next if you can make a start on all the other lazy vagabonds who don't like work.'[10]

Wages and food prices

Let us consider briefly the case of Hacienda Jonás. In table 17 I present the *agregados*' and *chapoleros*' daily wage, the average number of days

Year	Agregados' daily wage	Chapoleros' daily wage (9 tarros quota)	Average number of days worked by agregados per year	Price of a typical ration[a]	Family money income per year[b]	Food expenditure of family per year	Balance of family budget at end of year
1896	0.51	0.38	222	0.12	261	147	114
1897	0.54	0.40	273	0.12	322	135	187
1898	0.40	0.30	250	0.12	224	140	84
1899	0.47	0.30	238	0.14	257	167	90
1900	0.76	0.57	243	0.23	417	273	144
1901	1.20	1.00	247	1.15	685	1,354	−670
1902	4.35	3.50	234	2.62	2,362	3,151	−789
1903	10.90	6.00	239	5.33	5,554	6,539	−805
1904	14.75	8.25	247	7.45	7,744	8,771	−1,027
1905	13.10	9.00	220	7.15	6,537	8,804	−2,267
1906	13.57	9.00	217	6.00	6,647	7,425	−778
1907	13.96	9.00	147	4.58	5,090	6,249	−1,159
1908	16.55	9.00	223	5.00	8,042	6,593	1,449
1909	12.86	9.90	209	6.70	6,346	8,398	−2,052
1910	16.09	9.00	241	6.31	8,279	7,502	777
1911	16.65	9.00	210	6.25	7,612	7,820	−208
1912	21.45	9.90	160	7.62	7,505	10,297	−2,792
1913	19.50	11.00	204	6.68	8,787	8,488	299
1914	17.50	11.00	239	5.40	9,145	6,444	2,701
1915	15.00	10.00	222	6.76	7,470	8,347	−877
1916	21.50	13.50	236	6.96	11,120	8,560	2,560
1917	24.40	13.50	215	7.73	11,421	8,779	2,642
1918	—	13.50	200	7.46	—	—	—

a For a typical ration on Jonás, see table 19. However in calculating the rations the family had to buy I used these estimates: meat, 100 g per ration; kidney beans, 125 g; maize, 125 g; *panela*, 250 g; salt, 20 g. b Figures in paper pesos as they appear in the hacienda pay-rolls. From 1904 the paper peso was fixed at 10,000% of the gold peso. To obtain the equivalent in gold pesos, divide by 100.
Source: Archivo Jonás.

worked by *agregados* per year, and the price of a typical ration on the hacienda. The last three columns on the right are based on a very rudimentary hypothesis. I assume a typical family of seven members, of whom the father and the adolescent son work as *agregados*; the mother and four children under twelve years of age work in the harvest. I have not attempted to include in this calculation the work of the mother in the upbringing of the children and the housekeeping chores. Putting aside purely economic considerations, it would be a simple matter to show that the mother has to make the greatest single physical effort: as Juan de Dios Restrepo wrote, 'The men of Antioquia are only surpassed in the colonization of El Quindío by their women.'[11]

In my hypothesis the father and the first son each work the average number of days *agregados* work in the hacienda, but the father's wage is 1.0 to the son's 0.75. I assume that the mother and younger children work the average number of days worked by harvesters, which on this hacienda is 83 per year, and that together they count as two harvesters. To obtain the family money income I multiply the average number of days worked by *agregados* per year by the average wage and multiply the result by 1.75. The result is the annual contribution of the father and first son. The income of the mother and the other children is obtained by multiplying the average day-wage of harvesters by 83 and then doubling.

In the matter of food I assume that that obtained from the family plot is marginal, and that the family has to buy food at the same price as the hacienda pays. I establish the price of the typical ration (see table 17) and multiply by a factor of 4.75 units of consumption: father and first son, 2.0 units; mother, 0.75 unit; four smaller children, 2.0 units. This is the daily cost of food when no member of the family is working on the hacienda. As I assume that on the days worked on the hacienda the workers get the *ración*, I subtract the cost of this food.

The state of the family budget at the end of the year is only a rough guide to the welfare of the family over the years, and I do not think that it has much use beyond that. A more exact estimate would have to take family dynamics into account, with its change in the consumer—worker ratio; I have assumed a 'typical' family with a static ratio. But I do not think that it is risky to say that people suffered more in deficit years — eleven of the twenty-two analysed — and that in such times the consumption of clothing, tobacco, etc. was either maintained on a poor diet or through more labouring outside the hacienda. These figures thus would appear to indicate that between 1901 and 1912 family income probably fell to one of its lowest points in the history of coffee cultivation in that region.

No similar statistics are available for Cundinamarca. We may say only

Table 18. *Hacienda Santa Bárbara: money wages and panela prices, 1896–1900*

	Semester	Panela price index	Cosechero piece-rate wage index
		(1896 = 100)	
1896	2nd	100.0	100
1897	1st	100.0	100
	2nd	89.4	100
1898	1st	80.3	100
	2nd	35.3	100
1899	1st	58.1	100
	2nd	58.1	102
1900	1st	46.5	120
	2nd	84.1	163

Source: Archivo Herrera.

that the cash *jornales* of the *cosecheros* ran on a par with inflation until the outbreak of the War of the Thousand Days. There were even brief periods (such as that of 1896–1900) when the rise in the *jornal* rate overtook that of prices of basic foods like *panela* and meat.

Some evidence on the *jornalero's* diet

The little reliable information available on questions of the *jornalero's* diet only allows us to establish the nature of the daily ration given to them by the hacienda. However, since lengths of occupation varied considerably and a resident *jornalero* worked for only 200 days a year (he did not always receive food rations, as the *arrendatario* or *agregado* sometimes agreed to work on different terms from those of the seasonal workers), it is not possible to ascertain whether the *jornalero* received the same diet throughout the year.

According to the records of the Jonás estate, the daily ration of a peon on a ten-hour working day during the period 1896–1917 was made up as follows: 125 grams of meat, 125 grams of kidney beans, 500 grams of maize, 300 grams of *panela*, 20 grams of salt.[12] As the production of foodstuffs was immediately affected by abrupt changes in the market price, there was a tendency to resort to a substitute on many occasions. For example, maize might be substituted for *panela*, kidney beans for maize, and so on. The meat ration remained constant at 125 grams, and plantain or *revuelto* had no fixed limit.

Food rations formed a basic element in remuneration. When the first unions were established, one of their main demands centred upon the quantity and quality of the diet, which unquestionably improved as a result. In 1930, the workers on the Buenavista estate in Viotá achieved the following agreement: 'In cases where meals are provided by the hacienda, these rations should be made up of half a pound of meat, one and a half pounds of *miel* (for *guarapo*), one pound of maize, sufficient amounts of plantain, yuca, and *arracacha*, and rice twice a week.'[13] In 1934 on the Florencia estate in Viotá the following rations were agreed upon: 'Breakfast: black coffee made with *panela*, ¼ pound of meat, potato soup, and *mute* [*Zea mays L.*] and stewed plantain. Lunch: *arracacha* soup, potato, yuca, and others in sufficient quantity, ¼ pound of meat, and stewed plantain. Dinner: *mute* soup, ¼ pound of meat, and stewed plantain. Twice a week: rice broth for breakfast, 1¼ pounds of honey per day or an adequate amount of *guarapo* according to the worker's own preference.'[14]

In 1934 the Organización Campesina de Quipile came to terms with all the coffee haciendas in the *municipio*. The first point of the agreement stated: 'The food rations of the *arrendatarios* and workers on the estates will be made up as follows: Breakfast: two bowls of *mute* broth with peas and *arracacha*. Lunch: two bowls of *mazamorra* or *cuchuco* with peas, cabbage, and one-fifth pound of meat. Dinner *arracacha*, yuca, plantain, kidney beans, and *balú* in reasonable amounts, and one-fifth pound of meat. All of these dishes should be properly cooked and seasoned. The plantain should not be cooked in iron or copper pots unless they are enamelled. Each *arrendatario* should receive one litre of undiluted *miel* for each day worked in order to make *guarapo*. The preparation of food should be carried out as far as possible in hygienic conditions.'[15] The conflicts which arose as the haciendas sought to exert control over food production (in the hands of the *arrendatarios* and *agregados*) and the subsequent difficulty in meeting market prices led to new labour agreements through which the workers won a daily wage with all-inclusive costs ('*jornal a todo costo*'). According to this arrangement, the worker took responsibility for feeding himself. This system gave rise to the development of a 'services sector' on the estate itself. This was run by the wives of some of the *arrendatarios*, who were paid by the *cosecheros* for providing food. By the forties, the system of the *jornal* with meals included was already on the decline. An agreement made between the Communist-dominated unions in Viotá and the eleven large haciendas which were still on the scene in 1946 stipulated that 'The *jornales* and *quartilla* costs should be paid entirely in cash and not in part cash, part *dulce*.'[16]

Table 19. *Nutritional content of the jornalero's diet, 1896–1934*

	Calories per 100 g	Protein per 100 g	Daily intake of calories	Daily intake of protein
Hacienda Jonás 1896–1917				
125 g meat	232	18.7 g	290	23.7 g
125 g kidney beans	302	20.4 g	377	25.5 g
500 g maize	324	7.5 g	1,620	37.5 g
300 g *panela*	312	0.5 g	936	2.5 g
250 g plantain	142	1.2 g	355	3.0 g
Total			3,578	92.2 g
Hacienda Buenavista 1930				
250 g meat	232	18.7 g	580	46.7 g
750 g *miel–guarapo*	12	0.1 g	90	0.7 g
500 g maize	324	7.5 g	1,620	37.5 g
250 g plantain	142	1.2 g	355	3.0 g
250 g yuca	146	0.8 g	365	2.0 g
250 g *arracacha*	100	1.0 g	250	2.5 g
Total			3,260	92.4 g
Hacienda Florencia 1934				
625 g meat	232	18.7 g	1,450	116.8 g
750 g *miel–guarapo*	12	0.1 g	90	0.7 g
250 g plantain	142	1.2 g	355	3.0 g
250 g *arracacha*	100	1.0 g	250	2.5 g
250 g yuca	146	0.8 g	365	2.0 g
Coffee	5	0.3 g		
Total			2,510	125.0 g
Quipile 1934				
200 g meat	232	18.7 g	464	37.4 g
250 g plantain	142	1.2 g	355	3.0 g
250 g yuca	146	0.8 g	365	2.0 g
250 g *arracacha*	100	1.0 g	250	2.5 g
100 g kidney beans	302	20.4 g	302	20.4 g
1,000 g *miel–guarapo*	12	0.1 g	120	1.0 g
Total			1,850	66.3 g

Notes: The minimum daily diet for an adult worker should contain, according to WHO–FAO, 3,000 calories and 53 g of protein. These tables cannot be used to analyse the nutritional intake of the worker and his family throughout the year, although they do give a general idea of the food given to the workers, here for the most part seasonal ones. It must be borne in mind that in the areas where large meat rations are agreed, it is probable that the worker shared these with his family. *Guarapo* should be regarded as an alcoholic drink, not a food.

According to the Instituto Nacional de Nutrición, the average weight of *arracacha*, plantain, and yuca is 400 g, 300 g, and 850 g respectively. For these foods I have roughly calculated their 'sufficient amount'.

Source: The nutritive content of the food has been calculated using the Instituto Nacional de Nutrición, *Tabla de composición de alimentos colombianos*, Bogotá, 1954.

A notable difference between the workers in Antioquia and those in Cundinamarca and Tolima (and probably also Santander) is the important place in the diet of the latter of fermented alcoholic drinks. The term '*chichismo*' was given colloquially to a common form of alcoholism which existed (and still exists) in the coffee regions where the consumption of *guarapo* in 'sufficient quantities' formed an integral part of the daily working pattern. It was generally taken after lunch and the workers would often spend a good part of his afternoon in a state of drunkenness. The judicial statistics published in the *Gaceta de Cundinamarca* contain a number of references to offences of *aguardiente*-smuggling. The social unrest which flared up in Viotá between 1913 and 1919 reached its climax in the latter year with violent confrontations between the *arrendatarios* and *cosecheros* on one hand, and the 'Guardas de Aduanas' (excisemen) on the other. In this conflict the farm-workers received the backing of the *hacendados*.[17]

The *arrendatarios*: kulaks or proletarians?

An examination of the existing relationship between *arrendatario* and hacienda is essential to an understanding of the type of social formation which took place in the hacienda in Cundinamarca and Tolima. One of the most difficult aspects of the problem, once we have elucidated the essence of the abundant literature on the subject with its leitmotiv of 'feudalism',[18] is that of making even an approximate estimate which might show that, of the two sources of the *arrendatario*'s income, receipts from his activities as a small-plot peasant are greater than those received in cash for fulfilling his labour obligations. There are very few figures available to indicate the size of each plot, the volume of saleable production, and the sale prices of food in the village markets.

It has often been claimed that the institutional basis of servility rests in the power of the landlord to restrict the mobility of the labour force. However, our own evidence appears to indicate a very different explanation. The hacienda does not in fact impose a restrictive influence on the *arrendatario*; on the contrary, the latter prefers to stay on the estate. Moreover, the *arrendatario* has no direct personal obligation, since another person may carry out work on his behalf. The fact that this system was predominant and that the *arrendatario* subcontracted his work to other peons appears to support the view that his income as a peasant farmer was necessarily larger than his cash income as an *obligacionero*. This key fact is really not so surprising if we consider that in certain periods before 1935, the Communist party organized the '*peones voluntarios*' to fight, not against the haciendas, but against the *arrendatarios*! By March 1935 this policy was judged by the Communists to be unsatisfactory: 'the *voluntarios* are making more insistent demands on the *arrendatarios* than on the latifundist exploiters'.[19]

The *arrendatario* was not simply a *peón de asiento* but was in fact the true mediator between the merchant–*hacendado* and rural society. In this respect he was the backbone of the hacienda. The amount of his obligations underwent adjustment and refinement. In the twenties, the *arrendatario* struggled to establish a more equitable relationship between the size of his *estancia* and the amount of work to be provided in return. The more enterprising *arrendatario* had the opportunity of taking on greater work obligations in exchange for more land.

In such conditions the *arrendatario* supplied an important part of the hacienda's labour force (often subcontracted by him), and he acquired land of a size beyond the capacity of family exploitation. Thus he employed *jornaleros* who alternated between working his land and working in the hacienda's coffee plantations. The Communists who took note of this feature and saw the *arrendatario* as a 'kulak', initially mobilized the *peones voluntarios* against them. The documents which attest to the negotiations carried out between the *arrendatarios* on the largest haciendas, which experienced the most serious social disturbances (Buenvista, Florencia, Enterríos, and El Chocho), leave no room for doubt as far as the *arrendatario*'s social position is concerned. He was able to grow cane; used *trapiches* powered by mules; had pigs, horses for riding, and beasts of burden. He put up fences in his *estancia* when the hacienda was willing to pay half the expenses.

The documents published at the time speak for themselves. For example, Nicolás Ramos, *arrendatario* on the Chocho estate, 'put in 32 years of hard work on a plot of 60 *fanegadas* including mountain slopes'. He paid 9,660 pesos to have his 'obligations' fulfilled. He set up six ranches 'in which live 26 men, 19 women and 37 illiterates'. With the help of what Ramos called his 'army', he produced 5 *cargas* of yuca, 20 of *arracacha*, 6 of plantain, 14 of coffee, and 2 of *panela*, and 20 pieces of sawn-up wood. He had 2 *fanegadas* of pasture land with one cow, one horse and twenty chickens. He estimated improvements made at 2,000 pesos and the value of the land at 300 pesos, and he claimed to have 'paid the value of the plot 33 times over'.[20]

But in spite of these obvious kulak features, the *arrendatario* was greatly restricted by the rules and regulations of the hacienda. A group of *arrendatarios* on the La Viña estate in Viotá denounced the *hacendados* as 'men who don't care about anyone else, shameless, anti-Catholic and with no respect for the law and here we have seen them beat poor devils like Pío whom they had taken captive, and they tied him to a post in the yard where they tie up the animals for treatment and then they gave it to him, they gave him a whipping all tied up, and the poor man hadn't even done anything to offend them . . . there are several of us here who are on the [union] list and who don't make an effort to stand together to make a protest here on the hacienda against the weeding duty or to fix the price we should ask for the *cuadros*.'[21]

The conflicts between the *arrendatarios* and the hacienda arose out of the growing practice of selling peasant production surplus.[22] At first the produce of the *estancia* was necessarily shared according to the norms common to peasant economies, namely (*a*) family consumption, (*b*) funds for reinvestment in extending the plot or buying seeds, etc., and (*c*) the exchangeable surplus. On some haciendas the *arrendatario* managed to gain an agreement whereby he was able to substitute food products from his *estancia* for his labour obligations. However, in most cases the surplus could be sold in local markets, although there were still certain restrictions. For example they had to pay tolls (*peajes*) and duties (*aduanillas*) for the right to use the paths across the hacienda, and the *arrendatarios* had to be up to date with their working obligations to the hacienda. Finally, they were allowed to take their produce to market on only one day of the week, in spite of the fact that there were nearly always two market days weekly. Such restrictions not unnaturally provoked considerable friction and disturbances. The presence of political movements obliged *capataces* and *mayordomos* to increase their vigilance, to keep track of movements on the haciendas, to forbid the *arrendatarios* to give lodging to strangers, and to persuade them to inform the administration of any irregularities which might arise. Movements within the hacienda were restricted and other similar security measures were taken. Many complaints of such occurrences were reported to Congress as clear evidence of 'feudalism'.[23]

We should also turn our attention again to the situation of the *arrendatario* in order to understand why, from being a founding element of the hacienda, then a middleman between the hacienda and the *jornaleros*, he finally came to side with the latter in forming a united front of sufficient strength to destroy the hacienda.

Victor J. Merchán, the most notable leader in the Tequendama peasant movement, described recently how the decisive struggles in Viotá had begun on the largest of the estates such as Florencia and Calandaima–Buenavista.[24] Fortunately records still exist in the notarial archives in La Mesa, Tocaima, and Bogotá that provide an account of the negotiations carried out between the peasant leagues and unions and the haciendas.[25]

From these documents it is possible to make a detailed reconstruction of the basic relations in the pre-capitalist *arrendamiento* system, and to trace the origins of social conflict.

The practice of landlord absenteeism reinforced the brutal authoritarian attitudes of many *administradores* and *mayordomos*. Relations between these and the peasants were strained on the large haciendas. One of the most frequent demands made by the *arrendatarios* was that the hacienda should put an end to their abuse. The settlement agreed between the Cranes, owners of the Calandaima estate, and the Tequendama peasant league in 1930 is a classic example of its kind, and it is worth attempting here to give a clear and detailed account of its principal implications.[26]

First we will examine the exchange relationship between work and land: 'Clause 29: for the purposes of the settlement we should understand by *"estancia"* or *"parcela"* a piece of land of 40 *cuadras* with an area equivalent to 6.25 *fanegadas* [4 hectares]. By the terms "obligation" or "each obligation" we should understand the total services which a worker was obliged to render in return for the personal use of an *estancia*.' The following point makes this clear: in the event of the occupied land being larger or smaller than an *estancia*, it should be taken as understood that the obligation would be increased or decreased accordingly. For each *estancia* of 4 hectares, the *arrendatario* would pay 32 pesos per annum as rent.

The *arrendatarios* were divided into three categories according to the amount of obligations owed.

(*a*) The *'semanales'* (weekly *arrendatarios*), who could rent half an *estancia* by agreeing to work seven days per month on the hacienda. For this work they would be paid 3 pesos weekly or 32 pesos per year.

(*b*) The *'quincenales'* (fortnightly *arrendatarios*), who in return for an *estancia* agreed to work for 14 days in the month at the same rates of pay as the above.

(*c*) The *'semestrales'* (six-monthly *arrendatarios*), who were by far the most important of the *arrendatarios*. Their obligations entailed weeding 40 *cuadros* of coffee plantation and picking 465 *cuartillas* of coffee berries, each *cuartilla* weighing 50 pounds.

It is thus a relatively simple matter to estimate annual cash incomes received by each group of *arrendatarios* for this particular operation. This estimate obviously does not include family food, funds used for reinvestment or in the expansion of the land under cultivation on the *estancia*, or saleable surplus.

For each obligation fulfilled we should thus deduct an annual 32 pesos for the latter groups, and 16 pesos for the *semanales* who had a right to only half an *estancia*.

	Annual salary	Rent	Net annual income
Semanales	36 pesos	16 pesos	20 pesos
Quincenales	72 pesos	32 pesos	40 pesos
Semestrales	111.25 pesos	32 pesos	79.25 pesos

We may now reduce the income to average *jornales* by dividing it by the number of days rendered annually as obligations.

Semanales: 20/84 = \$0.24 pesos
Quincenales: 40/168 = \$0.24 pesos
Semestrales: 79.25/305 = \$0.26 pesos

These *jornales*, which varied from between \$0.24 and \$0.26 pesos, did not include a food allowance. It was stipulated that 'when, in this region, the *jornal* of the voluntary peons increases or decreases by 10% or more, there will be a proportional adjustment in what is paid in fulfilment of obligations'. It should be immediately seen that the average current rate of voluntary salaries [*sic*] in the region is approximately \$1.20 for weeding each *cuadro*, \$0.20 for harvesting one *cuartilla*, and \$0.60 for general duties'. It appears obvious that the rate for general duties was a simple average of other duties at \$0.20 per *cuartilla* and, with an average of 3 *cuartillas*, comes to \$0.60. The opposite is true of weeding, since two *jornales* are required for each *cuadro*.

If we calculate the salary content of the voluntary peon's income, where he pays off 305 *jornales* in one year, as in the case of the *semestrales* (i.e. weeding 40 *cuadros* and harvesting 465 *cuartillas*) he would earn 183 pesos at an average *jornal* of 60 centavos.

It is therefore evident that the *arrendatario* received the equivalent of 50 per cent of the cash salary paid to the voluntary peons. On the other hand, the 'peasant incomes' from their own plots of land must have been considerably larger to permit them to subcontract *jornaleros* who were to work off their obligations.

During the formation of an *arrendatario* hierarchy, there were still some who were unable to engage *jornaleros*. In such cases, these *arrendatario* were often forced to give back part of their *estancias* to the haciendas. This was due to their own inability to cultivate them fully, and not because the land itself was of poor quality.

The economic situation of the 1930s suddenly brought the *arrendatarios* into conflict with the haciendas. Two adverse events occurred simultaneousl:
The deflation which followed the economic crisis was felt strongly in 1931–2 and was reflected in dearer money, a fall in food prices, an influx of out-of-work labourers from abandoned public works in the peasant areas, and a fall in real incomes. Thus the prices of produce sold in local markets

were severely affected while the real rent paid for land increased. Settlements which had been agreed during a time of inflation became explosive in times of deflation. The responses of the Communist party came promptly: strike against work obligations and withhold payment of rents. Thus the most strategic social group, that of the *arrendatarios* was drawn into the conflict.[27] The *hacendados* and politicians in Bogotá were also quick to react and tried to turn this mobilization to their own advantage. The case of the Florencia estate, the leadership of Julio Ocampo Vásquez, and the policies of Carlos Lleras Restrepo, Government Secretary of Cundinamarca, are all indicative of the process through which an attempt was made to manipulate the agrarian unions.[28] By following very different paths, the Florencia estate and Ocampo arrived at a common objective. Ocampo intended to establish unionism whatever the cost, and Aristides Salgado, owner of Florencia, realized that unionism could be instrumental in solving certain practical problems, and in pacifying the *jornaleros* and *arrendatarios*. The 1934 negotiations were of prime importance. The hacienda agreed to support the union if it in its turn agreed to rationalize and organize labour in order to free the administration of the constant headaches caused by individual demands and complaints. The union would assume responsibility for hiring and firing workers and allocating jobs, for which service it would receive a small fee in the form of a contribution from the hacienda. It was also agreed to establish two unions of *arrendatarios*, one of coffee-producers, and, the other of *dulce*-producers. A social action committee, Comité de Acción Social, was set up at the instigation of Carlos Lleras, who was apparently the most active politician locally in that period, as well as the most adept at finding solutions for agrarian conflicts, at least from the government's point of view.[29]

At the other extreme was Jorge Eliécer Gaitán. With his populistic approach he proposed sharing out the latifundia in the Sumapaz region among the *arrendatarios*. Since there were discrepancies between the claimed boundaries of properties and the relevant deeds of ownership in Sumapaz, it was possible to question the rights of ownership of considerable tracts of land claimed by the haciendas. At the same time, the largest latifundio in the region, the El Chocho estate, had long since lifted the prohibition on coffee-growing on the *estancias*. The 'improvements' made to a plot were worth more than the land itself, and this was unquestionably a factor used to persuade the government to pass Law 200 of 1936, which laid down the principle that where the improvements were worth more than the land the right of possession of the improver should prevail over that of the landowner.[30]

In 1933, Francisco José Chaux, the Minister for Industry, remarked on the problem of proof of ownership, claiming that the 'deeds had not been adequately preserved in notary and registry offices as a result of civil wars, carelessness, disorganization, and pillage'. The result, he alleged, was 'the falsification of deeds, forgery, and the false representation of property boundary lines'.[31] In December 1935, Eduardo Zuleta Angel, a Supreme Court magistrate, presented an explanation to the House of Representatives. He claimed that virtually all of the land in question had been conferred by the Crown under different schemes but without adequate surveying, with the result that 'it is extremely unusual to find a square inch of land in Colombia which has not been claimed with a colonial title attesting to the ownership of private land, whenever some *colono* or other has some financial interest in it'. There was, according to Zuleta, a simple device for making such a claim; 'within a matter of weeks, the owners had found in village A . . . certain papers which presume to prove that the property had been ceded to his great-great-grandfather.'[32]

Lawsuits arising from boundary disputes were common. There are frequent references in notarial archives to legal actions which arose from confusion over ill-defined boundary lines, though it should be added that there are references to friendly settlements as well. To refer to only one example, the owner of the Ceilán estate (created in 1870 with the dividing up of the Calandaima estate) had to agree to an amicable redefinition of his boundaries thirteen years after his purchase of the property. But the poor definition of his boundaries on the mountainous side of the property (from the edge of the El Subia mountain range) was to prove a source of problems in 1948. An expert from the Consejo Departamental Agrario de Cundinamarca offered the following information: 'The waters of the rivers and streams on the Ceilán estate are very low in the summer, but do not dry up completely thanks to the fact that a forest has been preserved in spite of the attempted encroachments by potential settlers. These have so far been kept at bay by the establishment of a permanent police post manned by the Guardia de Cundinamarca and financed by the estate itself.'[33]

One of the principal aims of the activities of the Federación de Arrenda-tarios del Chocho in 1933 was the total cancellation of the deeds of owner-ship held by the owners. The Federación had made its case along rough legalistic lines and was thus obliged to accept the decision of the Head of the Department of Public Lands. The sensible study published by the Oficina General de Trabajo provides a clear indication of the type of problems in question.[34]

In Sumapaz there were clear signs of affinity between Gaitan's style of petty-bourgeois populism and the aspirations of *arrendatarios* like Ramos, who was mentioned previously. It only remained for the *arrendatario*, now freed from *obligaciones* but still hampered by anachronistic restrictions, such as tolls, to break the last remaining tie with the hacienda by expropriating its land. The strike against the exaction of *obligaciones* hit the *hacendados* hard. The unions adopted a more radical stance. Leaders like Ocampo became discredited, and the *hacendados'* momentary confusion was followed by police repression, the effects of which were much feared by men such as President López Pumarejo.[35] Once the tie of the *obligación* has been cut, the dual nature of the plantation—small-plot family economy was also put under pressure, until finally the family unit came free of its shackles. It only remained to 'fight for the land' and the *arrendatario* finally succeeded in casting off the 'strait-jacket' imposed by the hacienda. Thus there emerged a new type of small landowner dedicated to coffee production. However, it would be a mistake to conclude that all of the haciendas in Cundinamarca disappeared as a result of dramatic confrontations with *arrendatarios*, politically mobilized and organized into unions counting on the support of left-wing political groups, such as Gaitanism, the *Lopista* Left, and the Communist party.

By 1936, the conflicts had reached an end. But later, in the Tequendama region where peasant organizations continued in existence, the Communist unions addressed themselves to somewhat more modest objectives than the expropriation of latifundia. For reasons of political strategy, open conflict gave way to lawful bargaining carried out in an evident conciliatory spirit. A clear illustration of this tendency is provided by Point Nine of the Labour settlement between the unions of eleven *haciendas* in Viotá and the owners, signed in March 1946. 'Provision of land to landless workers who wish to establish their own plot. Division of land into plots in accordance with Ordinance 30, 1944'. In response to this agreement the following was agreed:[36] 'The *haciendas* which resolve to divide land for resale as plots should offer a first purchase option to their own workers – *arrendatarios* – in accordance with existing conditions. A similar procedure will be followed when the plots are offered in *arrendamiento*.' Moreover, both owners and workers agreed that the government should be responsible for defining the new plots in accordance with Law 100 of 1944, a procedure which had to be previously accepted by both parties in its entirety, as the only effective and plausible means of ensuring that the benefits of the division of land into plots should go to the present workers.[37]

Capitalism of feudalism? This has become an obsessive question, and it appears that every historian is obliged to give his answer. From the foregoing analysis it does not look like capitalism, but neither is it feudalism.

The extra-economic coercion of feudalism is absent. The resident labour is at liberty to abandon the hacienda; moreover, one way of penalizing this labour is to evict it. The resident labour wishes to remain on the hacienda, and many day-labourers are ready to fill any gap that occurs. We find a type of social formation that Juan Martínez-Alier has called 'Andean pseudo-servitude',[38] and it seems to me that this term matches what is here described. Certainly more detailed and profound analysis of the political and ideological ambiance of the coffee hacienda would disclose the elements which secured the legitimacy of the order it represented, the obedience of the workers to its rules, and the loyalty to it of the *mayor-domos* and the other intermediaries. But when this legitimacy was challenged by the spread of socialist ideas on the great haciendas of Cundinamarca and Tolima, their automatic response was an attempt to 're-feudalize' what had never been completely feudal. These coffee haciendas between 1870 and 1920 had sustained themselves in part by relying on the servile mentality of the *boyacense* peasants, first- and second-generation migrants. After 1925, feeling themselves menaced, they sought to defend themselves through recourse to this supposed servility, now so diminished that the recourse was no longer viable.

Why did the haciendas not establish a system based exclusively on wage contracts? In the years of foundation it seems to me that the scarcity of money and geographical isolation were the principal obstacles, and these led to the introduction of the alternative systems described. Why did they not take the option in the 1920s and 1930s, as a logical solution to the conflicts in which they were involved? I have no definitive and complete answer. Perhaps the basis of these systems consists in that financially the *arrendatario* is cheaper for the hacienda than the wage-labourer. Is this the *economic* truth? That is harder to establish. It may be that the opportunity cost of the land given over to the permanent labour force was not very high in terms of coffee production — the hacienda had other areas for the expansion of its plantation — while giving the residents this land guaranteed labour all the year round for maintenance and for part of the harvest. But even if one were to assume that the wage-labourer cost the hacienda less than the *agregado* or *arrendatario*, at least in Cundinamarca the appearance of militant agrarian organizations meant that the option was no longer available.

6. Inflation, devaluation, and export taxes, 1870–1904

Most Colombian historians agree that between 1880 and 1886 changes in economic policy and in the constitution bring the Radical period to an end.[1] Monetary policies – the creation of the national bank, the ending of the right of the commercial banks to issue currency, and finally the imposition of the *curso forzoso* (the forced acceptance of paper money) – are seen by these historians as mechanisms for redirecting investment towards production, reviving the economy, and promoting coffee exports. Political centralism and the new extended Presidential powers and term are seen as essential to national unity, gravely threatened by the federalist anarchy of the free-trade era.

I do not intend to give a full account of all these complexities, crucial as their interaction was in the formation of the contemporary Colombian state and in maintaining its legitimacy. I must concentrate on one part of the Regeneration's economic 'programme' and its impact specifically on the expansion of coffee.

I hope to show that economic policy did not have as its objective promoting coffee exports or channelling savings to investment in coffee. Nor did it have a long-term coincidental effect of encouraging the sector, and it is therefore not possible to attribute to it a positive role in the first cycle of expansion. In this chapter I shall show that the opposition to the new policies that came from bankers, importers, and exporters was not derived just from their being now relatively isolated from political power, whereas they had previously been the beneficiaries of official favour. This opposition was much more widely based, and it went far beyond what one would expect if it were just a matter of the mere immediate economic interests of these groups. What produced this homogeneous and united opposition, coming from elements of both parties, was an economic policy they considered vicious. This is rather a polemical statement in the context of Colombian historiography, where there is still a strong tendency to use political criteria to divide the periods, in a manner which conceals the significant discontinuities. Government depositions, and the proclaimed intentions of dominant groups are analysed, and conclusions are carelessly drawn that the origins of change are to be found there. It is of course safer to consider many other possible explanations before giving each element its weight. In the case before us here I consider that trends in

121

international prices, the availability of labour for the initial phases of expansion, the ecological conditions of the country, and the existence of a minimal transport system established in times before coffee are of far more fundamental importance in the rise and then the stagnation of coffee between 1870 and 1904 than the disconnected government policies between 1880 and 1899, policies that have their own origin in acute fiscal penury.

The forty years from 1865–70 to 1905–10 can be considered as the period in which the coffee economy was established in Colombia. The four fundamental features of the period were:

(*a*) The geographical diffusion of cultivation, which took place in a series of stages; in Santander from 1835 to 1900, in Cundinamarca and Tolima from 1870 to 1900, in Antioquia from 1885 to 1905, and finally in the areas of *antioqueño* colonization, a movement which began, it is true, in the seventies in Manizales, but which assumed significant proportion only from the middle nineties onwards.

(*b*) Despite the crises provoked by low prices, some acute, such as that from 1879 to 1883, and some prolonged, such as that from 1897 to 1910, coffee was able to maintain itself as one of the most important Colombian exports, unlike the products which preceded it.

(*c*) The period was one of stagnation and decline in foreign trade, with the combined value of imports and exports remaining more or less constant at U.S. $30 million per year, while the population grew in round numbers from 3 to 5 million from 1870 to 1912.

(*d*) It should be noted finally that the period was one of political instability; four civil wars on a national scale interrupted trade and hindered the geographical mobility of labour when they did not remove it more directly; also, by putting the heaviest of pressure on a Treasury already impoverished, and further weakened by the decline in foreign trade and its direct effects on the customs duties which were the main source of goverr ment income, they led to a fiscal bottleneck, which was practically irremovable while Colombia remained on the gold standard.

To complete this brief survey we should recall that after the 1847 Mosquera reforms, inspired by Florentino Gonzalez, Colombia went onto the gold standard and, in conformity with the classical theory of internation<u> </u>trade, operated during the free-trade period in accordance with a metallic or, better, bi-metallic (gold and silver) standard. This had a double effect:

(*a*) The depression of exports led to a recession, unemployment, and a restriction of the internal money supply, as the notoriously inelastic imports had to be paid for in coin.

(*b*) The changes in parity of the prices of gold and silver in the international market, not foreseen in the Colombian legislation of 1873, led to

an internal overvaluation of silver, which automatically produced an out-
flow of gold, as it was profitable to buy silver cheap on the international
market and import it into Colombia, where it fetched a higher price. The
trade was carried on by the export of gold coin. Although Colombia was
a producer of gold, which was one of the most important and constant
of its exports throughout the nineteenth century, adherence to the metallic
standard became impossible after the prolonged recession which followed
the collapse of tobacco in 1875. Between 1880 and 1886 the national
bank was created, and the introduction of paper money went some way
towards ending the gold-standard policy. That it did not do so completely
was first because in Santander, currently the most important coffee
region, neither producers nor merchants accepted paper money, and commercial transactions were carried out in silver and with bills backed by
gold[2] and, secondly, because paper money was made compulsory only
for internal transactions, and exporters and importers continued to negotiate
their bills of exchange freely in foreign currencies or in gold, just as they
had done before. In other words, the adoption of paper money was not
accompanied by suspension of external convertibility, which was a necessary
complement to a coherent policy of rejection of the gold standard.[3]

As regards coffee exports, there was a recession approximately from
1898 to 1911. With the necessary caution regarding the quality of the
different statistical sources, we may accept that between 1870 and 1910
coffee exports rose five times over, moving from 100,000 to 570,000
62.5-kilo bags. But the real expansion occurred between 1885 and 1898,
when exports rose from 120,000 to 531,000 bags. The stagnation between
1898 and 1910 is partly to be explained by the disastrous effects of the
1899–1902 war, particularly in Santander and Cundinamarca. It is even
possible that production may have fallen in many districts in these departments, with this fall being compensated for by increased production in the
new zones being opened to the south of Manizales and in Quindío. The
international depression in the coffee market between 1896–7 and 1910
must also have maintained this stagnation, preventing further investment
in haciendas in the zones of Cundinamarca and Santander. In the first
region it was thought that between 1903 and 1910, with the rate of exchange maintained at 10,000% of its value in the first months of peace,
there was no profit, and may even have been some loss, in exporting coffee
when the New York price stood, as it did, at between 8 and 10 U.S. cents
per pound.[4] In Santander the political and diplomatic problems with
Venezuela which led to the frequent closure of the frontier dealt a severe
blow to the possibilities of coffee expansion, as 90 per cent of the coffee of
that region was exported through the Maracaibo Gulf, due to the lack

of a viable route to the Magdalena river, a problem that still existed in 1930.[5]

The coincidence between the dates of the introduction of paper money and the expansion of coffee exports has led some economists writing in the recent past to propose the existence of a causal link between the economic policies of the Regeneration and the expansion of the economy based on what has been called the 'coffee bonanza'. These authors, whose contribution is undeniable,[6] argue that while the presence of railways, of cheap lands suitable for the cultivation of coffee, and of abundant geographically mobile labour was a significant factor, the policy of paper money is the most important key to an understanding of the period and of the type of economic development which took place. The introduction of paper money came as a response to a fiscal crisis, but in their view became a catalyst for the expansion of coffee and, in a positive development, for a form of income concentration compatible with the formation of an internal market for manufactured goods such as textiles, bottled drinks, and processed foods.

Their central argument is developed as follows: the issue of paper beyond the actual demand for money caused inflation and depreciation of the exchange rate, which stimulated exports, since internal costs rose less than the fall in the exchange rate. The mechanism by which this occurred was a redistribution of income. The inflation reduced the real income of the rural proletariat engaged in coffee production, and of those employed in the transport sector, while it favoured the producers in two ways, by increasing their profits by reducing the costs of production and transport, and by protecting their income if the external price should fall.[7] Although there was some concentration of income, at the expense of the majority of the population, the medium and small coffee producers benefited, and came to form a rural middle class which, despite its limited size, was a sufficient base to provide a market for infant industries, particularly those of Antioquia.

There are essentially two premises central to this argument: (*a*) that during the Regeneration a coherent economic policy was followed, not only from the point of view of monetary control, but also regarding the creation of an internal market, since 'a protectionist tariff policy was adopted, and this helped in allowing the additional national demand to be satisfied with goods manufactured nationally';[8] (*b*) that depreciation increased exports, since inflation protected the profits of the producers, as the costs of production rose more slowly than the price of coffee. Put more emphatically, the result of this policy was that the cost of producing and transporting coffee rose more slowly than the rate of depreciation.

From the point of view of our analysis this argument would lead to the conclusion that the coffee bourgeoisie (the major producers and exporters) managed to impose, through control of the state, economic policies which favoured their class interests and which were at the same time compatible with the national interest, in so far as this can be identified with a programme of industrialization.

My own conclusions are less optimistic; I shall argue that precisely because of the *lack* of a coherent economic policy, either in terms of internal consistency or in terms of the interests of the coffee bourgeoisie, inflation annulled the effects of devaluation; in other words, between 1880 and the first half of 1899 (that is, until the outbreak of the War of the Thousand Days) the costs of production rose *more* rapidly than the rate of depreciation. For exports to have been encouraged, a greater degree of devaluation would have been necessary, and it is possible that until 1899 the peso (paper money) may even have been overvalued.

If inflation wiped out the possible positive effect that devaluation might have had on exports this was largely because the issue of money was essentially determined by political necessity. The regulation of the exchange rate, while it followed in general terms the evolution of the fiscal and political situation and the resulting inflation, still depended fundamentally on the market for bills of exchange. The central government had more or less direct control over money supply through the issues of the national bank. Founded in 1880, government control of this institution had been strengthened in 1886 with the introduction of compulsory acceptance (*curzo forzoso*) of paper money, while the parity of the peso with gold was fixed independently of any government control.

The economic depression which followed the collapse of tobacco in 1875 played out its course in an unstable and explosive political situation. The national and local civil wars and the fragility of 'public order' made onerous demands on public expenditure, which, both in the Federal period and even more during the Unitary Republic could be only partially covered by the central exchequer. Once the conflicts were over, the sovereign states, and later the different departments, passed on their debts to the central government, as if they were individuals with rights under civil law to claim against the Executive for dereliction of duty.[9] 'The civil wars', said Núñez in his Presidential Message of 1882, 'and the general disquiet which preceded and followed them, have quite exhausted our fiscal resources.'[10] But the measured optimism which he showed in that year had no real basis: 'It is true that we have not yet subdued all those who seek to subvert the republic; but we are gradually approaching the happy state of scientific peace.'[11] Three further civil wars waited in the wings, each one, with the founding of the national bank, more inflationary than the last. Núñez himself recognized in 1888 that 'the national bank, as we all know only too well, has been our great source of finance during the last few years of transformation and transition, of fiscal penury and ever increasing scarcity of gold and silver coin'.[12] Thanks to the printing press, 'we have been able to meet, with relative ease, the heavy extraordinary expenses caused by the extreme circumstances of every kind through which the country has passed since the last days of 1884. It is more than clear that without this resort it would have been impossible to confront the difficulties, both political and fiscal, to which this government has had to find timely solutions.'[13]

The President attributed the fall in the rate of exchange to 'deficient exports. If these could be increased, the greater supply of bills of exchange would cause the exchange rate to rise.' Although he recognized that property prices had risen, particularly in the urban sector, due to these issues of currency, he spoke in defence of the issue of paper money: 'I cannot deny that objections can be raised to the use of paper money; but its appearance among us is more an effect of the nature of things than an imposition on the part of the government, as it has tended to make up the shortage of coin, contributed to the reduction of the imbalance of foreign trade by facilitating exports that would not have been made without it, and indirectly stimulated the production and consumption of national manufactures.'[14] It is difficult to accept that the policies adopted could at one and the same time have served both God and the devil, benefiting the growers and exporters of coffee and an exchequer expanding as a result of the war, the costs of political centralization, and the growth of the civil bureaucracy.

The cancelling of the right of commercial banks to issue their own notes and the monopoly granted to the national bank had, in the nineties, economic consequences unforeseen by Núñez in 1886. This was not only a result of the loss of prestige of the bank and its note issue, both attacked by politicians and the opposition press as a result of the scandal of the 'clandestine issue'.[15] but also because it placed directly in the hands of the government the power to issue notes at will, as it did freely after 1895 and with single-minded zeal during the three years of war.

The 'protective' tariffs after 1885 and the resulting increase in the price of imports, together with galloping inflation, forced the merchants in the importing business to restrict their operations and to eliminate the risks involved in the traditional system of acting as agents, at low rates of interest, for smaller traders. Nevertheless, the importers and bankers exercised a high degree of control over the bill market, and were to some degree able to resist the tendency towards devaluation, partly because they were creditors of the exporters, and partly because many exporters had only a marginal interest in the bill market because they dealt directly with the foreign houses. The degree of political instability which made the idea of 'scientific peace' no more than a dream was revealed in the incapacity of any socioeconomic group to control the state and impose policies congruent with the needs of economic expansion. It is evident that one of the implicit objectives of this policy was to reduce the economic power of the bankers and importers, and these in their turn responded with implacable and unremitting political and intellectual opposition.

If the introduction of paper money favoured coffee exports, how could we explain the stubborn resistance to it from the majority of *hacendados*, Conservative or Liberal? Why this anti-Nuñism *à outrance* on the part of the supposedly practical merchants? Was such opposition ideologically motivated? Was it inspired by 'inherited hatreds'? Was it a reaction of repugnance to the authoritarian methods used during the repressive onslaught mounted by Caro? Did it spring from scorn for a bureaucracy seen by those excluded from it as parasitical and job-hungry? These questions, the stuff of traditional political historiography, should by no means be neglected. An analysis of the debates over export taxes which occupied the parliamentary sessions from 1894 to 1898 reveals the force of the belief that the government was set on making its political enemies, the major coffee magnates, pay heavily for the disaffection and stubborn opposition they had shown, despite the conviction of those in government that their policies were designed to suit this particular class. More and more the bankers and importers were reduced to exploiting the possibilities offered by capital flight and by the preference for gold; and their activities, in turn, accelerated the inflationary spiral.

Bankers and importers such as the Sampers managed to accommodate themselves, with some difficulty, to the new situation, and even to profit from it; the larger banks linked directly to foreign trade, such as the Banco de Bogotá and the Banco de Colombia, not only managed to survive, unlike the provincial banks and the savings banks linked to internal trade, but grew in strength. At one stage towards the end of the century entrepreneurs, led by Nicolás Sáenz, tried to found a Banco de Exportadores to take advantage of the speculative opportunities offered by the bill market in the hands of the importers. Even if it had been true that inflation lowered the wage of labour in relation to the price of coffee, offering the coffee magnates higher profits, devaluation did not benefit them in that the majority were, as we have also seen, chronic debtors, with their debts generally in gold. Granted this, what weight should we attach to the second premise of the argument we are discussing – the view that devaluation and inflation favoured the coffee producers? It could still be true that, despite the lack of congruence between the objectives, and the relatively autonomou character of the different mechanisms which produced inflation and de-valuation, the costs of producing and transporting coffee rose more slowly than the rate of exchange.

A great deal more work needs to be done before a definitive view can be taken on this point, and given the paucity of the few available archives it may not be possible to reach any satisfactory conclusion. I have myself used the same sources as the authors whose thesis is under discussion, but I have reached very different conclusions.

Using series based on the accounts of Roberto Herrera Restrepo, I found that production and transport costs rose more rapidly than the peso price of coffee. In table 20 it can clearly be seen how real costs, obtained by dividing the index of total production costs by the peso price index of coffee, rise between 1879 and 1884, then show a falling tendency to 1894, and from then on once again rise rapidly. The short period of fall in real peso costs corresponds to a sustained rise of the dollar coffee price. It is evident that devaluation offsets the fall in the international price. If paper money had not existed, the index of real costs would have risen from 133 to 240 between 1894 and 1899, whereas in pesos it rose only from 98 to 163. I refer to a composite cost in which the two elements are the cost of wages on the hacienda and transport costs. The ratio of labour costs to the final peso price (column 6) remained at its lowest level between 1888 and 1893, but after 1894 it rose much more rapidly than the rate of depreciation. The brief fall in real wage costs must without doubt have been a great incentive to investment in coffee, which, as has been stated, was massive precisely in those years of low wages and high prices. The thesis of Urrutia and Bustamente is not, however, solidly based; it has only a partial validity for one short five-year span in the whole period, five years which also saw buoyant prices. Taking the whole series, 1879–99, their theory does not hold: for the period as a whole costs rose faster than devaluation; from the point of view of the coffee exporter, the paper peso became increasingly overvalued in relation to the dollar.

If my estimates and conclusions are correct, it is possible to understand why, despite the existence of economic conflicts between exporters and importers, no political breach occurred. On the contrary, the two groups formed a solid front against the policies of the Regeneration, at their most militant during the six-year Presidency of Caro. It is not merely that many importers were also coffee exporters, and that many from each camp were closely bound by family and social ties, but also that the policies pursued were lacking in coherence, and contradictory in their objectives, so that the rules of the game did not emerge with any clarity. The *hacendados* as employers did not benefit from inflation, and as debtors in gold they detested devaluation. A policy of promoting exports and penalizing imports was not always compatible with the need to increase fiscal revenues, as this could only be done, as we have already mentioned, if there was a prosperous import trade. It was utopian to pose borrowing abroad as an alternative in the middle of such a prolonged depression. Furthermore, devaluation itself aggravated the situation of the state in its role as a debtor in gold, obliging it to seek moratoria in the payment of interest and principal on external loans.[16] It is true that such a schematic analysis leaves out of account the political and ideological ingredients which continued to play such an important role in the course of events. For example, until 1892 the predominantly Conservative bourgeoisie of Antioquia supported the government, but as a result of the election of Caro it split along lines which cannot be interpreted in terms of the social and economic structure of that class. The example could be multiplied.[17] Even so, taking up the thread of our narrative, it seems that if the political project of the Regeneration was fragile the position of the great coffee *hacendados* and exporters was weaker still. The coffee-producers showed their weakness on three fronts: (*a*) they could not halt the trend towards rising costs in the 'labour market', (*b*) they had to accept the imposition by the river transport companies of a monopoly tariff calculated in gold, and (*c*) they could not profit from depreciation because it failed to keep pace with their rising costs, and because they owed debts in gold.

The comparison which can be made with the Brazilian case illustrates the point and provides a degree of clarification. In Brazil the interests linked to coffee were able to impose through the state a set of monetary and exchange policies aimed at solving the problems of the balance of payments, income distribution, and defence of the level of employment, by adjusting the rate of exchange in accordance with the evolution of the international coffee price.[18] In Colombia, in contrast, the coffee interest was still weak, and could not impose a similar policy; as we have seen, banking and monetary legislation after 1880 and trends in the restricted financial market were marked by incoherence.

The best indicator of the comparative situation is the evolution of the exports of each country; this reveals that in Colombia a little after the fall in prices the figure oscillates around half a million bags a year, in spite of the devaluation, right up to 1910, while in Brazil the expansion continues and between 1895 and 1910 exports double, growing from 7.2 million to 15.3 million bags. To make the situation even worse, Caro's government decided in 1895 to apply an export tax to coffee, and by 1897 this had

Table 20. *Indices of costs of production, exchange rate, and international price of coffee, 1879–99*

Year	(1888–90 = 100)		
	(1) International coffee prices	(2) Labour costs on hacienda	(3) Transport costs
1879	98	76	47
1880	103	76	47
1881	81	73	47
1882	70	71	60
1883	63	69	71
1884	67	69	71
1885	70	63	71
1886	69	67	72
1887	71	76	95
1888–90	100	100	100
1891	114	129	113
1892	113	150	119
1893	125	162	126
1894	111	185	121
1895	107	175	157
1896	104	195	164
1897	90	195	165
1898	77	195	176
1899	57	198	160

Note: The difference between my results and those obtained by Urrutia and Busta-mante derives from two causes. First, there are some very important differences in the costs of wages on the hacienda, and more serious ones in transport costs – here I was able to give the books a more thorough examination, which brought this out. The second source of error is a methodological one. Urrutia and Bustamante are comparing indices with different bases, which they have not themselves constructed – for example, they used McGreevey's world coffee price index which has base 100 in 1923–5! (For McGreevey's indices, see Urrutia and Arrubla (eds.), *Compendio*, p. 212.) There is a similar comparison of indices with different bases in their cal-culations of exchange rate and international price of coffee.

become an explosive issue. In the last section we shall examine this aspect of economic policy, and the response of the coffee bourgeoisie.

The conflicts on export taxes, 1895–1906

Taxes were imposed on the export of coffee and other products in March 1895, and were maintained, with significant modifications, until 1906, when they were removed, to reappear in 1927 in fulfilment of an agreement

		(1888–90 = 100)	
(4) Total costs	(5) Coffee price in pesos	(6) Ratio of labour costs to final peso price	(7) Ratio of input costs to final peso price
61	52	146	117
61	57	133	107
60	44	166	136
65	40	177	162
70	45	153	155
70	43.	160	162
67	44	143	152
72	50	134	144
86	63	120	136
100	100	100	100
103	117	110	88
120	108	138	111
130	162	100	80
148	151	122	98
175	143	122	122
179	125	156	143
179	112	174	159
185	113	172	163
178	–	–	–

Sources: (1) Taken from Beyer 'Colombian Coffee', pp. 368 et seq. (2) I have taken as base the average piece-work-unit wage paid on the hacienda Santa Bárbara. (3) These costs do not include payment of taxes after 1895, nor other extra transport costs recorded. (4) The composite cost, transport and labour on the hacienda, of a bag of coffee. Hacienda labour costs do not include extras such as administration. (5) Same as (1) multiplied by the rate of devaluation. For the rate of devaluation I have used the table cited in Appendix 4. (6) The result of dividing (2) by (5). (7) The result of dividing (4) by (5).

between the recently founded National Coffee-Growers' Federation of Colombia and the government. The history of the tax and the debates which it aroused is important, signalling as it does the changes and the political and ideological tensions within the ruling class. This class formed itself slowly from the local oligarchies led by the export-oriented merchants and major growers in Antioquia, Cundinamarca, and the Valle del Cauca.

Of these six legal dispositions only the second (Law 37, 1896) was approved by Congress, as a reform of the taxes initially imposed by Executive

Table 21. *Colombian and Brazilian coffee exports, 1880–1910 (in 000 60-kilo bags)*

Year	(1) Colombia	(2) Total *'suave'*	(3) Brazil	(4) Grand total
1880	107	4,847	5,568	10,415
1885	120	4,894	6,327	11,211
1890	–	4,096	4,444	8,540
1895	358	4,420	7,237	11,657
1900	–	4,982	9,454	13,941
1905	500	4,553	10,524	15,077
1910	570	3,976	15,324	19,300

Sources: (1) see table 2. (2), (3), (4) H. Roth, *Die Ubererzengung in der Welthandelsware Kaffee im Zeitraum von 1700–1929* (Jena, 1929), pp. 63 et seq.

Decree 75 of 22 March 1895; all the rest came directly from the President, using special powers under the terms of the state of siege.

The tax had been proposed by Caro to the Legislature in 1894, and received systematic opposition led by Rafael Uribe Uribe, who made an economic, social, and financial study on behalf of the coffee interests, to show that the tax would be inappropriate.[19] Congress rejected Caro's project, and the President had to wait until the outbreak of civil war in the following year gave him the chance to use his extraordinary powers to impose the tax 'to collect funds to restore public order'.

Opposition was widespread, as the taxes were not imposed on coffee alone. The initial decree of 1895 increased import duties by 15 per cent, and taxes on slaughtered cattle by 10 per cent, as well as introducing the coffee taxes mentioned. As a consolation for the latter measure, the government ordered that safe-conducts should be given to 'the owners or lessees of plantations' for them to supervise the harvesting and processing of the coffee, with the proviso that 'the authorities should distribute them with caution'. As is well known, local mayors and military chiefs were not only cautious — in many cases they refused to provide the required passes.

The gradual fall in prices which began to be felt at the beginning of 1896 made even more unpopular a tax which in Antioquia fell directly upon the merchant exporters who had made forward purchases.[20] It was not difficult to build a broad front of importers, exporters, and grower-exporters, all well represented in the Congressional debates of 1896, and these debates led to reductions in the taxes, and to the granting to the President of the right to suspend the taxes if the price fell any lower. August 1896 saw the presentation of a projected law authorizing the

Table 22. *Taxes on coffee exports, 1895–1906 (per 62.5-kilo bag)*

March 1895[a]	1.60 pesos gold for *pilado*
	1.20 pesos gold for *pergamino*
October 1896[b]	0.625 pesos gold for *pilado*
	0.50 pesos gold for *pergamino*
July 1897[c]	Temporarily suspended while the international market price remained below that prevailing in March 1895
September 1898[d]	Suspended permanently
April 1900[e]	Exporters obliged to sell 10 peso gold to the national treasury per 125 kilos of *pilado* exported at the rate of exchange set by the government, or alternatively to pay an *ad valorem* tax of 20% in gold
July 1900[f]	This tax removed and replaced by another: 3.20 paper pesos on *pilado*; 2.40 paper pesos on *pergamino*
1906	Taxes finally removed

Sources: a D.O., 22 March 1895. *b D.O.*, 4 November 1896. *c D.O.*, 20 July 1897. *d D.O.*, 3 December 1898. *e D.O.*, 30 April 1900. *f D.O.*, 18 July 1900.

Executive to 'eliminate in whole or in part the tax on coffee exports' in accordance with the international trend in prices for the product, and to earmark the tax, while it continued, for the development of the Giradot and Santander railways, and for the overall improvement of communications between the coffee-producing centres and the ports.[21] For the modern reader, the debates which opened that September are a curious mixture of traditional rhetoric and general principles of political economy. In the speeches made, one notes the concern of some professional politicians to insert into their party-political discourse some elements of economic and technical data. As this tendency spread, the lines dividing Liberals from Conservatives began to disappear, and the opposing factions found room for agreement, as they had done in the great debates over economic policy in the middle of the century. The representatives of the government in this debate became defenders, by virtue of their office, of a treasury in deficit and continually more in need.

We shall gain little insight into the problem if we examine the figures and statistics brought forward by the politicians. They were crudely distorted and exaggerated, even by such experts as General Uribe Uribe, owner of the hacienda Gualanday in Fredonia and more recently administrator of the famous hacienda Ceilán of Viotá. Guillermo Valencia's warning, delivered in those debates, should be taken seriously: 'Statistics among us are monopolized by a small number of people who shelter behind figures as though they were inexpugnable entrenchments.'[22] In the face of the current crisis — argued Valencia, in September 1896 — all work on new plantations had been suspended, and those who were small-scale growers (according to his figures this meant 80 per cent of producers in Santander and 50 per cent in Cundinamarca–Tolima and the Cauca) were facing 'early ruin'. 'Coffee', he went on, 'is in many parts of the country a means of exchange; in El Tambo, Cauca, it is exchanged for food.' Given that the recent expansion was owed above all to the high prices prevailing, it was absurd to impose duties on exports just when prices were beginning to fall. On the contrary, taxes should be imposed on 'brandy and jewels . . . I for my part am prepared to withdraw all the projects I have presented which have any bearing on the public treasury in exchange for the suppression of this tax.'[23]

Nevertheless, Valencia's central argument goes deeper: if the industry is being developed by small producers, and 'the hoe is the rifle's greatest foe', it is absurd to destroy the social forces working for peace. It is the unemployed, with neither possessions to defend nor work to do, who are for brusque and violent change. Coffee, Valencia concluded, is the industry of the poor, not of the rich; but he developed this very liberal argument with reference to the more ample doctrinal context of the encyclical *De rerum novarum* of Pope Leo XIII.[24] However, Finance Minister Ruperto Ferreira did not accept Valencia's proposition that coffee-growing was the industry of the poor. The position taken by the government in these debates can be summarized in three points: (*a*) the growers are not the 'class of the poor', because although cultivation may in the end spread to this class, it initially requires capital; (*b*) coffee is exchanged for gold, and this produces large profits which should be taxed; and (*c*) the government is prepared to lower the tax. According to Ferreira the tax was producing 800,000 pesos a year, and to remove it completely would be a blow which the Treasury would be unable to withstand.[25]

It is interesting to note the degree of confusion and lack of hard informat concerning the social organization of production, as the debaters struggled desperately to prove that coffee was 'the business of the poor or of the rich'. Those who opposed the tax sought to identify coffee with the 'poor classes', while for the government it was the business of 'capitalists'.

Regional factors also played an important part in the debates. Vergara y Velasco argued that coffee was 'a matter of life and death' in Santander, where the great majority of cultivators were poor families, and that the disparity between the taxes on *pilado* and *pergamino*, added to the fact that coffees obtained very different prices in the markets of Europe and the United States, depending upon the region from which they came, created a situation of injustice, penalizing the principal region of production, Santander; the tax as it stood was 'unworthy of a Christian nation'. Vergara contributed these figures: in Barranquilla 122,000 pesos in tax were paid on coffee with a declared value of 1,900,000 pesos (64 per cent), while in Cucuta 247,000 pesos were paid on coffee with a declared value of 1,800,000 pesos (13.3 per cent); 'the coffee which goes down the Magdalena river, and which fetches the best prices in Europe, paid half what was levied on the other'. He sought the imposition of a tax on bills of exchange.[26]

However, the central arguments came from Uribe Uribe, the development of whose ideas from free trade in the nineties to the subsequent adoption of a relatively well-defined position *circa* 1903–10 favouring the intervention of a paternalistic and socially conservative state to promote economic development and the social welfare of the popular classes in particular, and back around 1910 to his earlier free-trade views, exemplifies the ideological conflicts and tensions of important sectors of the ruling classes.

Núñez had sought to show the ingenuousness and inefficiency of the dogmas of the Liberals of the Manchester school, dogmas which continued to inspire the Liberal leaders who had not succumbed to Nuñism, and also without doubt an important sector of the Conservative party, who in the nineties would swell the ranks of the '*históricos*'.

The transition to more or less accentuated forms of state intervention would still, however, have to await the end of the Conservative Republic (1886–1930). The tensions observed within the thought of Uribe Uribe are a proof that the ruling class, or at least its dynamic elements, had to adjust their ideological schemes to the reality of a country of very secondary importance in international trade, and almost completely marginalized from the flow of international capital, mainly British in origin, which crossed the Atlantic to finance railways and commercial expansion in areas better integrated into the world market. The collapse of the export sector began to reveal with absolute clarity the failings of the Liberal recipe for a country which was weak even among those forming the peripheral area of world capitalism.

The commercial and fiscal crisis was a part of a social and political milieu of greater complexity. Religious and ideological debates raged, as did the problems of national integration aggravated during the period of free trade; conflicts of a purely party nature within and between the two major groupings themselves reflected a situation in which the social power of the rising groups, the merchants and great *hacendados* of the *tierra caliente*, had not yet succeeded in overcoming the local and national power of older groups of traditional latifundists. Furthermore, the Conservative line of thought, as developed by Julio Arboleda, José E. Caro and Mariano Ospina Rodríguez in the middle of the century, had successfully penetrated the most dynamic regional sector of the economy. The miners, merchants, *hacendados*, and politicians of Antioquia espoused with equal conviction and sincerity the ideas of economic free trade, federalism as a form of constitutional organization, Catholicism as the official state religion, and, naturally, a gradual form of progress which would not disturb the established social and political hierarchy, in a context of order among the 'lower ranks' of society, and the cult of manual or intellectural work of a practical bent.[27] To a certain degree, the relative weakness of one or another group in their regional or economic dominance obliged them to enter into implicit alliances which denied any of them hegemonic power; federalism was an implicit recognition of this fact. On the other hand, the survival of old party traditions, nurtured in family life from infancy, led to an early identification of political loyalties which in every region cut completely across class lines.

This society experienced severe political tensions as a result of the prolonged depression in international trade which Colombia suffered between 1875 and 1910. It was in this period that coffee began to figure significantly in the overall balance of trade, replacing other products. At the same time the principles of social and economic organization deriving from the middle of the nineteenth century were put to the test.

The first interventionist measures imposed by Núñez, regarding the tariff and the monetary problem, can be seen as an attempt to overcome the illusions nourished by the axiom of self-regulation of the economic system, assured by the laws of the market. One of the major problems for the understanding of the reorientation of values and attitudes in this period is related to the dynamics of political conflict; Núñez could only attract effective political support from intellectual and political circles which were dogmatically Conservative and pro-Hispanic, passionate enemies in the most concrete terms of French and Anglo-Saxon models, advocates of a Presidentia Republic that would be centralist, Catholic, and intolerant of opposition. In other words, during the Regeneration, state interventionism was intimately bound up with anti-Liberalism.

After the war and during the dictatorship of Reyes, Uribe Uribe — converted into one of the foremost figures of the regime — put forward the concept of state intervention implicit in the Brazilian model of coffee valorization of 1906. This approach, coloured by social ideas which he called 'state socialism', was certainly a precursor of later developments; he was the first to voice, before their time, new attitudes regarding the need of the state to play a direct role in the shaping of growth. However, given that Colombia's coffee economy was being automatically protected by the Brazilian valorization policy of 1906, the coffee interests continued to devote themselves to the preservation of the old Liberal scheme of economic development.

Let us look in a little more detail at the way in which Uribe Uribe expressed the interests, in the long and short term, of the Colombian coffee industry. He always put himself forward as the representative of the coffee interest in general, without making any distinction between the producers, merchants, agents, and financiers, who were emerging as separate groups. In some ways he managed to represent them all. His central idea on the subject, daring for those years, was similar to that of Pedro A. López: 'With coffee we shall be as invulnerable as the East Indies are with quinine!'[28] But the paradox is that men like López preferred to give their firm support to the pacifist group around ex-President Parra, while Uribe Uribe, the personification of the original synthesis of the economic interests of the coffee-growers with the ideals of parliamentary democracy, went on to become one of the great Liberal *caudillos* of the War of the Thousand Days.[29] The arguments put forward in his *Memorial* to Congress in 1894 consisted simply of the reaffirmation of the old principle of free exports: the coffee sector, and the producers and exporters of gold and bananas, were discriminated against because they had to pay a special tax for which no other producers were liable, as well as all the taxes to which all were subject, such as land taxes, tolls, import taxes, and so on.

He attributed to the introduction of paper money the undue rises in the price of essential foodstuffs which had led to a rise in the cost of labour. Real wages could not be forced down, as they were already at subsistence level. The price of transport was rising all the time, international prices were falling, and the coffee industry was still in its infancy. The proposed tax, the *Memorial* concluded, should be rejected as 'against economics and against patriotism'.[30]

Two years later, in the debates over the proposal to abolish the tax, Uribe exaggerated the scarce data available to give the impression that the coffee interests were national in scale: 'the fate of the coffee industry', he said, 'is of direct concern to one-quarter of the population of Colombia, and embraces in its widespread dissemination the whole of the country, whose future is depressed or accelerated in accordance with the decline or advance of that industry.'[31] According to his figures, the half-million bags exported 'give direct employment to one and a half million Colombians'

— a blatant lie from such an experienced planter.[32] More significant is the following assertion: 'everyone in this Chamber has links with coffee, unless he can prove otherwise; many of us possess plantations, others are thinking of acquiring them; some deal in coffee, many have close relatives tied up in the industry, and the rest, with very few exceptions, have connections of one kind or another with it'.[33] But the presence of the coffee interest in Congress was not at all illegitimate; there were no 'selfish' interests, and in any case involvement in the industry cut across party lines: 'At the foot of the petitions brought to the Congress by the coffee sector to protest against the tax we find a fraternal mixture of Conservatives and Liberals, just as their plantations lie side by side, and the owners live as good neighbours devoted to agricultural labour.'[34]

Uribe stressed that the coffee-growers lived in a world more exposed to risk and hazard than that of the cattle-fatteners or the potato-farmers. While they set up their plantations and awaited the first harvest the price situation could change radically. This happened when the good prices of 1888 led to an increase in supply by 1893 and 1894, and to a drop in prices. Besides, the market 'only allowed those to prevail who were best placed to withstand extreme falls in prices', which Uribe correctly predicted. Therefore it would be absurd to increase the costs of production by means of a tax. More gravely still, the Conservative governments were unable to provide adequate measures to keep internal prices down. In sum, the current situation was unfavourable (*a*) because of the rising cost of river transport 'equivalent to having thrust us back a further 200 leagues (1,000 kilometres) from the coast', (*b*) because of the progressive 'price increase and shortage of labour and foodstuffs, equivalent to a rise in the cost of labour', (*c*) because of 'the social and political insecurity which stems from bad government', and (*d*) because of the 'increases in municipal, departmental, and national taxes'.[35]

On the subject of daily wages there are flagrant contradictions between this and other speeches by Uribe. Uribe considered daily wages to be one of the principal contributors to the considerable increase in the costs of production, but as the cost of living had risen more rapidly than daily wages, wage-earners had not benefited, and their real wages had, on the contrary, fallen.[36]

Uribe did not accept the argument put forward by the government that coffee was an industry dominated by the rich, or as the deputy Neira put it, that 'the powerful coffee interests will always possess the means to make their influence felt and assure themselves of a majority in Congress'. Uribe's own estimate was that two-thirds of national coffee production came from 'small producers who do not export their produce directly'.[37]

He argued that the policy of the Regeneration had driven 50,000 inhabitants of Santander across the frontier to settle in Venezuela; when labour recruiters had gone to contract workers for the harvest 'the Ministry of War had published orders explicitly forbidding such activities; the workgangs have been called up into the army from transit towns and even from the departmental capital itself; moreover, this was occurring at a time when the development of established enterprises and the constant process of forming new ones had caused a tremendous increase in the demand for daylabourers; and as the whole process has taken place while there has been no significant increase in the total population, the owners of coffee groves have had to compete fiercely for the available hands, offering in competition against each other wages in advance, travel expenses, higher and higher salaries, better food, bargains of all kinds, and so on'. Despite this, many haciendas lost up to a third of the harvest due to lack of hands.[38]

At this point in the argument there is a clear element of rhetorical manipulation. Speaking of the small producers who produce 'two-thirds' of the coffee, Uribe is in fact describing the difficulties faced by *hacendados* such as himself, and dropping for the moment the thread of his defence of the day-labourers subject to more and more onerous conditions; on the contrary, he depicts a favourable situation in which the labourers control the labour market, or are at least in a position to dictate the terms of their hire, which is exaggerated, to say the least.

He attributes to the government's monetary policy the responsibility for 'the disappearance of credit', without which production loses its dynamism. Having identified his enemies, Uribe shields himself behind bipartisan utterances and references to undifferentiated national interests, and from that position launches a political and social attack on the policies of the Regeneration, its principles, and its leaders. He describes the men in government as a 'palace clique', intriguers, defrauders of the public treasury, owners of ill-gotten fortunes which for that very reason will not survive, as the proverb has it 'to the second generation'; he attacks the 'parasites' and latifundists who have their agricultural enterprises in the *tierra fría*, follow archaic and uncivilized methods and are astounded to learn that 'there are fertilizers for wheat'. He concludes that there is a struggle 'between good and evil . . . represented by the coffee-grower and the palace hanger-on'.[39] Uribe, then, attempts to describe what will years later become, in the splendid oratory of another great Liberal leader, Jorge E. Gaitán, the *país nacional* dominated by the *país político*: 'Tired of the errors and political crimes of the ideologues, the lawyers, the soldiers and the scholars, the professional politicians and the intriguers, we have come to believe that we shall not enjoy good government until we put it into the hands of the landed interest',[40] clearly identified by the speaker with the producers and exporters of coffee. During the whole period, the *país nacional* was contrasted with the *país de los políticos profesionales*, with this theme being particularly stressed during the governments of Reyes (1904–9) and Restrepo (1910–14).

The tax was not suppressed, but drastically reduced, as the Minister, Ferreira, had hoped. The international price of coffee fell in 1897, obliging Caro to suspend the tax at first temporarily and then indefinitely. During the War of the Thousand Days there were attempts to restore it with greater severity, but these failed.

The debates of 1894–8 remain as a testimony of the emergence of social groups who demanded policies which were less ideological, and grounded more in terms of the 'national interest'. Uribe's argument is placed in the context of a political, social, and economic rejection of the idea of intervention, and is an expression of the view that in order to emerge from the long depression of exports it was essential to return to the old system of free trade, and that *laissez-faire* should be reinstated by the *agricultores*.

To sum up, inflation annulled the positive effects which the consequent depreciation of the exchange rate or the rise in the tariff might have had. The export tax on coffee which began to be levied in the second quarter of 1895 increased internal costs by around 15 per cent. In these conditions the opposition of Liberal merchants and a faction of the Conservative party to the political economy of the Regeneration was not just a political matter. On the contrary, the political postulates of the opposition were part and parcel of the interests of coffee *hacendados*, exporters, bankers, and importers. The causes of the expansion of coffee in the nineties must be sought in the propitious conditions listed above – ecology, labour, entrepreneurial experience, good prices abroad, and cheaper ocean transport; they are not to be found in the practices of an economic policy that was far more concerned with resolving immediate fiscal problems than with anything else.

7. Crisis and transition towards the second cycle of expansion, 1903–10

Nothing could have been more discouraging than the political and economic state of the country when it emerged from the last civil war. The separation of Panama was to reproach the consciences of a whole generation. Once the links between the interior and the ports had been reopened, accumulated stocks proved so high that freight rates shot upwards. The coffee-growers, now the leading exporters, could not wait for better days, as they had to export to pay their debts. They seemed to understand that good prices had disappeared with the previous century. The government looked for pacts and compromises, between parties, between factions, between principles. The tariffs of 1903 and 1905 followed the protectionist pattern of the Regeneration. Attempts to return to the gold standard, suppress export taxes, and welcome what little foreign investment came near seemed to follow old free-trade dogmas. Coffee was the only export of importance, but the international market was very depressed, and there were serious doubts about whether it would expand again, or shrink everywhere as it was shrinking already in some districts. Perhaps a rubber or banana boom was coming. Nevertheless, the Brazilian valorization policy of 1906, and the recovery of prices after 1910, opened up a better future for coffee. The First World War closed European markets and increased dependence on the North American buyer, but the expansion of that market enabled it to absorb growing Colombian production without any trouble. In the second decade of the century there was some revival of the old haciendas, once again showing a profit. But it was really the hour of the small and medium cultivator. No sooner was he established on the slopes of the central cordillera than he was integrated into the network of monopsonic purchase, financed by large North American and European importers and roasters. A succinct description and analysis of some aspects of these preliminaries to the second cycle is the subject of this chapter.

Peace with all its horrors

It was not difficult for a man such as General Rafael Reyes, who had not participated directly in the civil war of 1899–1902, and who was a prominent figure in the ranks of the 'Históricos' at the end of the century, and a Conservative hero in the war of 1895, to come to an agreement with the

141

leaders of the failed Liberal 'revolution', Herrera and Uribe. Reyes and
Uribe had to make their first contacts in New York in 1901, when Uribe
was seeking, in the midst of the conflict, to buy arms and collect funds
while Reyes was maintaining his tactical withdrawal from politics but at
the same time keeping abreast in minute detail of the development of the
war.[1]

The Reyes administration faced many problems:[2] the misery and
decadence of the vast areas devastated by the war, economic recuperation,
the construction of forms of political compromise between the old historic
parties, and the control of feuds between *gamonales* throughout the
country all demanded his attention. His economic programme was an
inevitable compromise between free trade and interventionism. This
compromise meant an attempted return to the gold standard, the pursuit
of convertibility, the repudiation (at least in theory) of paper money,
liberty of means of payment, and the fixing of the exchange rate at
10,000%. His efforts to create a central bank, a little along the lines of
Núñez's national bank, soon ran into the resistance of the merchant
groups, who opposed him surreptitiously.

The highly protective tariff provided the basis for investment in the
textile, drink-bottling, and food-processing industries of Medellín, Cartagena,
Barranquilla, and Bogotá. Reyes was at the same time a leading representative
of those who wished to modernize the country by means of direct foreign
investment, as is demonstrated by his vigorous encouragement of mining
and railway projects, and the changes, which are described in chapter 8,
that he introduced in the legislation regarding public lands, greatly to the
advantage of the United Fruit Company.

The centralization of government income and new territorial divisions
which were to dismantle the pattern of the old sovereign states of Federal
times, the shadow of which had continued to weigh heavily on the departments during the centralist regime of the Regeneration, completed a
government programme which had initially received support from all
sectors of the ruling class.[3] The 'minorities law' permitted the Liberals
a moderate and reasonable participation in politics, at every level, and was
without doubt one of the major achievements of the regime. Uribe was a
roving Colombian ambassador in South America from 1905 to 1907, and
arrived in Brazil at a critical moment for the political economy of that
country, when the public discussions concerning the Taubaté Agreement
were in their final phase. This first attempt at coffee valorization in Brazil
put an end to more than half a century of free trade in the world coffee
market. The Agreement, the initiative for which came from the planters
of the state of São Paulo, allied to those of two other coffee-producing

states, Minas Gerais and Rio, broke with the established tradition of free trade, and was a daring economic experiment which led to the direct participation of the Brazilian state, controlled by the coffee interests, in the processes of economic development. Furtado has summarized in the following terms the principal elements of the system: (1) the government would buy up excess stocks of coffee to restore the equilibrium between supply and demand; (2) these purchases would be financed by foreign loans; (3) services on the debts would be covered by a new tax in gold on every bag of coffee exported; (4) the governments of the three producing states would check (for a period of two years) the expansion of production. For Furtado, this new policy symbolizes the political dominance of the coffee sector in the Brazilian state, a dominance which survived until 1930.[4]

Although the scheme was financially well conceived, and could be efficiently administered, one problem was insoluble in the long term. As a result of the control of the supply of coffee through retention of a part of production, prices returned to a level which made production profitable, again attracting investment and reinvestment in coffee and reinforcing the tendency towards disequilibrium between supply and demand. Demand became saturated long before all the potential resources in land and labour could be put to the production of coffee, and in these conditions, retention of stocks led to unbearable inflation, with prices tending to fall in the long term, as in fact occurred in subsequent decades, until Brazil abandoned its unilateral attempts at coffee valorization during the depression of the thirties.[5]

The Agreement was described by Uribe with great clarity, coherence, and detail in a series of articles published in the *Revista Nacional de Agricultura*, the journal of the Sociedad de Agricultores de Colombia (SAC), a body of which he was one of the leading members. Of the influence of the articles on thinking within the government and among growers there can be little doubt. The Agreement was for Uribe a clear sign of 'state socialism', and he saluted it as such with enthusiasm: 'What should concern every country', he wrote, 'is its policy of economic development. Against the old and sterile free-trade routinism which limits the action of the state merely to the keeping of order, is raised the new spirit of generations raised in the school of misfortune, who have a more modern conception of the essence and nature of the functions of the state, and therefore demand its direct intervention on behalf of the collective welfare of the people.'[6]

But such interventionism is not 'artificial'; the government of Brazil was acting to bring about a gradual equilibrium between supply and demand, with coffee prices rising to remunerative levels, and therefore allowing

this 'natural law' to express itself more fully. What is more, the measure
was one of national defence. Uribe's interest in developing a nationalistic
argument was pioneering, and allows us to see in him one of the first
representatives of a national bourgeoisie with a well-defined class conscious-
ness. His sympathies were clearly on the side of the producers, who had
hitherto been in a position of disagreeable subjection *vis-à-vis* the bankers
and international intermediaries: 'It must be noted that precisely because
the coffee trade is monopolized by a very small number of people, principall
in the United States, they share Brazil's interest in pushing up the price
so long as the consumer continues to buy.' The Agreement was a brilliant
protectionist defence, and Brazil 'is going to attempt a legitimate defence
against the inevitable oppression of the anonymous American or European
speculator who has been getting the best of both worlds, by exploiting
both producers and consumers'.[7]

But how practicable was this kind of protective policy for Colombia?
Clearly the factor of overriding importance was that Brazil was producing
75 per cent of the world harvest, and was thus in a position to control
supply; its position was very different from that of the Central and South
American countries which, like Colombia, favoured the valorization scheme
without participating in the risks or the costs involved.

The enthusiasm for 'state socialism' which Uribe Uribe showed with
regard to the Taubaté Agreement was something far removed from Colombi
reality at the time. In Brazil the major coffee interests, and in particular
those of São Paulo, had been able to establish their hegemony over other
groups, and controlled national politics until 1930 not only because they
were well served by the decentralization of the Old Republic, but because
they could and did manipulate the world coffee supply. On the other hand,
countries such as Colombia, where a coffee sector had appeared with a
fair degree of differentiation and growing internal importance, played only
a passive role in the international market, and the same kind of internal
political hegemony was not merely impracticable, but unthinkable. For
these reasons, Uribe slowly came back to the free-trade school, although
without abandoning his nationalism. He felt that independently of the fate
of the Taubaté Agreement 'Colombia couldn't lose' with coffee, for, if
the Agreement worked, prices would be good, and if it failed, Brazilian
production would suffer a tremendous jolt, which would affect supply
and cause prices to rise.[8] His proposals for 'what is to be done' in Colombia
are extremely illustrative: once the problems of exchange-rate stability
could be solved, long-term credit for agriculture and lower transport
charges would both be assured. He ingenuously suggested to the growers
of Antioquia and Santander that they should move to the coast, nearer

the ports, to Bolívar and Magdalena, to found their plantations there, and he called for a prompt solution to the technical and legal problems concerning land-ownership. 'All lands not legally owned and registered and not taxed belong to the nation', and in this way it would be possible to establish which lands were available to colonists, and which belonged to private owners.[9]

The problem of organizing colonists is a key one: as a good *criollo* he sought the encouragement of Spanish and Italian (white) immigrants, because 'I will not hear talk of Chinese and coolies', and finally revealed himself as opposed to large plantations (of over 100,000 bushes). If Colombia wished to remain in the world market, the ideal type of producer was 'the small family farmer, with 2,000 to 10,000 trees, working with a manual pulping machine of national manufacture; on the river banks we can set up central processing plants paid for by entrepreneurs not involved in production who buy the beans for export'.[10]

In this last respect Uribe mentioned *en passant* one of the most important sociological changes in the history of coffee production in Colombia, to which we shall address ourselves in chapters 8 and 9. The appearance on a massive scale of medium and small producers confronted the haciendas, already facing the problems we have described, with competition they found it difficult to meet. Although many were reorganized and went on to prosper, their weight in overall production was increasingly marginal. In a way, the *hacendados* failed but coffee did not. The coffee bourgeoisie, at whose heart were the *hacendado*–exporters, did not disappear. It simply shifted its ground from production to commerce; capital no longer went to control land and labour, but to control the internal coffee market. This fascinating process, marked by advances and retreats, spectacular bankruptcies, and solid and discreet consolidation, will be discussed later in this chapter, where we shall describe the mechanisms and systems adopted by the coffee bourgeoisie, in alliance or in conflict with the bankers and the great foreign coffee roasters, in order to control the market.

To President Marroquín is attributed a witty *bogotano* phrase, uttered on the occasion of the signing of the treaty which put an end to the War of the Thousand Days — 'Peace has arrived with all its horrors.' It is not known whether Ignacio de Márquez, an *antioqueño* coffee *hacendado* and exporter, was in equally good humour as he expressed his fears that the imminent peace could occasion him considerable losses. In the week in which the two parties signed the peacy treaty aboard the U.S.S. *Wisconsin*, he wrote to his brother: 'Peace arrived with all its horrors: everything has fallen disastrously, coffee, retail prices, wages, freight charges, cattle prices.'[11]

Even in a relatively unmonetarized economy a prolonged war can have a substantially inflationary impact, as San Tzu taught five centuries before Christ.[12] As a result of the War of the Thousand Days, food prices in the cities rose between twenty-five and thirty times in relation to prices in 1899; the money supply multiplied twenty-three times between 1899 and 1902.[13] As we have seen before, a dominant trait in the export and import trade was speculation with the exchange rate. In the last years of the war the speculators were offered golden opportunities by the shifts in military fortunes and the true and false reports which reached the commercial centres. The war was a continuation of the political situation which developed in the last years of Caro's government: then the government had not been strong enough to impose its will conclusively, and the opposition was not strong enough to win the elections. The war took the course which the Liberal leader Uribe Uribe had predicted: 'The government does not have the power to halt the revolution; but the revolution does not have the power to defeat the government.'[14]

As peace approached, the merchants were faced with the problems of finding solutions to the devaluation and to the settling of accounts between debtors and creditors. Should they return to the gold standard? How should the devalued notes be redeemed? What should the rate of exchange be in relation to gold? These and other uncertainties produced violent and unforeseen fluctuations in the money market; the rate of exchange fell to 4,000 per cent and shot up to 20,000 per cent from one day to the next.[15] In the atmosphere of panic and speculation which produced in Medellín in 1904 the first substantial failures in projects of industrial investments,[16] it was hoped that the new government would produce a clearly defined fiscal and monetary policy. Reyes took the pragmatic course of fixing the rate of exchange by law at the level at which it showed signs of settling in the first months of the peace, at 10,000 per cent. He thus gained the sympathy and support of large-scale commerce, and of many local notables.[1] In Antioquia the monetary part of the wages was still paid well into the century in the old notes, while in Cundinamarca some *hacendados* asked to be allowed to return to the old and proven system of paying with their own nickel and tin coins due to the shortage of notes.[18] In these first years of peace which were almost as hard for the peasants and workers in the coffee sector as those of war, the merchants were going through a period of readjustment. Between 1903 and 1923, when the Banco de la República was founded, monetary policy was the reverse of that followed during the Regeneration. The year 1903 saw the firm beginnings of a return to the gold standard. The state took upon itself the obligation to pay for the paper issued, on the principle that 'the compulsory paper which replaced the metal coin is a national debt'.

In pursuit of this principle it was necessary to create new sources of income. In 1906 one-quarter of these were taken up by the amortization of the debt; in 1907 half went to the same end. The government, through different agencies, bought up the notes by paying one-hundredth of their face value in gold, and burnt them in public. For a number of reasons the system did not function adequately — political pressures, the poverty of the exchequer, favouritism, and corruption. The government was therefore obliged to support its amortization efforts by reviving the very sort of institution which it had appeared most essential to destroy: it created the Banco Central in the very image of the Banco Nacional of Núñez, which in the eyes of the politicians and the merchant community had been a scandal, nothing more or less than an office of the Treasury of the national government. This measure created resentment and without doubt hastened the fall of Reyes.[19]

To continue the amortization of the paper currency, new fiscal resources were brought to bear in 1909: the income from the emerald mines of Muzo and Coscuez, the rent of the silver mines of Marmato and Supía, and 2 per cent of import duties. Little was achieved with the mines; whatever the private profits were, the government gained little. Lawsuits followed which were not resolved before the thirties. Thus the Treasury took on a load that was too heavy, particularly after the fiscal centralization had been decreed. This measure aimed at weakening the political bastions in the provinces, but it was accompanied by other measures which involved the central state in a costly expansion of its bureaucratic machinery. All this made the fiscal deficit more acute at an already critical time, with foreign trade depressed, service on foreign debt due to be resumed, and the issue of paper money constitutionally prohibited after 1910.

Difficulties in production and transport

At the beginning of the century many *hacendados* thought that the history of coffee would be a failure like that of indigo and tobacco. In 1906 the *Revista Nacional de Agricultura* asked its readers to meditate on the question 'coffee is a bad business, but is there any other?'[20] Four years later a Bogotá *hacendado* thought he had the answer — the future was in bananas; Cundinamarca would be relegated to a 'potato republic', with Turmequé as its capital.[21] Others were less inclined to foresee a final catastrophe, but were by no means optimistic. 'The coffee business', wrote another commentator, 'has seen many fortunes and lives sacrificed for the good of the country, after providing wages, bread, and a roof for our poor people; it stimulated the mechanical arts and commercial life of such centres as Girardot, Honda, Barranquilla, and Cartagena; it provided cargoes for railways and river transport, and profits for banks and gold for the public Exchequer; even in its present state of decline the coffee industry is sustaining the rate of exchange of the compulsory paper currency at between 10,000 and 12,000 per cent.[22]

What was the basis of this 'decline'? In September 1910 a table of costs was presented in the same journal, according to which a *hacendado* lost 960 pesos per *carga* (4.8 pesos gold per 62.5-kilo bag) when the New York price was at 10 cents per pound. 'Everyone is hoping to sell his coffee grove', the report stated, and if the *hacendados* continued to produce it was because they had debts in coffee or in gold with their agents. Tied to these contracts, the *hacendados* received from 20 to 50 per cent less for their coffee than did 'the respectable trading houses'.[23] Some sought to explain the situation not simply in the purely economic terms of costs and prices, but as arising from the lack of prestige of Colombian coffee in the world market, and especially in Europe. Once the shipment of coffee had started again, the first exports were of stocks which had been stored in the warehouses of the ports or the sheds of the haciendas, and its condition had deteriorated from damp and bad storage conditions. Furthermore, many plantations, twenty and thirty years old, partially abandoned from 1900 to 1903, were producing coffee of inferior quality. The coffees of Cundinamarca and Tolima, which before the civil war had fetched prices in London similar to those of the prized Costa Rican coffee, were now selling at almost half the price of the latter.[24]

The policy of a stable exchange, a healthy exchequer, and a resumption of payments on the foreign debt energetically pursued by the Reyes government worked against the expansion of coffee in its former 'speculative' manner. The impact of the railways on coffee expansion before 1920 has recently been exaggerated.[25] By 1898, the end of the first cycle of expansion, in Cundinamarca and Tolima there were only 65 kilometres of track constructed; in Antioquia between 1885 and 1904 only 57 kilometres were built, from Puerto Berrío towards Medellín. Not only was the total number of kilometres constructed small; their location did not always affect coffee. Most of the zones of the Tequendama, all the Sumapaz area, and the Chaparral and the Rionegro regions expanded without railways. According to Roger Brew, the south-east of Antioquia did not receive the benefits of rail transport until well into the twentieth century.[26] Angelópolis was not reached until 1917, and Fredonia not until 1918. By

1915 these districts had already four million coffee trees planted.[27] The tracks were few and unconnected, and it was frequently necessary to load and unload cargoes. Transport costs in Antioquia were not substantially reduced until 1930. Until the La Quiebra tunnel on the Ferrocarril de Antioquia was opened in 1929 the two separate lines were linked by a two-kilometre stretch of road.[28] Railway freight charges were clearly much lower than those of mule or steamboat. From 1909 to 1911 in Medellín, for example they remained constant at 9 pesos per kilometre/tonne by river and 2.5 pesos per kilometre/tonne by rail.[29] Nevertheless, the greater part of the distance was covered by traditional means. Table 23 shows that, compared to the price of coffee, transport costs did not fall to any great extent.

Furthermore, the river companies were able to charge monopoly rates. These were controlled by the merchants of Barranquilla and Cartagena, and by some foreign investors; the *antioqueños*, more far-sighted than the Bogotá merchants, had also invested some money in them. The small British railways, like that of La Dorada, also enjoyed a monopoly and this affected the coffee-growers considerably. In 1906 the Sociedad de Productores de Café denounced the 'alliance' between the Cartagena and Barranquilla navigation companies, and asked the growers and exporters to use the Cartagena companies exclusively in an attempt to break the pact.[30]

When the Reyes government decreed premiums on coffee, gold, and rubber exports, to be paid by granting reductions at 5 per cent on import duties, the coffee-growers requested that instead of these premiums the tax on river transport be eliminated and replaced by the concession of a subsidy to be given to the companies if they would reduce their rates by 40 per cent.[31] Taking direct action, the *hacendados* instituted a boycott which had positive results: between April and May 1906 they forced the tariff of 40 pesos in gold per tonne from Giradot to the coast down to 25 pesos in gold per tonne.[32]

Agitation against the rates charged by the railways was also constant. The La Dorada line was the object of one of the most sustained and systematic press campaigns of the period — 'the most expensive railway in the world'. According to the *hacendados*, its freight charges were five times higher than those of the La Sabana railway. In the same year, 1906, another boycott took place, this time against the Girardot railway, with the slogan 'it might be cheaper to take your coffee to Girardot on your own mules'. 'The Colombian coffee industry', they said, 'was about to disappear, less as a result of the lack of means of communications than as a result of the monopolies enjoyed by the railways and the river transport companies.'

Table 23. Cost of internal transport of 62.5 kilos of coffee in Colombia, 1885–1932

	Antioquia[a]			Cundinamarca[a]		
	Price per bag	Cost of transport	%	Price per bag	Cost of transport	%
	Pesos paper money					
1885				23.06	3.52	15
1890				54.33	5.05	2
1895				71.20	7.74	11
1896	61.20	7.83	13			
1899				55.45	7.91	14
	Pesos gold					
1904	12.00	3.88	32			
1905				14.40	3.12	22
1908	16.56	4.10	25			
1910				21.88	2.60	12
1918	23.60	2.41	10			
1922					3.25	
1932[b]	14.02	1.92	14	10.09	0.80	8

a The costs for Antioquia are those for coffee from the south-east brought to Puerto Colombia; and in the case of Cundinamarca, Sasaima coffee until 1899, and afterwards that from the south-east, both to Puerto Colombia. b Railway freights only.
Sources: 1895, 1890, 1899: Archivo Herrera, Roberto Herrera R., Libros de Contabilidad. 1896: Archivo Ospina. Correspondencia. 1904: Vida Nueva, Medellín, 5 November 1905. 1905, 1910: R.N.A., no. 4, 31 May 1906; nos. 2–3, 1 September 1910. 1908, 1918: Vásquez, Correa & Co., correspondencia. 1922: Augusto Ramos, O café, p. 284. 1932: FNCC, Boletín de Estadística, year 1, no. 2 (April 1932), 48, and year 2, no. 6 (April 1933), 170 (railway and river costs only).

At the end of 1906 the railway had to reduce its freight charges by 25 per cent; a year later a similar agreement ensured that the charges would remain at the same level.[33] Within each *comarca*, the maintenance of the bridle paths was the responsibility of the *hacendados*. In Cundinamarca, for example, they rebuilt the bridge over the Sumapaz river which linked Fusagasugá with the road to Girardot, after it had been destroyed in the civil war, and built roads to Subía, and from Viotá to Portillo.[34]

Finally came the problems of the seasonal movement of labour. The growers had to put pressure on the government in order to get a reduction from the railway companies of the La Dorada, La Sabana, and Giradot lines of 75 per cent on third-class tickets for the workers who went to harvest the coffee.[35] They were sporadically subject to competition for labour from the United Fruit Company, and lamented that many peasants and peons went to the Magdalena plantations, tempted by a higher daily wage, but 'not knowing the suffering that awaits them'.[36]

General Benjamin Herrera, Liberal hero of the 1899–1902 civil war and a planter in the banana zone, spoke up publicly in defence of the 'fruitful labour of the United Fruit Company',[37] but in 1920 the first Congresso de Cafeteros unanimously approved a 'formal protest' against the company 'for its monopoly of the banana business on the Atlantic coast', and asked for greater liberty for that industry. The coffee-growers resented the fact that concessions and liberal terms were offered to foreign companies (with interests in railways and bananas), while the coffee sector which continued to contribute the greater part of national exports could not impose conditions which would favour its development.[38] But coffee continued to expand; new social groups had appeared in the countryside: peasants or owners of peasant stock and mentality, for whom coffee-growing was not a speculative undertaking but a way of life.

But during the Regeneration, particularly during the six-year Presidency of Caro (1892–8), during the war (1899–1902), and during the Quinquenio (1904–9), the fate of private finances was closely linked to control of political power. This was an era of large-scale corruption and major scandals; Alberto Lleras Camargo, with a sharp eye for the differences between one oligarchy and another, has recently put forward a new formulation of the thesis that it was in this period that a new oligarchy rose to power.[39]

Jorge Holguín was perhaps the most complete representative of the era and of an oligarchy at once politically reactionary, at times short on scruples, and set on *embourgeoisement*. On 15 June 1912, Enrique de Narváez Quijano, the representative of the interests of Fould & Cie, sold to 'General Jorge Holguín, banker' seven large coffee haciendas and five blocks of land in Nilo and Tibucuy, auctioned on behalf of old and insolvent clients;

it was the transaction of the century, with Holguín paying £68,000 sterling.
Ten years later Holguín was the largest individual cultivator of coffee in
Colombia.[41] In 1896 Uribe Uribe had accused him of representing the
interests of parasitic *altiplano* latifundism and of the underworld of government finance; by 1912 Holguín had passed over to the side of the coffee
latifundists, probably under the benevolent eye of Uribe himself. The date
of Holguín's purchase is significant. Prices were again remunerative, and
many of the old haciendas were being revived. Jonás, for example, had
twelve *tongas* in production in 1915, with 142,575 trees; three and a half
years later, in January 1919, it had twenty *tongas* with 194,500 trees.[42]

But Holguín, as Uribe Uribe prophesied, was a rentier rather than an
entrepreneur. The entrepreneurs of the coffee trade were now elsewhere,
controlling the market, concentrating their resources of capital and talent
against isolated and dispersed producers who occupied places of weakness
and vulnerability in the social scale. But before examining this new group
of speculators and their essential role in the second cycle of expansion, we
must consider one of the elements of technique which were to be as decisive
in letting the small coffee plot flourish as was the existence of peasant
proprietorship itself. This was the spread of the small hand depulping
machine.

In a historical perspective that would stress success rather than failure,
perhaps there is no better example of success in the difficult struggle of
Colombian industry from 1860 on in Antioquia and Cundinamarca than
that of the small iron-foundries which produced agricultural machinery for
what Luis Ospina called 'the simple classes'.[43] From time to time the iron
works of Amagá and La Pradera had exaggerated ambitions of producing
rails on a grand scale, and even rolling stock, but these and other more
modest enterprises had a more important and definitive function in helping
to consolidate the family unit of coffee production. The small depulping
machine, although it wasted many good beans and did not produce a high-
quality coffee, did enable the small producer to sever for ever the umbilical
cord that tied him to certain haciendas or processors, and put him in direct
contact with the small-town middlemen. The foundries of Amagá and La
Estrella (Caldas, Antioquia) had served a torpid market for small items of
sugar-mill machinery, but in the nineties the demand from the coffee
fincas in Antioquia and the centre of the country gave them new life. Many
produced machinery for haciendas – Pelton-wheels, large depulpers, different types of dryers and threshers – but at the turn of the century the
small hand depulper was their principal line of business.[44] Coffee machinery
produced in the *antioqueño* foundries and moved to the Antioquia Railway
showed a spectacular rise: 1905, 1.8 tonnes; 1908, 4.9 tonnes; 1911, 269

tonnes; 1914, 585 tonnes; 1919, 914 tonnes.[45] Antioquia in 1915 had 5,670 depulpers and 8,048 coffee *fincas*, or 0.70 depulpers per *finca*. In 1922 the ratio had risen to 0.97.[46]

The study of the society and economy produced in the areas of dense coffee production and based on the medium and small cultivator requires a much closer analysis that I shall undertake in the next two chapters. Here I shall end with a rapid analysis of the formation of monopsonic groups in coffee marketing: when the peasant producer emerges these are already organized and experienced.

Opportunities for speculation

The most favourable opportunities were still in imports and in exports. This was no new discovery, and an organizational base already existed for further entrepreneurial schemes for coffee exports. The commercial houses which had begun as importers established in Barranquilla, Honda, Medellín, Bogotá, and other places had been acquiring experience in the coffee export trade since its beginnings; they had been increasingly forced to accept coffee in payment for imported goods.[47] The reorganization of trade implied initially the reorganization of these old family-based firms, some of which had been established since the tobacco days. Firms began to emerge in the coffee sector which specialized in buying the beans in the inland markets, and processing and exporting them along with other products, principally gold, panama hats, and hides.

The marketing of coffee became separated from its production as the hacienda began to give way to new units of production. This does not imply that all the haciendas disappeared at a blow or that the wealthy and the socially prominent did not continue to invest in the cultivation of coffee. Little by little the system of purchasing and processing the coffee for export became defined. It showed a high degree of concentration, and powerful financial control was exercised by the commercial houses in the interior. These characteristics were largely a product of the evolution of the international market, dominated by the United States, in which there were appearing signs of monopolistic concentration, particularly among the roasters and the wholesale distributors.

This was immediately reflected in the structure of the Colombian coffee market, in commercial practice, and even in the design of means of communication. In the twenties the Pacific railway would unite the districts of Caldas and Quindío with the port of Buenaventura, from where coffee would be shipped to San Francisco and through the Panama Canal to New Orleans and New York.

Though at the beginning of the century it had still appeared that the European market should be taken into account by the Colombian producers and exporters, by the thirties the hegemony of the United States in the marketing and consumption of Colombian coffee was clearly expressed in the techniques of processing. These were adapted to suit the particular idiosyncrasies and tastes of that market.[48] The commercial history of the important coffee-exporting firm of Vásquez, Correa & Co., of Medellín, illustrates the whole range of commercial and financial practices, and contributes to a clarification of the relations between the groups of the bourgeoisie who specialized in coffee exports, finance capital, and the organization of foreign buyers.[49] This *antioqueño* firm, like most others in the country at that time, whether industrial, commercial, or service companies, functioned on a family basis with a legal and mercantile type of organization which maintained elements of the classic nineteenth-century enterprise, despite the fact that from an initially broad range of activities there generally came a transition towards more rational and specialized division as the assets were successively divided among heirs. The firm established agencies for the purchase of coffee in practically all the coffee-producing municipalities of Antioquia, but was forced by the shortage of national capital to seek loans to increase the scope of its activities from firms already well known to Colombian merchants, Schloss Brothers of London, Tardiff & Cassou of Paris, and Amsinck of New York.

In 1907 Luis M. Botero & Sons, the representative in Antioquia of Amsinck, which at the time was fighting its way into the Colombian market, proposed that Vásquez, Correa & Co. should work for the New York firm, which offered better terms for credit than could be obtained from domestic banks, and a wide range of possibilities for the importing and exporting of different goods. Nevertheless, Vásquez, Correa & Co. began to work instead with Schütte & Gieseken, a firm which had its general headquarters in Bremen and New York, and was equally active in the North American and European markets.

To describe the mechanisms of marketing in sufficient detail for our purposes we need only say that these foreign houses provided their Colombian colleagues with funds to purchase coffee and other products direct from the producer, leaving them in relative freedom as to their own organization and trading practices, but demanding of them payment in these commodities. The Colombian firms, however, ran all the risks of the operation except for one, which was taken by the North American importers, and which was of extraordinary importance, given the particular nature of the Colombian trade — proof of enshipment, in this case in Puerto Berrío, was sufficient to discharge the obligation, so that if for any reason the price of the product on the international market fell while the coffee was between Puerto Berrío and its final destination, the loss was assumed by the importer.

To reduce the sometimes devastating effects that a trade war between different buyers could have, the foreign houses tended to develop policies of agreements and joint operations between various Colombian houses. One frequently finds in the correspondence of Vásquez, Correa & Co. propositions from New York or Bremen offering the firm larger loans or more advantageous conditions if it would associate with other Colombian firms for particular buying operations. The foreign houses also tried to break down the regional division of markets by urging the Colombian houses to enter new markets, or buy in those controlled by others groups, often with counter-productive results.

For example, between 1911 and 1913 there was a bitter conflict between a group of *antioqueño* firms and Pedro A. López & Co., the largest buyer and exporter of coffee in the interior of the country. While the former tried to gain ground in Caldas, Tolima, and Cundinamarca, López & Co. tried to break into the Antioquian market: 'In view of the fact that the agent of Pedro A. López has begun to buy coffee and hides in Fredonia and that he has done so by putting the price too high, it was agreed that the company should take on this competition once and for all, and instructions were given to Don Enrique Vásquez to keep the price if necessary 2 or 4 pesos above that being paid by the other gentleman.'[50] It need only be added that López & Co. was backed by Lazard Frères of Paris and London.[51]

But the trade war was carried on not only at inter-regional level. It was possible that within a single market, such as that of Antioquia, different firms might enter similarly into competition in an attempt to gain control. To avoid this, special organizations were created. Vásquez, Correa & Co. participated in a secret commercial company based in Medellín, and known among its members as the 'Negocio de X y Y', or the 'X and Y business'. X stood for coffee: Y for hides. The company took in all the coffee region of Antioquia, and its objective was to eliminate competition among buyers.

The company had considerable weight in the market. Between 1908 and 1911, years for which a small archive exists, the Negocio X and Y bought roughly 65 per cent of the coffee exported from the department of Antioquia.

Negocio X and Y: Purchase of parchment coffee in Antioquia 1908–1911

31 May 1908 to 27 March 1909	5,780 tonnes	(10 months)
8 April 1909 to 26 February 1910	5,750 tonnes	(11 months)
4 May 1910 to 12 January 1911	5,770 tonnes	(9 months)
Total	17,300 tonnes	(30 months)
Monthly average	576 tonnes	

If this figure is compared with the monthly average carried by the Ferrocarril de Antioquia in 1913, which was 800 tonnes,[52] it emerges that the Negocio X and Y had purchased 65 per cent of the *antioqueño* crop.

The company was formed in 1908 and the purchase of coffee and hides was carried on separately. In August 1908 shares in the coffee business were distributed in the following way: Vásquez, Correa & Co., 28 shares; Londoño Bros., 22; Angel López & Angel Jaramillo, 17; Escobar & Co., 17; Hijos de Félix A. Correa, 17; Luis M. Toro, 16; J. Escobar y Baltazar Ochoa, 14; Carlos Nauts, Enhart & Co., 8; Mejía & Echeverría, 8; and Cortés Duque & Co., 6. The total number of shares was 153.

Each partner provided, in order to purchase the coffee, 'a sum of money' in accordance with the number of shares he held; the company updated the coffee inventories twice weekly; and the different partners could buy and sell among themselves. Once a particular lot of coffee had been finally assigned to a partner, he could dispose of it freely, exporting it through his own agents or selling it to another exporter. The field of action of the company was confined to the internal, not the export, market.

The mechanisms of control were rudimentary but effective: (*a*) fixing of the purchase price in the markets of the coffee *municipios*; (*b*) purchase and administration of threshing plants; (*c*) renting of bags to the partners (expensive and scarce at the time);[53] (*d*) manipulation of the mule freight rates through commercial tactics. For each purchase of coffee the firm itself set the exchange rate and guided itself as regards external prices by the bulletins of Fould & Cie of Paris. In 1909, once the business was firmly established, the partners began to study the possibility of setting up a shoe factory in Medellín.

As the society was a secret one, each partner had to have his own agent in each municipality, so that it appeared to the producers and small middlemen that there was competition between the different agents and processers. Orders were passed in code to the agents of each partner, and the sender invented ingenious schemes so that not even the agents would know of the secret. For example, when orders went out to lower the price to a municipality where two or more partners had agents, the orders were sent out with three days' or a week's delay between one and the next, so that any suspicion of collusion might be dissipated.

Thus in November 1908 a circular explained the procedure in the following terms: 'The notification of the previous prices [forced down] is to be sent out to the townships by telegraph during this week, before next Saturday; it has also been agreed that some houses should pass the word that they are suspending purchases until further notice, stating in the telegrams they send that there is likely to be a big fall in the price, not only in the exchange rate, due to the present crisis, but also because coffee itself is falling. The decision that some houses should order prices to be lowered and that others should suspend purchases was taken with the principal objective of disorienting the agents [of each house] regarding the existence of the society.'[54]

The organization also concerned itself with the rates for land transport: 'The Administrative Junta of the Negocio X and Y, in today's session, decided that all the houses should instruct their agents in the towns of the interior to begin to despatch their coffee to this town (Medellín), or other towns along the way as the case may be. If we do this it is likely that transport costs will rise somewhat, but on the other hand we shall avoid the loss of interest payments represented by the deposits in the towns in the interior, and justify a fresh reduction in the price of coffee in those towns; it is also very likely that when the summer comes we shall be able to work the combination the other way round, lowering the transport rates and pushing up the prices, but in that case we shall have already bought most of the harvest and we shall be able to transport it here and on to the coast at cheap rates.'[55]

Naturally enough, there appeared in the national press accusations of monopoly on the part of the buyers, although there was no lack of authoritative commentators who decided that to speak of buyers' monopolies and agreements to lower the prices in the coffee municipalities was at best a fantasy, at worst a sign of demagogic agitation.[56] Tables 24 and 25 demonstrate the effect of the imposition of prices in the *municipios*. It can be seen that as the harvest approaches the prices are pushed down, although there is no corresponding fall in the external price.

Between 15 May and 22 November 1908 orders were given for eleven consecutive price reductions (table 24) which did not correspond to any fall in either the international price or the rate of exchange. These reductions range from 26 per cent (Amagá, for example) to 33 per cent (Valparaiso, for example). Price differentials between municipalities clearly follow transport costs to Medellín, where the coffee was traded between the participants.

The coffee thus acquired at monopsony prices was exported by Vásquez, Correa & Co. to their agents in New York. The tremendous variation in profit rates from one month to the next is a proof of the risk implicit in the export business and shows the need to export in large quantities, as the net profit per bag is relatively low. During this short period, the second half of 1908 (the most important in Antioquia for the coffee merchants, as it was the period of the main harvest), the rate of exchange and rate of transport charges were unchanged. A minimal alteration in

Table 24. Prices fixed by the Negocio X and Y for parchment coffee in the second half of 1908 (pesos per arroba)

Municipio	15 May	18 June	19 June	23 June	4 July	31 July	20 Aug.	Main crop (Oct.–Jan.)				
								6 Oct.	7 Oct.	14 Oct.	4 Nov.	22 Nov.
Andes	145	150	140	130	120	125	115	120	115	120	115	105
Amagá	175	–	165	155	145	150	135	140	135	–	–	130
Angelópolis	175	–	165	155	145	150	135	140	135	–	–	130
Abejorral	160	155	–	145	135	–	120	–	–	–	–	–
Aguadas	155	145	–	135	125	–	110	–	–	–	–	–
Bolívar	135	125	–	115	105	–	90	105	100	–	95	90
Concordia	140	130	120	115	–	110	115	110	–	105	100	–
Fredonia	165	160	–	150	140	150	135	–	–	145	135	130
Jericó	160	150	–	140	130	135	120	125	120	125	120	110
Jardín	145	150	140	130	120	125	115	120	115	120	115	105
Libornina	145	135	–	125	115	–	100	–	–	–	–	105
La Ceja	172	162	–	152	142	–	135	–	145	–	–	140
Medellín	185	185	–	120	155	165	150	–	160	–	155	150
Montebello	–	–	–	145	135	–	120	–	–	–	–	115
Pácora	150	140	–	130	120	–	105	–	–	–	–	–
Santo Domingo	–	–	–	160	150	–	135	–	–	–	–	130
Sa. Roque	165	–	–	155	–	140	–	–	–	–	–	130
Sopetrán	165	155	–	145	135	–	120	–	–	–	–	115
Santa Barbara	160	150	–	145	135	–	120	–	130	–	–	125
Sonsón	175	165	–	155	145	–	130	–	–	–	–	140
Titiribí	165	155	–	145	135	–	120	–	130	–	–	125
Tamesis	150	155	160	145	135	125	130	115	125	125	120	110
Valparaiso	150	140	135	125	130	120	125	110	120	115	110	100

Source: Archivo Ospina, Vásquez, Correa & Co., correspondence.

Table 25. *Profit margin in coffee exported by Vásquez, Correa & Co., 1908*

Month	Total sold[a] (60-kilo bags)	Cost (pesos gold per 60-kilo bag)			Sale price			Net income			Profit per bag	Profit as % of total cost
		Purchase	Transport	Total	Total pesos	Pesos gold		Total	Per bag			
July	1,057.5	8.75	5.61	14.36	18,811.26	17.79		17,122.2	16.19		1.83	12.94
August	766.4	7.09	5.61	12.70	13,249.3	17.29		11,972.20	15.62		2.92	22.99
September	–	–	–	–	–	–		–	–		–	–
October	1,360.7	7.57	5.61	13.17	23,680.06	17.40		21,399.70	15.73		2.56	19.44
November	1,481.5	7.33	5.61	12.94	26,977.60	18.21		24,498.15	16.40		3.46	26.73
December	1,139.8	7.09	5.61	12.70	19,361.20	16.99		17,430.06	15.29		2.59	20.39

a Only to Amsinck, New York.
Source: Archivo Ospina, Vásquez, Correa & Co.

either of these two variables meant larger or smaller profits. Despite the ability to control the price of purchase it was not easy to adapt to such alterations: there was a delay between the time of purchase and the time of sale (which was in many cases the moment the exporter received notice of enshipment at Pto Berrío), during which time fluctuations might occur. But the greatest uncertainty, and one over which there was no control, came from variations in the external price. The need for a secret organization of a monopsonic nature is therefore evident; its weak point was that it demanded access to credit. In a speculative situation originating in manipulations of the price or of the exchange rate, or rising transport costs, a firm might choose to hold the coffee and store it in the hope that improved market conditions would allow the hitherto expected rate of profit to be made, but this option was open only to firms which had liquid funds and could dispose of them with relative autonomy.

Initially the *antioqueño* entrepreneurs considered that the weakness of their commission houses lay in the fact that they were intermediaries, and in the second decade of the century the more powerful firms decided to open offices in New York as agents and importers. In 1913 Vásquez, Correa & Co. informed the New York houses of this plan, to be told immediately that all their lines of credit would be withdrawn.[57] It was explained to them that such funds should not be seen as bank loans, for the commission houses were not in the business of lending out money for interest, but of financing the purchase and export of coffee and other products. In view of this situation, capital had to be acquired in Colombia itself and, taking advantage of the 'black list' operated as a result of the First World War by the United States government against some of the biggest coffee-importing houses in New York mostly German in origin, Vásquez, Correa & Co., Alejandro López & Co., Pedro A. López & Co., and other Colombian groups set themselves up as importers and agents in the very centre of the world coffee market. The *antioqueño* banks, such as the Banco Sucre, played an important role in this venture.[58] Everything went well until the crisis of 1920.

8. Private appropriation of public lands in the west

Antioqueño colonization deserves the attention it has received as a decisive episode in Colombian history. The society which emerged from it on the hillsides, river banks, and valley slopes situated between the Cauca river basin and the peaks of the central cordillera found integration and economic progress in the early years of the twentieth century through the cultivation, processing, packing, and transport of coffee.[1]

Naturally enough, a slow-maturing crop such as coffee did not appeal to colonists who had set themselves, days and even weeks away from the nearest outpost of civilization, the task of carving a living out of the *monte*. Coffee had to wait until communities had been established, supported by a subsistence agriculture of maize, beans, yuca, and bananas, and until improvements had been made to the bridle-paths used to transport the pigs which were fattened for the distant towns of Medellín and Bogotá. Before the frontier provided a stable economy it offered only the chance of survival to a population which in its land of origin was growing more rapidly than any other in the Republic, in a poor environment of waste lands and steep and eroded terrain. At the same time adventurers arrived to seek buried treasure from previous indigenous civilizations, and search the forests for wild rubber.

The frontier protected its inhabitants from the vicissitudes of politics, and from wars, recruiters, requisitions, and similar outrages, while the struggle against nature and isolation bred unpolished but comradely habits. It would be very difficult to deny that these factors made for a more egalitarian ethos in the society produced by *antioqueño* colonization than in those of the *altiplano* or the Atlantic coast – it was an ethos of axemanship, effort, and achievement. But it would be equally difficult to ignore other factors which were important, and whose concealment has led to the creation of a legend of *antioqueño* colonization which has been ideologically manipulated to suggest not only a nineteenth-century Arcady but a subsequent society blessed with every advantage, or at least with those advantages stemming from a just distribution of land and of political and economic opportunity.

It is possible that the structure of social classes in Antioquia, transplanted to the areas of colonization, may have become somewhat blurred in the initial period of the collective struggle to settle down and survive with a

161

minimal degree of civilization. The values of solidarity and egalitarianism certainly governed conduct in the initial phase of *guaquería*, rubber, pigs, and cacao. But as the population expanded and one frontier gave way to another, there appeared in the areas of original settlement a type of economy oriented to the principles of capital investment. The occupation of the lowlands along the river banks saw the formation of cattle and sugar-cane latifundia; near such centres as Pereira the first relatively large-scale plantations of sugar-cane were founded, with their *trapiches* and their systems of wage labour. It was in these circumstances that there flourished with all their colourful vigour the original characteristics of the stratified society which had left the south of Antioquia in search of opportunity. In this chapter I shall lay great stress upon these aspects, which took shape and meaning as frontier settlements became the centres and points of logistical support for new openings. The importance attributed in this chapter to land accumulation, *gamonalismo*, and violence is a reaction to the 'white legend' of *antioqueño* colonization; however, I have no desire to replace it with a 'black legend', which would invalidate arguments concerning the greater degree of social mobility, or the dynamic character of the *fundadores* as entrepreneurs.

From the beginning the process of colonization came to be dominated by the elite of Medellín, who were able to finance it and to mould it socially. As the demographic and geographic base of colonization grew, and it began to acquire characteristics of autonomy, the support of the commercial elite of Medellín remained crucial in three aspects: (*a*) for credit and supplies, (*b*) for political support, decisive if the state were to grant public lands to the organized settlers, and (*c*) for legal and political support when the colonists entered into conflicts over the precise location of their boundaries with the older *latifundistas*.

The dynamic of colonization tended to produce a uniform pattern of social structures. Once the first wave of colonists had become established (Sonsón and Abejorral in 1780–1810), the directors of that colonization, with family connections among the Medellín elite, became independent, acquired land, and began to accumulate capital through trade. They were then equipped to direct a second wave of colonization (Salamina, Neira, and Manizales in 1835–50). This second colonizing movement entered into conflict with the Concesión Aranzázu administered by a commercial company based in Medellín, González & Salazar. After lively legal and political proceedings, this second colonizing group emerged as the elite of Manizales and attempted to control the third phase of colonization, modelling themselves on their forebears, when they entered the Quindío region in 1875–1910.

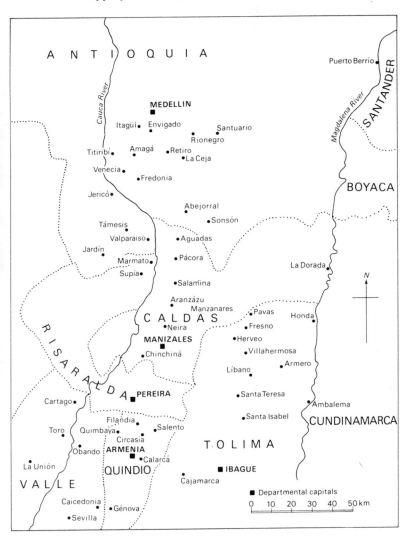

Map 4. Municipalities important in the coffee economy of the 'antioqueño country'.

(*Source:* Instituto Geográfico Agustín Codazzi, *Diccionario geográfico de Colombia* (2 vols. (Bogotá, 1968), vol. 1, p. 75.)

All the same, Quindío colonization comes closer to the egalitarian and democratic pattern than that of the regions of central Caldas. A look at the biographies of the principal founders, their social and geographic origins, their economic position, and even their political affiliation shows that they were not well connected with the Manizales or *antioqueño* elite. Furthermore, the Quindío depended administratively and politically on Popayán, not on Medellín, and it attracted colonists from a variety of regions, including Tolima, Cundinamarca, and Boyacá.[2] As we shall see, the Empresa Burila, in contrast with González & Salazar, failed in its aim of speculating with lands whose value increased through demographic pressure. Thus Quindío colonization differed from the earlier settlements of which it was the demographic and geographical continuation.

Parsons laid down the basic lines for the interpretation of *antioqueño* colonization. He notes the importance of latifundism and capitalist forms of colonization, but to my mind he still fails in one area to correct the too-rosy versions of the process. He scarcely goes into the problem of un-official peasant colonization, which escaped the official registers, and on the structure of the *colonias agrarias* he relies too much on the letter of the law and popular legend.

Looking at the figures, it is clear that the great majority of peasant colonists are not recorded. This suggests the existence of a critical problem in this frontier society; insecurity of title, which meant for thousands of *colonos* that they remained at the mercy of *gamonales* and local store-keepers, which generated an atmosphere of uncertainty, a breeding-ground for certain patterns of crime and violence related to land and work. The conclusions of recent anthropological studies[3] seem to me plausible: the violence of the Quindío of the middle years of this century was a magnified form of a pattern of crime already present in the initial stages of colonizatio: Naturally, this interpretation does not imply denying the importance of the usual range of passions and interests which are bound up in the political process – questions of religion, sectarian emotions, the electoral system with its competition for access to bureaucratic spoils (the police, the school-masters, the judges) with which every *gamonal* must secure his pre-eminence There has been no study yet of this unofficial colonization; the *colonias agrarias* would be a good point of departure, for in them one can see most clearly the vital importance of title to the *colono* and how ability to secure titles is a touchstone of the local power of the *gamonal*, and how it is at the root of the struggle of the *colonias* to secure official recognition. A short inquiry into the principal types of conflict present in the *colonias* lays open a world of resentments, rivalries, and violent antagonisms not at all like the picture Parsons describes: 'These new colonies, especially in Caldas and Tolima, were closely knit, fraternal, agrarian associations in which cooperative clearing, seeding and harvesting, and the sense of communal responsibility were highly developed.'[4]

In this chapter I do not intend to provide an exhaustive account of the sociological complexity of *antioqueño* colonization, but to attempt to clarify the meaning of its central feature: the appropriation of land. There were four mechanisms through which such appropriation took place:

(*a*) by gaining title to public lands through the legal processes of adjudication and concession,

(*b*) by special concessions or adjudications granted to the *colonias de poblamiento*,

(*c*) the transfer of title of privately owned land by commercial companies, and

(*d*) by extra-legal occupation by poor colonists excluded from 'official colonization'.

Colonization was not a socially selective process of migration and settlement, but one that included all social classes. It was shaped by four major historical agents. First, there were the capitalist colonizers, including social groups with family or commercial connections with *antioqueño* elites, principally of Medellín or Sonsón, who enjoyed access to credit, information, legal protection, and social prestige, enabling them to direct the process of migration and settlement and take political action in its name. Colonization was for them a means to social and economic ascent, and they employed the practices of mercantile capitalism to these ends. Secondly, there were established landowners who, as the colonizing movement gained momentum, created commercial companies with the objective of speculating with their land as it gained value. Thirdly, we must consider the groups of peasant families who made up the mass of colonists, driven out of Antioquia by the economic conditions prevailing there. The term 'peasant' is here reserved for the group to which it is most generally applied — family units who obtain their basic subsistence income working independently on their own plots, which they cultivate without the aid of wage labour contracted outside the family. These are the poor colonists. But, fourthly, there were also other poor colonists who managed to obtain land by submitting themselves to certain types of political organizations called *colonias de poblamiento*, which obtained legislation in their favour regarding public lands.

For reasons of economy we shall refer in this chapter to the four groups who accounted for the bulk of official colonization as (a) colonizers, (b) companies, (c) poor colonists, and (d) *colonias*. *Antioqueño* colonization can to a large extent be studied by following the nature of the conflicts and pacts between these different agents of colonization.

Legislation relating to public lands

The society that arose from *antioqueño* colonization on the slopes of
the central cordillera is also the focal point of analysis of agrarian policy.
For persons as far apart intellectually and politically as the Liberal historian
Nieto Arteta and the Conservative statesman Mariano Ospina Pérez, the
coffee-growing society of western Colombia signified the democratization
of access to land, the existence of small properties without the necessity
of agrarian reform.[5]

For both Liberals and Conservatives in the nineteenth century the
colonization of land appeared to resolve the social problem in a very simple
fashion: surplus lands for surplus people. But what shape of society would
these frontier regions produce? Juridical ideology and agrarian legislation
in Colombia derives from the two Liberal currents of thought on property
in land and agricultural production, formulated by the great reforming
bureaucrats of Carlos III, Jovellanos, Olavide, and Aranda. One can say of
Colombian Liberalism, as of Spanish, that its agrarian programme was
worked out at the end of the eighteenth century.[6] At the same time, this
connection was denied by the Liberal reformers of the mid nineteenth
century, determined to do away with all trace of the 'colonial' or the
Hispanic. Spain was for them decadent, 'feudal', wretched, and idle
Castille:[7] they had forgotten the Spain of the Enlightenment or of the
Cortes of Cádiz, even though the essence of their subsequent agrarian
policy was to be found there. From Jovellanos derived the idea that all
collective property, such as Church lands, and all obstacles to a free market,
such as *mayorazgos* (entails granted by the Crown) and *censos*, represented
a drag on the economy, and that a free market in land was the basis of
prosperity. The failure of this individualistic solution to the problem of
men without land and lands without men led Aranda and Olavide to another
conclusion, that property was not an individual right but a social institution
– hence the right and the need to support collective colonization schemes
and to expropriate absentee and unproductive landlords in favour of the
real cultivators.

While idle state lands could absorb those seeking land there was no
conflict in Colombia, and the Republic's legislation could contain at the
same time the individualist principles of its Civil Code and the older Hispanic
tradition of royal ownership (*tierras realengas*) and appropriation of land
through work. When in the 1920s and 1930s demographic pressure was
directed towards lands not in production but to which large landowners
had titles, attempts would be made to solve the problem by falling back
on Aranda's theories of the social function of property and the necessity of

expropriation. Of course, these doctrines were given a more fashionable origin – the latest French Juridical theory.

In his report to the Bolívar legislature of 1879, Francisco J. Balmaceda argued that 'without property there cannot be civil society, nor lasting peace, nor development of public wealth, nor morality among the masses', and he proposed the free distribution of public lands and the exemption from military service of the cultivators.[8] The principles of Liberalism thus concisely stated should have found their guarantee in the distribution of state lands, seen by the enlightened oligarchy as an answer to the problems of economic development and political stability. Social democracy was to be based on a middle class of literate farmers.

Social reality moved in a different direction. Liberals such as Diego Mendoza and Anibal Galindo had seen the experiment fail. Mendoza discovered the gradualism which Mariano Ospina Rodríguez had earlier advocated, and which in agrarian policy Salvador Camacho Roldán would endorse years later. According to Mendoza, it was necessary first to pass through an inevitable first phase in which the protagonist would be the large-scale proprietor, the only one capable of exploiting considerable extensions of land economically, especially in the development of livestock. In the second phase inheritance would divide properties, and *latifundismo* would die a natural death.[9] Thus, *antioqueño* colonization can also be seen as the test of the Liberal principal which aspired to create a democracy based on the smallholder.

Without doubt peon labour was not as widespread or as important here as in Cundinamarca, but the other characteristics observed by Anibal Galindo in the formation of new latifundia out of public lands were to be found – the 'feudalization' of the land through *gamonalismo*, the gestation of a social group which profits out of the 'surplus value' which society and social progress bring to erstwhile empty lands.[10]

The regulations and legislation regarding public lands, and the available statistics, present a confused and varied picture of official colonization. If we accept that between 1873 and 1936 – two dates which marked changes in legislation which had important repercussions in the appropriation of public lands[11] – some three million hectares of land in the regions which these colonizing movements were incorporating into the civilized world passed out of public patrimony, then it is immediately clear that the theme merits an effort to free from this tangle of legislation and confused and unreliable statistics some general trend, some important historical insight into the formation of the modern Colombian society.

The question of public lands has not aroused the interest of historians. This is curious, given that the number of hectares taken into private ownership through the various systems designed to make public lands available was many times greater than the paltry amount which passed into private hands from the religious corporations between 1861 and 1877.[12]

Although *antioqueño* colonization occupies a central part of this history, it would be a mistake to limit the phenomenon to it alone, as it also existed in significant proportions in the Llanos de San Martín, as in the plains and hills to the south of Tolima Grande, in the Sumapaz region and, at the beginning of the twentieth century, in the banana zone of the Magdalena; it would later play an important role in the Sabanas de Bolívar. If we limit ourselves to Antioquia, we must take into account, along with the principal current of migration towards the south and south-east, the occupation of lands by cattle latifundia in the Cauca, Magdalena, and Porce basins.

The notorious poverty and neglect of the municipal archives of the nineteenth century, compared with those that survive from the Colony, is a major disadvantage facing the historian of the period. It is of course one more reflection of the political instability, bureaucratic incapacity, and institutional fragility of that century. This has important repercussions for our analysis. It is not by chance that the expropriation of Church lands, which is a problem closely linked with high political and religious struggles and the career of General Mosquera, figures so frequently in discussions of the accumulation of land and the formation of the Republic's latifundio. Similarly, the abolition of the *resguardos* has attracted attention, much of it focussed on the politics of the decisions rather than on the demographic realities, particularly miscegenation, that lay behind them.

In many substantive aspects Republican legislation concerning public lands maintained the tradition of the Colony. Public lands were essentially the *tierras realengas*; the state was the original owner of all landed property, and in principle private persons could establish ownership by economic occupation.[13] The general backwardness of the country, the absence or precariousness of means of communication, the isolation of the different regions, and the lack of population in the valleys and basins of the great rivers were all barriers to the economic exploitation of these lands until around 1870.[14]

Between the Congress of Cúcuta of 1821 and the issuing of the Código Fiscal in 1873, the laws that were passed took into consideration diverse situations, and offered a variety of solutions for the transfer of public lands. Immediately after Independence, the public lands, along with the *secuestros*, formed a fund against which *vales* were issued to the soldiers who took part in the liberation struggle. These fell into the hands of the generals and other high-ranking officers, many of whom managed to make

deals whereby the state redeemed the *vales*, distributing to the holders
land with boundaries more or less defined.[15] The process of assignment of
lands to Republican soldiers is very well known. From the Independence
period until the middle of the century it was one of the most important
mechanisms for the redistribution of public land, first in favour of the
generals and other high officials and later in favour of merchants.[16]

Until 1873 the most important use to which these public lands were
put was as a preferred guarantee for the external debt, but the debt was
renegotiated in that year without such a provision, although the foreign
bondholders were awarded two million hectares of *baldios* in compensation.
The way was clear for the concession of public lands for purposes directly
related to agriculture and livestock-farming. The renegotiation of the debt
was merely the backdrop to a situation too glaringly obvious to go unnoticed by the legislators: more than 90 per cent of the land titles issued
to pay the external debt had not been adjudicated.

It is important to give a clear account of the subject, as it has led to
unfortunate confusions in the reading of statistics and in the interpretation
of the commentary made by Anibal Galindo.[17] There is a world of difference
between the issue of a title, whether by a *vale*, a *bono*, or in some other
way, and the concession of land. If the holder of a bond wished to exchange
it for land, he was obliged to defray the costs of survey and demarcation;
once he had done this, he could convert his bonds or *vales* into land after
complying with administrative procedure. If the property was made over to
him he became a *concesionario*, different from an *adjudicatario*, who for
our purposes may be defined as a cultivator who obtained the ownership
of public land by virtue of permanent occupation (dwelling and labour),
and who was subject to different administrative procedures.[18]

In 1874 Galindo, the national Director of Statistics, announced that
title had been issued for 1,653,000 hectares in order to redeem the external
debt, and that only 96,364 hectares had been finally adjudicated. Only
5.8 per cent of the titles had therefore been taken up.[19] The market for
bonds was depressed and land bonds stood for long periods at 20 per cent
of their nominal value.[20] The market did not find such bonds attractive,
and few of the bonds issued actually resulted in adjudications taking place.
The state had to float its loans on something else: land was a poor guarantee.

Another function attributed to the policy of disposal of public lands
was that of attracting foreign white colonists; few themes recur with greater
frequency in the Memorias and Mensajes from the middle of the century to
around 1870.

In the end neither the Independence generals nor the original holders
of the land bonds became *concesionarios*. The soldiers sold their bonds either

in private transactions or through the Montepío Militar, and the 'English bonds' found their way into the hands of the merchants. Thus, for example, ten Bogota merchants, seven of whom were among the forty richest men listed in the capital in 1878, became between 1865 and 1899 *concesionarios* of 208,000 hectares in Sumapaz, the Llanos de San Martín, and Colombia (Huila), as set out in table 26. By comparison, this makes up a greater area than was granted to the *antioqueño colonias*; according to Parsons these received 195,750 hectares.[21]

According to Emiliano Restrepo, himself a holder of large concessions in the Llanos, the *bonos territoriales* of the public debt worked out at 30 centavos a hectare, the *vales* for lands from Independence times stood on the London market at around one shilling a hectare, and in public land auctions the price paid for lands in government paper represented some 15 centavos a hectare. When survey costs were included, the average costs worked out for extents over 500 hectares at 50 centavos a hectare.[22] Using these 1870 data, an outlay of 10,000 pesos, the price of a good house in the centre of Bogotá, could secure a latifundio of 20,000 hectares. This very low price, and the low valuation of land bonds, shows the risk inherent in this sort of investment. It would not be prudent in the present state of research to pass any judgement on the economic function these speculators were performing. Speculators they certainly were, but in a highly risky sort of operation, particularly in areas like the Llanos, the Sumapaz region, or Huila. The entrepreneurial role of those who obtained concessions in those parts has still to be studied, but it was clearly rather a different business for them than it was for those who were in a good position to take advantage of rising values in the central cordillera.

The accumulation of land by the merchants of Medellín and Bogotá (and in passing we should state that Camacho Roldán & Co. were the principal agents in Bogotá dealing in concessions on behalf of the merchants of Medellín and that activity in this area was intense between 1873 and 1896) gathered pace in the seventies, encouraged by the Código Fiscal of 1873 and the admittedly hazy prospects of development on a large scale of agriculture and livestock. The extraction of quinine and rubber and the establishment of cattle-ranching were making their entry, as yet little noticed, on the scene, with high costs and proportionate risks, although at that time there was a far from systematic pattern of capital investment in these activities.[23]

The legislation of the 1870s on public lands represents another partial break with colonial legislation. Now there was not so much stimulus intended for organized nuclei of settlement, complete with a political and administrative hierarchy that the state could immediately recognize; on

Table 26. *Adjudication of public lands to ten bogotano merchants, 1875–95*

Name	*Municipio* or region	Extent (hectares)
1. Bernardo Herrera R.	Pandi	3,500
	Colombia	7,183
	Llanos de San Martín	10,000
2. José M. Saravia	Pandi	24,224
	Llanos de San Martín	12,915
	Llanos de San Martín	4,554
3. Inocencio Vargas	Pandi	1,000
	Pandi	7,209
4. Vargas and Lorenzana and Montoya	Cunday	7,594
	Llanos de San Martín	4,853
5. Mariano Tanco	Junin	7,000
	Llanos de San Martín	5,181
6. Marcelino Gutierrez	Llanos de San Martín	5,999
	Llanos de San Martín	6,000
	Llanos de San Martín	8,228
7. Indalecio Liévano	Caparrapí	5,000
8. Emiliano Restrepo	Llanos de Villavicencio/San Martín	4,236
	Llanos de Villavicencio/San Martín	1,118
	Llanos de Villavicencio/San Martín	2,971
	Llanos de Villavicencio/San Martín	6,029
	Llanos de Villavicencio/San Martín	10,000
	Llanos de Villavicencio/San Martín	1,143
9. Andrés and Joaquín Rocha Castilla	Ataco–Chaparral	6,500
	Ataco–Chaparral	2,000
	Ataco–Chaparral	6,000
	Ataco–Chaparral	1,200
10. José Bonnet	Llanos de Villavicencio/San Martín	4,861
	Llanos de Villavicencio/San Martín	2,530
	Llanos de Villavicencio/San Martín	2,930
	Llanos de Villavicencio/San Martín	4,134
	Llanos de Villavicencio/San Martín	4,788
	Llanos de Villavicencio/San Martín	14,857
	Llanos de Villavicencio/San Martín	4,788
Total		200,867

Source: Memorias del Ministro de Industrias (5 vols., Bogotá, 1931), vol. 3.

the contrary, the emphasis was placed on individual occupation.[24] After 1870 few *colonias* were created, and those that existed faced serious obstacles in obtaining official municipal status, which would have carried with it recognition of their right to distribute land to their inhabitants. This contradiction between individualistic legislation and the collective practices of occupation of land produced, in cases like those described in the next chapter, an exacerbated municipal patriotism and fierce rivalries between *municipios*. Taking all lands allotted to *colonias* between 1823 and 1931, while 65.5 per cent was distributed before 1871, between 1871 and 1905 the percentage falls to 22.6 and between 1906 and 1931 to 11.8. Individual appropriations follow a different pattern: 1823–70, 36.7 per cent; 1871–1905, 44.5 per cent; 1906–51, 18.7 per cent.[25]

Between the Código Fiscal of 1873 and Law 200 of 1936 more than ten important decrees and regulations were issued affecting basic aspects of the public-lands policy.[26] Among these aspects were the nature of the *concesionario* or *adjudicatario*, the maximum acreage that could be acquired in any one transaction, the geographic location of the lands, the height above sea level, the administrative mechanism of application and adjudication, conditions of the granting of land, and the rights of cultivators and third parties.

Until the 1905 legislation was passed the basic principles of public-land policy were laid down in the 1873 Código and in Law 48 of 1884. They were as follows:

(*a*) Public lands would be acquired, whatever their extent, by cultivation, and the state would protect the cultivator.

(*b*) Cultivators with a house constructed and land under crops were *poseedores de buena fé*.

(*c*) Should the cultivator lose the property through a civil suit he could be evicted only after he had been compensated for the value of any improvements.

(*d*) In any civil suit against a cultivator title deeds were admissible only if they dated back at least ten years.

(*e*) The land would revert to the state if ten years after the concession or adjudication it was still not being exploited.

(*f*) In any concession of public lands, the rights and property of any cultivators or *adjudicatarios* who might be on that land were automatically safeguarded.

(*g*) The zones in which public lands could be obtained by concession were geographically limited to exclude those near to centres of population.

(*h*) The system of concessions remained in force, with the acceptance of the principle that the public lands should be used not only for the payment of the internal public debt, but also for the development of infrastructural projects such as railways and roads.

(*i*) The geographic limitations imposed upon the granting of concessions referred only to applicants who were holders of bonds, not to those few who paid for their concessions in cash.

(*j*) With the intention of favouring those who cultivated the land the Código established that the area adjudicated could be up to twice the area actually cleared and under tree crops. The effect of this measure was in fact neutral, as the majority of poor settlers could not undertake such permanent crops as cacao, coffee, and sugar-cane. In the circumstances, most peasants remained outside the advantages which the law in theory offered them. It is important to make clear that the law established that those who had permanent crops (*cultivos permanentes*), would receive free either an extent equal to that cultivated or 30 additional hectares, if they could prove an occupation of five years. This principle of ceding a free additional 30 hectares was applied also to cattle-raisers and those who fenced their crops, and not in the fashion erroneously stated by McGreevey, who assumes that the 30 hectares were the total extent ceded to cattle-raisers with five years' occupation.[27]

Even so, the legislation passed from 1873 onwards was an advance on what had gone before. In 1870 an expert on the subject, Salvador Camacho Roldán, had reported that the small cultivator had a right to a maximum of only 6 hectares, and urged the government to create mechanisms to 'put within the reach of the poor classes the possibility of acquiring small amounts of land to cultivate as owners'.[28] At the other end of the scale the situation was by no means satisfactory: 'The government doesn't know that some properties even exist, let alone who owns them . . . private citizens get hold of the property and it is passed from hand to hand until there is a perfectly documented series of acts of ownership all based on an original usurpation all the more dangerous for its having occurred in the distant past, for this makes it difficult to investigate.'[29]

One of the most serious and intractable obstacles was the disadvantageous position of the independent colonist *vis-à-vis* the public administration. The legal processes involved in establishing the boundaries of a property and gaining legal title to it could be as expensive as the property itself. Not only was information regarding the law required, but also the time and money to contract the services of lawyers and surveyors, and to provide witnesses of suitable status. These things were beyond the reach of the majority of peasants, who generally had recourse to legal processes only when they were threatened with eviction. This oppressive situation played a part in the formation of latifundia worked by colonists; the new land-owners could often give positive proof that they had considerable areas of land under 'economic occupation'. The fact that the jurisdiction over public lands and their administration was continually passing from one Ministry to another added to the difficulties of the colonists. Until 1886, when this administration was finally centralized, the federal states were in some cases free to control autonomously the concessions they had themselves received from the central government.

The theory that public lands should be earned by economic exploitation continued to figure in legislation. In 1905 the continued issue of land bonds was forbidden, but it remained legal to redeem those which had been issued; the holder could receive in redemption lands at least ten kilometres away from centres of population, roads, or railways.[30] In 1907 new legislation, openly aimed at encouraging cattle-ranching and banana plantations, principally in Magdalena and Bolívar, limited to 500 hectares concessions of land more than 600 metres above sea level, and to 5,000 hectares land below this level.[31]

Many dispositions remained dead letters, and the legislation was widely ignored. Laws which stipulated that lands should revert to the state if they were not cultivated or sown as pasture within a given period, or which set minimum and maximum limits, were rarely if ever invoked. There were occasional short-lived panics among bondholders regarding the possibility of such reversion, resulting in falls in the market value of bonds, but the state seldom set out to annul concessions systematically, despite its ample power on paper to do so. This was in part because it lacked the necessary administrative machinery.

The Presidential Message of 1916 sounded a note of alarm:

'It is true that there is in existence no rigorously exact record of lands which have been adjudicated or alienated or of those which belong to the nation; successive administrations have not retained or kept in order either deeds of adjudication or the plans which those who acquire the land through adjudication or by other means should have presented; nobody knows for sure how many titles have been issued which can be used to acquire land, nor how many have been redeemed, for which reason frauds have frequently been attempted or carried through in these areas at different times.'

The Message called for the reorganization of the administration and control of public lands, and requested with urgency 'that measures be prepared to put an end to the vertiginous process of acquisition of land, which not only constitutes the dispossession in advance of generations yet to come, but must become a found of perpetual conflict and litigation'.[32]

A year later Law 71 of 1917 was approved.[33] Restricting to a total of 20 hectares the area which could be awarded to colonists with permanent crops, the law rationalized the procedure under which public lands could be acquired, but placed the poor petitioner in a difficult situation by requiring him to produce three witnesses who were themselves owners of

real property. This discriminatory clause was eventually removed in Law
74 of 1926,[34] a law directed towards resolving such social conflicts as
had been foreseen in the Presidential Message of 1916, and which was the
most important legal antecedent to Law 200 of 1936.

Statistical aspects

The statistical register of transfers of public lands should be approached with
extreme reservations, and it is only used here for want of a more reliable
source of information. While it is not precise, it does help us to understand
trends in the private appropriation of public lands.[35]

Public lands were alienated in three major ways:

(*a*) to *colonias*,

(*b*) to private *concesionarios* in redemption of bonds and *vales*, and

(*c*) to lesser private *adjudicatarios* in accordance with the principle
that public lands could be appropriated by economic exploitation.

Confining ourselves to the categories recognised by the legislation, we
arrive at the situation shown in table 27. Between 1823 and 1931 a total
of 1,235,000 hectares was adjudicated in Antioquia and Old Caldas.[36] of
which only 17 per cent went to *colonias*. Approximately 65 per cent of
these concessions were made before the coffee era. These figures suggest
that the Código of 1873 did not so much favour organized or independent
colonization as the development of a modern tropical agriculture through
the granting of liberal concessions; if so, it was unsuccessful. By the end
of the century it was already becoming evident that official prodigality
had served only to create vast and unproductive latifundia and that the
fundamental problems facing the development of capitalist agriculture were
not 'colonial' hindrances to the private appropriation of land. The average
size of concessions leaves no room for doubts concerning the creation of
latifundia:

Period	Average size (over 1,000 hectares)	Average size (under 1,000 hectares)
1823–70	11,518	491
1871–1905	3,400	416
1905–31	2,003	59

Some clarifications and emphasis are needed here. First, more than one
adjudication may have been made in favour of any one individual. Secondly,
given the conditions prevailing in a particular region, a holding of over 400
hectares can be considered a latifundio; for example, in Quindío a coffee

Table 27. *Adjudication of public lands in Antioquia and Caldas, 1823–1931 (hectares)*

Concessions	1823–70	%	1871–1905	%	1906–31	%
To *colonias*	138,692	27	48,000	10	25,000	12
To individuals (more than 1,000 ha)	310,996	60	295,820	59	88,153	41
To individuals (less than 1,000 ha)	64,775	13	159,467	31	103,344	47
Total	514,463	100	503,287	100	216,497	100

Source: Memorias del Ministro de Industrias (5 vols., 1931), vol. 3.

plantation of 80 hectares can be termed a hacienda. Thirdly, for the period 1823–70 the number of concessions over 1,000 hectares was twenty-three times greater than the number under 1,000. In the period 1871–1905 it was eight times greater, and in the period 1905–31 it was thirty-four times greater.

Given that half the total land granted had been distributed by the time the coffee take-off occurred, it would not be surprising if subsequent notari archives showed a fragmentation of ownership due not only to inheritance but also to sales. Colonization created a dynamic land market. Rapid population growth increased land values. Acquiring public lands cheaply, generally by redeeming depreciated bonds, and selling lands so acquired when conditions were favourable, speculators accumulated capital, mainly in Antioquia and Caldas. Because of legal difficulties involved in acquiring land, many independent colonists had to make sacrifices in order to save up to buy the land from the original *concesionarios*.

Although it is difficult to categorize the quantities of public lands given in concessions or adjudicated in terms of the area of each grant, some idea of this can be obtained. The figures in table 28 were obtained by following the categories employed in the agricultural censuses. If we arbitrarily define a small property as one of less than 10 hectares, and a 'medium-sized family holding' as between 10 and 49 hectares, the figures for Caldas show that only 16.7 per cent of concessions were for small properties, and 47.1 per cent for medium-sized family holdings. As for the percentage of land granted to these 64 per cent of *adjudicatarios*, if we make two generous assumptions simply to illustrate general trends – the first that eac proprietor received only one concession, and the second that each grant was the maximum possible within each category — the amount of land given in small properties is as follows:

Antioquia: 34 × 4.9 = 166.6 ha + Caldas: 134 × 4.9 =   656.6 ha
        28 × 9.9 = 277.2 ha +   157 × 9.9 = 1,554.3 ha

Subtotal   = 443.8 ha   2,210.9 ha

                                              2,654 ha

For medium-sized family holdings we have:

Antioquia: 28 × 19.9 =   557.2 ha + Caldas: 403 × 19.9 = 8,019.7 ha
        90 × 49.9 = 4,491.0 ha +   414 × 49.9 = 20,658.6 ha

Subtotal   5,048.2 ha +   28,678.3 ha

                                          = 33,726.5 ha

Total   36,381.2 ha

Summarizing our results:

Adjudications to *Latifundistas* in Antioquia and Caldas   1,022,555 ha or 96.7%
Adjudications to small holdings   2,654 ha or 0.3%
Adjudications to medium-sized holdings   33,381 ha or 3.0%

In other words, peasant colonists obtained directly *at best* 3.3 per cent of public lands given in concessions to private individuals through legally established procedures. If we take into consideration public lands granted to organized groups of local inhabitants, the total comes to approximately 212,000 hectares, or one-fifth of the total concessions to private individuals. The absence of efficient systems of rural survey, official neglect, and the general ignorance concerning vast areas obliges us to assume that many poor colonists managed to settle and survive outside official programmes, and outside official statistical records. For example, the 128,000 hectares claimed by the Empresa Burila were occupied, if the imprecise figures available are to be believed, by anywhere between 1,000 and 4,000 families of poor colonists in the jurisdiction of Armenia and Calarcá alone, without even considering those of Sevilla and Caicedonia.[37]

The structure of land-holding derived from these figures cannot be described as democratic or egalitarian. The general pattern of land transfers in *antioqueño* society is shown, on the contrary, to be much the same as that prevailing elsewhere in the country.

Of course, of the million and more hectares registered, some 700,000 were not located in areas of dense population. These formed the basis for a capitalist colonization centred on cattle-ranching, in the Cauca,

Table 28. *Number of public-land adjudications by size: Antioquia and Caldas, 1827–1931*

Size (ha)	Antioquia	Caldas	Caldas + Antioquia	Total Colombia	% of total in Caldas + Antioquia
0–4.9	34	134	168	311	54
5–9.9	28	157	185	316	58
10–19.9	28	403	431	748	57
20–49.9	90	414	504	1,942	30
50–99.9	90	289	379	689	55
100–199.9	50	180	230	448	51
200–499.9	87	92	179	498	36
500–999.9	60	35	95	307	31
1,000–1,999.9	43	14	57	221	26
2,000–4,999.9	67	15	82	307	27
5,000–9,999	16	4	20	81	25
More than 10,000	8	7	15	36	42
Total	601	1,734	2,335	5,904	40

Source: Memorias del Ministro de Industrias (5 vols., 1931), vol. 3.

Magdalena, Nús, and Porce basins. But what must be made clear is the existence of a social structure which shared essentially the same class characteristics as have been attributed to the traditional latifundist– minifundist society of the east of Colombia.

Conflicts between poor colonists and the *antioqueño concesionarios* who were opening up the mountain slopes for cattle were continuous and violent at the end of the nineteenth century.[38] In 1892 the priest of Yolombó wrote to the President of the Republic denouncing monopolistic speculation in public lands along the railway line from Puerto Berrío to Medellín. Sixteen well-known merchants of Medellín had bought up 60,000 hectares, to the detriment of small *colonos* who were forced into the Yolombó area 'owing to the increase in the population of this department, the rising price of food, the monopoly of land, the erosion and sterility of many parts, and the hateful and usurious rates which landlords impose on their *agregados*'.[39]

Apparently the government decided to apply the law and suspended the concession of public lands near the railway to holders of *bonos ter-ritoriales*. S. Ospina wrote at this time to Pedro Nel Ospina: 'In the matter of the bad articles in the regulations on public lands, for the moment they are not prejudicing us, but Fernando Restrepo é Hijos, who have claimed some 35,000 hectares in the vicinity of the Puerto Berrío railway, a grant that has now been suspended. The undersigned does not see how this can prejudice us; I suppose Tulio wrote to you at their instigation asking that this suspension might be revoked and the articles changed, so that they can go forward with their claims. Indeed I hope that you can arrange the passage of the projects on public lands, coal-mines for the railway entrepreneurs, and use of the roads by them which have been mentioned. These would be a notable benefit to us.'[40]

9. Sociopolitical elements in *antioqueño* colonization

The population of Antioquia (including the areas of *antioqueño* colonization) increased from 395,000 in 1870 to 525,000 in 1883 and to 923,00 in 1905.[1] The rhythm of urbanization was also brisk, with the population of the three most important cities in the areas of colonization, Manizales, Pereira, and Armenia, growing from 11,195 in 1870 to 53,324 in 1905.[2]

Manizales in 1850 was contributing to the *trabajo personal subsidiario* (obligatory male labour, generally of three days per year, on municipal roads and public works) a mere 550 men: 'The agriculture of the district produces each year 8,000 *fanegas* (i.e. *almudes*) maize, and consumes the same amount, with perhaps 800 cattle, 300 horses and 4 [sic] pigs in the area. There is no factory of any kind ... Nor is there a school.'[3] Its population grew as follows:[4]

1851	2,789
1870	10,362
1884	14,603
1905	24,700
1912	34,720
1918	43,203

By 1880 Manizales was a centre for the diffusion of coffee cultivation, although the size of plantings was still modest. Its strategic location between Cauca and Antioquia, and between Antioquia and the centre of the country contributed to make its principal economic activities 'transmit goods and imports', with secondary activity in the exporting of gold, hides, and coffee. The town was already attracting merchants from Medellín, who were setting up local branches for their import–export houses.[5]

By the beginning of the second decade of the twentieth century the population centres and the whole region of colonization were attracting attention because of the feverish rate at which economic growth was proceeding. Quindío, with its fertile lands, sloping terrain, and exceptionally propitious climate, was being covered by 'groves of coffee which benefit and sustain without effort the poor families who live in the district'. The number of *trapiches* worked by water power was growing, and already in the coffee industry there were complaints about the 'lack of hands'.[6]

Of all these centres, originally *fondas* where two roads crossed, 'Armenia is without any doubt the one which has progressed the most rapidly in the

180

country, from a lowly *fonda* to a *cacerío*, and then to a *cabecera de distrito*.[7] this spectacular advance took place over only twenty-three years, from 1889 to 1912. By this time the large firms engaged in threshing and drying coffee were gaining notoriety, as were the trusts which monopolized and controlled the trade in coffee from Armenia itself and the neighbouring municipalities of Calarcá, Circacia, and Montenegro. On the first Friday of every month the cattle market opened and the town filled with 'well-dressed and cheerful folk . . . and 100- and 1,000-peso notes circulate, and what is more, the much-sought-after pound sterling fills the wallets and pocketbooks of this labouring race of Titans who have dragged themselves up from a state of misery by their own efforts'. For the observer, these towns reflect 'the customs, the tastes, and the styles of a city of Antioquia transported at a blow to the Quindío valley . . .'.[8]

In the twenty years from 1910 to 1930 Caldas became the leading coffee-producer in the country. By 1913 it was already clear that the bulk of the coffee produced in Caldas was coming from the area to the south of Manizales. In that year it provided 160,000 of the total of nearly 200,000 bags which the department as a whole sent to the market. Pereira was still the second coffee centre after Manizales, but soon the 'poor colonists' who were clearing the Quindío mountain slopes would mercilessly overtake it.[9]

Coffee was not, however, the basis of the prosperity of Pereira; as far as agriculture was concerned, sugar-cane and livestock were far more important, while its commercial houses, moneylenders, and agents were moving into the Quindío region, perhaps taking advantage of the resentment provoked among Armenians by the pseudo-aristocratic airs put on by some of the new Manizales oligarchy.[10]

In 1913 Pereira boasted 370 hectares under cane, employing 306 labourers, and 6 refining plants and 17 *trapiches*, worth a total of 100,000 pesos gold. Two enterprises alone possessed more than half the land and the machinery. There were also five cattle haciendas with 9,500 of the 11,590 head of cattle registered that year.[11]

It would be difficult to argue that the railway was the cause of this development, for it reached Caldas slowly, as it did the rest of the country. Merchandise was transported on mule-back or by ox-cart as far as the ports of the Cauca or the Magdalena, although naturally the integration of the producing regions with the Cauca railway (1918–25) and the construction of the aerial cable from Manizales to Mariquita–Honda (1921) must have contributed to the continued expansion of the coffee, cattle, and agricultural activities which had started decades earlier.[12]

The later take-off towards a coffee-based economy was in the end vital for the survival and prosperity of the *finca familiar*. In these regions, in contrast to those we have already examined, the role of the haciendas as centres of diffusion and control of coffee agriculture was only modest. The capitalist colonizers sought first to monopolize the lowlands to which access was easy, and left to the poorer colonists the distant and densely wooded hills which would become with time the most productive land for coffee.

Colonizers and companies: alliances and conflicts

There were many lawsuits, some of them long and complicated, between the colonizers and the companies, and reprisals were sometimes taken outside the terms of the law. At times also the companies resorted to violence against poor colonists, destroying or setting fire to their new properties, and provoking similarly violent reactions.[13] The history of the initial conflicts between colonizers and colonists on the one hand and with the González & Salazar company on the other form part of the confused myth of an 'open' colonization in Manizales, Neira, and Salamina. The basis of litigation was naturally the possession of vast tracts of fertile but uncultivated land which the company claimed with an eye to speculatio with the higher prices created by the colonization itself. To find a definitive solution the central government itself had to intervene, along with the political and merchant elite of Antioquia. Between 1851 and 1853 the bases for an agreement among the litigants were drawn up, with the participation of Finance Minister José M. Plata. In accordance with the 185 agreement the company was to cede to the colonization programme and to the nation, without cost, approximately 40 per cent of the area to which it held title. It thereby lost about 80,000 hectares, but it kept 120,000 which had gained considerably in value in recent years, and which formed a fund for commercialization.[14] Between 1853 and 1871 there took place within the company (in which leading colonizers from Manizales were now very active) a famous lawsuit involving 21,000 hectares of excelle land in the area formed by the Claro and Chinchiná rivers and the central cordillera.[15] This was the result of the interpretation of the pact of 1853 establishing the definitive borders of the Concesión Aranzázu, which had passed into the hands of the company, and as we follow it through we shall gain an insight into the solidarity of interests between the company and the new elite of Manizales.

The 1853 agreement had laid down that the southern border of the concession should be the Chinchiná river. According to the map in official use, drawn by Codazzi in 1852, that river ran to the south of Villamaría.

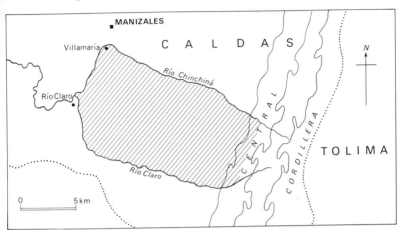

Map 5. The Concesión Aranzázu—Colonia Villamaría land dispute, 1851—70.

The inhabitants of this village, established in 1850 and recognized by the Asamblea del Cauca in 1852, argued that Codazzi was victim of 'an error made in bad faith' (*un error de mala fé*), and that the river which flowed past Villamaría to the south was the Claro, while the Chinchiná lay to the north, separating the village from Manizales. The lawyers for the colonists of Villamaría accused Marcelino Palacio, the founder and *procurador* of Manizales, of colluding with the company to confuse Codazzi, inducing him to change the names of the rivers, and in the process gaining 21,000 hectares for the company.[16] Palacio was the representative of Moreno & Walker, a firm which was a partner in the company, and these factors were complicated by political issues. The Chinchiná was the official boundary between Gran Cauca and Antioquia (the provinces of Buga and Córdova respectively), and to complicate matters further Villamaría had received from the central government a special concession of 7,680 hectares for its inhabitants.

The lawsuit dragged on for the rest of the decade, and was on the point of being settled in 1860, but the declaration of war on the federal government by Tomás Cipiano de Mosquera, President of the sovereign state of Cauca, placed the President of the Republic, Mariano Ospina, in a difficult situation. He could either respect the 1856 resolution, which had implicitly recognized that the land occupied by the inhabitants of Villamaría was public by granting the concession to which we have referred, and thus alienate the Manizales elite, who were pressing for a favourable solution, or give way to the claims of that elite. The new political and military situation forced him to adopt the latter alternative, given the strategic importance of Manizales.

The Radicals, building on Mosquera's triumph, produced copious legislation on public lands at the 1865 Convention of Rionegro. They decided that the area of Villamaría was public land before the village was founded, and that it came under the jurisdiction of Cauca, as Ospina had recognized in his 1860 resolution. But the company did not admit defeat, despite a further executive resolution in 1864 confirming the decision taken in 1860. It continued to apply pressure through its lawyer Pablo Marulanda until the Minister of the Treasury, Salvador Camacho Roldán, decided in 1871 that the lands of Villamaría had been expropriated from the company, and ordered an indemnity to be paid in the name of the nation.

A number of the new latifundists of Manizales involved in the land market came to direct the other major land concession, whose titles dated back to the colonial period. With this one too colonists came into conflict. The Concesión Burila at the end of the nineteenth century covered an area of 120,000 to 130,000 hectares between the south-east of Quindío and the north of the Cauca valley.[17] Colonists had been entering the area and clearing the land since the middle seventies, giving rise to a number of lawsuits, which were settled by the Supreme Court in 1888 in favour of the Caicedo family. As a result of this judgement members of the Manizales group proposed to the family the formation of a commercial company to take advantage of the fact that the movement of population into the Valle de la Vieja to the south was increasing the value of the Burila lands.[18]

The Caicedo family accepted the proposal. A commercial company was constituted, and issued 1,000 shares, of which 400 remained with the family which owned the land, 400 formed a 'fund for development operations', and 200 were bought from the family at their nominal price. The transaction was described by the manager of the enterprise in his 1890 report:

'by subscribing and buying shares in the company nobody is giving money to a third party, but simply contributing to a capital stock in which shareholders will have proportionate participation . . . There are few partnerships which result in the formation of a powerful limited company, with a considerable capital base, without the partners themselves having to contribute it. The truth of the matter is that the forerunners of the enterprise [Lisandro and Elisario Caicedo] have based their venture in the Burila lands which they own on the sound expectation that colonization will enhance the value of their reserves. A great number of people who have begun to cultivate public lands contiguous to those of the company are waiting impatiently for the site of the town to be laid out, so that they can put up buildings there.'[19]

This plan was never implemented, and the 400 *fanegadas* destined for the commercial and administrative centre of the new colony were never released. Nor was it possible to establish how the *dotes* (shares converted into demarcated holdings) were distributed. Each share gave the right to 200 *fanegadas*, or 130 hectares, and no partner could obtain a block of more than 3,250 hectares (25 shares). Apparently Marcelino Arango, who had married a Caicedo heiress and who was the major individual share-holder and principal 'executive' in Manizales, lost interest in the scheme. The inflow of population advanced much more rapidly than had been planned, invading the lands of the company itself.[20] Between 1910 and 1911, for example, representatives of Calarcá and Armenia petitioned the national government for authorization to grant title to colonists occupying Burila land. Unfortunately the figures they provided are very imprecise: they reported that between one and four thousand families of colonists had been settled there for some time.[21]

In 1905, 180 colonists signed a petition to the Minister of Public Works requesting him to declare as public the lands they were occupying, with houses and crops, in the Burila grant. The company, by claiming these lands, 'causes great damage to this neighbourhood [Calarcá], as they occupy a considerable area which serves for its expansion, and where many colonists have already settled, although afraid that in the future they or their children may be exposed to controversies which would lead to the loss of the fruits of their labour in different kinds of lawsuits which will perhaps have no real *raison d'etre*'.[22]

The lawsuits continued into the thirties, and the company finally lost its rights.[23] Research remains to be done to establish how much land was distributed in *dotes*, how much was sold on the market, and how much was occupied and passed into the ownership of colonists through their labour.

Concesionarios, independent colonists, and 'organized' colonists

Before giving a general résumé of the social structure which emerged in the course of the *antioqueño* colonization, I shall describe briefly the relationships between the recipients of large concessions and the independent and 'organized' colonists, and the procedures and conditions inside the *colonias*.

The evidence in this section contrasts strongly with the idyllic picture often painted of the Juntas Repartidoras and the Comisiones Agrarias. Colonization cannot be treated as if it were carried on solely by the *fundadores* and *notables* who established themselves in the agrarian colonies once the first distributions of land had been made by the Juntas. If we take the 195,000 hectares which Parsons uses as a base we would have to conclude that no more than 4,000 families benefited throughout the whole area open to colonization, and this figure is clearly unacceptable.

In the pages which follow I discuss four types of conflict common in the appropriation and distribution of public lands which suggest the existen of a considerable number of colonists who were not officially registered. They may even have been the majority. As we shall see, local control of power was the *sine qua non* in this process of distribution.

The first type of conflict shows the means used by *fundadores* to appropriate for themselves the 'improvements' (*mejoras*) made by poor *colonos*, and I illustrate this with the cases of Belalcazar and Manzanares.

The second case, the conflict-ridden one of Soledad and Fresno, illustrates the way in which the surveyors and the *fundadores* who controlled the Juntas de Repartición manipulated the 'municipal patriotism' which the fixing of boundaries aroused. They distributed land among their clientele, their family, and their friends, and in so doing reduced internal social conflicts to a minimum. But their proceedings gave birth to municipa feuds and rivalries which later are caught up in departmental party struggles Here we can see the origins of certain varieties of *cacicazgo* and the seeds of future violence.

The third case, that of Armenia and Calarcá, is similar, but introduces a new element: the collusion of the local authorities, the Municipal Council, which in the distribution of land and granting of title had replaced the Juntas with the new landowners. The interesting feature here is that the internal social conflict once again disappears with the creation of an external enemy, this time not a neighbouring municipality, but the Compañía Burila. Thus, while the *gamonales* validate or attempt to validate the titles of substantial landowners and speculators to lands which should have been distributed 'democratically' among the real inhabitants and small farmers of the municipality, they find at the same time in the lands of the Compañía Burila, either idle or under *de facto* occupations, an outlet for the aspirations of the poor, to whom they give their full political backing.

The last case is that of the *concesionario* with a large concession, advised by surveyors who had considerable experience and knowledge of local conditions and who themselves, as was notoriously the case of Buenaventur and Arana,[24] would personally benefit handsomely. Such a *concesionario* was able to employ legal sophistries, with the support of the local authoritie to evict colonists in *de facto* possession. Eviction was often carried out by force, and validated later by the judges and *alcaldes*. The case examined is that of the Río de la Vieja valley.

Whatever the situation, violence was never absent. The struggle to make headway in a frontier society where all institutions were weak and vaguely defined, and where social relations were marked by ambiguity, fostered a kind of individual violence recorded in the crime statistics and in the chronicles of some of the *fundadores*. Among the thirteen events worthy of mention in the founding of Armenia (which when it was a *corregimiento* of Salento had to endure the names of Hunger's Edge (Filo de Hambre) and Cuyabro), two were *hechos de sangre*: the first mortal wounding and the 'first man to be killed in the *plaza*'.[25] In most of these situations there is no sign of the presence of the large capitalist colonizer or the large old-established landowner, such as we find in Sonsón and in the central zone of Caldas. In these regions of the Quindío and north-east Tolima, on the other side of the central cordillera, land was the means of economic and social ascent for men who came from further down the scale. Of great local influence, such men were not known in the provincial capitals until the electoral and political services they could perform became interesting to the notables there. As has already been stated, they were not directly related by family with the established elites. Many came from the decadent mining regions of the west, lands of old, even sixteenth-century, settlement: Marmato, Supía, Salamina, or south-east Antioquia. They were looking for gold. For an idea of the make-up and size of one of these colonies let us take the settlement of Pavas in the *municipio* of Villahermosa. According to the register of the Agrarian Commission, when the land was distributed it contained 761 inhabitants, of whom 555 were 'children less than 21 years old', who had no right to land. Of the inhabitants 206 settlers were given lands; 47 single men, 13 widows, and 146 married men. The average age of the adults was thirty-four, and the plots distributed varied from 32 to 87 hectares (proportional to the size of the family), the most frequent size being 52 hectares.[26]

For a long time the only proof of property was the minutes of these commissions, so that the destruction of these documents was a favourite device of those who wished to deny such colonies any legitimate existence or to dispute the property rights of a given group of colonists. Only a few rare historians have looked on these archives with a reverence equal to that of the settlers themselves. In 1890 the inhabitants of Armenia failed to obtain recognition as a corregimiento from the municipality of Salento, although they had succeeded in 'obtaining the services of a deputy' who would arrange in Popayán that Armenia should become head of a district.

Ironically, Salento then became a subordinate *corregimiento* of Armenia, and when the Salento municipal archives arrived in Armenia on a donkey, there was public rejoicing:

Dejó de ser pueblo
y pasó a ser ciudad
esta villa nuestra,
de casualidad

Ya viene el archivo.
Ya viene y se va
y con tantas vueltas
se nos va a acabar.

Díganle a Circacia,
Filandia y Calarcá,
que el 'Cuyabro' tiene
Distrito en propiedad.[27]

(This town of ours has ceased to be a village and become a city. Here comes the archive; how it comes and goes; all this coming and going will wear it out. Tell Circasia, Filandia, and Calarcá that Armenia is now a properly recognized district.)

In the war of 1876, it was not by chance that the first thing General Casabianca did when he entered Salento was to destroy its archives.[28]

Founders and poor colonists in Belalcazar and Manzanares

'In the year 1888 Señores Pedro Felipe Orozco and Climaco Pizarro originated the foundation of the village now called Belalcazar. Señores Pedro and Jorge Orozco spread the word throughout the department of Antioquia, principally around Támesis, calling the attention of all hard-working men to the opportunity, urging them to go into the Cauca and join in this philanthropic work which their nephew had undertaken.'[29]

Thus begins a petition of a group of *colonos* to the Governor of Caldas in 1906. The subsequent history of the foundation is a typical one. Once the land was cleared and the first crops planted, the founders sold out to lesser men, who in order to take up possession forced out the occupants, who described their situation as follows: 'now that these men have in their possession the fruits of our labours, it can be said of us, as they have stolen our work, that these men and the authorities they sustain treat us like slaves'.[30] Then in 1904–6 comes open conflict. There are physical assaults, attacks on crops, cattle, houses; there are threats and ambushes, of a sort that prefigure the mid-twentieth-century violence described by Jaime Arocha.[31] There is open collusion between the new medium proprietors who wish to dislodge the *colonos* and the local authorities. What is not clear from the memorandum is the actual recruiting mechanism employed by the Orozcos. The petition initially describes them as 'protectors of the poor', which perhaps implies that their role included distributing seed and tools and perhaps making some advances for the journey and the first few months of life in the colony.

In Manzanares the situation was similar, though with some additional elements. In July 1879 the inhabitants of Manzanares addressed the President of the Union, seeking guarantees for the land which the nation had granted to cultivators in the village in 1866.[32] On 27 January 1880 they became more explicit, and denounced the fact that 'egoism on the one hand and bad faith on the other caused deviations and fatal consequences in the adjudications, and one of the surveyors was the first to violate them, buying and selling lots of land, contrary to article 10 of the Law of 2 April 1871, naming fictitious *adjudicatarios* and giving less to those who should have received more, more to those who should have received less, and letting himself be guided by his own preferences and favouritism'.

In view of this many adjudications were annulled. But annulment was no answer, as it affected 'many very poor people with large families . . . as the land-dealers and speculators are beginning to try and take our land from us, claiming that it belongs to them and saying that the latest adjudications are null . . . and thus they intimidate the poor'. As if this were not enough, the petitioners continue: 'we also attach a certificate as proof of the loss of the archives which were kept in the building which was used as a public office . . . among the archives stolen was that of the Comisión Agraria, including the documents which we could have presented as proof of the legality within which the latest members of the Comisión proceeded'.[33]

In this account two of the major figures of organized colonization emerge: the surveyor and the *gamonal*, the *técnico* and the *político*. Working closely as allies, they redistributed the lands of the colonies to their personal advantage and to that of their favourites, relatives, and henchmen. Such manoeuvres were more complex than they appear at first sight. The *gamonales* had recourse to provincial legislation in their municipal struggles. One of the classic mechanisms was the arrangement of municipal boundaries, which came under the provincial assemblies. If an order (*ordenanza*) could be approved changing the boundaries of a *municipio de colonización*, then the inhabitants of one *municipio* could be favoured at the expense of those of another when the law regarding concession of land was applied.

The 'grudge' between Fresno and Soledad

These points are illustrated in the conflicts between Fresno and Soledad.

In August 1892 the inhabitants of Fresno sent a *Memorial* to the Congress of the Republic putting forward the following facts:[34]

(*a*) That in 1857 Colonel Anselmo Pineda had fulfilled the steps requisite to declare as public land a large stretch near the Herveo plateau, and established there the settlement of Fresno, which already had 200 colonists.

(*b*) One year later the government had created the municipality of Fresno, and made it a grant of 7,680 hectares to be distributed among the inhabitants in accordance with the terms of the Recopilación Granadina; 'there was still not the remotest intention of founding Manzanares, Soledad, Marulanda, or any other municipality in the vicinity of Fresno'.

(*c*) In 1871 the Asamblea de Tolima created the municipality of Soledad, separating it from Fresno.

(*d*) 12,000 hectares were ceded to Soledad in that year.

(*e*) In view of the expansion of Fresno, the national government granted it a further 20,000 hectares in 1879, and at the time of writing 27,680 hectares were under cultivation 'without a square inch of land left waste'.

(*f*) The surveyor Joaquín Buenaventura was charged with making the plans for the boundaries between Soledad and Fresno, and decided to take 6,000 hectares from Fresno to add to the 12,000 granted to Soledad, as a result of which the inhabitants of the latter settlement 'have made their intentions plain by actually invading the land belonging to Fresno, which has caused and continues to cause endless disturbances . . . and incalculable damage, above all by inflaming the bitter hostility which Fresno and Soledad feel towards each other'.

In this suit over boundaries the national government seemed initially to favour Fresno, but a second *ordenanza* from the Departmental Assembly of Tolima decided in 1892 to accept Buenaventura's case and, as a consequen 'half or more than half of the territory of Fresno passed into the hands of the inhabitants of Soledad'.[35]

Collusion in Calarcá

In October 1909 the Municipal Council of Calarcá asked the national government if it could grant to Luis Felipe and Cristobal Jaramillo 5,032 hectares of public land in payment of a municipal debt, and if this was possible within the terms of Law 56 of 1905, or Law 36 of 1907, which gave Calarcá land to distribute among its inhabitants.[36]

Although the same Council reported in 1909 that there were still at least 1,500 hectares uncultivated and without title issued, and in December of the same year took the decision under the terms of Law 36 of 1907 to demarcate and distribute the surplus lands to new inhabitants as they arrived, there were continual complaints from the municipal representative (*personero*) and the parish priest between 1908 and 1909 that 'the Council has suspended the measuring out of land without any reason, causing the gravest of harm'.[37]

In fact what was going on under cover of the exchange of communications was the transfer of vast tracts of land to established and influential *hacendados* such as the Jaramillo brothers. In December 1910 the Council no longer mentioned municipal debts, as it had done fifteen months earlier, but argued that 'the brothers Luis Felipe and Cristobal Jaramillo and others who clear land and set up their *fincas* believing that they were protected' were 'in possession in good faith'. Therefore the authorities of Calarcá were consulting the Ministry as to whether they might be given title to a quantity of land very much greater than that stipulated in the law.[38]

In 1907 Pedro Henao, one of the *fundadores* of Calarcá, wrote to the Ministry, hoping that his 'efforts would not be in vain'. He wished 'to show the people of Calarcá that I have tried to favour them, and to show those who seek to swindle them out of their land that they are impotent'. He stated the case of a number of colonists who were working land which 'is said to belong to the company working the *Salina de Platarica*; the intention is to throw them off, for they are besieged by so-called owners with titles to many times over the 300 hectares to which they are entitled'.[39]

In 1904 and 1905 the Governor of Caldas wrote to all *alcades* ordering them to seek to solve agrarian conflicts swiftly, and to support colonist cultivators who had been occupying land for more than a year, even against the presumed owners.[40] Telegrams seeking the aid of national authorities began to proliferate, as did orders from the central government instructing the *alcades* to defend the interests of the cultivators. Priests and in some cases *personeros* appear to have been the standard-bearers in this amorphous movement which was gaining strength towards 1910. Telegrams such as this are common in the archive of *baldíos*: 'Through judicial orders police evicted us violently lands Risaralda. We seek justice. Colonists', or this one from Calarcá, dated 23 November 1911, 'Despite papers conceded Municipal Council dated only 1908, awaiting definitive judgement we were evicted from improvements possessed twelve years permanent crops houses buildings which were destroyed by machete by local *alcalde*, police. Colonists.'[41]

Evictions in the Río la Vieja

On 4 December 1887, the inhabitants of Filandia sent to the national authorities a *memorial* denouncing a plan by José M. Marulanda, Sotero Suárez, Florencio Echeverría, and Juan A. Botero[42] for acquiring, by means of concession deeds or land bonds, lands on the right bank of the La Vieja river. There were already many small cultivators established there, with houses built and crops planted. The colonists argued that the lands in question could not be alienated under the provisions of Law 48 of 1882, as they were situated close to centres of population (Cartago, Pereira, Filandia) They sought official protection against 'those who, armed with their capital, throw off the land men with families who are at present occupying it, thus discouraging immigration to the state, which is growing every day'.[43]

In 1889, after many such denunciations and complaints, the Finance Ministry issued a resolution to prevent 'a handful of speculators in land bonds from gaining control of vast expanses of land at the expense of the inhabitants who live there and cultivate the soil'. The resolution referred to Salento and Quindío; the colonists of Salento had been petitioning the government for some time.[44] On 28 April 1891, the *alcalde* of the district wrote to the Finance Minister:

'In the vast tracts of public land which fall under our jurisdiction there are hundreds of people established and cultivating crops . . . As the region within the La Vieja basin is very beautiful, and known to be fertile, many people have been gripped by ambition, and others are working together to expand their possessions, and have come to believe that they own as much land as takes their fancy, much of it uncultivated. In this locality there are rich men and many more poor ones who can only achieve anything over a long period; for this reason the former have been enlarging their holdings until we are facing a situation in which the latter have no chance of increasing theirs. This has led to continuous quarrels amongst them, and as in these mountains and woods the majority are ignorant, and have no idea what the law might be on this subject, they are being abused by a certain class of individuals with influence and money who unfortunately are sometimes successful over some social classes; this works directly against the unfortunate families who come to these parts with nothing but their physical strength and faith in the fertility of the soil. Your Excellency will understand that it is necessary to give the poor settlers wide-ranging guarantees, for as they lack resources of their own they seek protection in the law from the attacks of the wealthy with their money behind them.'[45]

It was in this atmosphere that the serious conflicts between colonists and landowners were incubated, and they continued from 1905 to 1915, with the money of the '*ricos*' eliminating the protection which the law offered to the '*pobres*'. On 21 February 1912, for example, sixty families of cultivators from La Cristalina, Pereira, wrote to the Ministry describing themselves as cultivators of sugar-cane, coffee, *plátano*, and pasture on lands they had held without interruption for more than thirty years. They told how 'a Sr José Pío Durán appeared with his lawyer Jesús M. Salazar and claimed the land on the basis of a later title deed'. The colonists complained that these gentlemen 'woo over the *alcalde* of Pereira' and that this official had decided to order that they should be forcibly evicted, 'going so far as to order that our houses should be destroyed by fire to avoid any payment for improvements'.[46]

In 1914 the representative of Belalcazar also complained that there were 'innumerable conflicts, clashes, and quarrels between the inhabitants of the town, some of whom call themselves colonists and cultivators, while others are *concesionarios* of public lands belonging to the nation and located in this district'.[47]

Manuel M. Grisales, one of the *fundadores* of Manizales, originally a natural ally of the peasant colonists, became in time an ardent disputer of their rights to the land; by then he was in the fortunate position of being able to make his money and influence speak. In 1892 the aged Grisales acquired with land bonds 2,000 hectares on the banks of the La Vieja near the town of Filandia, where hundreds of colonists had long been established with 'houses, specially sown pasture for over a thousand head of cattle, and crops of other kinds such as plantations of sugar-cane, *plátano*, cacao, coffee, and tobacco'. Grisales had first sought adjudication of the land in 1877, and between that date and the resolution of 1892 there were, according to the colonists, a series of violations of procedure and of civil law. Grisales increased his claim to 5,000 hectares, with the land in question 'mostly very distant from that mentioned and requested in the adjudication'.

In 1886 the Finance Minister declared the provincial adjudication corrupt, and ordered the 'defects noted to be rectified'. Grisales swiftly complied with various brief formalities in the prefecture of Salento, 'rectified' the errors, and was rewarded with the definitive adjudication in 1892.[48]

Final considerations

What Alejandro López called the struggle between the axe and legal papers (*hacha y papel sellado*) was not confined to *antioqueño* colonization. In Cundinamarca, especially in the Sumapaz region, both legal and rougher conflicts between colonists and landowners were very frequent from the end of the nineteenth century until well into the twentieth. In northern Santander there is also evidence of the sort of collusion in which local political authorities tilted the balance in questions of land distribution:

'On the twentieth of the present month [January 1894] Captain Tobías Alvarez stationed a squad of the National Guard here under the orders of Ramón González Valencia, and the latter, with the support of Elías Calderón, the *alcalde* of San Cayetano, and of the judge of the same municipality, is intimidating and evicting the colonists on the public lands called La Contenta and Pan de Azucar, claiming as a pretext a judicial proceeding for which no law authorizes the use of armed force. Fdo. Pedro S. Martínez, Gabriel and Federico Rincón.'[50] The meeting in 1914 on the plains of Pandi of an *alcalde* making a visual inspection of public lands and the *hacendado* Vargas de la Roche and his mounted guard could figure in an anthology devoted to the Wild West.[51]

The accounts of the travellers who crossed the districts between Cali and Medellín in the last third of the nineteenth century differ somewhat. We have the optimistic view of Röthlisberger to balance against the more guarded and sombre opinions of Brisson.[52] The difference of opinions regarding conditions of life in the region colonized by the *antioqueños* has certainly continued, and lost none of its vigour. A technical report would show that in the fifties the *caldense* coffee-growers were better off than the *minifundistas* of the highlands of Boyacá or Nariño, but would note that their income was much lower than that of unskilled workers in the cities. The dispersion of wealth and of income is not less there than it is in other areas in the country.[53]

In this section we have shown that the small farmer lived in a society which was far from egalitarian and under institutions which were never stable. It remains true that nobody could prevent very many colonists from settling and surviving despite title deeds, subclauses, judgements, edicts, evictions, threats, mortgage deeds, and bills of sale. Thousands of families established themselves silently and unperceived near the new settlements with their 'palaces of mud and zinc', the roads, the new haciendas, and the old latifundia. Many had to face one usurper or another from time to time if they were to survive, but without doubt they all suffered from the weakness of axe against paper. In this stratified, but dynamic and ambitious society, the coffee smallholder was born, destined for a hard and precarious life. The public land archives are full of *memoriales* such as this, which reveals in 1929 the existence of a 'legal problem' which had begun as soon as the land had been occupied:

'I am making this petition to you because the [twelve] individuals named above, all of them growers of coffee, in order to improve their economic situation seek to obtain loans from the Banco Agrícola Hipotecario at low interest, and thus to free themselves from the suffocating pressure of the speculators and loan sharks who take advantage of their needs,

buying their harvests in advance at ridiculous prices, so that the real
workers never get out of debt, while they live subject to the damnable
conditions which their exploiters impose upon them.'[54]

By around 1910 all the *municipios* mentioned in this chapter had become
important coffee-producing centres in Caldas and Tolima. The former
department was becoming a centre of rapid diffusion of coffee cultivation.
From 1913 onwards it doubled its production every six years, until at
the time of the Depression it was producing a third of the national crop.
The Quindío had become the most densely coffee-growing region of the
Republic.

The transition from a subsistence frontier to one based on coffee was
rapid, but very unequal in its effect. For example, the municipalities of
Caldas continued to suffer very high rates of infant mortality and tropical
disease into the second half of this century.[55] In addition prostitution
and venereal disease followed the seasonal cycle of the harvest.[56] Peasant
poverty found some relief, though, and the region became much better
integrated into the communications network of the country. In 1917–18
the Pacific railway reached Pereira. In 1917 it had carried only 8,633 bags
of coffee; in 1919 this increased to 76,470; in 1921 to 218,292. In 1922
Manizales was connected with Mariquita, near the Magdalena river, by the
aerial cargo cableway, owned by the English La Dorada railway company.
The 72-kilometre line could carry ten tonnes an hour, and lowered costs to
37 pesos a tonne. In that year comparative costs per tonne via the Pacific
and via the Atlantic from and to Manizales were as follows:

	Pacific	Atlantic
Manizales–New York (1 tonne coffee)	69.80 pesos	68.29 pesos
New York–Manizales (1 tonne merchandise)	130.00 pesos	126.00 pesos

Thus coffee chose the cable route, despite problems between the cable company and the river steamers, which preferred Caracolí to La Dorada.[57] But
in the 1920s the construction of the railway was enthusiastically carried
on towards Manizales, which was reached in 1918. A year later Armenia
was connected with the Pacific railway by the line to Nacederos.[58]

The majority of the population (65–70 per cent) was still rural, although
the towns grew with the coffee. The threshing was centralized; the buyers'
agents reached into the small municipalities.[59] All the same, though Manizales,
Armenia, and Pereira had the look of substantial towns, and boasted
200,000 inhabitants between them by 1938.[60] The tone of town life was
still very rural. The fire in Manizales in 1925 revealed problems that were

to become very evident later on. According to the Governor's *Informe*, 'The industrious working people, like the members of our high society, worked very hard and efficiently to put out the fire. But part of the populace, made up of vagabonds and thieves from the lower depths, people with records known to the police and the courts, gave itself up to robbery and showed itself quite unworried for the fate of the threatened city.'[61]

The region's coffee, its principal wealth, was not processed with the minimum care needed to obtain the premium price of 'Medellín' grades. Only Aguadas and Pácora in the north produced this quality and earned the premium. 'Caldas is losing large sums of money by the unscientific way it prepares its coffee for export.' In the Quindío the indebted peasants sold their coffee wet, and the intermediaries and storekeeper buyers dried it out in the sun. They paid the growers 30–40 per cent less than the going price for dry coffee; drying it in the sun could take two or three weeks, depending on the weather.[62]

In 1928 the enthusiasm for railways and cables was interrupted by the first signs of crisis, severely affecting the departmental budget.[63] The political change of 1930, the end of 'Conservative hegemony', further intensified the electoral struggle for increasingly scarce municipal and departmental resources. The atmosphere was propitious for the mobilization of new social groups, which had scarcely come on the scene before they suffered the affliction of widespread unemployment. For the agricultural elite of Manizales it was essential now to cut production costs and at the same time improve quality, principally through better processing. But, as Antonio García noted, the productive sector had a very rustic and primitive technology, routine-bound and 'irrational'. Through its peculiar family origins work appeared costless (*el trabajo aparece sin valor*), and in times of falling prices 'it is not possible to surpass the small *finca* either in its capacity to resist crisis or in the processes it uses for selecting the beans'.[64] In a later chapter we shall see how escape from the crisis of the thirties was found through the consolidation of the small farmer, by policies deliberately adopted at national level.

The intense commercialization of agriculture, in a market structure integrated vertically by monopsonistic buyers, did not bring about a fundamental change in the peasant base. It did not, as is so often axiomatically affirmed, create a rural middle class with sufficient size and purchasing power to stimulate industrial investment. Income from coffee was very concentrated, and, as we shall see, the free-trade orientation in economic policy reaffirmed itself rigorously in the 1920s, at the time of the great Caldas expansion. Economic policies at this time, when looked at from the point of view of income distribution or their impact on the general development of the country, were not very different from those of the tobacco-boom years 1852–65. The integration of the small producer into the money economy was superficial.

Peasant-family labour involved in the widening coffee frontier had no private money cost, although this work represented the most important source of social capitalization in the country. Peasant society had no need of liquid funds to expand the crop because 'it financed itself'.[65] Liquid funds irrigated the system of commercialization and transport. In the real coffee zones profits were concentrated in the hands of a chain of intermediaries. From time to time these also exploited the weakness of the legal title of substantial numbers of small cultivators to their own advantage.

10. Coffee expansion and the strengthening of the Liberal model of development, 1910–50

The continuous growth of the production of coffee between 1910 and 1960 is the most decisive phenomenon in the recent economic history of Colombia. The country became the second most important world supplier of coffee, and the most important supplier of mild coffees. The impact of coffee expansion on economic growth, on the diversification of the productive and occupational structure, and on the distribution of income among classes, groups, and regions is therefore central to contemporary historical analysis. Given the present state of research, it is impossible to give a full and precise account of this impact and of the multiple relationships between the coffee sector and the rest of the sectors of the Colombian economy. Many themes still remain unstudied and require the slow construction of time-series and the systemization of basic document sources. Even then, it would be odd to write about coffee in Colombia without making ample reference to the external parameters by which it is circumscribed.

During the First World War, Colombia became a first-order coffee-exporting country. The annual average of production between 1915 and 1917 was 800,000 bags of 60 kg. The annual rate of growth of Colombian production from 1915–17 to 1970–2 was 4.2 per cent,[1] against an annual growth of world consumption averaging 2.2 per cent for the same period. It was logical that the highest rates of growth should have been reached in the earlier periods. From 1915–18 to 1930–2, it was 9.93 per cent per annum; in the decade 1930–2 to 1940–3, 3.66 per cent; between 1940–2 and 1957–9, 2.42 per cent. Between 1957–9 and 1970–2 the rate of growth fell to zero, reflecting the success of the policy of stabilization of supply laid down by the International Coffee Agreements of 1962 and 1968. The price increase of the years 1975–7 has done away with the programmes of 'development and diversification' adopted by stages after 1960. It is possible that between 1975 and 1985 Colombian production may increase by 20–25 per cent. With new cultivation techniques, the expansion of land in coffee may not exceed 100,000 hectares – a little less than 10 per cent of the land of 1975.

In this chapter, the term 'Liberal model of development' refers to a capitalistic economic system based fundamentally, although not exclusively, on the principle of self-regulation through the market. State intervention

198

is not aimed at transforming the existing structures, but rather at palliating the most traumatic effects of property and income concentration and of cycles in the world market. This means that the private sector predominates in the formulation of macroeconomic policy, and that state interventionism, no matter how widespread its activity, functions according to the requirements of the private sector.[2] Three sub-periods can be distinguished in the period from the First World War to the Korean War.

(1) Until 1929, there was a resurgence of *laissez-faire*. The system based on coffee export shows the same mixture of positive and perverse symptoms which are attributed to the tobacco boom of the nineteenth century:[3] extraordinary concentration of income, massive imports of final consumer goods, the gold standard, strong foreign participation in the control of marketing, and accelerated development of the transportation infrastructure. But there are basic differences: coffee cultivation was developed on a geographic and productive scale never known by tobacco. In terms of the area cultivated, employment, and geographical location, coffee was, at least until 1940, the leading sector of the economy; its contribution to GDP was much greater than that of any other sector except non-coffee agriculture.[4] But the world market in the first half of the twentieth century had changed much from the market of 1850–75. The international economy which had consolidated itself between 1870 and 1914, the classical imperialist period, suffered three grave collapses: the First World War, the Depression of 1929–33 and the Second World War. In these forty years, Colombia depended for its development on a single product, coffee, and on one market, the United States. Between 1910 and 1960, coffee represented between 60 and 80 per cent of the value of Colombian exports, and the United States imported between 80 and 90 per cent of Colombian coffee exported.

(2) The world crisis stimulated industrial development in final consumer goods – an effect of drastic changes in economic policy that were meant to resolve the fiscal and balance-of-payments deficits now thrown into sharp relief. In this period, coffee exports continued to expand, and Colombia consolidated her position as the second world producer of coffee. Several elements contributed to this industrial development, the most accelerated the country has experienced. There was the entrepreneurial experience that had been gained in the industries sporadically founded since the beginning of the twentieth century. There was devaluation, which made imports more expensive and native industry competitive. Protectionist policy had some impact, although a recent study has demonstrated that its effect was minimal compared with that of devaluation. Demand had increased, particularly in urban areas, encouraged by the direction of public

expenditure. Industrial production costs were low: labour, raw materials, and machinery were cheap, and, taken together, these could give a high rate of return. The government, in its attempts to reconstruct the old agrarian economy, imposed restrictions on the freedom of the banks to invest in industry, but entrepreneurs nevertheless expanded by reinvesting their profits, and in addition showed themselves able to absorb the higher costs implied in the 1935 tax reform.[5]

(3) By 1945 an industrial sector had come into being, not through a coherent policy, but rather through a combination of favourable local circumstances and policies designed to overcome the Depression. Colombian industry was the result of the ability of entrepreneurs to take advantage of such favourable conjunctures, to invest when and where the rate of return was high. The entrepreneurs and industrialists who were prominent in 1945 adhered unconditionally to the tenets of the Liberal model, whose efficacy they had seen confirmed. However, post-war market conditions, the dynamics of industrialization in a period of unfamiliar diversification and of renewed foreign investment in industry, coloured their aspirations of building capitalism along classical free-enterprise lines.[6] After the war, two substantial social and economic changes made a widening of the sphere of state intervention inevitable. First, accelerated urbanization threatened to dislocate the bases of the political system; secondly, rapid import-substitution now made exchange-rate and tariff policies critically important. With the depression of coffee prices in 1955–7, a 'structural' crisis of the balance of payments would make interventionist policies even more pronounced.

Coffee tied the Colombian economy to the world market, and through coffee were expressed the limitations and possibilities of a particular type of dependent capitalism. Accepting this view, in contrast with those which presuppose a semi-colonial or neo-colonial connection, implies shifting the emphasis of one's analysis from the loss of political sovereignty and from the terms of trade and the different elasticities in the demand for coffee or manufactured goods. One has to look at the structure of coffee production and how coffee is financed and traded, and one has to understand the formal and informal mechanisms that concentrate income from coffee.[7] Among these one must pay particular attention to the Federación Nacional de Cafeteros.

In the following pages I will present an account of the development of the twentieth-century Liberal model. Here the first stage, from 1910 to 1930, marks the return to nineteenth-century Liberal policies, but in a context of a more centralized state and in an atmosphere of lessened ideological pugnacity – the role of religion, still considerable, is less of a

bone of contention than in the previous half century.[8] The crisis of the
Depression, while creating conditions that encouraged industrialization
and greater diversification, did not alter the Liberal model fundamentally,
although the economic function of the state became increasingly indispensable and multifarious. My argument is that the structural condition
of coffee expansion supported the Liberal model of development.

The resurgence of *laissez-faire*, 1910–30

With the caution characteristic of his statements, Ospina Vásquez argued
the establishment of an industrial protectionist policy from the period of
Reyes, who 'effected the protectionist system outlined by Núñez'.[9] After
Reyes, Ospina Vásquez remarks, 'protectionist policy was a generally
accepted fact'.[10] The basis of such general approval was perhaps that
'protection had not appeared as a form of state intervention . . . The
mechanism of protection through the customs hides its true nature.'[11]
But by mixing up the economic principles of these policies with the need
for state intervention, Ospina notes that the Liberals took interventionism
as their standard, and that 'Manchester Conservatives' appeared, suspecting
that behind such theories 'socialism' was hiding.[12] Even so, much of their
inspiration was derived from the Conservative Republic. Perhaps a kind
of mercantilism was the basis on which many Conservative circles accepted
protectionist principles. Ospina's postulates, and his documentation of
the polemics of 1912–13 and those occurring after 1920, make abundantly
evident a very important dimension of the prevailing economic ideology
of the era. Through force of habit, from repetition and misuse of language,
certain ideas ended up by being regarded as essential aspects of the economic
structure itself.[13] A more consistent argument seems to me to be that
protectionism was a disguised method of increasing state revenues in an
age in which between 60 and 80 per cent of the state income was derived
from tariffs. It is likely that the degree of effective protection was quite
low. In themselves, the tariffs do not indicate the degree of effective
protection.[14] The economic policies had as their central object fiscal and
monetary soundness, and the resolution of the problems of the internal
and external public debt.

The return to the gold standard was a much slower and more arduous
process than had been initially foreseen. The peso was overvalued. The rate
of exchange remained generally stable during these years. Only in unusual
circumstances, as in 1919–20, was there a temporary devaluation.[15] But
internal prices and wages were increased after the First World War, and
faster between 1926 and 1929.[16] This overvaluation, based on a system

based partially on the gold standard, cancelled the customs protection; and in effect the increase in internal demand, a result of urbanization and of coffee, was met with cheap imports. Why did the export sector not push for a devaluation which would set the rate of exchange at market price? Speculative interventions were very frequent in a money market that until 1923 still lacked a central bank. The demand for gold greatly exceeded supply. Differentials in the rate of exchange existed from one place to another in the Republic – mainly between the Atlantic coast and the interior.[17] Antioquia was a producer of gold, mostly under control of British firms which were exporting it. But it seems to me that there are two peculiarities in the marketing of coffee which explain the exporters' lack of interest in devaluation. First, in many cases, they were creditors for the importers, and secondly, vertical control of marketing allowed them to impose too low a level of purchase prices: in 1920, the dominance of peasant farms in the supply of coffee was evident, but while functioning in a vertically controlled marketing system, they did not form the basis of the internal market as has so often been supposed – they remained on the margin of the market economy. The beneficiaries were the intermediaries and the storekeepers, not the original small producers.

It is important to underline this structural base of *laissez-faire* policy. Coffee income returning to the country was not applied to the amortization of investment in coffee, nor to reinvestment in this sector. The peasant base of production grew its own basic food necessities; the demand for other foodstuffs, drinks, and clothing would be maintained at the traditional low levels. In other words, the productive sector represented no pressure on the balance of payments, and remained at the edge of international price oscillations, as long as it neither demanded imported goods nor drew much of the money supply.[18] There is a disarticulation between the productive sphere and that of marketing and export. Income from coffee was applied to imports of consumer goods for high-income groups and to imports of mass consumption goods for the urban and semi-urban popular classes, and to a much lesser degree for the peasants. One must bear in mind that per capita income was very low (U.S. $100 per year between 192? and 1929),[19] so that aggregate demand was concentrated in high-income groups, and in the cities, which had grown substantially in this period.[20] The advantages of an overvalued rate of exchange are evident for the importer able to satisfy an increased demand in spite of the low per capita income, offering goods at competitive prices. The close links between the coffee-grower and the subsistence economy maintained production costs at the lowest possible level, and devaluation as a means of promoting exports was unnecessary. The overvalued rate of exchange thus allowed an increased import capacity. This explains why, in spite of the differential tariffs, and opportunities in the area of investment in textile manufacture and in other industries after the First World War,[21] the increase in aggregate demand resulting from the extraordinary expansion of coffee exports would basically be satisfied with imports. According to a recent study, imports as a percentage of domestic demand were in 1927–8 as follows: textiles, 81; paper, 81; rubber, 99; chemicals, 52; non-metallic minerals, 75; basic metals, 97; metal products, 82; non-electrical machinery, 88; electrical machinery and transport equipment, 100.[22] The Kemmerer Mission of 1923, which represented the purest Liberal and monetarist orthodoxy, must have clearly understood the impact of this overvaluation, and for this reason rapidly abandoned its desire to obtain a reduction in the tariff.[23]

The crisis of 1920 and the penetration of American monopsonies

In failures, one can also clearly see the lines of this *laissez-faire* scheme; in the coffee crisis of 1918–20, all the large Colombian coffee-exporting companies went bankrupt, and the monopsonistic control passed into North American hands. The state no more intervened than it had when Montoya & Sáenz went bankrupt in 1857.

Between August and December 1918, that is in four months, coffee prices rose by 71 per cent in New York as a result of two coincidental events: a sharp drop in supply due to frost in Brazil and the sudden reopening of European demand when the Armistice was signed in November. During the first quarter of 1919, the price remained high; in the six months from April to August of the same year, it rose an additional 21 per cent, and at this point began a gradual and sustained decline. In June 1920, it was again nearly at the same level as that of April 1919, but in the four following months it fell by 45 per cent.[24]

Colombian exporters were not prepared for this development. Subtracting the costs of maritime transport, insurance, and commissions, the rise in the price represented in 1919 an additional income of U.S. $40 million on the Colombian balance of trade. Internal monetary difficulties made it almost impossible to buy up the harvest that year. In Manizales the shortage of currency was such that local commerce had to be organized on the basis of a return to barter, with the use of *café pilado de primera clase* as a means of exchange. To solve this scarcity of currency the government decreed that pounds sterling would be legal tender for all payments to the national Treasury, a measure of 'genius', attributed to the Minister Esteban Jaramillo, but in fact inspired by the British Minister in Bogotá, who could see that in the re-establishment of trade after the First World War British interests were being displaced by those of the United States, and thought it a good time to encourage Colombia towards this entry into the sterling area. The Treasury in London thought this step a little naive, and somewhat dangerous: a significant build-up of sterling balances in Colombia might lead the Colombian authorities to demand at some stage that they be converted into gold. The measure was defeated in the tribunals, much to the relief of the British Legation.[25]

But between May and June 1920 the merchants of Bogotá, Medellín, and even Manizales were gripped by 'import fever'. Employing letters of credit put out by companies like Pedro A. López and Vásquez, Correa & Co., and very liberal credit lines extended by national and foreign banks, they bought with reckless extravagance. The trade surplus which Colombia enjoyed with the United States, and which caused the peso to rise against the dollar, disappeared in the second half of the year. As a wave of conspicuous consumption overtook the *haute bourgeoisie* of the expanding cities, the central government launched itself into grandiose plans for public works. The river transport companies and port authorities were unable to handle the goods which flooded down upon them. When prices began to fall in the middle of 1920, the national banks were driven to the point of suspending payments, and had to go to the English and North American banks for support. The Banco López of Bogotá, the Banco Sucre of Medellín, and the Banco del Ruíz of Manizales all received considerable injections of dollars to keep them solvent, and ended up in the control of foreign interests.[26] The Bank of New York and the Battery Park National Bank announced that they were seizing the coffee shipped by the companies of Alejandro Angel, Vásquez, Correa & Co. and the Antioquian Commercial Co. The government, whose budget was heavily dependent on customs duties, was in alarming straits in 1921, and the payment of army, police, and judicial salaries was delayed. Service of the national debt was not paid, and by the end of the year the fiscal deficit reached 14 million pesos.[27]

All the Colombian firms in New York went bankrupt in 1920. There were many causes, but two of the most important reveal the extreme vulnerability of this kind of financial speculation. The fall in prices which began in May 1920 took the firms by surprise with large stocks which they had bought at prices between two and three times higher than those which the market was now showing. The extraordinary congestion of river transport on the Magdalena, and in addition a severe drought, delayed shipping, while prices continued their headlong fall. The firms had been buying coffee in the Medellín market from October 1919 to May 1920 at 6.50 pesos per *arroba* on average, and by December 1920 the price had fallen to 2.10 pesos.

In order to meet their obligations, Vásquez, Correa & Co. took receipt between September and October 1920 of U.S. $1,291,000 from their branch in Medellín. Banks, local commerce, and even the state government of Antioquia, through its Casa de Moneda, came to their aid, but in vain. At the end of 1921, after a complicated series of agreements between the creditors, the assets of the firm were auctioned off in New York; the proceeds did not pay off 15 per cent of the firm's liabilities. The bankruptcy hearings began in Medellín in 1923 and were concluded in 1927, with the family connections between the partners and two leading politicians of the Ospina family (Pedro Nel Ospina and Mariano Ospina Pérez) provoking criticisms and press debates along party lines.[28]

After this débâcle, the predominance of North American monopolies was marked until the forties, as can be seen in Appendix 3. The banks themselves came to finance the purchase of coffee direct from the producers, through the activity of powerful firms acting throughout the Latin American market, such as the Great Atlantic & Pacific Tea Co., and its subsidiary the American Coffee Co. The Commercial Bank of Spanish America (which had begun life modestly in London in 1881 with the name of Casa de Comisiones de Enrique Cortés & Cía) was established and absorbed in 1926 by the Anglo-South American Bank, also recently established. The same period saw the founding of the Banco Mercantil de las Américas and the National City Bank.

Linked with the Commercial Bank were the Parga Cortés, an important Tolima family of coffee-growers and politicians. At harvest time the Anglo-South American Bank would receive instructions to buy coffee and export it to San Francisco. It had close links with the Cundinamarca *hacendados*, who were influential in forming public opinion in the twenties, and also in the infant national coffee *gremio*, whose relatively small exports (never more than 5,000 bags of 60 kilos) they financed.

The most important business in Colombia of the Banco Mercantil de las Américas was the purchasing and exporting of coffee; the familiarity of the future President, Alfonso López Pumarejo, with this field, acquired in his father's firm, led him to the position of general manager in the critical years from 1918 to 1920. The City Bank bought for another leading New York house, Amsinck.[29] Other firms, such as Huth & Co., used Colombian firms as a front to mask their own activities. In Manizales they used Carlos Pinzón & Co.[30] and in Antioquia it was held that the Tolima firm Francisco Pineda López was actually in the hands of Amsinck.[31]

It is difficult to argue from a study of the purchase market that competition between these firms to control different municipalities necessarily led to better prices for the producer. Between the peasant who sold his coffee in the markets of the interior and these firms there was a chain of intermediaries who were better placed to profit from a trade war (see fig. 4).

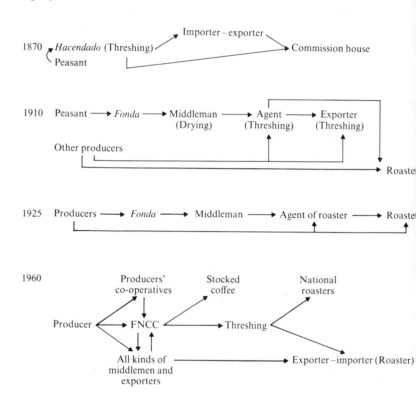

Fig. 4. The structure of internal marketing.

It is not surprising that towards the end of the twenties voices were raised in the circles of the coffee bourgeoisie of Antioquia in condemnation of the monopolistic presence of the North American roasters in the Colombian markets. It is significant that Rafael Ospina Pérez should have described these firms as 'the claws of Yankee imperialism' in a letter published by *El Tiempo* of Bogotá.[32] Despite this, the process by which a Colombian elite, closely linked with finance capital, gained control of coffee in the name of the coffee-growers and of the 'national interest' was to develop slowly. Independently of the nationality of the exporting firms, which may anyway have been a mere facade, the trade continued to be in the hands of a handful of firms which had undoubtedly developed somewhat the rudimentary logic of the Negocio X and Y of Medellín.[33]

The 'Colombian Renaissance'

The growth of foreign trade between 1905 and 1929 shows a curve similar to that experienced in the *laissez-faire* period from 1850 to 1875; the movement of continued growth was more evident after 1916, by which time the levels of the 1885–1910 period had been far surpassed.

Table 29. *Colombia: index of growth of foreign trade, 1905–29 (U.S. dollars)*

Three-year period	Annual averages (1905–7 = 100)		
	Imports (c.i.f.)	Exports (f.o.b.)	Coffee exports
1905–7	100	100	100
1916–18	221	270	352
1927–9	1,150	902	1,473

Source: Banco de la República, *XLII y XLIII Informe Anual del Gerente a la Junta Directiva* (2 vols., Bogotá, 1965–6), vol. 2, p. 190.

The expansion of coffee production in the twenties was based on traditional methods of cultivation of an extensive nature, with low technology, but with costs of production kept low, as the majority of peasant producers maintained a standard of living which bordered on subsistence level. Between 1920 and 1930 coffee production doubled, and the resulting increase in employment, demand, and savings was the principal cause in the expansion of means of payment, given the policy of monetary restriction and exchange stability maintained by the Banco de la República. Inflation in those years, moderate in comparison with that of the Regeneration or of the present day, was not a decisive factor in the expansion of coffee production, given that after 1922 external prices recovered and remained at profitable levels until the crisis of 1929. It was therefore possible for exports to increase despite the fact that the rate of exchange specifically favoured the importers of consumer goods and foodstuffs.

The great geographic and occupational mobility of the labour force which arose out of the expansion of the internal market and of coffee production after the First World War had unforeseen consequences for the economic organization and the social, political, and institutional life of Colombia. Modern forms of social organization spread through the centres which felt the impact of accelerated economic growth, such as the banana

plantations along the Magdalena, the oilfields of Santander, and the commercial and industrial centres of Giradot, Bogotá, and Medellín.[34] By the
end of the First World War Colombia had the seventh largest volume of
foreign trade in South America; by 1927 she had moved into fourth place.
Between 1913 and 1928 the volume of exports increased fourfold, while
that of imports rose fivefold. In three years only, from 1924 to 1927,
bank deposits doubled, and in the summer of 1928 Colombian bonds were
still standing at the price at which they had been issued in the New York
market. Means of payment tripled between 1923 and 1928, while the cost
of living in Bogotá increased by 10 per cent per annum.[35]

The expansion of economic and financial activity made itself immediatel
felt in public revenues. In that period 56 per cent of government income
came from customs duties, and these rose from U.S. $22 million in 1922
to $75 million in 1927. In 1925 there was, perhaps for the first
time in history, a genuine current surplus in the government budget. In
this decade it was clear that the Colombian policy of public investments
was not independent, but a consequence of the need to export capital
from financial centres, principally New York;[36] these centres brought
heavy pressure for the provision of a transport infrastructure at all levels,
whether national, departmental, or municipal. Plans abounded to expand
road and rail networks, augment or replace rolling stock, build bridges,
improve and develop ports, install greater electrical capacity, and build
aqueducts and canals along the Magdalena.

A thick slice of the U.S. $40 million 'mortgage credit' went to large mer-
chants and landowners, who clearly did not invest the money in the land.
Production in much of this sector was completely dislocated by the freedom
to import. By the end of 1928 the debt attributable to these investments
in progress was nearly U.S. $200 million. Between 1928 and 1929 there
came the first manifestations of a regionally based political crisis, due to
the geographical location of public works, while the world financial crisis
found concrete expression in the repatriation of capital. As the Treasury saw
its coffers empty, programmes of public works were abandoned; bureaucratic and political conflicts within the governing party became more acute,
and there was an abrupt end to the paradise of adventurers, contractors, and
bankers of dubious standing,[37] most of them North American, who had
invaded the country after 1926.

Before the fall of the New York stock market in 1929, the Colombian
economy had experienced its own crisis in and after September 1928.
The confused measures of 1929 only aggravated the situation, and when in
1930 the wave of the world depression wrought its full effect upon Col-

ombia's export and import structure, it only proved the wisdom of the old saw that no situation is so bad that it cannot get worse.

By 1929 it was clear that agricultural production for internal consumption had fallen to hitherto unheard-of levels during the happy years of the boom. The food necessary to sustain urban centres had to be imported,[38] while the accumulated deficit in the trade balance (excluding oil and bananas) came to $220 million between 1925 and 1929. The contraction of the public works budget was dramatic: it was $48 million in 1928, $36 million in 1929, and $14 million in 1930. Deflation accelerated and money in circulation fell by 20 per cent between 1928 and 1930; even so, the government deficit of $7 million in 1927 rose to $16 million or more in 1929.[39]

In the twenties there began a process of integration of the regional elites, of Bogotá, Antioquia, and Valle principally, and the creation of bourgeoisie at a national level. During the 'dance of the millions' from 1926 to 1928 it was hardly able to accommodate itself to the government. Even more, the integration of regional sectors into a national ruling class showed itself in sharp divisions within the Conservative party, which continued to administer public affairs in accordance with the traditional practices of clientelism and *caciquismo*.[40] The modernizing projects of the bourgeoisie clashed with the interests of traditional politicians, who sought to continue their nineteenth-century role in the organization of '*empleomania*'. Despite the fact that, since the times of Reyes, Uribe Uribe, and Restrepo, landowners', bankers' and exporters' groups had been expressing their dissatisfaction with the archaism of professional politicians,[41] this intermediate social stratum was very well entrenched in the administration, and was the only one which could win elections. All in all it was still the legitimizing base of the Colombian political system. It was therefore necessary that regional economic interests in their process of national integration, seeking to modernize the state apparatus and give it an orientation which would allow the process of decision-making regarding economic policy to be rationalized, should come to an accommodation with the bureaucrats, *caciques*, and political professionals who derived their position, prestige, and power from their connections with the government and their access to budget funds. This clash of interests between the bourgeoisie and professional politicians should not be taken too far. Powerful families such as the Ospinas or the Holguíns were greatly influential within the Conservative party, but in the more modest provinces and local communities the political minnows followed a logic alien to that of the 'Leviathans'.[42]

The contraction of the public works budget brought to a head these frictions between competing groups. An example of this was the dispute between Finance Minister Esteban Jaramillo, the representative in Abadia's cabinet of the rising capitalists of Antioquia and of North American banking groups (supposedly opposed to British financial interests), with 'the Minister of Works, Dr Sotero Peñuela, an ignorant and half-barbarous political "boss" from Boyacá, [who] opposed the whole scheme with the obstinacy of a man unaccustomed to give or even have reasons for the policy of local interests'.[43] The apple of discord was the creation of the Consejo de Vías de Comunicación, promoted by Jaramillo, who had already gone so far as to place upon it three North American advisers; Sotero Peñuela opposed the project violently and publicly. However, these were only the preliminary skirmishes in the division of the Conservatives in the 1929 elections. The alliance of the Conservative oligarchies (Bogotá–Medellín–Cali) was broken when the 'Bogotá–Medellín axis' decided to support the poet Valencia against the Cauca valley General, Vásquez Cobo, and the Archbishop Primate played the role of a political novice.[44] The situation in that decade of agitation was well summed up by the British Minister in Bogotá:

'Modernism, based upon loans and foreign participation, offers Colombia nothing but political and social dangers engendered by the weakening of the old respect for the Church and the Conservative traditions, economic subservience, and in consequence, an appreciable step nearer to diplomatic absorption into the orbit of the United States. These effects of the Colombian renaissance are now making themselves felt, and the Church is the loser at every step.'[45]

To summarize: from the beginning of 1929, inflation and bureaucratic and political chaos discredited and divided the government party. Between January 1929 and January 1930 the price of coffee on the world market fell by 50 per cent, and the 40,000 workers engaged in public works projects began to lose their jobs. In 1931 the price of industrial and banking shares declined to a half or a third of their previous value; debtors were unable to pay. Urban unemployment increased, and the most recent migrants, least well equipped to face the crisis in the towns, temporarily deserted them and returned to the countryside.

The end of the *belle époque* saw the birth of the hopes and illusions of some sectors of the working classes, of rural labourers, artisans, and the lower ranks of the bureaucracy. The strikes, social protests by the unemployed, and movements of solidarity which gathered momentum between 1929 and 1934 began to lose energy and impact, and ended by collapsing from lack of organization and dedicated leadership, and, naturally, in the face of repression by the government. Rebel strongholds were still in existence in a few Communist-dominated rural areas in 1936, but by then

Liberalism was on the ascent with its proposals for social reform and economic modernization, and a populist rhetoric which displaced and left stranded political movements of socialist and Marxist orientation. The coffee zone in the south-east of Cundinamarca was invaded by social agitation. Its geographic dependence upon Bogotá, and its social dependence on an important group of the oligarchy in the capital, gave it a national importance which was reflected in the casuistic legal reforms of 1936.

In this atmosphere, charged with brusque and unforeseen changes in policies, orientations, and values, in part a product of the unusual growth in foreign trade in the economy as a whole after the First World War, there was bound to be a realignment of political and social forces and a restructuring of the relations between the dominant class as a whole and the state apparatus which had been mediated, as we have seen, by a traditional political system based almost exclusively upon professional politicians who represented the interests of the dominant economic groups, and a federal system of *caciques*, clientelistic demands, and corruption.

The atmosphere of optimism if not of complete freedom from concern which the oligarchies of the twenties found when they broke through the shell of provincialism to discover the *país nacional* was of short duration. They soon had to face regional conflicts of a political and social nature sparked off by economic growth, and then by the world depression, in a different context from that of the traditional model of two-party conflicts. New social agents appeared on the political horizon, and disturbing and disquieting symptoms signalled the possible fragility of the political structure. Optimism gave way to uncertainty, as it appeared that there was no solution within a general framework of continuity. Nothing was so eloquent in this respect as the maladroitness of the Archbishop Primate in the 1930 elections. But any socialist alternative was a long way beyond the horizon, and the middle classes were not strong enough to propose a different programme for the nation. The crisis, in these circumstances, allowed the coffee bourgeoisie to weld its class interests to the state in a form as indissoluble as an old Catholic marriage then was.

After the crisis of 1930 and as a result of the abandonment of the gold standard in September 1931, the imposition of exchange controls, the regulating of gold exports, and legislation concerning moratoria for private debtors, the English banks began to lose ground in the banking and coffee business,[46] while the North American roasters began to buy directly from the important internal markets. Processing was increasingly absorbed into the marketing rather than production side, and more than ever oriented towards the tastes of the North American market. Table 30 reveals the

Table 30. *Markets for Colombian coffee exports, 1863/7–1965/9 (percentage distribution)*

Five-year average	U.S.A.	Europe	Others
1863–7[a]	26	74	–
1873–7[a]	40	60	–
1883–7[b]	65	35	–
1893–7[b]	44	56	–
1903–7[b]	72	28	–
1915–19[c]	91	7	2
1925–9[c]	92	7	1
1935–9[d]	77	19	4
1939–43[e]	93	4	3
1944–8[e]	92	3	5
1955–9[f]	81	17	2
1965–9[f]	47	49	3

Sources: a Van Delden Laërne, *Brazil and Java*, p. 413. *b* Beyer, 'Colombian Coffee', pp. 368–71. *c* FNCC *Boletín de Información y Estadística*, 1, 2 (April 1932), p. 40. *d* Ibid. 5, 23 (May 1942), p. 596. *e* Ibid. 8, 29 (July 1949), p. 23. *f* Revista del Banco de la República, no. 517 (June 1970), pp. 168–9.

extraordinary importance (already noticeable in the nineteenth century) of the United States as the buyer of Colombian coffee. After the First World War, and from then until the end of the fifties, exporters to the United States shaped the coffee market in Colombia. The increasing participation of European countries in the twenties and thirties was halted by the Second World War. Until the thirties this pattern of trade led to many problems in Colombia's trade policy: some of Colombia's imports, mainly textiles from Manchester, had to be paid for in dollars earned by the sale of coffee in the United States.[47]

Gradual Interventionism, 1930s–1950s

The Colombian state has historically played a feeble role in the articulation of agro-exporting sectors with the world market. At the beginning this role was strictly limited by Liberal orthodoxy to making possible the development of the productive structure oriented 'towards the exterior', or, according to the view taken at the time, towards the strengthening of the 'links with civilization', the export of gold and the products of tropical agriculture, and the import of the consumer goods, as capital and immigrants never reached this tropical region in the quantities desired. The social structure and the state experienced considerable transformations with the economic growth which this integration brought with it, and the functions of the state necessarily expanded as economic policy penetrated fields which had hitherto been closed to it. The relations between the state and the coffee bourgeoisie have to be understood in the broader framework of the functions of the state in the development of an infant and dependent capitalism with all its inherent limitations, contradictions, and frailties. Whether during the orthodox *laissez-faire* era or in the period of interventionism and *dirigisme*, the state is supposed to be the political organization capable of articulating the internal productive structure towards the world market, and absorbing and attenuating through its economic policy the cyclical disruptions of that market. This function of articulating internal production towards the world market and responding to crises or booms of external origin through the state is the political and historical expression of a new and weak bourgeoisie which held political power along the lines of the Republican model, but was incapable of sustaining itself on the internal market, finding on the contrary that agro-export activity was the only path to economic growth and, it might be argued, to national integration.

In the era of the 'minimal' state, mechanisms for the appropriation of the land, the organization of the labour force, and the construction of a transport system were favoured and supported. However, we have seen in earlier chapters that, despite the general orientation towards the export of agricultural products, the place of coffee was both modest and insecure, while the absence of a hegemonic class found expression in civil wars and political instability. By 1930 profound changes had taken place in the socioeconomic and demographic structure of the country and in the spatial distribution of the population. The peasants were migrating to the towns, the seats of commerce and of textile, food, and bottled-drink factories, of administration, artisans' workshops, schools, universities, and barracks. In 1870 5 per cent of the population lived in the towns, and by 1938 this figure had increased to 30 per cent.[48] Such a change implied equally far-reaching transformations in the occupational structure and in geographic mobility, and these factors were creating significant tensions in the coffee regions of the east. The sporadic shortage of hands and the resulting inter-regional competition for the labour force was intensified by the attractiveness of public works programmes, which offered not only the temptation of a nominally higher wage, but also escape from restrictions on personal free-dom such as those which gave a 'pseudo-servile' character to peonage in the haciendas of Boyacá and the coffee districts. Industry was growing considerably with the expansion of the market, and was protected by monetary and tariff policies after 1931. Its contribution to the GNP was 7 per cent in 1925, as against 17 per cent in 1953. The leap forward in industrial growth took place between 1947 and 1953, when coffee earnings accumulated during the war were prodigally distributed between industrial monopolies and large-scale importers.[49]

By this time regional imbalances were mainly explicable in terms of the production and internal marketing of coffee. The old centres of regional power, the preserves of military and political *caudillos*, Gran Cauca, Boyacá and Santander, were definitively relegated to a subordinate role. The new pattern of regionalism was shaped by the distribution of coffee cultivation and by the localization of industry in the towns which bordered the coffee belt: the Cali–Medellín axis to the east, and the capital, Bogotá. The principal port for coffee exports was Buenaventura, dependent upon Cali, while imports came on the whole through Barranquilla. When the 1929–30 crisis began, the pre-eminence of coffee in the balance of trade was overwhelming, particularly if one discounts oil, gold, and bananas, the other important exports, as the income they generated did not return to Colombia, despite the exchange controls applied as a result of the abandonment of the gold standard. All these changes affected the atmosphere in which the coffee bourgeoisie was recreated. In fact, this social class was in no way reminiscent of that described in previous chapters.

The world depression and the rise of the coffee *gremio*

Colombia, unlike many other Latin American countries, faced the world crisis without suffering severely traumatic effects in its political system, and it rapidly recovered from its adverse effects. The kind of exporting economy described above contributed to this relative stability. The direct producers felt the fall of the *external price* only remotely, since their income was barely above subsistence level. It would have been quite different if, in place of peasant farms, the base of Colombian production had been composed of large haciendas.

Between 1928 and 1933, there were two crises differing, if not in their effects, at least in their causes. The first was the fall in the coffee price due to the exceptionally large Brazilian harvests between 1928 and 1930, which swelled their stocks to record level and caused prices to fall from mid 1928.[50] It is possible that without the world crisis coffee prices would have become depressed in any event during the 1930s, although it is difficult to know if this would have occurred with the same severity. The second crisis is directly related to the international depression, and was felt in the suspension of credit and foreign investment, and in rapid capital

repatriation. Schematically, it can be stated that the two crises over-
lapped, the one commercial and the other financial, although obviously
these two were tightly interlinked in 1929. But the commercial crisis
was less severe than the financial. According to the tables on foreign trade
between 1923 and 1934, the total value of Colombian exports fell by 39
per cent, but exports of petroleum, gold, and to some extent bananas
and platinum had no impact on the balance of payments, so that the only
effective exports were coffee exports. The decrease in the value of these
between 1923 and 1934 was 26 per cent in dollar terms. Devaluation was
sufficient to enable the exporters to maintain their profit, since the border
of coffee cultivation was constantly pushed back through peasant 'self-
finance'. Net inflow of foreign exchange was sufficient to meet industrial
demand. Towards 1934 the symptoms of economic recovery were evident.

The economic measures taken to face the world crisis show the extreme
vulnerability of the Colombian economy, ever more dependent on the
North American market. They also show the dominance of the coffee-
exporting group. It would not be an exaggeration to state that macroeconomic orientation was based on the interests of this group. In effect,
the financial crisis principally affected the state and the banking and credit
system. The initial response was on the most orthodox lines: maintenance
of the gold standard and monetary parity and deflation. This policy, laid
down in its principal tenets by the second Kemmerer Mission of 1931 by
means of seventeen law projects, of which eleven were presented to
Congress and implemented by the government, concentrated initially on
decreasing public expenditure by means of sharp budgetary reductions, and
on limiting the general level of consumption.[51]

The pressure of public opinion for a moratorium on payment of the
external public debt clashed head-on with rigid thinking that preferred
resorting to short-term foreign borrowing to alleviate the balance-of-
payments problem, and to internal borrowing for a partial and transitory
solution of the fiscal deficit. A detailed study of how these credit negotiations were carried on would perhaps further reveal the degree of governmental submission to conditions injurious to national sovereignty.[52] The
economic effects of this policy were unemployment and the exhaustion
of reserves: from U.S. $64 million in 1928, they fell to $14 million in 1931.
With the abandonment of the gold standard and the consequent devaluation
of the peso, economic recovery began, and the levels of internal demand,
public expenditure, and employment rose to their old levels. These measures
were accompanied by a moratorium on private debts, the establishment of
exchange controls, and the suppression or limitation of payments in gold
and foreign exchange.[53] In commercial policy one can better appreciate

the overwhelming influence of the coffee export sector, implicit ally of the commercial interests of the United States. Tariff policy was directed towards stabilizing the commercial balance through the introduction of discriminatory tariffs against the countries holding deficits with Colombia. The formulation of a dual tariff was advocated by the Manager of the Federación Nacional de Cafeteros, Mariano Ospina Pérez, and by other influential politicians such as the ex-minister and petroleum lawyer Alberto Urdaneta Arbeláez. A study of the negotiation process for the commercial treaty with the United States, signed in October 1935, shows that the crisis strengthened the agro-exporting model of development, in spite of industrial diversification. On this point, it is important to draw attention to some aspects of the industrial development of the years 1930–45.[54]

α   A recent study of the industrialization of this period shows that, rather than protectionist policy, the 41 per cent devaluation between 1932 and 1935 was the most important stimulus to industrialization. This devaluation was proposed as a means of facing the negative terms of trade, and it simultaneously favoured coffee-exporters and already installed industries, as imports grew more expensive. Under none of the four Liberal administrations (1930–46) are there signs that a deliberately industrialist policy was being developed. The second Kemmerer Mission, and later the discussion over the ratification of the new commercial treaty with the United States (1934–5), made the limitations of an excessive protectionist policy manifest as did popular urban pressure against the rise in the cost of living. Explicit evidence abounds that 'the sacrifice being demanded of the consumer' limited the level of protection fixed in the tariff of 1931 and its later revisions. As the ECLA demonstrates, the policy of economic development through public expenditure was oriented towards reconstructing the agrarian economy, especially that being developed in commercial units: wheat, rice, cotton, copra, sugar, and tobacco.[55] Credit legislation was oriented towards favouring the marketing of crops, and it developed production while at the same time prohibiting long-term finance, which was precisely what was required by industry.[56] Further, during the Alfonso López government, in a heated atmosphere of political polarization, the industrialists threw themselves into opposition.[57] The government advanced what was according to the ECLA a premature tax reform, the burden of which fell more heavily on the industrial enterprises and higher income groups in the cities,[58] and brought in some additional measures of labour legislation. It uttered accusations that tariffs were 'an instrument of abusive exploitation', used by businessmen educated in the 'old Conservative school of privilege' who lacked a modern mentality: they associated taxes, which they should in fairness pay, and workers' rights with Communism.[59] The fairness of the tax reform was based, according to López, on the hope that through it 'flourishing industry' would return part of its abnormal earnings, obtained under shelter of high protectionist tariffs.[60] 'Our policy', wrote President López, 'is revolutionary without being Marxist class-based, but it in no way tries to challenge the existing order. It does not conspire against capital, nor does it seek an opportunity to do away with private property, giving the factories to the workers and the haciendas to the peasants.' His objective was to disabuse the capitalist of 'the bourgeois hope that it is possible to avoid the strife and struggle of economic interests' and 'to try to persuade him to join the new world which has appeared without his consent'.[61] This realistic policy was little appreciated by the industrialists, precisely because of the sociological characteristics López noted: firms and businessmen were the same before and after the crisis. What is certain is that without the 'premature' tax reform, the level of public expenditure would have fallen, increasing urban unemployment and decreasing demand. Industry could afford this reform because it remained within a very low cost structure, especially as regards wages. Along with the substantial cattlemen and farmers, the industrialists were the beneficiaries of the concentration of income which was accentuated during the Liberal Republic.[62] In this context there was little chance that either directly or through state intervention there would arise conflicts between the coffee-exporting sector and importers and industrialists. There was industrial development, but in the words of the President who considered himself to be the most industrialist of Presidents, Alfonso López Pumarejo, 'a predominantly exporting country, and one lacking major industry, cannot aspire even to the most limited autarky, and must increase its economic ties and extend the network of reciprocal interests between the foreign buyers and the national sellers'.[63]

In this milieu, a private body such as the Federación Nacional de Cafeteros de Colombia played a vital role, and its development can be studied in parallel with the process of widening state functions. The FNCC is perhaps the most difficult of institutions to define, and political scientists have asked themselves if it is a bureaucracy, an interest group, or a quasi-official body.[64] The Supreme Court of Justice laid down the legal doctrine that it is a private company entity carrying out essential public functions for the national interest,[65] and in documents of the international organizations, the Federación is described as a semi-official body. As a bureaucracy, the FNCC seems to be more efficient than other organizations carrying out parallel functions, such as the Ministry of Agriculture, given its apolitical nature and its administrative stability.

In recruitment and promotion of administrative personnel, the FNCC has the modern characteristics of a civil-service-type structure. But anyone who intervenes in the decision-taking process becomes entangled in traditional patterns. There is intermarriage between coffee-*hacendado* and coffee-export families. The FNCC contains such traditional elements in its top management, and these gradually adjust to changes in their decision-making functions, as they adjust in their relations with the professional internal administration staff.[66] Without denying that these sociological traits help towards a fuller understanding of the functions of the Federación it seems more important to concentrate on the nature of the FNCC's relations with the state, and to study its role in the distribution of coffee income. I discuss this in the final chapter of this book.

The remote origins of the FNCC can be traced back to the Sociedad de Agricultores de Colombia — founded in the 1870s by Salvador Camacho Roldán — a landowners' organization which spread the fundamental precepts of Liberal economic orthodoxy and the rudiments of tropical agriculture, provided information concerning the state of the international market, and oriented literate opinion in the centre of the country towards economic policies favourable to agricultural development. It aimed at removing the political, social, and economic obstacles which agriculture faced. From 1904 to 1906 the members of the society were largely the big coffee-growers of Cundinamarca and Tolima, but the coffee depression between 1907 and 1910 led them to attempt once more to represent wider sectors.

The participation of politicians, whether great landowners and *hacendado* or simply those who aspired to such a status, was notorious in the first years of the organization. The agricultural and commercial congresses of 1911, 1920, 1926, and 1927 were attended by many leading politicians, ex-Presidents, ex-candidates, and Governors, the representatives of regional interests, illustrating the links between agriculture and the politicians, in the absence of a more organic institutional connection. The 'pressures' from the different groups were in those days far more diffuse and unstable, and passed through Congress itself.[67] One feature became rapidly apparent: the large landowners rapidly took up Uribe Uribe's argument that representative groups should be of a 'technical' rather than a 'political' nature. They defined themselves as the 'producing classes', outside the ambiguous and unproductive world of the professional politicians. This exclusion of partisan politics was only partial, as important regional and national leaders participated actively in these societies, and it had a precise and restricted connotation: it sought to create, beyond party affiliations, a group and class identity, and thus to protect the group against the instability inherent in political involvement. These landowners' 'clubs' were able to operate while direct state intervention was unnecessary or undesirable. But the modernization of the twenties brought their policies and their representatives out of the confines of the clubs. Such factors as the occasional incompatibility of long- and short-term interests and the gradual appearance of new economic groups at the helm in the nation promoted attempts to operate through more formal and stable organizations, and to create more systematic relationships between the state, political circles, and public opinion.

The initiative for the creation of a special organization to represent the coffee-growers came principally from the *hacendados* and politicians of Bogotá and Antioquia. After two special meetings, the first in 1920 and the second in 1927, the institution was finally created with the income from a modest tax on coffee exports.[68] Whoever studies the first three years in the life of the FNCC is bound to emerge surprised by its weak and uncertain character. Its slight income was paid by the national Treasury with considerable delays, and its leaders limited themselves to 'federating' members, frequenting the waiting rooms of the different Ministry offices, and making releases to the press. The group seemed to be thinking in terms of a federation of growers of all kinds, great or small, and to be seeking legitimacy as a trader in the internal market: its organizational and financial resources were insignificant, and regional groups still had considerable power and autonomy. As a result of the 1929–30 crisis the FNCC underwent a profound reshaping of its character and style of leadership.[69] The federation of producers rapidly became the spokesman for the large producers and exporters. Its internal structure changed and by 1934 and 1935 the FNCC was a closed institution controlled from above.[70] Modifications were introduced into its statutes which remain in force today and which are the basis of the stability of its general management, and of the absolute control by that management over the organization. It has had only two general managers in the last forty years. Its formal structure is that of a 'wheel of fortune': half the members of the municipal committees are elected by departmental committees, with half of those in turn elected by the national committee. The national committee is elected by the national coffee congress, which is made up of delegates elected by the departmental committees. Besides these elected members, different proportions of delegates were admitted *ex officio*, such as Ministers and Governors.[71] Alfonso López attempted to 'officialize' the FNCC by changing the proportion of government members and members elected by the national coffee congress, but this change in the composition of the coffee hierarchy had few practical results, and the state majority was finally abandoned in the fifties.[72]

The principal functions which the Federación sought to perform in the first years of its existence were mostly related to the market. Intellectual authorities such as Alejandro López (who as a result of pressure from the President would be manager of the Federación for the brief period from November 1935 until July 1937) wrote in 1930 that it was necessary to leave production itself free of interference, and concentrate efforts in the spheres of trade, finance, and propaganda.[73] This policy was carried out during the period of consolidation. Analysis of the legislation concerning coffee shows clearly how the FNCC was successful in achieving legislation favourable to the rationalization of the market:

(*a*) through the organization and development of the Almacenes Generale de Depósito, the Caja Agraria, and the bonos de prenda agraria,[74]

(*b*) the regulation of the types and grades of coffee for export, oriented to the North American market and aimed at guaranteeing a standard of quality which, with prices depressed and in reply to the Brazilian valorizatio programme, would displace Brazilian coffee while sacrificing the difference in price (leading to an expansion of the market in return for a lower price, a profitable policy in the long term and one which was the basis of the penetration of European markets in the sixties),[75]

(*c*) pressures to obtain rates of exchange favourable to the 'coffee dollars', particularly in the critical years from 1932 to 1936,[76] and to devalue in step with competitors, particularly Brazil, from 1931 to 1935,

(*d*) pressures on behalf of those debtors who had become insolvent between 1931 and 1933,[77]

(*e*) the creation of special offices for advertising and the promotion of exports in Europe and the United States,[78] and

(*f*) the directing of international coffee policy in particular alongside or against Brazil, which was bearing the full cost of the valorization programme for coffee until 1937 saw the 'price war' begin.[79]

The degree to which the policy of restricting the coffee supply, for which Alfonso López Pumarejo pleaded from 1933, was based on his experience as an export banker or on doctrinaire principles is a question yet to be studied. The fact remains that policies of widening cultivation and increasing exports, underwritten by the devaluation of the peso, made much more sense if levels of employment, income, and import capacity were to be maintained. What was suitable for the producing countries taken together, and especially for Brazil, which was carrying the heaviest load of intervention in the market to restrict supply, did not necessarily offer advantages to countries protected by this policy, as was Colombia.[80] Brazil's policy of destroying stocks had as a consequence a differential price decrease between the Santos 4 type and Manizales coffee. The price differential of

Colombian coffee over Brazilian evolved as follows: 1913–17, 24.65 per cent; 1918–22, 20 per cent; 1925–7, 20.52 per cent; 1928–32, 19.16 per cent; 1933–7, 13.22 per cent. This made Colombian coffee increasingly attractive in the world market.[81] In view of this situation, Brazil decided to abandon its valorization policy in 1937, a year in which 17.2 million bags were destroyed. Paradoxically, the result was an increase in the differential to 30.17 per cent in 1938, and 36.45 per cent in 1939, although Brazil had increased the total volume of its exports from 12 million bags in 1937 to 17 million in 1938. What occurred was that 'the differential was restored by allowing Brazil's [price] to fall and not by increasing the price of the milds . . . the relatively low levels of coffee prices had induced many roasters to improve their blends by inclusion of the milds'.[82] Thus, Colombia compensated for the fall of unit value by increasing the volume of supply, and by its increased participation in a more differentiated buyer's market. The polemic between Alejandro López and Mariano Ospina from 1933 to 1937 was a rehash of arguments first brought to the fore by Uribe Uribe as a result of the Taubaté Agreement in 1906. Again, the Colombian solution seemed the same, although in 1937–8 the basis of reasoning was completely different. It was no longer 'Brazil protects us', but rather, as the coffee lobby insisted after the publication of the Coffee Census of 1932, 'the internal cost structure protects us'.

The crisis in the management of the FNCC during the brief period in which it was headed by Alejandro López is a key to the understanding of the broadening of the range of action of the FNCC to include intervention in the internal market and in exports. Leaving aside personal aspects and the political conflicts in which the FNCC became embroiled during the last years of the managership of Mariano Ospina Pérez, and the expressions of dissatisfaction on the part of some major producers and exporters regarding the exchange rate, the basic problem to be resolved was that of establishing an internal market structured in such a way that it could operate with some autonomy *vis-à-vis* the external market, which at the time was showing all the signs of a growing imbalance between supply and demand, aggravated by the restrictions on German trade and the almost complete closure of the European markets after 1939. López the President and López the manager took a view consistent with their interventionist posture, and pushed through the acceptance of an agreement for 'price parity' with Brazil, which would regulate the supply of Colombian coffee in accordance with the relative evolution of Brazilian and Colombian coffee prices on the international market. Between October 1936 and April 1937 the Banco de la República was authorized to finance the scheme. In those months the

FNCC acquired 353,000 bags before the policy was abandoned as a result of the inflationary pressures it unleashed and, naturally, of the political pressure brought to bear by the more orthodox groups.

The sudden resignation of Alejandro López from management of the FNCC signalled the failure of the policy of retention of stocks; the Banco de la República refused to continue to finance it (Ospina's group was strongly influential in policy-making in the Banco) and President López's interventionist scheme was completely discredited.[83] Nevertheless, this first intervention in the market as a result of this parity agreement with Brazil was to serve as a model for the subsequent policies.[84]

In the six basic measures described above, realized to rationalize the market and to favour the interests of the exporters, the FNCC did not act as a pressure group using its own mechanisms within a pluralist democracy, and competing against other groups to obtain a favourable decision for the interests that it defended. Here one might first question the existence of such a pluralistic democracy, a matter outside the scope of this book. For the present, it is enough to see the origin of certain tendencies that after 1957 would be made abundantly evident: the appropriation by the FNCC of functions which at least in theory were reserved for the state. This appropriation of state functions began as a result of the Second World War: between 1935 and 1939, and principally due to the clearing agreement with Germany, European participation in Colombian exports of coffee reached 19 per cent.[85] The closing of the European market in 1939–40 and the strong imbalance in the 'international statistical situation' – large stocks and overproduction – was a sharp blow to the Colombian coffee economy. In 1939, an increase in North American demand lowered the stock level in the country, and the attempts at dumping on the North American market by Latin American producers placed the price level at one of the lowest floors of its entire history: Colombian coffee was quoted in New York at an annual average of 8.38 U.S. cents per pound in 1940. In April, the Colombian government decreed an export bonus which implied a subsidy of U.S. $2 million.[86] The German invasion of the Low Countries aggravated the position of the producers when it became clear that the United States could not consume all the coffee supplied. For Latin America, coffee was the principal item of her total exports, and in many countries political stability depended directly on the conditions of the coffee market. It does not seem at all illogical to conclude that the Pan American solidarity sought by the United States in confrontation with the Axis powers led to the Inter-American Coffee Agreement.[87] With the failure to fix a price ceiling, in spite of excess of supply over demand, a doubling of prices between October 1940 and October 1941 was allowed to occur. Another political reason could be cited in 1962 to explain why the United States entered the International Coffee Agreement: the Cuban revolution.[88]

The Fondo Nacional del Café: state functions performed by the coffee *gremio*

With the approval of the government and of the Congress of the Inter-American Coffee Agreement came the creation of the Fondo Nacional del Café, which offered to the FNCC the chance to intervene more directly and massively in the internal market. The Fondo was technically an account in the Treasury which handled special taxes on bills for the export of coffee, and it was intended to finance the purchase and storing of coffee in order to meet the upper limits set upon exports by the pact. The warehouses and storehouses multiplied; the FNCC set up modern processing plants in the busiest coffee-trading centres, and with the agreement of the government set a rate of exchange at which every exporter was obliged to sell his coffee dollars to the Banco de la República, and slowly began to remove differentials in the internal price in pesos at the different buying points throughout the country. The policy of the thirties was pursued: to improve the quality of the crop, and disseminate among producers more efficient methods of processing. Between October 1940 and December 1953 the FNCC bought 11.9 million bags, which represented 18 per cent of the total exports.[89] The mechanism was a simple one: the Fondo was financed by a tax, and a private group operated it, buying, selling, and storing coffee. The costs and risks were assumed by the national Treasury.

Meanwhile the restricted supply of imports was leading to inflationary pressures. Since the authorities wished to maintain an exchange rate favourable to industry and importers, they resorted to a device of immobilizing foreign exchange earnings by the sale of dollar bonds of two-year terms, with interest payable by the Fondo Nacional del Café, whose financial position seems to have improved.[90] The role of the FNCC as a direct exporter was still limited, and its relations with private exporters close and non-competitive. The FNCC controlled the licences for exports indirectly, and sold to exporters part of the stocks it accumulated. The FNCC regulated the market and defended the income of the growers, at least maintaining them at subsistence level, and paying somewhat subsidized prices as it enjoyed the support of the state to finance the retention of coffee which could not be sold on the external market. On the other hand, by not applying pressure for a more equitable distribution of the currency earned by the coffee sector, which could have been achieved by a more

favourable exchange rate, it favoured the industrialists, who devoted themselves increasingly after 1945 to 'import substitution', and also the large-
scale importers. The international terms of trade of the post-war period
were favourable, so that frictions between the groups involved in the
export–import sector were reduced. Nevertheless, the heavy inflation
after the war brought with it urban agitation and popular discontent,
channelled by the Liberal and populist leader Gaitán.

The Fondo was not dismantled when the quota agreement came to an
end in November 1945. In part this was because the post-war coffee
market continued to be very unstable and it was possible that new retention
schemes would be required. The European markets reacted very slowly in
the era of the Marshall Plan, which placed great emphasis on economic
reconstruction and paid only secondary attention to the acquisition of non-
essential consumer goods such as coffee.[91] Thus it was in the period of
the forties that the FNCC acquired the financial power which, since 1946,
has allowed it to make bilateral agreements with European governments;
to intervene massively in the markets, fixing prices and purchasing coffee;
to invest money in the only Colombian maritime company, in which it
held the majority of shares after 1946; to extend the network of Almacenes
Generales de Depósito; to manage the official coffee policy in the international field; and to create fertilizer industries. In the fifties the FNCC
considerably expanded its technical and agricultural assistance departments.
The financial base of this expansion was in the 'mixing' of the patrimonies
of the FNCC and the Fondo Nacional del Café.[92]

The brief price stability that lasted while the Inter-American quota pact
was in force ended in 1946. A glance at the international coffee panorama
after the war aids comprehension of the sharp tensions to which Colombian
economic policy was subject. From 1946–7 to 1962–3, the year in which
the First International Coffee Agreement came into force, the market was
very unstable; there were six- to eight-year cycles, within which occurred
marked fluctuations of prices from year to year and from month to month.
Before the Second World War, the average annual volume of coffee production in the world was 38.1 million bags, and that of consumption, 26.6
million; for 1961–2, these figures increased by 85 per cent and 65 per cent
respectively. The enormous surpluses were retained in the producing countri
The principal reason for the increase in supply was the opening of the Paraná region in 1950: between 1955 and 1962, Brazil doubled its production
and accumulated more than 60 million sacks in stocks, forcing a Colombian
stockpiling which rose in the 1960s to a level around 6 million bags. In
spite of this absolute increase in Latin American production, the region's
participation in world production fell from the pre-war figure of 90 per cent

to 80 per cent, which shows accelerated coffee expansion in the African countries.[93] After the war, prices and volumes showed an inverse tendency: the average quotation of the 1941–5 period doubled in 1948–9; in 1950, a pronounced increase in prices began, reaching its peak in 1954, when the bad frosts of Brazil at the beginning of the year caused prices to rise to 90 U.S. cents per pound in March; with a slight tendency to fall, the quotation was maintained in 1956–7, and from then on, it began to fall until it reached 39 cents in 1963.[94] The post-war oscillations and the depression of 1957–62 have been the subject of intense argument and analysis to identify the characteristics of the Colombian economy of the period. It suffices to say that, in this period, economic policy and the interests it defined had become much more complex: accelerated import substitution, the modernization of commercial agriculture and transportation, and urbanization all contributed to form a structure whose rhythms of expansion and contraction were interlinked with the movements of the price of coffee, which represented almost 70 per cent of the total value of exports. In 1960–6, Colombia was still the country where coffee most dominated the export sector, followed by Ethiopia, Rwanda, Uganda, and Haiti.[95]

The depression of coffee income after 1957 seemed momentarily to stimulate a redefinition of Colombian economic development strategies. By these years the two alternative models that in Glade's nomenclature correspond to the orthodox and neo-orthodox approaches were formalized. In this case these were expounded by the World Bank report of 1950 and the ECLA analysis of 1957 respectively.[96]

In practice, economic policy maintained an intermediate position between the two, since from 1940 a state industrialist tendency emerged, of which the Instituto de Fomento Industrial, the Empresa Colombiana de Petróleos, and Acerías Paz del Río were the offspring. In addition, state participation proved vital for the development of the railroad, telecommunications, and maritime navigation system. After 1960, it was increasingly evident that industrial growth would not relieve either the strangulations of the balance of payments, or the problems of employment and redistribution of income, all of which ended up by giving renewed impetus to the Liberal strategy in which the external market again acquired its position as the leading sector of the economy. The improvement in the terms of trade in the 1970s reinforced this tendency and facilitated a clear redefinition of economic policy in terms of international efficiency. This still derives from the old theory of comparative advantage.

The great directions of Colombian coffee policy, and the role assigned to the FNCC, are clearly integrated in the strengthening of the free-enterprise economy. In 1957, the FNCC began to intervene massively in the internal market and in coffee exports, using a scheme which greatly resembled the one I described for the 1940s. Coffee policy was integrated without difficulty into the Liberal scheme of the economy, although it acquired a growing rationalization and sophistication. To use the language of Weber, it would be necessary to make it clear that this is a matter of greater 'formal rationality', which does not correspond to greater 'substantive rationality' in terms of the national interest, but rather in terms of those specific interests of the foreign and national importers, exporters, and bankers which ensure a greater control of marketing. But the evolution of this Liberal model would be difficult to understand without referring to the changes in the social structure of coffee agriculture. In chapter 11 I shall give an outline of the evolution of coffee cultivation in the twentieth century, and of the role of the FNCC after 1957.

11. The international cycle and coffee policies confronting the peasant, 1930–70

General characteristics of coffee production, 1930–70

Since its beginnings, coffee cultivation has developed with other kinds of cultivation and with cattle. Of the 4.5 million hectares contained in Colombia's coffee zones in 1970, a little less than one-fourth were planted with coffee, which clearly reflects land usage within the productive units of the coffee belt: while the mean farm size was 15.05 hectares, the mean coffee-grove size on each *finca* was barely 3.53 hectares. These figures show the inherent limitations in a treatment such as the one I undertake in this final chapter: to treat coffee cultivation separately from its immediate agricultural environment. To understand the changes in the organization of the production of coffee in Colombia during the twentieth century, one must of course also analyse the relationship between these changes and the tendencies and events of the world coffee market, together with the role which is assigned to coffee in the Liberal model of development.

My intention is first to outline the more general trends which have become apparent in the productive sector. I shall consider then to what extent such tendencies may have been responses to changes in the structure of the international coffee market.

For the student of Colombian coffee history, 1932 stands out as the year which marks the shift from the 'pre-statistical' to the 'statistical' period, with the publication in that year of the Coffee Census. Naturally there was no sharp break between the two periods, rather a gradual process dating back to the nineteenth century and arising out of the various attempts to organize agricultural statistics on a more scientific basis.[1] Moreover, the technical superiority of the reports and censuses made after 1932 should not necessarily be taken to imply that these may be relied upon without question, since the figures available may well have been manipulated by the FNCC with the aim of providing support for its own policies.[2]

Having stated these reservations, we may now move on to suggest the 1960s as the period in which the first major changes in the productive structure took place. These appear to have resulted directly from the conscious efforts of the coffee authorities to bring about certain reforms, and there are clear indications that 'traditional' techniques in coffee

227

husbandry were beginning to give way after the sixties to new intensive techniques of production. It is hardly an exaggeration to say that the First Programme of 'Development and Diversification in the Coffee Zones' (1965) marked the beginnings of an 'agricultural revolution'[3] in this sector.

From the first modest and hesitant steps taken in the second half of the nineteenth century, coffee production followed the course of development which I described in chapters 4 and 5. The original technical base was primitive and static; the coffee crop increased as a result of the expansion of the agricultural frontier; land and labour were extensively utilized and increases in the total product were a function of the corresponding increases in, and in static proportion to, the area under cultivation and the labour force employed. The use of manure and fertilizers was virtually unknown and planting and replanting rarely conformed to the application of established agricultural principles. We have seen in previous chapters how this type of agriculture experienced favourable development under conditions of productive techniques and social relations that can, today, only be described as archaic: newly established haciendas reproduced (and modified in accordance with the nature of coffee production and with new ecological and geographical conditions) the basic patterns of agricultural organization which had been established in the highland regions and on the peasant farms which came into existence on a massive scale during the *antioqueño* colonization, and which also assumed significant proportions in eastern Colombia.

It would appear undeniable that the haciendas played an important role in pioneering coffee production and in expanding the frontier, but, as a result of the nature of the socioeconomic organization and political and financial problems which accompanied them, they were rapidly supplanted by the peasant units. In table 31 we can observe the absolute and relative increases in the number of *fincas* between 1932 and 1970, and the average size of the coffee grove within the *fincas*.

At all events, the peasant units in the coffee zones, with substantial backing from a strong subsistence sector, showed considerable resilience in withstanding the effects of price cycles and the administrative problems associated with seasonal labour shortage, itself a product of the highly seasonal nature of coffee production. Marginal productivity was hardly of major concern for the smallholding peasant, while other factors such as the certainty of finding reliable outlets on the coffee market (at whatever price) and the low risk involved in quasi-permanent investment in the coffee plantation, were positive elements in the development of the coffee sector based on peasant economies.[4] There seems no doubt that coffee production developed along somewhat rustic lines, still employing, in some places,

Table 31. *Variation in the number and average size of the coffee plantations by departamentos, 1932–70*

Departamento	Number of coffee *fincas*			Mean size of coffee planting (ha)		
	1932[a]	1955[b]	1970[c]	1932[a]	1955[b]	1970[c]
Antioquia	28,589	33,203	50,169	2.23	3.5	3.09
Caldas	40,174	45,930	45,485	1.95	4.1	4.63
Cundinamarca	13,812	29,749	41,330	2.70	3.1	2.47
Tolima	12,771	27,197	23,801	4.70	4.3	5.73
Valle	20,069	23,975	17,116	1.90	3.9	7.41
Subtotal	115,415	160,054	177,901	2.69	3.78	4.66
Boyacá	1,333	10,496	21,396	3.17	1.4	1.39
Cauca	12,477	17,559	41,761	0.87	1.4	1.92
Huila	4,471	17,746	13,503	1.98	2.5	3.55
Magdalena	682	2,088	838	8.00	8.3	17.04
Nariño	3,811	7,070	11,769	0.92	2.1	1.46
N. Santander	7,972	6,207	9,334	3.13	4.7	4.89
Santander	3,045	11,454	18,608	6.12	2.2	3.39
Subtotal	33,791	72,620	117,209	3.46	3.23	4.81
Others	–	2,000	6,708	–	–	–
National total	149,206	234,674	301,818	2.38	3.3	3.54

Sources: a FNCC, *Boletín de Información y Estadística*, no. 5, February 1933.
b ECLA/FAO, *Coffee in Latin America*, vol. 1. c FNCC, *Censo Cafetero de 1970* (2 vols., Bogotá, 1970).

techniques which had fallen out of use in the Antilles by the end of the eighteenth century,[5] but this does not appear to have seriously hindered development until the 1960s and, indeed, may have favoured Colombia with regard to her competitive position in the world market.

The question which now arises is whether or not the peasant household is destined for extinction. Before attempting to outline an answer to this question, we shall first pause to consider the relationship which exists between the transition from extensive to intensive agriculture, and the changes which have taken place in the world market structure.

As we saw in the previous chapter, a mere glance at the coffee price curve on the international market shows sharply fluctuating prices. It has been estimated that between 1902 and 1950 the average year-to-year fluctuation in the Brazilian coffee price was around 21 per cent. According to my own estimates, the coefficient of inter-annual variation of the price

of Manizales coffee in the New York market was 65.3 per cent between
1902 and 1972, and in the sub-periods 1902–29, 36 per cent; 1930–56,
66.9 per cent; and 1957–72, 14.1 per cent.[6]

External cycles and internal structures of production

Economists have succeeded in identifying clearly definable price cycles,
among them the so-called biennial coffee cycle which results from the
apparent alternation in coffee cultivation between a good crop one year
followed by a mediocre crop the next. These coffee price cycles appear to
bear a closer relation to fluctuations in supply than to variations in the
pattern of demand. Coffee consumption, which may be defined as a 'habit'
falls significantly only if high prices are maintained for prolonged periods;
and demand tends to be inelastic. The causes of these cyclical fluctuations
are mainly to be found in the relation between prices and supply, due
largely to those peculiarities in production which have been comprehensive
discussed in other chapters but which, for convenience, may be summarize
as follows: once equilibrium between supply (production plus stocks)
and demand has been reached, prices are liable to rise sharply if production
is suddenly cut back, a phenomenon frequently observed after damage
to the Brazilian coffee crops caused by severe frosts. As a consequence of
this situation, coffee-growers respond to rising prices first by improving
their care and harvesting and then by making new net investments. As a
result of the time-lag which occurs between investment and production,
supply meets demand only after a period of some years and new investments may still be feasible even after prices show some sign of falling.[7]
In a country like Colombia, given the 'cost structure' of the peasant sector,
it is possible for production to continue at the same high level for a considerable period before the effects of the crisis make themselves felt in
the economy as a whole.

As we have already seen, the interventionist measures carried out by the
Brazilian government after 1906 had the effect of protecting Colombian
production and promoting the expansion which took place after 1910.
At times of cyclical depression, the *hacendado*'s high overheads obliged
him to maintain production at a constant level while attempting to force
down wages. The peasant units could retreat from the crisis by falling
back on subsistence farming. It could be argued that the relative absence
of serious political conflict within the Colombian ruling classes may also
be attributed to Brazilian protectionist policies: the 1929–32 crisis which
played havoc with the various political systems throughout Latin America
left Colombia virtually unscathed. However, the principal reason for this

situation seems to have been that the worst of the crisis could be withstood by the smallholder if additional measures were taken to modernize transport and marketing systems. The logic of increasing supply at times of low prices allowed Colombia to capture a larger share of the world coffee market: 12.3 per cent in 1930/2 and 20.0 per cent in 1943/5. This had the effect of strengthening the policy of the FNCC in encouraging the proliferation of the peasant unit, symbol of social democracy.

The peasant: from hero to villain

The 1932 Census transformed the family farmer into something of a hero. This figure then became an object for exploitation by the big coffee-producers, who were attempting to carry out a policy which enjoyed considerable support in the country, namely that of leaving the techniques and methods of cultivation in their primitive state in the hope that they would develop spontaneously, while attempting to modernize transport and the structure of warehousing, credit, and finance facilities for domestic and export–import trade. Thus, the expansion of the coffee frontier continued to depend largely on the labour of the family producer between 1930 and the 1950s. By then the preferential system accorded to the African countries by their European colonial or ex-colonial masters had led to the strengthening of their coffee-planting, a development which represented a serious threat for the Latin American nations. Colombia, meanwhile, was experiencing the symptoms and effects of the industrial-ization and modernization which took place in the post-war period. An ideology of development began to take shape, nourished somewhat in-coherently by traditional protectionism, the reports of international agencies and experts, and the passing policies which emerged in response to each new crisis. The various experts have attempted to show that in the field of agrology, the peasant coffee-cultivator was nothing but a burden for the sector, while economists have concluded that the peasant producer was basically inefficient. In order for Colombia to maintain her competitive position in the international market (and coffee after all was virtually the sole generator of the foreign exchange required to finance her import-substitution programme), it was essential to give a vigorous shaking-up to the productive structure, and to abandon the idea that it was sufficient to rely on the spontaneous responses of a rustic agricultural sector. A rapid transition towards an intensive, highly productive agricultural sector now became the priority.[8] But these new plans could not be put promptly into practice due to the prevailing conditions of economic crisis, the scarcity of resources, and the absence of any coherent policy for Latin American

Table 32. *Coffee exports: Colombian and world, 1932–72 (000 bags)*

Year	Coffee exports		Colombian as % of world
	Colombian	World	
1930	3,118	25,725	12.1
1931	3,017	27,895	10.8
1932	3,184	22,654	14.1
1933	3,281	26,347	12.5
1934	3,143	25,318	12.4
1935	3,786	27,166	13.9
1936	3,981	27,605	14.4
1937	4,060	25,128	16.2
1938	4,262	30,133	14.1
1939	3,774	29,039	13.0
1940	4,457	23,390	19.1
1941	2,912	28,553	10.2
1942	4,310	27,858	15.5
1943	5,252	25,710	20.4
1944	4,923	24,710	19.9
1945	5,150	26,070	19.8
1946	5,661	29,416	19.2
1947	5,339	28,742	18.6
1948	5,588	32,197	17.4
1949	5,410	34,236	15.8
1950	4,472	29,229	15.3
1951	4,794	31,840	15.1
1952	5,032	32,230	15.6
1953	6,632	34,617	19.1
1954	5,754	28,918	19.9
1955	5,867	33,698	17.4
1956	5,070	38,394	13.2
1957	4,824	35,125	13.7
1958	5,441	36,231	15.0
1959	6,413	42,168	15.2
1960	5,938	42,386	14.0
1961	5,651	43,778	12.9
1962	6,561	46,225	14.2
1963	6,134	48,906	12.5
1964	6,412	46,721	13.7
1965	5,651	44,969	12.6
1966	5,566	50,328	11.1
1967	6,094	50,342	12.1
1968	6,588	54,605	12.1
1969	6,478	54,466	11.9
1970	6,509	52,095	12.5
1971	6,569	52,629	12.5
1972	6,528	57,179	11.4

Source: International Coffee Organization, *Coffee in Colombia* (London, 1973; mimeographed).

coffee-producing nations as a whole. Although the outlines of a modernization programme were already to be found in a 1956 ECLA/FAO report.[9] it was still necessary to subsidize the coffee export economy by means of favourable monetary and exchange policies in 1962. The hero of the thirties became the villain of the piece in the sixties. He was not held responsible for the inflation attributed to the low levels of productivity prevailing on the coffee *fincas*.

Behind this formulation of coffee policy, there was a coherent conception about the restructuring of the producing sector which would be undertaken in later years. On this point, it is interesting to put the problem in historical perspective: it seemed as if the 'democratic' way of *antioqueño* colonization, centred on the medium-sized *finquero*, was exhausted, and that it would stifle the economic development of the country. This pattern had been firmly imposed on that of the hacienda, which, as the most-capitalized great unit, did not show signs of Kautskian superiority over the peasant *fincas*. Are we now, in looking at the 1960s, in the presence of another break, as significant as that of the rise of the family *finca*? From the economic point of view, are we facing a change of direction of the secular tendency of productivity?

It is worth while summarizing the aspects on which the new classification of coffee agriculture were founded. The characteristics of the 'traditional' methods of cultivation and production are: (*a*) intensive use of labour with low productivity (social division of labour is expressed within the family structure; cultivation methods are mediocre and 'traditional'); (*b*) extensive use of the soil due either to a low seeding density (1,000 to 1,500 trees per hectare) or to the abuse of inter-planting, which exhausts the fertility of the soil; (*c*) low use of fertilizers: 12 kg/ha in 1956; (*d*) low control of soil erosion; and (*e*) scant use of pesticides.[10]

Before listing the characteristics attributed to the 'modern' method, several clarifications are needed: inter-planting as well as the diversification of cultivation on the *finca* were official policies between about 1930 and 1955, years in which an attempt was made to 'protect' the cultivator from the cycle by preaching diversified use of land to him. As can be seen from table 33, there is an inverse relationship in the ratio of *finca* size to size of coffee grove: small *fincas* tend to specialize in coffee, which makes it clear that this kind of cultivation produces the most income and is probably the least risky. Diversification of cultivation within the *finca* can be effected by coffee groves and complementary cultivation or pasture on separate lots; by inter-planting within the coffee grove, usually *plátanos*, or by a combination of the two methods. In general, the peasant *fincas* inter-plant *plátanos*, yuca, and maize in the coffee grove and plant some

Table 33. Use of land on coffee farms by farm size (hectares)

Farm size	Total farm area	Total area under coffee	Land under other uses					Total land under other uses	% of total farm area under other uses
			Other permanent crops	Annual crops	Pastures	Fallow land and forests	Other land		
Less than 1	20,386.4	16,975.7	842.2	420.7	1,439.3	706.6	1.9	3,410.7	17.38
1 to 1.99	61,561.7	40,020.7	4,668.3	2,548.0	9,845.3	4,378.7	100.7	21,541.0	33.78
2 to 3.99	160,102.0	85,976.3	13,960.6	7,478.7	36,521.2	15,793.6	371.6	74,125.7	46.89
4 to 9.99	457,043.9	189,248.4	38,516.6	21,006.4	142,094.0	64,754.9	1,423.6	267,795.5	58.68
10 to 15.90	383,312.6	130,803.3	29,186.9	15,959.6	138,944.0	66,758.8	1,660.0	252,509.3	65.92
16 to 49.99	1,223,088.1	312,016.5	80,097.5	44,544.2	512,037.1	268,916.8	5,476.0	911,071.6	74.52
50 and over	2,255,062.2	295,359.8	111,657.0	56,210.2	1,200,873.3	572,855.2	18,106.7	1,959,702.4	86.88
Total	4,560,556.9	1,070,400.7	278,929.1	148,167.8	2,041,754.2	994,164.6	27,140.5	3,490,156.2	76.53

Source: FNCC, Censo Cafetero de 1970.

additional lots with sugar-cane. But as the 1970 census does not give information on the intensity of inter-planting on these *fincas*, one must
be careful in interpreting the low productivity of their coffee groves.
Under the extensive traditional systems, the differences in physical
productivity of land among units according to size are not very large on
average.[11] Bearing in mind the use of all land in each *finca*, the small
units tend to use more intensive systems. Colombian coffee cultivation
until 1970, especially in the *veredas* on which new cultivation techniques
have not been introduced, show the same configuration observed in the
regions in which the latifundio–minifundio complex predominated:
Higher land productivity in the small units and higher labour productivity
in the large units.[12]

Since it has been empirically demonstrated that land productivity
determines, in Colombian coffee cultivation, the productivity of the rest
of the factors,[13] new cultivation methods tend to increase land productivity
to the maximum. According to the established definitions, a modern
plantation must (*a*) multiply the traditional seeding density (1,200 coffee
trees per hectare on average) by a factor of 3 to 5; (*b*) eliminate the use
of shade trees or use only *plátanos* and increase the use of fertilizers;
(*c*) use more productive botanical varieties. I will mention later the principal
advantages that these methods offer the investor, but for the moment it
is worth noting another aspect of the historical evolution of Colombian
coffee cultivation: the displacement of the coffee frontier towards the
central cordillera, which culminates in the hegemony of the '*antioqueño*
country'. The phenomenon tends to be interpreted mainly as a function
of the entrepreneurial capacity of the *antioqueño* and of the social organization, a view I criticize in chapters 8 and 9. Without ignoring the importance of a peasant society in consolidating a seasonably variable and
labour-intensive cultivation on land of excessively steep gradient, the
natural fertility of the soil must be brought into the explanation. Regional
differences of productivity are much more important and statistically
significant than difference in land productivity according to the size of
the whole *finca* or of the coffee plantation. In table 34 one can see the
marked inter-departmental differences in relation to the national average.

Natural fertility: a neglected factor in social and economic history

The secular movement of coffee from areas of low fertility towards areas
of high natural fertility, in addition to its obvious implications for the
regional structure of the country, helps one to understand better the
economic nature of coffee cultivation. On the basis of table 34, I obtained

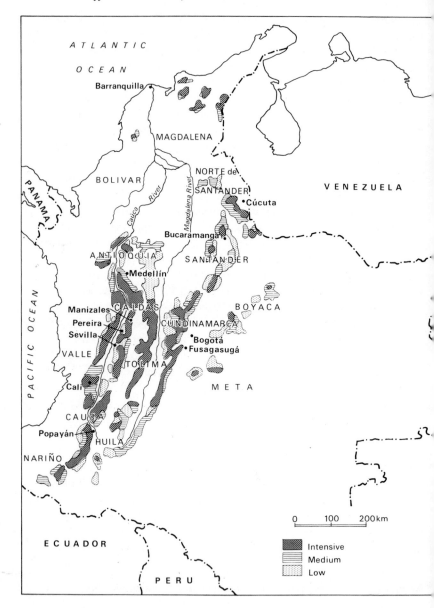

Map 6. Coffee cultivation zones, *c*. 1960. (*Source*: FNCC, Colombian coffee map.)

Table 34. *Yields of parchment coffee by departamento, 1922–70 (tonnes/hectare)*

Departamento	1922[a]	1926[b]	1932[c]	1955[d]	1960[e]	1965[f]	1970[g]
Antioquia	0.861	1.141	0.668	0.706	0.721	0.472	0.588
Boyacá	0.546	1.612	0.368	0.386	0.546	0.511	0.391
Cauca	N.D.	1.165	0.373	0.525	0.389	0.376	0.374
Cundinamarca	0.810	1.158	0.668	0.412	0.524	0.447	0.508
Huila	N.D.	0.725	0.454	0.496	0.359	0.550	0.458
Magdalena	0.933	0.998	0.263	0.450	0.311	0.580	0.429
Nariño	N.D.	1,095	0.421	0.238	0.510	0.254	0.378
N. Santander	1.125	0.927	0.702	0.471	0.397	0.288	0.340
Santander	1.125	1.104	0.574	0.513	0.387	0.328	0.451
Tolima	0.539	1.079	0.522	0.646	0.428	0.337	0.507
Valle	0.588	2.593	0.709	0.776	0.621	0.593	0.612
Caldas	0.625	1.077	0.889	0.850	0.649	0.738	0.731
Risaralda	–	–	–	–	–	–	0.593
Quindío	–	–	–	–	–	–	0.855
National average	0.730	0.970	0.668	0.653	0.526	0.509	0.541

Sources: a Jorge Ancízar, 'La industria del café en Colombia', *R.N.A.*, nos. 239–40 (May–June 1924). b Monsalve, *Colombia cafetera.* c FNCC, *Boletín de Información y Estadística*, no. 5, February 1933. d ECLA/FAO, *Coffee in Latin America.* e DANE, *Directorio General de Explotaciones Agropecurias, Censo agropecuario 1960* (Bogotá, 1964). f DANE, *Encuesta agropecuaria nacional 1965* (Bogotá, 1966). g FNCC, *Censo Cafetero de 1970.*

the coefficient of variation of the departmental productivities in relation to the national average and, surprisingly, in spite of the limitations and methodological differences of the censuses and inquiries used (excluding that of Monsalve, which does not have any statistical value), I arrived at these results: 1922, 30 per cent; 1932, 26; 1955, 25; 1960, 23; 1965, 27; and 1970, 25. That is, over time the degree of dispersion of regional productivities in relation to the national average has not varied significantly. On this first conclusion, I decided to research the dispersion of departmental productivity, using the census of 1970, one technically superior to the rest, taking three statistics: the average size of coffee-planting on each coffee *finca*; the productivity of the coffee grove; and the average monetary income. I used the seven size ranks of the coffee groves of the same census, and the results can be seen in table 35.

The conclusion is that as the coefficient of inter-departmental variation of productivity of the land (coefficient B) maintains itself more or less constant, independent of the sizes of the coffee plantations, the cause of the variations of productivity is more a natural one than a technical or economic one. This also indicates low capitalization, and the very under-developed technical base of Colombian coffee cultivation. It focusses attention on the empirical difficulty of tracing a divide between 'efficient' and 'inefficient' units according to the size of the coffee groves. The co-efficient C, of monetary income, seems to be a function of the size of the coffee grove (coefficient A) and secondly of physical productivity. In other words, until 1970, the average differential productivity of coffee land cannot be attributed to the fact that some 'efficient' units use fertilizers, better cultivation methods, and superior botanical varieties, but rather that they are located in better lands and climates.

The *Programa de Desarrollo y Diversificación*

The fundamental transformation proposed from the 1960s in the different programmes of 'development and diversification' was to improve the cultivation techniques and botanical varieties in the *comarcas* where fertility and the rest of the ecological conditions are more appropriate. The first steps to the transition towards intensive coffee cultivation were taken in these years. They had positive results, if one bears in mind the short-term production aspect, as we will see below. I still do not think it can be said that one end result can be known beforehand: the disappearance of the peasant units labelled 'inefficient'.

Beginning in 1962 a pilot programme of diversification in Caldas was attempted. The green light to a coherent policy of diversifying cultivation

Table 35. *Coefficients of inter-departmental variation of productivity, size of coffee grove, and monetary income according to size group* (1970)

Size of coffee grove (ha)	Size of grove (A)	Productivity (B)	Monetary income (C)
Less than 1	25	20	49
1–5.99	31	19	69
6–9.99	29	20	47
10–19.99	34	20	52
20–49.99	41	23	65
50–99.99	46	26	70
Over 100	46	26	66
National average	51[a]	25	108

[a] Excludes Magdalena, where the size of coffee groves is far above average and would distort the standard deviation.
Source: Based on M. Palacios, 'Coffee in Colombia: Its Economic, Social and Political History, 1870–1970', unpublished D.Phil. thesis, Oxford University, 1977, App. III, table 1 (p. 300).

in the coffee zone and of increasing the productivity of the coffee plantations to overcome the crisis of 1957–62 was given in 1965 by the International Coffee Organization, which recommended that, in order to shore up income levels, the coffee-producing countries should restrict production, increase productivity, and attempt to diversify crops in the coffee zones.[14] To these ends, a special fund was created. In Colombia, the FNCC set up a new division whose purpose was to carry out the programme of development and diversification, placing greater emphasis on the importance of the role to be played by the Subgerencia Técnica. The first obstacle to be faced was the problem of 'peasant mentality'. The small producer refused to accept the new agricultural and supervisory demands placed on him by the new programme and he resisted attempts to persuade him to raze his 'traditional' *cafetal* to the ground in order to plant his land with new varieties, and to adopt new techniques of husbandry. The new agriculture was regarded as both risky and costly in spite of the relatively generous credit facilities which were made available.

Thus, while the 1965–7 programme dealt mainly with the units classified as 'family *fincas* of less than 20 hectares', the Five Year Plan launched in 1973 pragmatically disregarded the coffee-*finca* size, concentrating its attention instead on the microeconomics of the costs and output of the various crops which would take the place of coffee, and of the new varieties of coffee itself. Experts of the FNCC have recently arrived at comparative estimates in terms of tons of *pergamino* coffee per hectare produced by the 'traditional' as opposed to the 'modern' unit of production. The moder unit is considered to produce above 1,000 kilos per hectare. If we consider that, in 1970, the national productivity average stood at only 541 kg/ha, then it is apparent that the Colombian coffee sector must still be considered largely 'traditional'.[15]

In 1970 38.3 per cent of all coffee *veredas* displayed average productivit levels equal to or greater than the national average of 541 kg/ha. Of these *veredas* 5.2 per cent (955) had average productivity levels in excess of 1000 kg/ha, while 2.6 per cent (472) had over 876 kg/ha. Of these two groups 80 per cent of the *veredas* were situated in Antioquia, Viejo Caldas and Valle.

	Number	%
Less than 300 kg/ha	3,281	18.1
301–375 kg/ha	2,903	16.0
376–500 kg/ha	4,939	27.3
501–750 kg/ha	4,648	25.7
751–875 kg/ha	869	4.8
876–1,000 kg/ha	472	2.6
Over 1,000 kg/ha	955	5.2
Total	18,067	99.7

Source: FNCC, *Boletín de Información y Estadística*, no. 45 (1971), p. 34.

If we take three *municipios* in which the Programa de Desarrallo y Diversificación has been operating we arrive at the results shown in table 3 In order to give some idea of the results provided by this programme, we need only mention that in 1974 an area of 132,000 hectares which was under cultivation and using these new intensive techniques (10 per cent of the country's total coffee area in that year) produced approximately 30 per cent of the national crop. Thus far, it would seem difficult to make any serious criticism of the plan. However, if we stop to consider that, of the 132,000 hectares mentioned above, only 8 per cent belonged to owners who could be classified as 'family units' then we may appreciate the extent to which the 'green revolution' has tended to produce appreciable changes in the social structure. Furthermore, its stated objective of modernizing methods of cultivation, and the productive units themselves, will lead logically to the disappearance of the peasant coffee-producer, whether or not by a process of assimilation.[16] For example, in 1970 the cost of cultivating one hectare of coffee land controlled by the new system stood at around 40,000 pesos (including the price of the land) while the average family holding at that time earned a total monetary income of 5,600 pesos.[17] Thus it would indeed appear to be true that the new style of

Table 36. *Area yields per hectare in three coffee municipios under the Programa de Desarrollo, 1970*

Finca size (ha)	1970 yield (kg/ha)					
	Fredonia (Ant.)		Palestina (Cal.)		Caicedonia (Valle)	
	No. *fincas*	Yield	No. *fincas*	Yield	No. *fincas*	Yield
Less than 1	250	797	106	1,010	4	1,023
1–1.99	204	688	29	917	20	1,200
2–5.99	289	1,358	120	1,633	125	2,019
6–9.99	77	1,463	61	1,791	109	1,782
10–19.99	104	3,428	58	4,751	166	4,497
20–49.99	65	705	51	982	140	835
50–99.99	36	664	23	1,121	41	798
Over 100	26	2,467	22	2,150	32	1,540
Total	1,051	739	470	1,027	637	851

Source: Based on figures given to author by Dr Alberto Ararat, Director of the Division of Estudios Económicos Especiales of FNCC, and taken from unpublished figures from the Censo Cafetero of 1970.

agriculture requires 'enterprising men with a modern mentality', as the FNCC experts had claimed.

The *'empresario'* figure was coaxed into existence by offers of cheap credit and technology supported further by an attractive minimum purchase price, as well as the more traditional advantages, such as (a) security of property rights, since there was to be no 'agrarian reform' in the coffee regions; (b) very low direct taxes with numerous opportunities for tax evasion; and (c) the constant appreciation in the value of assets in the prevailing climate of inflation. Although this plan had gained some momentum, it would be unrealistic and ingenuous to believe that its very success would not be the cause of some considerable apprehension among FNCC authorities and some politicians. The new technique also makes investment more attractive, since the capital return no longer takes four to five years as it did for the old haciendas. From the opening of the plantation until the first commercial crop there is only a 22 to 24 months' wait, although the full-sun method rapidly exhausts the life of the coffee tree. On average these must be replaced after eight years.

The eclipse of the peasant?

Meanwhile, we may ask what is happening to the Colombian coffee peasant. If he is indeed in the process of being eclipsed by a new type of producer, how and where is this occurring? Since we must rely on the available demographic evidence and the 1970 coffee census in order to debate this question, it is very difficult to arrive at a satisfactory answer. A first impression is that the small cultivator continues to proliferate at relatively high growth rates in the 'marginal' coffee *departamentos* such as Boyacá, Cauca, Huila, Magdalena, Nariño, North Santander, and Santander. For example, in 1932 there were in these *departamentos* 34,000 coffee *fincas*, representing 23 per cent of the nation's *fincas*. In 1970 there were 117,000 *fincas*, or 39 per cent of the total number, although their share of national total production increased from 18 per cent in 1932 to only 20 per cent in 1970. This clearly implies a lower output per unit, and an evident strengthening of the minifundio peasant sector. Thus, if for the sake of argument we classify as minifundias those *fincas* which in 1932 possessed fewer than 5,000 coffee trees and in 1970 comprised less than 3.99 hectares (any other comparison is rendered impossible by the lack of homogeneity in the figures from the two censuses), and we see that whereas these *departamentos* contained 21 per cent of all minifundia in 1932, in 1970 this figure had increased to 43 per cent.[18] Thus, while in some more dynamic regions a concentration of production had taken place and modern units had ousted the traditional ones, in the 'marginal' areas the numbers of peasant units had continued to multiply. Whereas in the *veredas* where modernization has taken place the differences between 'efficient' and 'inefficient' production are patently obvious, in the 'marginal' areas the line between the two is almost imperceptible.

Of what does the peasant base of Colombian coffee cultivation to which I have been referring in these chapters consist? Before separating out the various aspects of the question, I want to broaden the definition of the term presented in the initial chapters. The connotation of 'peasant' in the coffee economy refers to the fact that the family is almost exclusively the only source of work on the *finca*; the *finca* produces coffee and food for the basic diet; coffee is produced for the market, but as a means of satisfying other necessities; in this sense only the *finca* provides the basic needs of the family. Finally, as Shanin put it, 'The economic action is closely interwoven with family relations, and the motive of profit maximization in money terms seldom appears in its explicit form.'[19] One of the central problems of historical analysis is to determine if the peasant unit producing a cash crop having a national marketing network conserves its 'self-perpetua' characteristics, or if it dissolves on coming into contact with mercantile relationships and in the face of the capitalist orientation in productive investment described above. In a wider theoretical perspective, one would have to ask oneself if the peasantry as a transitional 'petit-bourgeois' class, according to the orthodox Marxist, contains within itself the capitalist germs which end up destroying it in the process of social differentiation in which a minority group becomes bourgeois, and the majority becomes proletariat, losing ownership of land and converting itself into a source of labour and the basis of the internal market for the capitalist sector. With the available data, and the very rudimentary character of Colombian agricultural statistics, it is impossible to reach a satisfactory conclusion on the tendencies of socioeconomic mobility in the coffee regions. For example, according to table 37, in thirty-one representative coffee-growing municipalities emigration (as in Boyacá) is an escape valve for the rural 'pressure cooker', to use the expression of the Colombian sociologist Orlando Fals Borda. Further, the ratio of day-wage-earners to owners decreased between 1938 and 1970, although it is probable that at least 50 per cent of the owners were also day-wage-earners themselves. This makes manifest the existence of forces which counteract the tendencies towards proletarization in the coffee municipalities.

On the other hand, it is likely that, given the great geographical and regional diversity of coffee production in the 'marginal' departments, the coffee-growers there are closer to a type of stable peasant economy than those in the most productive regions. There the land market, the increase in productivity, and the impact of urbanization and marketing are dissolving the subsistence units. It seems to me that at this level of analysis we are still very far from having convincing answers; insistence on premature answers closes the path for the research indispensable in this area. On the other hand, if we try to introduce our peasant coffee-grower into the descriptive schemes elaborated by Weitz,[20] we discover that he maintains discontinuous characteristics in the three stages which should mark the transit of farm evolution: subsistence, mixed, and specialized.

Composition of output: one dominant cash crop and auxiliary crop (specialized)

Purpose of production: domestic and market supply (mixed)

Work schedule: very low (subsistence)

Capital investment: very low (subsistence)

Income: low (subsistence)

Income security: high/medium as a result of the internal support price of the FNCC (mixed and specialized)

Ratio of income to value of output: high (subsistence)

Farmer's professional know-how: specialized (subsistence or specialized)

Naturally, the intermediate gradations between the peasant family farm and the modern family farm, and between the peasant family farm and the day-labourer without land are very numerous. Of the 300,000 coffee-producing families no less than 50 per cent have to supplement their

Table 37. *Trends in social differentiation and migration in 31 coffee-growing municipios, 1938–73*

	Ratio: $\frac{Jornaleros}{Owners} \times 100$			Growth rate of population		
	1938	1951	1964	1938–51	1951–64	1964–73
Antioquia				2.06	3.68	2.0
Amagá	383.3	409.9	454.1	0.94	2.43	0.67
Andes	300.0	264.2	252.5	3.08	−1.26	0.18
Fredonia	261.8	329.7	276.2	−1.99	1.29	−0.95
Támesis	331.6	190.0	264.1	−0.08	1.12	−0.14
Venecia	851.8	425.0	501.2	0.03	1.04	−0.96
Caldas				2.58	2.45	−0.18
Manizales	408.9	–	–	3.03	4.40	0.44
Armenia	453.6	–	–	3.43	4.73	0.66
Calarcá	437.6	–	192.6	2.98	0.50	−1.00
Santa Rosa	153.1	–	317.0	2.92	3.12	−5.78
Valle				4.71	3.48	2.63
Caicedonia	254.1	–	222.9	2.86	1.12	1.61
Sevilla	258.6	–	168.1	4.63	−1.86	4.97
Tolima				1.54	1.80	0.77
Chaparral	199.1	–	102.6	−5.64	8.20	0.03
Cunday	348.3	–	141.8	0.87	−0.54	0.02
Líbano	298.7	–	108.5	1.23	1.84	−2.58
Icononzo	764.9	–	112.6	0.34	3.40	−2.34
Villarrica	–	–	148.9	–	−1.19	0.28
Cundinamarca				2.52	−2.78	10.61
Anolaima	495.6	90.2	110.3	0.71	−4.73	−3.98
La Vega	387.5	176.6	156.8	0.72	0.21	−2.88
Quipile	398.2	122.9	117.6	0.03	0.24	−1.15
Yacopí	93.3	42.3	103.5	8.59	−1.75	6.08
Fusagasugá	220.4	116.5	100.9	−2.26	3.26	3.04
Arbeláez	143.2	130.5	170.6	0.85	1.49	−2.53
Pandi	266.3	146.6	144.2	2.32	−7.85	−1.03
Pasca	339.8	122.0	101.5	2.99	9.63	−1.28
Tibacuy	1,938.0	122.0	98.4	−0.01	2.16	−1.25
La Mesa	724.5	178.4	158.9	0.15	1.71	−3.14
El Colegio	900.6	118.1	167.5	1.47	1.43	−0.46
Viotá	2,328.3	172.7	147.7	1.02	1.56	−1.00
N. Santander				0.49	2.88	2.84
Chinácota	312.6	–	141.9	−2.48	1.16	3.79
Salazar	459.3	–	120.5	−2.05	1.05	0.90
Santander				1.53	2.25	1.32
Rionegro	526.9	–	169.7	1.30	0.32	−0.81
		Total national		2.23	3.22	2.76
		Rural national		1.29	1.31	−0.22

Source: Based on *Censo de Población* for 1938, 1951, 1964, and 1973.

subsistence income by day-wage labour. To determine the importance and function of this peasant economy in Colombian coffee agriculture, one must distinguish two aspects. First, there is the participation of these units in total production; secondly, their wider function in the fixing of the labour costs in the sector taken as a whole. In regard to the first aspect, there is evidence to show a drastic reduction in the percentage participation of peasant family farms in the national harvest. Here I think it is realistic to equate the producers of less than 120 *arrobas* in 1970 with the cultivators who in 1932 had planted less than 20,000 coffee trees. The participation of this group declined thus:[21]

	% of total number of *fincas*	% of total crop
Peasant *fincas*, 1932	98.0	60.0 to 73.0
Peasant *fincas*, 1970	71.3	29.5

Can one conclude in regard to the second aspect that the economic function of these units is growing weaker? The official ideology always pictures the small *finquero* as if his only function were that of direct producer. But it is clear that the peasant coffee-grower is also the labour reserve. In accord with economic theory, and in the absence of any rural union organization in these regions, the wage level is very low because it is probably determined by the labour productivity prevailing on the small *finca*. That is, it is determined by the level of the 'shadow wage' of the small peasant.[22]

The low productivity of peasant coffee cultivation reflects two additional problems: the first is the highly seasonal character of the crops, which in the face of a lack of alternative sources of employment in the low season of the year limits family income;[23] the second is the regional structure of coffee cultivation. It is purely academic to advise the small growers of Cauca, Nariño, or Santander that in place of coffee they migrate to the cities or change their type of planting: coffee, due to its secure market, and to the topographic characteristics of the land on which it is cultivated, does not have a high opportunity cost, social or private; rather, it produces a relatively fair income for the peasant. Perhaps the same can be said of coffee cultivation in many individual *comarcas* of zones elsewhere, more densely planted with coffee.

Thus, if we wish to say that there is a surfeit of peasant labour, it is necessary to identify those areas where such a situation exists. In the traditional minifundio regions where the terrain defies mechanization, coffee still appears to be the most profitable and marketable crop. In view of this fact, it is somewhat unrealistic to discuss questions of the high opportunity costs of producing *arabigo* coffee rather than engaging in the cultivation of pineapple or tomatoes, or in raising cattle, which appear to be the principle feasible alternatives in the main coffee regions, if we are to judge from recent entrepreneurial experience. Meanwhile, questions of 'efficiency' also remain largely academic when the existing economic structure offers the peasant coffee-producer no viable alternative to his present situation, if we discount the possibility of emigration to the cities, with all the associations of poverty and unemployment which this suggests.

In historical perspective, it should also be mentioned that modern techniques suffer from one major deficiency, namely their inability to prevent the exhaustion of the soil. If present short-term maximization policies are continued over the next decade or so, it may be necessary to extend further the geographical boundaries of coffee production.[25] If the present tendency to concentrate resources and investment in particular regions persists, it is probable that the peasant coffee economies in the now 'marginal' regions will continue to produce a subsistence living as they have always done, defending their own interests by expelling the surplus demographic elements which endanger their existence. A good historical example of the capacity for resistance of the peasant *finca* faced with competition from the modern plantation is given by sugar-cane agriculture in the last one hundred years.[26]

It is still not yet possible to offer certain conclusions on the dominant tendency in the agrarian structure of coffee. In order of importance, four development patterns are beginning to take shape. (*a*) In the areas of dense coffee cultivation of the central cordillera, the importance of the family farm is disappearing in the face of the competition of medium-sized and large units which utilize new intensive techniques of cultivation. (*b*) Another group of peasant family *fincas* is turning into commercial family *fincas*, and the peasants into farmers integrated into the economic and social life of the urban centres, not necessarily of cities like Calarcá, Armen or Pereira, but rather of municipalities like Montenegro, Palestina, Chinchiná, Sevilla. (*c*) In these same areas, the relative and increasing poverty of the majority of the small producers is evident. The economic function of this group of *finqueros* (who operate 55.6 per cent of all coffee *fincas* but only hold 5.31 per cent of the land and 13.2 per cent of the area in coffee groves) is changing. From direct producers, they are transforming themselves rapidly into temporary day-labourers. (*d*) In this group are included the *minifundistas* of the marginal departments; these differentiate themselves from the former in that they do not face the competition of modern units, but on the contrary are integrated into apparently stable peasant economies, in which coffee cultivation, in spite of the low levels of physical productivity, does not represent a high opportunity cost, either for the individual grower, or for the national economy taken as a whole. Nevertheless, the dramatic changes of the 1970s, which began with the execution of the Programa de Desarrollo y Diversificación with its goal of raising productivity and restricting total production, and with the sharp increase in internal purchase prices and the resulting increase in supply, could arrest or alter these tendencies. If, in this struggle for survival, the peasant units in the zones of dense cultivation adopt techniques inter- mediate between the old traditional extensive and the new intensive methods (for example, increasing the planting density by a factor of 2.0–2.5), it is probable that they can continue to be integrated into a system which has been described as 'agrarian capitalism without capitalists'.[27]

Coffee policies and world coffee strategies since 1960

The principal objectives of the 1973–8 Plan de Desarrollo y Diversificación were to concentrate production in optimal ecological areas, stimulate food production for the internal market and for export, promote the creation of manufacturing industries in the coffee zones, and finally to try to encourage migration from the *comarcas* of greatest density of population towards the geographic peripheries in the coffee belt. This plan was part of a much wider economic policy whose general outlines express the necessity of implementing nationally the world strategy of control of supply and of increase of productivity.

Although it has been sufficiently proved that the inequality in the distribution of the ownership and tenancy of land is the principal cause of the inequality of income distribution in agriculture, it is evident that with the urbanization and industrialization occurring after the Second World War, a much more complex urban–rural structure appears in which inter- sectoral movement exists, so that the price of productive factors is not determined exclusively within the agrarian economy.[28] But in this field, economists offer only hypotheses which cannot yet be fully proved. On the other hand, one must make schematic and simplified allusion to the two great basic propositions which for several decades have competed in explaining the underdevelopment of Latin American agriculture, which coincide in characterizing it as one of low general productivity and in- elasticity of supply, and one which shows tendencies of stagnation or deterioration in the real per capita income of the majority of the rural population.

The first analysis seems to have two variants: first the *agrarista*, which considers the dimensions of the inequality of tenancy and ownership of land and attempts several levels of agrarian reform. In Colombia, this

school has always been very weak politically, and the two attempts at
agrarian reform have been unsuccessful; one could even ask if they deserved
the name. The application of the laws of 1936 and 1961 only resolved the
legal aspect of appropriation of either *tierras baldías* or land whose title
was in dispute between peasants and landlords. The second, 'structuralist',
variant includes the social dimension of the agrarian problem, but tends to
state it in more economic terms: it aims at the use of resources according
to more efficient standards, which allow factor productivity, total producti
and rural income to increase simultaneously through a combination of
redistribution of property, credit, some planning of what is to be planted,
irrigation, and infrastructure works. The Peruvian agrarian reform would
be a good example.

At the opposite extreme appear the different 'economic' points of view,
which start from the belief that the basis of the agrarian problem is the low
rate of return from agriculture. This results from overall economic policies
('cheap food' or, rather, low wages in the cities) which combine price
controls, import subsidies, and other measures inhibiting capitalist investment in agriculture and redistributing income in favour of the urban economy.[29] The ideological and political implications of these points of view
are well known, and one can doubt totally or partially the validity of
their arguments. Colombian coffee cultivation is necessarily a case apart.
Coffee is neither a food nor an industrial input destined to supply an urban
market, but rather the principal generator of foreign exchange for the
country. As such, it is bound up in general economic policy and in this
last section I want briefly to discuss the directions of these policies, trying
to emphasize the elements of power they reflect.

The power of the FNCC, 1958–70

What is the essence of this power, historically the expression in concrete
form of the free-enterprise capitalism which has been dominant in Colombia? The study of the FNCC allows us to identify the means which
private enterprise had at its disposal to promote a policy in accordance
with its specific interests, even through state bodies. The formal and inform
power of the body is based on these four elements: (*a*) its ability to act
as a quasi-state entity in areas such as legal initiatives and the regulation
and application of the law (this is seen in the fact that legislation pertaining
to coffee is largely the work of the FNCC itself); (*b*) in the quantity and
quality of the economic and financial resources over which it has dis-
cretionary control (this is the case with its administration of the Fondo
Nacional del Café, and its legal immunity regarding the handling of liquid

funds in foreign currency, despite exchange controls and the increasingly speculative nature of its investments); (c) in its character as an oligopolic agent in the internal coffee market (for this purpose it uses the liquid funds which come from the commercial operations it carries out in the name of the Fondo, and the practically unlimited credit available to it from the central bank over long periods of time, as in the sixties); finally (d) its possession of a number of institutionalized monopolies, such as up-to-date information on the statistical, financial, commercial, and legal situation of the complex international coffee market, and the internal statistics regarding the production, movement, and export of coffee, which it manipulates in accordance with its commercial needs. The level of coffee stocks is a state secret, and one needs only a pen to tailor statistical series to fit a given commercial situation. And the FNCC retains a monopoly on the sale of green coffee to Colombian roasters for supply to the internal market; this has become a matter of considerable financial and economic importance over the last twenty years.

We have already referred to the growing role which the state is playing through the FNCC in the strengthening of a capitalist coffee sector. We shall concentrate here on the complex nature of the FNCC and on the tensions arising out of its different functions, tensions which are themselves reflections of wider contradictions in the Colombian socio-economic model, of the splits between different agents active in the economy, and of the possible alternatives for democratization of the state. For those with a taste for oversimplification and easy answers it is worth noting that the majority of coffee-producing countries can quite properly be classified as belonging to the broad category of dependent capitalist economies; nevertheless, they have developed institutional mechanisms different from those of Colombia as far as coffee is concerned. Although it could be argued that there too the 'universal logic of capital accumulation' is in operation, the relationships between the different sectors of the coffee economy contrast with the Colombian case. In Brazil, Mexico, and various African countries only private groups produce and export coffee, and the management of coffee policy lends itself less to ambiguity than it does in Colombia; the same applies to the internal market. The type of institutional arrangement prevailing in Colombia is also found, in a more rudimentary form, in the majority of coffee-producing countries in Central America.

Let us now examine the way in which the evolution of the coffee market has progressively delivered into the hands of the FNCC the instruments of power which it controls today. The years 1957 and 1958 were years of falling prices and acute economic depression, and of the turbulent transition from a failed 'populist' military dictatorship to the regime of restricted democracy of the National Front. Economic policy followed its exhausting 'stop–go' course, manipulating administrative controls on imports and exchange restrictions, and necessarily creating tensions in other bodies such as the Asociación Nacional de Industriales and the Federación Nacional de Comerciantes.

The Fondo Nacional del Café was not dismantled with the disappearance of the quota agreement, but rather grew in strength, for 1958 saw the creation of a new tax (*impuesto de retención*), which was to be thenceforward the principal source of finance for the Fondo (and one of the mechanisms controlling internal supply, by stabilizing the peso income of the producer). This 'tax' is a percentage of *pergamino* coffee or its cash equivalent which must be deposited without compensation against the quantity of coffee exported, and with this security, and a practically unlimited credit line with the Banco de la República, the FNCC was able to intervene in the internal market, and on occasion to displace temporarily the large buyers and established exporters. From that time onwards (bearing in mind that we do not go beyond 1970 in this study) the FNCC has bough directly (or through its co-operatives, set up in the sixties) between 70 and 80 per cent of the national harvest. The FNCC is the only important stockpiler of coffee, with capacity estimated at six million bags, stored in modern and technically advanced facilities. Its share of exports from 1958 to 1970 varied between 25 and 35 per cent of the total. The FNCC opens up and holds onto new markets, paying the high costs of advertising and eliminatin, the differentials between nominal quotations for its own coffee and that of Central American countries. These tactics were successful in Europe during the sixties. Given the logic of free enterprise, it is probable that pressures will soon make themselves felt from the financial sector and from private exporters for the FNCC to allow them to operate freely in the European market, now that it has been captured, just as they do in the North American market. Finally the FNCC retains a monopoly on sales in 'non-traditional markets', principally Spain and the countries of Eastern Europe, and commercial management of the compensation agreements. But not all the operations of the FNCC are external. The coffee it does not export on its own account can be (*a*) sold competitively, generally by auction, to private exporters, (*b*) sold to the national roasters, usually at a loss, with the objective of increasing internal consumption and opening up a new market, or (*c*) stockpiled.

Now, how does the body participate in overall decisions regarding coffee policy, and with what results? For the political scientists, a fascinating field of research would be to investigate who really holds the initiative in decision-making concerning the coffee sector. From a purely institutional

point of view, the structures of the Colombian state exhibit a growing
tendency towards complexity, as they receive demands from groups whose
interests are more and more incompatible in the short and medium term.
Given its effects on the economy (in the fields of monetary and exchange
policy) policy-making regarding coffee has been forced to abandon the
closed offices of the FNCC and the Banco de la República.

The principal institutional instruments of coffee policy are (*a*) the
internal support price, (*b*) the coffee rebate (*reintegro cafetero*), and
(*c*) credit for producers.

All these instruments are closely related to each other and to monetary
and exchange policies, and are the result of economic situations difficult
to control, and originating in the external cycle, but also of political
pressures from the different agents who are directly or indirectly affected
by measures relating to the coffee sector. Suffice it to say that it is not the
Colombian Congress which controls coffee policy, but the state bureaucracy
and the higher bureaucracy of the FNCC.

The *internal support price* is the price which the FNCC pays for *pergamino*
coffee in the primary markets in the country. The price used to be fixed
exclusively by the FNCC, but since 1967 this function has been taken over
by a committee composed of the Manager of the FNCC and two Ministers.
Although the internal price would appear to be a function of the external
price (expressed in pesos), it tends, on the contrary, to isolate the producer
from external fluctuations. It is in fact a price set with regard to administrative criteria, and does not take the market situation into account: in
periods of acute depression, such as 1958–63, it served to maintain levels
of income and employment in the coffee zones, producing considerable
inflationary pressures which have attracted much attention in economic
literature and in the press in Colombia.[30] The combination of the internal
price and the coffee rebate is what determines the margin of profitability
for the private exporter, and forces him to enter the market or leave it.
It is evident that the internal support price is not the minimum price paid
in the different markets of the country, as the question of quality plays
a part; private buyers have considerable liberty to classify coffee as the
lower or supposedly lower grades of the 'FNCC type', and this fact, which
favours the private buyer and exporter, must be taken into account. The
FNCC also seeks to ensure that the internal price is maintained in real
terms, and that major inequalities do not exist in the rate of exchange
between coffee and the products which the grower buys. It is probable
that without the FNCC coffee-growers in general would have received
less income, and that it would have fluctuated more over time. The FNCC
at least offers something which they desire: stability and security. This

is an important element in understanding the representative character of the FNCC and its prestige, as far as the growers are concerned.

Now, as we shall see, this does not mean that coffee policy does not tend to concentrate income, at the level of production as at the level of marketing. In other words, the maintenance of real income for the majority of growers is not necessarily incompatible with a concentration of income at sectoral, regional, and, obviously, socioeconomic levels.

Nobody except the writers of the pamphlets put out as propaganda by the FNCC seriously refers to the *coffee taxes* as such. They are not a source of fiscal income as other taxes are, nor are they treated as other taxes are. These taxes are:

(1) The general export tax, with which the FNCC began to supplement its small budget in 1927; it was increased in 1937 and abolished in 1972, but it was always insignificant in value.

(2) Different forms of *ad valorem* taxes. From 1935 to 1939 a tax on coffee transactions in dollars was in force, and this was reintroduced in 1940, surviving until 1944. It was replaced in 1951 by the so-called 'coffee differential'. This was a tax applied specifically to dollars earned from the export of coffee; the issuing bank exchanged these dollars at a lower rate than those earned from other exports. In 1957 the differential was suppressed, to be brought back in the crisis of 1962. Decree 444 of 1967 replaced it with an *ad valorem* tax which was to fall gradually from a peak of 26 per cent of the value of the coffee rebate. As is well known, these 'taxes' do not reach the Exchequer, with the exception of a modest proportion, estimated by experts as 11 per cent during the sixties.[31] This means that approximately 90 per cent of these 'taxes' are administered by the FNCC through the Fondo Nacional del Café account.

(3) The most important of all is the deposit tax, created in 1958 as part of the Mexico Agreement, in which the majority of coffee-producing countries agreed to maintain prices unilaterally, regulating supply and thus making non-exportable stocks self-financing.

Table 38 gives the total weight of all these taxes in coffee income, and reveals the way in which the 'taxes' could become an independent variable in relation to the other instruments for controlling supply. In other words, one should ask to what extent the FNCC – which must have, as an organizational principle, an implicit interest in increasing the quantity of financial resources at its disposal – has sufficient room to manoeuvre to combine internal prices and 'taxes' in such a way as to achieve simultaneously two objectives: the state's objective of controlling supply by making production a less attractive proposition, and its own objective of increasing the volume of its resources.

Table 38. *Distribution of coffee earnings per pound, 1958–72 (U.S. cents and percentages)*

Year	Average f.o.b. value of coffee exports per pound		Average FNCC support price per pound of green coffee[a]		Average value of 'taxes' per pound of green coffee[a]		Average FNCC costs and charges per pound of green coffee[b]		Average FNCC deficit or profit per pound of green coffee	
1958	43.9	100.0%	29.32	66.8%	8.97	20.4%	1.06	2.4%	4.55	10.4%
1959	42.6	100.0	27.47	64.5	10.53	24.7	1.07	2.5	3.53	8.3
1960	42.3	100.0	29.07	68.7	10.81	25.5	1.08	2.6	1.34	3.2
1961	41.2	100.0	31.90	77.4	8.56	20.8	1.10	2.7	−0.36	−0.9
1962	38.2	100.0	24.08	63.0	5.16	13.5	1.10	2.9	7.86	20.6
1963	37.3	100.0	28.00	75.1	10.31	27.6	1.12	3.0	−2.13	−5.7
1964	46.4	100.0	36.20	78.0	11.44	24.7	1.13	2.4	−2.37	−5.1
1965	46.0	100.0	24.07	52.3	9.44	20.5	1.14	2.5	11.35	24.7
1966	44.7	100.0	25.43	56.9	15.49	34.6	1.15	2.6	2.63	5.9
1967	39.9	100.0	21.71	54.4	13.86	34.7	1.15	2.9	3.18	8.0
1968	40.3	100.0	23.69	59.0	13.61	33.8	1.16	2.9	1.74	4.3
1969	40.1	100.0	24.85	62.0	14.11	35.2	1.17	2.5	−0.03	−0.1
1970	54.2	100.0	28.16	52.0	19.17	35.3	1.18	2.2	5.69	10.5
1971	46.0	100.0	26.89	58.4	15.95	34.7	1.19	2.6	1.97	4.3
1972	49.8	100.0	29.72	59.7	19.27	38.7	1.20	2.4	−0.39	− 0.8

a Obtained by using the rate of exchange given by the International Monetary Fund in *International Financial Statistics.* b Cost of milling, handling, storage, materials, and internal transport.
Source: International Coffee Organization, *Coffee in Colombia* (Doc. JAP/cp/mh) (London, 30 July 1973), App. table 10.

Furthermore, as the FNCC has, through the Fondo Nacional del Café, an unlimited credit line with the issuing bank, it is in the fortunate position, unlike any other commercial organization, of facing no problems of lack of liquidity. When these problems appeared in the sixties they were solved by issuings of currency, and the price paid was inflation.

The characteristic of the FNCC perhaps allows it to establish an autonomous strategy for investment and the expansion of its resources; the table could also be interpreted in this way. Such an interpretation is possible if we confine our attention to the column furthest to the right: negative or very low margins on sale are followed by figures which are 'abnormally' high. This suggests that it would be worth inquiring into the conduct of the FNCC as a private association *vis-à-vis* other private exporters. To what extent is this degree of variation made possible by the manipulation of the two variables, the internal support price and the level of 'taxes'? (The level of sophistication of the policy is such that it is possible to maintain a high internal price, and even to agree, as happened from 1959 onwards, on a formula for sharing out the additional increments in the internal price (as a function of the external price), and at the same time to maintain an upward trend in the 'tax' level.) It appears that this was possible in the seventies, when a good part of the increase in the international price got through to the producer, but the policy of containment of supply was based on increases in the deposit tax to levels undreamed of in the sixties, reaching a peak of 80 per cent!

The FNCC also has the organizational resources to channel part of its profits towards the regional bodies which are its real link with the producers and one of the most solid bases of its legitimacy, and to meet the expectations of the largest producers.

The 1959 agreement between the FNCC and the national government (with its subsequent modifications) is a good example of the way in which the FNCC also has the ability to appear as a pressure group which makes demands on behalf of its associates and the most important coffee regions. These agreements formalized specific formulas for the percentage distribution of additional increments in the coffee price between the direct producers (through an increase in the support price), the Departmental Committees (through education, health, and housing programmes in the areas where coffee production was dominant), and the Fondo Nacional del Café.[32]

To conclude our speculation regarding the real power of the FNCC, I should like to put forward some propositions for future analysis and research

The dual character of the FNCC is evident; it emerges concretely in the appropriation of state functions and resources by a private association, itself organized on highly hierarchal principles, with strategic decisions in the hands of a very small group, and on the other hand in the use which the state makes of the association to stabilize its coffee policy, that is to say, removing it from the hands of the professional politicians. Institutionally, it might look as if the FNCC were a semi-official body, dependent upon the monetary authorities (the Monetary Council) and the national government (the President and the Ministries of the Treasury, Foreign Affairs, and Agriculture). Despite its participation in the coffee market and in private enterprise through funds which are public in origin, these things endow it with a peculiar nature. How long will it be able to sustain these tensions? It is very difficult to say. It is probable that its very superiority of bureaucratic organization will allow it to maintain its present status. But it is also probable that the financial groups will mount a campaign to 'liberate' the internal market once more, and unleash their concentrated power against the scattered producers, perhaps accepting the taking of coffee policy into the state sector. But if one thinks of a democratic variant, a tendency to democratize the structures of the state, there may be another viable alternative, which would consist of making official the intervention in the internal market and in the export of coffee, leaving the FNCC intact as a bureaucratic organization, semi-autonomous but without control over the Fondo Nacional del Café. This, as table 38 shows, would make possible a more equitable distribution of coffee income, as the profit margins, which as we have seen depend more on administrative rules than on the free play of competition, could be distributed by means of public expenditure policy. These resources are considerable. Taking as a base the annual average from 1958 to 1972, the income of a six-month period could finance the Five Year Programa de Desarrollo y Diversificación, which as we know, is financed by foreign borrowing; and this is just an example of what might be done.

What should appear as an anachronism is that the state is feeding its funds into a new Negocio X and Y; I say 'should' because, despite the rhetoric regarding the democracy of the Colombian state, such a description can be judged only by its efficiency. From the form in which this business is structured, it may be concluded that the political and extra-market elements dominate over the purely economic ones of competition.[33] This raises the question of whether these political questions should be decided by a private entity in the name of the state. But once this question is resolved, the most important political problem still remains: how to distribute a magnitude of 6 per cent (1958–72) of the total income of Colombia's principal export?

The figures speak for themselves: looking at the total values shown in table 39, one can appreciate the extent of power to which I refer. Column 2 represents more than 300,000 producers, of whom 21,000 account for at least 58 per cent of the income; the last column refers only to the FNCC and another nineteen private enterprises.

From the previous remarks, which are necessarily made somewhat disjointed by difficulties of access to information, one can see that the subject is yet to be explored. The special kind of relationship between the FNCC and the Colombian state, the delegation of state functions to an entity which is at one and the same time a semi-official bureaucracy and the foremost Colombian monopsony fully expresses one of the possibilities which we have classified as the Liberal model of development.

If the forces of capitalism are held only to operate fully once the nation is integrated and politically centralized, or if in other words they require the existence of the national state, then the historical process in Colombia in the last century, taking the country's coffee history in its broadest perspective, shows a definite evolution in that direction. The change of emphasis in this book, from the detailed description of the local universe and its particular vigour to the general analysis of state policy, sets out to reflect and emphasize that evolution. What is peculiar to Colombian capitalism, as a system and as a process, is its close links with the rural world, the 'archaic' or 'pre-capitalist' world of the peasant, and at the same time its need to survive in the world of international capitalism exporting a typical *produit colonial*. These apparently contradictory linkages might make it seem impossible for the system to survive economically or for the nation state to come into its own. All the same, the system has been able to work. Even though this book cannot reach any final conclusion, its argument is that in the Liberal model of development there must be found some basic elements of the answer, some of the reasons why the system has worked. This model is the expression of the power of a social class which for more than a century has been strategically located at the intersection of these two worlds, the rural and the international. Recent statistics point to the weakening of peasant society, although only in the next decade will it be possible to know with certainty what are the real tendencies in the social and regional structure of coffee. If the peasant coffee economy is eclipsed, the so-called 'weak' state will expand some of its functions to relieve the problems of coffee-growing, of productivity, and the international price cycle. In spite of tensions in the power structure, tensions that derive from the growth of 'nationalist' ideology and from the appearance of more modern units of production, it does not seem that these are strong enough on their own to threaten the base which sustains the class which anachronistically is still called 'the oligarchy'. In the identification of the national

Table 39. Distribution of coffee earnings, 1958–72 (U.S. $000)

Year	Total coffee exports	Producers' income	Average value of taxes	Average costs and charges	Average deficit or profit
1958	460,715	307,757.6	93,985.9	11,057.2	46,071.5
1959	473,004	305,087.6	116,831.9	11,825.1	39,259.3
1960	464,578	319,165.1	118,467.4	12,079.0	14,866.5
1961	434,467	336,277.5	90,369.1	11,730.6	–11,729.7
1962	463,403	291,194.9	62,559.4	13,438.7	95,461.0
1963	446,257	335,139.0	123,166.9	13,387.7	–25,436.6
1964	548,136	427,546.1	135,389.6	13,155.3	–27,954.9
1965	539,144	281,882.3	110,524.5	13,478.6	133,168.6
1966	507,591	288,819.3	175,626.5	13,197.4	29,947.9
1967	509,923	277,398.1	176,943.3	14,787.8	40,793.8
1968	558,278	329,384.0	188,697.9	16,190.0	24,005.9
1969	607,510	376,656.2	213,843.5	17,617.8	– 607.5
1970	735,657	382,541.6	258,951.3	16,184.4	77,244.0
1971	690,009	402,965.3	239,433.1	17,940.2	29,670.4
1972	865,958	516,976.9	335,125.7	20,782.9	6,927.6

Sources: Table 38 and FNCC, Boletín de Información y Estadística, nos. 46–7 (1972–3), p. 30.

interest with the 'defence' of the coffee price there are plenty of signs of nationalist rhetoric. In the relative decline of the peasant producer, a result of the 'green revolution' in coffee-growing techniques and the rise of the modern producer, one can see signs that the system is capable of solving – at least, in the medium term – the problem of maintaining the competitiveness of Colombian coffee in international markets, through an increase in productivity.

A final comment. The analysis of this book ends in 1970, the date of publication of the last coffee census. The years since then have seen a significant fall in the level of stocks, with the consequence of rising prices on the world market. The Brazilian frosts of 1963, 1969, and 1972 were the main cause of this. World stocks as a percentage of world consumption fell from 116 in the coffee years 1959/60–1961/2 to 80 in the years 1969/70–1971/2 (the coffee year runs from 1 October to 30 September). Then in 1975 Brazil suffered the 'frost of the century', and stocks again fell sharply to a level of 46 per cent of world consumption in 1975/6– 1976/7.[35] The price that the consumer had to pay shot up all over the world, and the reader accustomed to a cup or two a day knows exactly what that meant. In Colombia, as was the case with most Latin American producers, the rise in world prices was translated into higher prices for the producer. Plans to reduce supply were shelved, the intervention of the FNCC in marketing grew, and the question of coffee once more became the nerve centre of public debate. The change in the structure of Colombian coffee production, already apparent in the 1960s and the subject of the last two chapters, continued with accelerating pace. The precise impact of higher prices on the Colombian economy cannot be evaluated here, and their impact on the coffee growing regions themselves must await the results of the coming 1980 coffee census. All that can be said at present is that the Brazilian frost of 1975 has already made invalid many estimates of future production, including one used in this book according to which Colombia would produce some 10 million bags in the 1980s. The 1977–8 harvest is estimated at 11.5 million bags. The reader will, I hope, find some interesting parallels between this boom and others that have occurred over the last century. Once again one bottle-neck for legal exports has been the inefficiency of the official ports, overcome by flourishing illicit points of export. From these not only contraband coffee leaves the country, but other stimulating productions of tropical agriculture as well, such as marijuana. Here too the initiative of Colombians in the 1970s repeats that of their forebears in the coffee market of the 1870s in exploiting a new area of comparative advantage.

Appendix 1. Sample of coffee estates in Cundinamarca and Antioquia, 1870–98

Hacienda	Municipio	Extent (ha)
El Chocho	Fusagasugá	6,400
Calandaima	Viotá	2,792
Florencia	Viotá	1,740
San Antonio	Anapoima	1,700
Misiones	El Colegio	1,234
Java	Viotá	1,104
Ceilán	Viotá	1,060
Liberia	Viotá	960
La Loma	Venecia	897
Jonás	Fredonia	832
Golconda	El Colegio–Anapoima	690
Liberia	Viotá	687
La Argentina	Viotá	648
Los Olivos	Viotá	576
Las Granjas	El Colegio	555
La Granja	Fredonia	473
La Amalia	Fredonia	403
Costa Rica	Viotá	384
Argelia	Viotá	333
La Ruidosa	Viotá	321
San Pedro	Fredonia	320
Gualanday	Fredonia	294
Atala	Viotá	256
Santa Bárbara	Sasaima	256
Escocia	Viotá	250
La India	Venecia	230
Arabia	Viotá	228

Sources: Based on documents in Oficina de Registro de Instrumentos Públicos, La Mesa and Fredonia; ANC, Notarías de Bogotá; Archívo Histórico de Antioquia, Notarías de Medellín.

Appendix 2. Piece-rate wages on two coffee haciendas, 1879–1933

Year	Hacienda Santa Bárbara[a]	Year	Hacienda Jonás[b]
1879	0.059	1918	0.15
1880	0.059	1919	0.15
1881	0.057	1920	0.18
1882	0.055	1921	0.23
1883	0.053	1922	0.36
1884	0.053	1923	0.72
1885	0.049	1924	1.08
1886	0.052	1925	1.12
1887	0.059	1926	1.08
1888	0.074	1927	1.08
1889	0.075	1928	1.35
1890	0.082	1929	1.08
1891	0.100	1930	0.81
1892	0.116	1931	0.81
1893	0.125	1932	0.81
1894	0.143	1933	0.86
1895	0.135		
1896	0.150		
1897	0.150		
1898	0.150		
1899	0.153		
1900	0.202		
1901	0.270		
1902	0.510		
1912	6.00[c]		

a Piece-rate in paper pesos per *arroba*. *b* Daily wage of a *chapolero* in pesos gold; quota: 9 *tarros*. *c* Equivalent to 6 centavos gold.
Note: The *cosechero* on Santa Bárbara was paid an additional ration of *miel* (to make *guarapo*). The *chapolero(-a)* on Jonás under a 9-*tarro* quota (70 kg approximately) received a full ration of food, i.e. three meals a day. For wages on Jonás 1896–1918 see table 17.
Sources: Archivo Herrera and Archivo Jonás.

Appendix 3. Concentration of the coffee export trade (percentage controlled by 20 leading companies), 1933–70

Year	Total Colombian exports[a]	Total number of export companies	20 leading companies				
			Percentage exported	Number of foreign companies	Percentage exported by foreign companies	Percentage exported by Colombian companies[b]
1933[c]	2,867,804	180	80.69	10	47.30	33.39
1940–1[d]	4,401,289	61	90.60	6	35.19	55.41
1944[e]	4,923,305	50	90.26	6	27.75	62.51
1954[f]	6,924,877	74	84.06	4	18.11	65.95
1961[g]	5,560,742	65	92.86	6	15.07	77.79
1966[g]	5,565,333	22	97.5	5	17.9	79.6
1970[g]	6,508,660	31	98.84	3	11.87	86.97

a 60-kilo bags. b Includes FNCC. Companies are defined as Colombian according to their formal legal status only.
Source: FNCC, Boletín de Información y Estadística: c No. 8 (January 1934), p. 234. d No. 23 (May 1942), pp. 580–91. e No. 26 (December 1945), pp. 181–3. f No. 34 (July 1955), p. 38. g Nos. 46–7 (1972–3), p. 26.

Appendix 4. Foreign exchange rates in Colombia, 1870–1970

Exchange rates, 1870–1913: paper pesos to the pound sterling

December of the year	Bogotá	Medellín
1870	5.00	5.05
1871	—	5.10
1872	—	5.04
1873	—	5.12
1874	5.20	5.19
1875	5.30	5.32
1876	5.45	5.05
1877	5.25	5.36
1878	5.40	5.32
1879	5.60	5.50
1880	5.25	5.66
1881	5.80	5.75
1882	6.00	6.24
1883	6.30	6.43
1884	6.50	6.40
1885	6.80	6.72
1886	7.00	7.42
1887	9.10	9.20
1888	10.10	9.85
1889	9.75	9.60
1890	9.50	9.40
1891	9.50	9.50
1892	10.05	10.00
1893	12.20	12.30
1894	12.90	13.20
1895	11.95	11.85
1896	11.90	12.00
1897	12.60	13.50
1898	15.85	15.80
1899	32.50	30.00
1900	54.60	53.50
1901	235.00	172.60
1902	460.00	375.00

December of the year	Bogotá	Medellín
1903	505.00	557.50
1904[a]	5.50	4.87
1905	5.20	5.22
1906	5.00	5.25
1907	4.72	4.91
1908	4.59	5.02
1909	4.77	4.95
1910	5.06	4.83
1911	–	4.93
1912	–	4.93
1913	–	4.99

a Pesos gold from 1904 onwards.
Note: The Colombian monetary unity is the peso divided into 100 centavos. In 1880 the paper peso was introduced and in 1904 the peso gold was reintroduced equivalent to 100 paper pesos.

To obtain the value of the peso to the £ sterling I have used the average quotation of 5.00 pesos to the £ sterling which prevailed about 1870, and to this figure I have added the Colombian foreign exchange premium, using for Bogotá the Banco de Colombia, 'Cuadro que indica el premio que han tenido en Bogotá los giros sobre Londres . . .' (n.d.), p. 45, and for Medellín, López and Rodríguez, *Estadísticas de Antioquia*, pp. 161–2.

It is worth mentioning that there were different monetary units at the end of the century with different values in terms of the pound. For instance, in his report of 1888, British Vice-consul Dickson in Bogotá gave these estimates: value of gold exported, 5 pesos to the £ sterling; value of silver exported, 6 pesos to the £ sterling; exports from Cúcuta (where the peso silver 8/10 was never displaced by the paper peso as the monetary unity), 6 pesos to the £ sterling; the remainder of exports, 9 pesos to the £ sterling. All imports were calculated by the Colombian customs houses at 5 pesos to the £ sterling. See Dickson, *Report on the Commerce*, P.P., vol. 78 (1889), pp. 587–8.

Principal exchange rate, 1910–36: pesos to the U.S. dollar

December of the year		December of the year		December of the year	
1910	1.03	1920	1.18	1930	1.03
1911	1.00	1921	1.09	1931	1.03
1912	1.01	1922	1.05	1932	1.05
1913	1.05	1923	1.03	1933	1.57
1914	1.08	1924	1.00	1934	1.55
1915	–	1925	1.01	1935	1.75
1916	–	1926	1.02	1936	1.75
1917	–	1927	1.02		
1918	0.85	1928	1.02		
1919	0.98	1929	1.03		

Source: Banco de la República, *XLI y XLII Informe Anual del Gerente, 1965–1966*, vol. 2, p. 146.

Exchange rates, 1937–70: pesos to the U.S. dollar

Last quarter of the year	Coffee export rate	Other exports rate	Principal selling rate	Free rate
1937	1.80	1.82	1.83	—
1938	1.74	1.75	1.77	—
1939	1.74	1.75	1.77	—
1945	1.74	1.75	1.82	—
1946	1.74	1.75	1.82	—
1947	1.74	1.75	1.82	—
1948	1.95	1.95	2.15	2.68
1949	1.95	1.95	2.15	2.86
1950	1.95	1.95	2.04	3.08
1951	2.19	2.50	2.59	—
1952	2.29	2.50	2.51	3.70
1953	2.38	2.50	2.51	3.41
1954	2.38	2.50	2.51	3.50
1955	2.50	2.50	2.51	4.16
1956	3.18	2.50	2.51	6.86
1957	4.28	5.31	5.97	6.22
1958	4.84	5.98	7.22	8.23
1959	5.03	6.82	6.40	7.01
1960	5.38	7.09	6.70	7.23
1961	5.72	8.62	6.70	8.82
1962	6.96	10.92	9.00	11.09
1963	7.01	9.98	9.00	9.99
1964	7.42	12.74	9.00	12.77
1965	8.50	13.50	13.51	18.29
1966	9.94	13.50	13.50	16.30
1967	12.13	15.76	15.82	—
1968	13.50	16.88	16.95	—
1969	14.28	17.85	17.93	—
1970	15.28	19.10	19.17	—

Note: In 1967 the heavily differentiated coffee export rate, first established in 1951, was abolished and in its place a special export tax was levied on coffee. But from the table it seems that the IMF assumes some sort of real value for the coffee export rate, probably taking into consideration this export tax and the *reintegro cafetero*. The Banco de la República gives the following values for the coffee export rate: 1967, 15.76 pesos; 1968, 16.88 pesos; 1969, 17.85 pesos; and 1970, 19.09 pesos. See *Revista del Banco de la República*, vol. 45, no. 541, p. 2088.

Sources: International Monetary Fund, *International Financial Statistics*, June 1954, pp. 72–3; supp. to 1963/4 issues, p. 46; 1972 supp., p. 120.

Weights and measures

cuadro: an area 40 metres square or ¼ of a *fanegada*
fanegada or *cuadra*: 0.64 hectare or 1.5808 acres
hectare: 2.47 acres
legua: 5 kilometres

almud: about 120 kilos (with local variations)
arroba (25 *libras*): 12.5 kilos
carga: usually 125 kilos or 10 *arrobas*
cuartilla: see glossary under *tarro*
kilo (kilogram; abbrev. kg): 2.2046 English pounds
libra (16 *onzas*): 0.5 kilo
saco: 62.5 kilos or 5 *arrobas*
tarro: see glossary
tonelada: 1,000 kilos or 80 *arrobas*
tonne: 1,000 kilos

Glossary

General terms

agregado: worker on *antioqueño* and *caldense* coffee haciendas allowed to
    cultivate a patch of land as part of his wage
anticresis: giving over to a creditor a property and its produce until the
    debt is paid
aparcero: share-cropper, called *viviente* in Santander and *compañero* in
    Antioquia
arepa: a kind of bread made of maize, common in *antioqueño* regions
arrendatario: worker on *cundi-tolimense* coffee hacienda who receives a
    small plot of land in return for his obligatory labour on the coffee
    plantation
audiencia: the highest court in the vice-royalty
baldíos: public lands
bochinche: riot, disturbance
cacique: local political boss; also called *gamonal*
capellanía: chantry endowment
censatario: owner obliged to pay *censo*
censo: ecclesiastical mortgage, usually perpetual
cestero: see *cosechero*

chapolero(a): see *cosechero*

colono: originally, service tenant on hacienda; later, colonizer or squatter on public lands

comarca: district

compañero: see *aparcero*

concertado: service tenant in the highlands

corregimiento: colonial and republican administrative unit; below the *municipio*

cosechero: coffee-harvester, usually a woman or a child; also *chapolero*, *cintudero*, *almudero*, *cestero*, etc.

cuchuco: a soup based on wheat

departamento: main political and administrative division of the country; there are 22 *departamentos* in Colombia

desamortización: expropriation by the state of lands and properties held by corporations, in practice by the Church

dulce: unrefined brown sugar (Antioquia)

ejido: common land belonging to a *municipio*

encomienda: grant of a number of Indians (to an *encomendero*) during the colonial era, as tribute-payers usually in workforce

enganche; *enganchador*: practice of labour contracting; a labour contractor

estancia: plot worked by an *arrendatario* for his own sustenance and profit

finca: estate, usually small or of medium size

fonda: in *antioqueño* country, a rural dry-goods and retail shop; usually receives coffee as means of payment and is a centre of local credit

fundador: in *antioqueño* colonization, founder of a settlement or *pueblo*

gamonal: see *cacique*

gariteros: workers responsible for preparing rations

graneos: the end-of-season coffee crop

gremio: an economic interest group; a trade organization

guaquería: despoiling of Indian tombs, especially in Quindío, in search of gold

guarapo: non-distilled liquor from sugar-cane; basic in the *arrendatario* and peon diet on *cundi-tolimense* coffee haciendas

guardiola: machine for drying coffee (from the Costa Rican inventor de la Guardia)

jornal: daily wage of the peon

jornalero: day-labourer

machete: long knife for agricultural work

mazamorra: a soup based on maize

miel: sugar-cane juice

mitaca: the smaller of the two coffee crops of the year

mute: a soup based on maize

mulero: mule boy

mestizo: half-breed of European and Indian blood

minifundia: very small land-holdings

municipio: the small administrative unit centred on a city or *pueblo* with jurisdiction over the surrounding countryside

oidor: *audiencia* judge

panela: loaf of unrefined brown sugar
peon: worker in agriculture on public works
peón de asiento: see *arrendatario*
pepeos: the coffee production of the infant tree
personero municipal: official *municipio* representative
pueblo: a small rural town
quina: cinchona bark; quinine bark
rancho: in Colombia, a humble rural dwelling
resguardo: Indian reservation
rocería: clearing land by burning before planting
secuestros: confiscations of Spanish-owned property at the time of Independence
tablón: naturally defined area of coffee plantation (Cundinamarca)
tarro: a basket, varying in size, used in picking coffee in Antioquia; called *cuartilla* in Cundinamarca and Tolima
tierra caliente: hot lowlands (below 1,800 metres)
tonga: naturally defined area of coffee plantation (Antioquia)
trapiche: simple mill for sugar-cane
vales: bonds
vecino: inhabitant, especially white or *mestizo* living in Indian *resguardo* village
vecino rico: in Santander, a local well-to-do person
vereda: the smallest rural unit; rural neighbourhood
viviente: see *aparcero*

Coffee terms*

clean coffee: see 'green coffee'
coffee pulp: covering of the coffee berry; it is removed during depulping operations and can be used as compost
depulping: initial phase of processing during which the pulp of the fresh coffee berry is removed
drying: process of drying parchment coffee in the sun or in drying machines or *guardiolas*
excelso coffee: principal grade of green coffee; represents 95% of Colombia's coffee exports
green coffee: fully processed coffee ready for export. In Colombia green coffee represents 80% of the parchment coffee and 20% of the berries processed. Also known as 'clean' or 'threshed' coffee.
mild coffee: type of coffee derived from the *arabica* variety
nursery: place where seedlings are prepared; consists of seed-boxes and seed-beds
parchment coffee: coffee in semi-processed stage, still retaining the thin skin or parchment
processing: the whole series of stages through which the coffee passes from the time it is picked (in the berry) to the time it is ready for export (as green coffee)

* See ECLA/FAO, *Coffee in Latin America: Productivity Problems and Future Prospects*, vol. 1: *Colombia and El Salvador* (E/CN 12/490) (1958), p. 100.

pruning: series of operations designed to influence the growth of coffee trees or shade trees for the purpose of obtaining the highest possible coffee yield. In Colombia the most important of these are: (*a*) elimination of unproductive shoots by light pruning (*deschupone*); (*b*) pruning proper, i.e. removal of superfluous shoots on a scale greater than in (*a*); (*c*) topping, i.e. shaping of the tree by limiting its vertical growth to a height of 1.60–1.70 m, thus facilitating its horizontal development and picking; (*d*) shade pruning, i.e., pruning of shade trees

replanting: replacement of withered, unproductive and weak trees within an established coffee plantation

threshed coffee: see 'green coffee'

threshing: final stage of processing; it consists in the final removal of the parchment

washing: stage in processing which follows fermentation and which is designed to remove the mucilage

weeding: operation designed to eliminate weeds; usually the hoe is used and, to a lesser extent, the *machete*

Notes

Abbreviations

ANC	Archivo Nacional de Colombia
DANE	Departamento Administravo Nacional de Estadística
D.O.	*Diario Oficial*
ECLA	Economic Commission for Latin America
FAO	Food and Agriculture Organization
FNCC	Federación Nacional de Cafeteros de Colombia
P.P.	Parliamentary Papers
PRO, FO	Public Record Office, Foreign Office
R.N.A.	*Revista Nacional de Agricultura*
SAC	Sociedad de Agricultores de Colombia

Chapter 1

1 G. Colmenares, *Historia económica y social de Colombia, 1537–1719* (Cali, 1973), pp. 185, 277–9.

2 S. Camacho Roldán, in *El Agricultor*, no. 5 (October 1884), p. 200.

3 By the coefficient of exports I mean the percentage of exports in GDP.

4 On the negative effects of foreign trade in the second half of the nineteenth century, see W. P. McGreevey, *An Economic History of Colombia, 1845–1930* (Cambridge, 1971), pp. 157–81. This work met with widespread criticism in a seminar on Colombian economic history held in Bogotá in July 1975. These proceedings are to be published in L. Ospina Vásquez et al., *Historia económica de Colombia: un debate en marcha* (Bogotá, forthcoming).

5 This topic has been analysed by three of the most influential Colombian historians: L. E. Nieto Arteta, *Economía y cultura en la historia de Colombia* (Bogotá, 1942), I. Liévano Aguirre, *Rafael Núñez*, 2nd edn (Bogotá, 1958), and L. Ospina Vásquez, *Industria y protección en Colombia, 1810–1930* (Medellín, 1955). See also F. R. Safford, *The Ideal of the Practical* (Austin, Texas, 1976).

6 Liévano, *Núñez*, pp. 175–8.

7 Ospina, *Industria*, pp. 206–8.

8 D. C. Johnson, 'Social and Economic Change in Nineteenth Century Santander, Colombia', unpublished Ph.D. thesis, University of California at Berkeley, 1975, considers that Santander was a laboratory of 'utopian radicalism' from the 1850s on (pp. 4, 16–17). According to Johnson this mid-century Liberalism found its inspiration not in the European revolutions of 1848, but in the Enlightenment, in Independence, and in the local legacy

of the Comunero revolt of 1781 (p. 50). He also holds that M. Murillo
Toro was not a complete free-trader, but rather a pre-Marxist socialist
after Sismondi (pp. 28, 33, 36). This socialist side of Murillo Toro is also
stressed by G. Molina, *Las ideas liberales en Colombia, 1849–1914*, 2nd
edn (Bogotá, 1971), pp. 70–82, following R. Quiñones Neira, *Manuel
Murillo Toro* (Bogotá, 1936). Ospina Vásquez considers his socialism an
aberration of his last years. See Ospina, *Industria*, pp. 250–2.

9   J. M. Samper, *Derecho público interno de Colombia*, 2nd edn (2 vols.,
Bogotá, 1974), vol. 1, pp. 290, 293–4.

10   R. L. Gilmore and J. P. Harrison, 'Juan Bernardo Elbers and the
Introduction of Steam Navigation on the Magdalena River', *Hispanic
American Historical Review*, 28 (August 1948), pp. 342–3; F. R. Safford,
'Empresarios nacionales y extranjeros en Colombia durante el siglo XIX',
Anuario Colombiano de Historia Social y de la Cultura, no. 4 (1969),
pp. 97–8.

11   L. F. Sierra, *El tabaco en la economía colombiana del siglo XIX*
(Bogotá, 1971), pp. 105–9.

12   W. J. Dickson, *Report for the Year 1888 on the Trade of Colombia*,
P.P. 1889, vol. 78, p. 597; S. Camacho Roldán, *Notas de viaje* (Bogotá,
1890), p. 103.

13   On Santander, see for example *Ordenanzas espedidas por la Cámara
Provincial de Santander en sus sesiones ordinarias de 1850* (Socorro, n.d.),
pp. 29–50; *Constitución Municipal i Ordenanzas espedidas por la Lejislatura Provincial de Santander en sus sesiones de 1853* (Sorocco, 1854),
p. 244; *Ordenanzas de la Cámara Provincial del Socorro espedidas en
1850* (Socorro, 1850), pp. 21–2; ibid. *1852* (Socorro, 1852), p. 5. On roads
in Cundinamarca, see *Informe del Secretario de Hacienda del Estado
Soberano de Cundinamarca a la Asamblea, 1865* (Bogotá, n.d.), p. 10;
Memoria del Gobernador de Cundinamarca 1858 (Bogotá, n.d.), pp. 12–
13; *Informe del Presidente de la Junta Administradora del Camino de
Occidente* (Bogotá, March 1888), pp. 5–9; *Los doce códigos del Estado
de Cundinamarca* (3 vols., Bogotá, 1859), vol. 1, pp. 63, 272–4. On roads
in Antioquia see R. J. Brew, 'The Economic Development of Antioquia
from 1850 to 1920', unpublished D.Phil. thesis, Oxford University, 1973,
pp. 91–3.

14   On the problems of tolls on merchandise passing through the state of
Magdalena that Santander merchants had to pay, see *Informe del Presidente
del Estado de Santander, 1874* (Socorro, n.d.), pp. 3–5, and *Informe del
Presidente del Estado de Santander, 1875* (Socorro, n.d.), pp. 7–11.

15   Camacho, *Notas*, pp. 25–7.

16   Dickson, *Report on the Trade*, p. 594.

17   J. F. Rippy, 'Dawn of the Railway Era in Colombia', *Hispanic Americ*
Historical Review, 23 (August 1943), pp. 650–3. The most important work
on railway development in Colombia is that of A. Ortega, *Ferrocarriles
colombianos: resumen histórico* (2 vols., Bogotá, 1920), and *Ferrocarriles
colombianos: la última experiencia ferroviaria del país 1920–1930* (Bogotá
1932).

18   'Economic anarchy produces political anarchy which in its turn make
economic anarchy worse', wrote Nieto Arteta (*Economía*, p. 116). M. Deas

has called attention to this politico-economic interaction in the relationship between fiscal crisis and breakdown of public order. See Deas, 'Crisis fiscal y "orden público"', in Ospina et al., *Historia económica*.

19   F. Schurmann, *Ideology and Organization in Communist China*, 2nd edn (Berkeley, 1968), pp. 405–12.

20   Sierra, *El tabaco*, pp. 128, 168, 170.

21   D. C. Johnson, 'Social and Economic Change', pp. 176–81.

22   Data on cotton exports from Banco de la República, *XLII y XLIII Informe Anual del Gerente a la Junta Directiva* (2 vols., Bogotá, 1965–6), vol. 2, p. 189.

23   Juan de Dios Carrasquilla to B. Koppel, Bogotá, 30 March 1880, in U.S. National Archives (microfilm): Despatches from U.S. Consuls in Bogotá, 1850–1905, T116.

24   D. C. Johnson, 'Social and Economic Change', p. 166.

25   M. Rivas, *Los trabajadores de tierra caliente*, 2nd edn (Bogotá, 1972), pp. 288–93.

26   Dickson, *Report on the Trade*, p. 592.

27   Based on data provided by Sierra, *El tabaco*, p. 111.

28   A thinker like M. A. Caro, the principal ideologue of the Regeneration, is hard to consider as in the same current as the Porfirian *científicos* like Sierra, Bulnes, and Limantour. Caro, unlike these, was essentially anti-liberal in the de Bonald and de Meistre tradition, and his notion of power derives from Suarès, though perhaps unconsciously. On Caro's thought, see the analysis of J. Jaramillo Uribe, *El pensamiento colombiano en el siglo XIX* (Bogotá, 1964), pp. 314–49.

29   See F. H. Hinsley (ed.), *The New Cambridge Modern History, XI: Material Progress and World-Wide Problems, 1870–98* (Cambridge, 1962), pp. 25–34.

30   According to Ospina Vásquez, the 'example' of Porfirian Mexico had a powerful influence on Conservative leaders. Jorge Holguín, Jorge Roa, Pedro Nel Ospina, Carlos Martínez Silva, and Rafael Reyes, among others, visited Mexico at the end of the century. For Reyes it was certainly a model. See Ospina, *Industria*, pp. 330–1.

31   E. J. Hobsbawm, *The Age of Capital* (London, 1976), pp. 303–6.

32   F. R. Safford, 'Commerce and Enterprise in Central Colombia, 1821–1870', unpublished Ph.D. thesis, Columbia University, 1965, p. 13.

33   D. Bushnell, *El régimen de Santander en la Gran Colombia* (Bogotá, 1966), pp. 155–6, 169–70, 175–6; R. Carr, *Spain, 1808–1939* (Oxford, 1966), pp. 65–72.

34   P. Monbeig, *Novos estudios de geografía humana brasileira* (São Paulo, 1957), p. 157.

35   *Colombia: relación geográfica, topográfica, agrícola, commercial y política de este país*, 2nd edn (2 vols., Bogotá, 1974), vol. 2, pp. 34–5.

36   M. Romero, *Cultivo del café en la costa meridional de Chiapas* (Mexico City, 1875), pp. 217–40; C. F. Van Delden Laërne, *Brazil and Java: Report on Coffee-Culture in America, Asia and Africa* (London, 1885). On Costa Rica, see C. Hall, *El café y el desarrollo histórico–geográfico de Costa Rica* (San José, 1976), based on her D.Phil. thesis, 'Some Effects of the Spread of Coffee Cultivation upon the Landscape of Costa Rica in the

Nineteenth and Twentieth Centuries', Oxford University, 1972. On Guatemala, see S. A. Mosk, 'The Coffee Economy of Guatemala, 1850–1918: Development and Signs of Instability', *Inter-American Economic Affairs*, 11 (1955). On Venezuela, see J. V. Lombardi and J. A. Hanson, 'The First Venezuelan Coffee Cycle, 1820–1855', *Agricultural History*, 44, 4 (October 1970), pp. 355–66.

37   S. Bolívar to J. A. Páez, Bogotá, 16 August 1828, in V. Lecuna (ed.), S. Bolívar, *Obras completas* (3 vols., Havana, 1950), vol. 2, pp. 944–5.

38   *Escritos de dos economistas coloniales: don Antonio de Narváez y la Torre y don José I. de Pombo*, 2nd edn (Bogotá, 1965), pp. 30, 35, 144–5, 215–18.

39   Comisión Corográfica, *Geografía física y política de las provincias de la Nueva Granada* (4 vols., Bogotá, 1957–9), vol. 3, pp. 29, 71, 85, 116. For an earlier period see B. V. de Oviedo, *Cualidades y riquezas del Nuevo Reino de Granada*, 2nd edn (Bogotá, 1930), pp. 164–5, 177; F. Silvestre, *Descripción del Reino de Santa Fé de Bogotá*, 2nd edn (Bogotá 1968), pp. 46, 58, 61; G. Giraldo Jaramillo (ed.), *Relaciones de mando de los virreyes de la Nueva Granada* (Bogotá, 1954), pp. 129, 177, 215– 16; L. Febres Cordero, *Del antiguo Cúcuta*, 2nd edn (Bogotá, 1975), pp. 203–29.

40   Felipe Pérez, *Jeografía física i política del Estado de Santander,* 3rd edn (2 vols., Bogotá, 1863), vol. 2, p. 82; M. Ancízar, *Peregrinación del Alpha*, 2nd edn (2 vols., Bogotá, 1970), vol. 2, pp. 198–205.

41   R. C. Beyer, 'The Colombian Coffee Industry: Origins and Major Trends, 1740–1940', unpublished Ph.D. thesis, University of Minnesota, 1947. Chs. 2 and 3 of this work deal with early transport problems.

42   A good example is provided by Nicolás Sáenz's donation of 514 technical books to the Biblioteca Nacional in 1902. Sáenz was well known in Cundinamarca and Tolima for being one of the most vocal supporters of coffee trade and cultivation among the pioneers of that product. A study of this process of orientation towards 'the technical and the practical' among the New Granadian elite, before coffee and clearly Bourbon in origin, is F. Safford's already cited book *The Ideal*, pp. 49–98.

43   Brew, 'Economic Development', pp. 15–21.

44   ANC, Consulados: Correspondencia consular: Liverpool, vols. 6 and 8; New York, vols. 20–2. See also the report of Miguel Samper, Londres, vol. 4, p. 197.

45   See table 3.

46   Based on Roth, *Die Ubererzeugung in der Welthandelsware Kaffee im Zeitraum von 1700–1929* (Jena, 1929), appendix.

47   Comisión Corográfica, *Geografía*, vol. 3, p. 71.

48   See table 3.

49   The prices are annual averages based on New York prices. A series for 1858–99 was reproduced by S. Camacho Roldán in *Escritos varios* (2 vols., Bogotá, 1892), vol. 1, pp. 555–6. A more complete series based on the same source for 1825–1945 is to be found in Beyer, 'The Colombian Coffee Industry', pp. 366 et seq.

50   D. C. Johnson, 'Social and Economic Change', p. 183.

51   Comisión Corográfica, *Geografía*, vol. 3, pp. 25, 29, 71–85, 115–17.
52   A. Ramos, *Industria cafeeira na America hespanola* (Rio de Janeiro, 1907) in his *O café no Brasil e no estrangeiro* (Rio de Janeiro, 1923), pp. 339–40.
53   H. Arboleda C., *Estadística general de la República de Colombia* (Bogotá, 1905), pp. 174–5; Dickson, *Report on the Trade*, p. 588; J. P. Eder, *Colombia* (London, 1913), p. 76.
54   *Informe del Presidente del Estado Soberano de Santander, 1878* (Socorro, n.d.), p. 27.
55   'Circular sobre el fomento de la agricultura', *El Agricultor*, no. 6 (November 1884), p. 208.
56   The classic work remains that of J. J. Parsons, *The Antioqueño Colonization in Western Colombia*, 2nd edn (Berkeley, 1968).
57   An optimistic *ex post facto* vision is very current and tends to prevail among economists. A good example of this is to be found in R. W. Harbison, 'Colombia', in W. A. Lewis (ed.), *Tropical Development, 1880–1913* (London, 1970), pp. 73–86.

Chapter 2

1   M. Deas, 'A Colombian Coffee Estate: Santa Bárbara, Cundinamarca, 1870–1912', in K. Duncan and I. Rutledge (eds.), *Land and Labour in Latin America* (Cambridge, 1977), pp. 269–98; D. Bustamante, 'Efectos económicos del papel moneda durante la Regeneración', *Cuadernos Colombianos*, no. 4 (1974), pp. 561–660; M. Urrutia, 'El sector externo y la distribución de ingresos en Colombia en el siglo XIX', *Revista del Banco de la República*, no. 541 (Novembér 1972).
2   M. Urrutia, *Historia del sindicalismo en Colombia* (Bogotá, 1969), pp. 47–51.
3   A. Lleras Camargo, *Mi gente* (Bogotá, 1975), p. 48. In the context of this work, a poor work of history but a valuable ideological text, 'peasant' would perhaps be understood as 'señor campesino' as opposed to 'aldeano' (p. 21).
4   See among others A. Parra, *Memorias* (Bogotá, 1912), S. Camacho Roldán, *Memorias*, 2nd edn (2 vols., Bogotá, 1946), E. Rodríguez Piñeres, *El olimpo radical* (Bogotá, 1950), and A. J. Rivadeneira, *Don Santiago Pérez: Biografía de un carácter* (Bogotá, 1967).
5   M. Samper, *La miseria en Bogotá y otros escritos*, 2nd edn (Bogotá, 1969), pp. 39, 102.
6   *D.O.*, 1 April 1874, p. 1.
7   J. M. Cordovez Moure, *Reminiscencias de Santa Fé y Bogotá* (Madrid, 1957). This is a series of chronicles of political and social life in the Colombian capital in the nineteenth century; they appeared in different magazines between 1891 and the author's death in July 1918. This 1957 edition, carefully prepared by Elisa Mujica, contains the prologues to the different collections which appeared between 1893 and 1904. In that of 1893 José M. Marroquín stated: 'we old men feel irresistibly drawn towards the past, hungry for memories and openly hostile to the future', and to the con-

temporary historian this seems more a social problem which affected the elite of Bogotá than a symptom of a geriatric condition. The poet Pombo wrote with ill-concealed joy that 'Bogotá is nothing more than a city with more pawnshops than regular commerce.' But at the very time he was writing, a legitimate merchant, Pedro A. López, a protégé of the Samper family, had become so important in Honda that he decided to move with his family to the capital to set up a store in the Tercera Calle Florián and speculate in coffee, not as a pawnbroker. See Hugo Latorre Cabal, *Mi novela: Apuntes autobiográficos de Alfonso López* (Bogotá, 1961), pp. 207–8. The *raizales* (original inhabitants of the city) did not resent trade in itself, as this had enjoyed great prestige since the days of the Colony, but the success of the 'new class', expressed in the power of money. See also Rivas, *Los trabajadores*, p. 306. On J. A. Silva, himself a merchant *malgré lui*, and the 'aristocratic–literary' *soirées* in which the enlightened merchants of the city participated, see R. Maya, 'Mi José Asunción Silva', in J. A. Silva, *Obras completas* (Bogotá, 1955), and A. Miramón, *José A. Silva*, 2nd edn (Bogotá, 1957). The best work on Mariano Ospina Rodrígue despite its constantly laudatory tone, is E. Gómez Barrientos, *Don Marianc Ospina y su época* (2 vols., Medellín, 1913–15).

8   Ospina, *Industria*, pp. 206–7.

9   H. Rodríguez Plata, *La inmigración alemana al Estado Soberano de Santander en el siglo XIX* (Bogotá, 1968), ch. 3; J. J. García, *Crónicas de Bucaramanga* (Bogotá, 1896), p. 186; C. Martínez Silva, *Capítulos de historia política de Colombia*, 2nd edn (3 vols., Bogotá, 1973), vol. 1, pp. 193–203.

10   J. L. Helguera, 'Antecedentes sociales de la Revolución de 1851 en el sur de Colombia (1848–1849)', *Anuario Colombiano de Historia Social y de la Cultura*, no. 5 (1970), p. 57.

11   From among the many contemporary accounts, see esp. A. Cuervo, *Cómo se evapora un ejército* (Paris, 1900), which offers a version of the 1860 war from the point of view of the Ospina government, and S. Camacl *Memorias*, vol. 2, pp. 151–231, which describes the attitude of the young Liberals to General Mosquera from the time when he entered the city of Bogotá as victor in September 1861 until the Convention of Rionegro, 1863.

12   Samper, *La miseria*, p. 32.

13   *D.O.*, 4 August 1875, 17 November 1876, 15 December 1896. See also *Informe del Gobernador de Cundinamarca 1877* (Bogotá, 1877); Banco de Bogotá, *Trayectoria de una empresa de servicio, 1870–1960* (Bogotá, 1960), p. 44; J. Holguín Arboleda, *Mucho en serio y algo en broma* (Bogotá, 1959), pp. 31–3, and *21 años de vida colombiana* (Bogotá 1967), ch. 49.

14   M. A. Caro, *El Centenario de 'El Tradicionista'*, ed. C. Andrade Valderrama (Bogotá, 1972), pp. 24, 103.

15   Martínez Silva, *Capítulos de historia política*, vol. 1, pp. 97, 165; Ospina, *Industria*, p. 248.

16   *Informe que presenta el subsecretario encargado del Ministerio de Gobierno de Colombia al Congreso Constitucional de 1894* (Bogotá, 1894). The author describes a 'Liberal conspiracy' which ends in the

expulsion from the country of Santiago Pérez and Modesto Garcés, and the confinement in San Andres Island of a number of Liberal leaders, as well as the suspending of the newspapers *El Relator* and *El Contemporaneo*. On the behaviour of Don Santiago Pérez, see Rafael Uribe U. in *Anales de la Cámara de Representantes*, 21 December 1896. See also the *'Mensaje de 1894'*, in *D.O.*, 20 July 1894. Press censorship was becoming progressively tighter; *D.O.*, 12 January 1897, 14 January 1898.

17   See p. 17.
18   'Informe del Comandante de Policía de Cundinamarca', in *Gaceta de Cundinamarca*, 23 June 1890.
19   ANC, Consulados: Correspondencia consular, Londres, vol. 2, ff. 1–7, 265–360, 458–552, 708–85; Liverpool, vol. 8, ff. 1–72, 117–86, 253–329, 530–91, 831–930; New York, vol. 25, ff. 1–142, 238–358, 392–559.
20   Archivo Ospina, S. Ospina to G. Arboleda, Medellín, 4 September 1888.
21   Ibid., S. Ospina to J. Arboleda, Medellín, 8 May 1893.
22   Ibid., S. Ospina to T. Ospina, Medellín, 4 September 1888.
23   Ibid., S. Ospina to T. Ospina, Medellín, 14 August 1888.
24   Ibid., S. Ospina to P. N. Ospina (in Guatemala), Medellín, 15 January 1888.
25   Ibid., P. N. Ospina to T. Ospina, Medellín, 15 September 1888; Ospina Hermanos to J. M. Restrepo G. and A. Villa, Medellín, 11 August 1891; Ospina Hermanos to J. M. Amadador, Medellín, 12 August 1891.
26   Ibid., Ospina Lalinde to F. Escobar, Cali, 30 August 1892. (Ospina Lalinde was a firm formed by Ospina Hermanos, Gabriel Lalinde Hermanos, Eduardo Vásquez, Eduardo Uribe U. & Co. and Ramón Restrepo.) In a letter from S. Ospina to Tulio and Mariano Ospina Vásquez, Medellín, 13 February 1894, the family pronounces its final judgement on Pepe Sierra, with whom it has maintained a complex relationship of alliance and rivalry in the liquor auctions: 'As regards Sierra, we don't believe either in his friendship or in his hostility: he is a mercenary who would help us if it suited his convenience.'
27   L. Ospina Vásquez attributed this element to what he called 'the *antioqueño* mode of being', a theme on which much has been written. See also F. R. Safford's already cited work on values, *The Ideal of the Practical*.
28   Archivo Ospina, S. Ospina to P. N. Ospina (in Guatemala), Medellín, 15 February 1888, S. Ospina to T. Ospina, Medellín, 20 August 1888.
29   These were the codes for the telegraph: 'I hope to return' = defeat for the government; 'I hope to return soon' = serious defeat for the government; 'Need money' = serious *pronunciamiento*; 'I am writing' = Santander; 'Answer me' = Boyacá; 'Regards' = Cundinamarca; 'Embraces' = coast; 'Please reply' = Tolima; 'Remember me' = Cauca; 'Cable me' = Antioquia; 'Good' = General Reyes; 'I am the same' = Caro left office; 'Advise me' = Magdalena river. Telegrams *en claire* were to be signed 'Nel'. Those were the codes from Bogotá. From Medellín to Bogotá the possibilities were even simpler: 'Come back' = defeat for government; 'Come back soon' = serious defeat for government; 'We have sent money' = *pronunciamiento*; 'We have sent money immediately' = serious *pronunciamiento*; 'Good' = General Vélez entered government service; 'No news' = forces

have left; 'Best wishes = river boats; 'Remember me to every one' = revoluti
has captured river boats.

30   These were basic elements and situations. The theme of civil wars has
not aroused much interest in recent Colombian historiography. For a
bibliographical introduction, see A. Tirado Mejía (ed.), *Aspectos sociales
de las guerras civiles* (Bogotá, 1976), although it is incomplete. A penetratir
analysis of the interactions between society and civil war, and the political,
psychological, and cultural ambiance in which civil war took place, and of
problems of political and military leadership and recruiting, is M. Deas,
'Poverty, Civil War and Politics: Ricardo Gaitán Obeso and his Magdalena
River Campaign in Colombia, 1885' (forthcoming).

31   Archivo Ospina, S. Ospina to T. Ospina, Medellín, 16 December 1893.

32   Ospina, *Industria*, p. xl.

33   *Manuelita una industria centenaria, 1864–1964* (Palmira, 1964), p. 3?
J. de D. Carrasquilla, *Segundo Informe Anual que presenta el Comisario
de la Agricultura Nacional al Poder Ejecutivo para concimiento del Congres.
año 1880* (Bogotá, 1880), p. 50; P. Eder, *El Fundador* (Bogotá, 1959),
pp. 449–51.

34   J. J. García, *Crónicas*, pp. 81–90, 140–1, 168, 206–7.

35   Carrasquilla, *Segundo Informe*, p. 32.

36   Ibid. p. 33.

37   Ibid. pp. 17–174.

38   Ibid. p. 51.

39   Ibid. p. 93.

40   *D.O.*, 10 August 1875. The government also distributed free the work
of E. Martínez, *Memoria sobre el café* (Mexico City, 1875) (Carrasquilla,
Segundo Informe, p. 17).

41   Eder, *El Fundador*, p. 448.

42   Camacho, *Escritos*, vol. 1, pp. 555–6.

43   The freight on one tonne of coffee from Sabanilla to London fell
from 70 shillings in January 1880 to 40 shillings in March 1883 and
remained at around 40 shillings until the end of the century (data provided
by M. Deas from ledger 'Ventas de Café' of R. Herrera Restrepo). Tariffs
on imported coffee in the U.S.A. evolved as follows: July 1832–May
1861: free; May 1861–December 1862: 4 cents/lb; December 1862–
December 1870: 5 cents/lb; December 1870–May 1872: 3 cents/lb; after
May 1872: free again. As part of the retaliatory commercial policy of the
time, Colombian coffees paid 3 cents/lb between 1892 and 1894. At
that time Colombia may have sent 90% of its coffee to England, and perhap
the rest to the U.S.A. as 'Maracaibo' coffee. See Van Delden Laërne, *Brazil
and Java*, pp. 466–7, Beyer, 'Colombian Coffee', pp. 253–7, and E. T.
Parks, *Colombia and the United States, 1765–1934*, 2nd edn (New York,
1970), pp. 267–71.

44   Camacho, *Escritos*, vol. 1, pp. 555–6, and Beyer, 'Colombian Coffee',
pp. 368 et seq.

45   The collection of this *prima* appears transiently in Roberto Herrera's
accounts in 1887. See also R. Uribe Uribe, *Discursos parlamentarios*, 2nd
edn (Bogotá, 1897), p. 192.

46   I refer to the volume of sale and mortgage transactions registered in

the Oficina de Registro de Instrumentos Públicos y Privados of La Mesa.
See also Camacho, *Memorias*, vol. 1, pp. 197–9.

47   Carrasquilla, *Segundo Informe*, p. 42.
48   Ibid. pp. 60–2.
49   'Memoria', *El Agricultor*, no. 11 (May 1892), pp. 481 et seq.
50   See p. 42.
51   For the conversion of paper money into pesos gold I used (for the
Bogotá area) Banco de Colombia, *Cuadro que indica el premio que han
tenido en Bogotá los giros sobre Londres por moneda corriente colombiana,
1874–1906* (Bogotá, n.d.), p. 45. But for the business of Roberto Herrera
I used the rates given in his books.
52   See pp. 42–9.
53   Nearly all the laws and regulations concerning mortgage or land banks
failed to have the slightest effect – for example, those of 14 January 1874
and November 1874 which created the Banco Hipotecario del Estado de
Cundinamarca 'with the aim of providing loans to owners and farmers at
reasonable rates of interest and for long periods'. An ironic commentary
on banks of this nature is given by E. Santamaría, *Conversaciones familiares*
(Le Havre, 1871), p. 341. J. Quijano Wallis founded in 1883 a Banco de
Credito Hipotecario in Bogotá which was confiscated by the government
in the war of 1885. See J. M. Quijano W., *Memorias autobiográficas, his-
torico-políticas y de carácter social* (Rome, 1919), p. 43, and Banco de
Bogotá, *Trayectoria*, pp. 85–6. The *hacendados* of La Mesa founded
another mortgage bank, the Banco del Tequendama, which was liquidated
in September 1888; see *Gaceta de Cundinamarca*, 24 October 1888. For
Antioquia, see Brew, 'Economic Development', pp. 79–80.
54   Carrasquilla, *Segundo Informe*, p. 42.
55   Archivo de la Amalia, I. de Márquez to C. Ponthier, Medellín, 4 July
1899.
56   Ibid., I. de Márquez to A. J. Gutierrez, Medellín, 18 May 1901.
57   See p. 51.
58   Carrasquilla, *Segundo Informe*, p. 77.
59   *Informe del Gobernador de Cundinamarca, 1877*, pp. 8–12, 64–5,
166–294.
60   Archivo Ospina, T. Ospina to Enrique Cortés & Co. (in London),
Medellín, 15 August 1893. From this correspondence it can be seen that
the Ospinas cautiously began their coffee-planting in 1887. It appears that
commercial contact between the Ospinas and the Liberal merchant Enrique
Cortés dates from the time Mariano Ospina Rodríguez exported coffee
from Guatemala. They also sent Cortés gold.
61   Ibid., S. Ospina to T. Ospina, 16 December 1893.
62   S. Ospina to T. and M. Ospina, 15 January 1894.
63   S. Ospina to T. Ospina, 16 December 1893.
64   Unless there is indication to the contrary all the references to Roberto
Herrera and to his Hacienda Santa Bárbara are taken from his account
books. This is a private archive. The account books are arranged by years.
Volume of production may differ here from volume exported, as transport
was slow. Probably this explains discrepancies between the data here and
those extracted by M. Deas from the book 'Cuentas de Café', which I was

unfortunately unable to consult. The accounts and tables presented here have been formed from the very diverse accounting of Herrera Restrepo ('Diario Mayor', 'Balances', Inventarios', etc.) and the hacienda accounts are found in various parts under headings 'coffee', 'Santa Bárbara', 'exchang bills', etc. Wages are usually entered weekly.

65   This is the peso of 20 g silver of 0.90 weight, as opposed to the *peso fuerte* of 25 g; it was the older *'peso de ocho decimos'* ('piece of eight').

66   Deas, in Duncan and Rutledge (eds.), pp. 285–90.

67   Ibid. pp. 290–1.

68   Taken from a description of the hacienda written by Herrera. This includes area, number of trees, labour force, use of land not in coffee, machinery, estate roads, transport costs, and total production.

69   The basic 'new economic history' contribution to this problem is A. H. Conrad and J. R. Meyer, 'The Economics of Slavery in the Antebellum South', *Journal of Political Economy*, 66 (1958), pp. 95–130. Another very influential contribution has been R. W. Fogel, 'The Specification Problem in Economic History', *Journal of Economic History*, 27 (1967), pp. 283–308.

70   Bustamante, 'Efectos económicos', p. 613.

71   McGreevey, *An Economic History*, pp. 230–1. See also Camacho Roldán's optimistic calculation at the end of the 1860s, in *Escritos*, vol. 2, pp. 581–3.

72   McGreevey, *An Economic History*, pp. 230–1.

73   Average productivity in Colombia in 1970 was 541 kg of parchment coffee per hectare.

74   Conrad and Meyer, 'The Economics of Slavery', pp. 98–9. The risk I refer to is more technical than theoretical. To base conclusions on one set of accounts, without being able to find a comparable series (these sets of documents have rarely survived), is necessarily a doubtful procedure. The argument that the value–capital formula cannot be employed because the service tenure on which the hacienda is based is pre-capitalist – an argument with which I am in agreement and wish to explore in succeeding chapters – is not pertinent here, because Herrera was not a feudal lord in Poland, but a capitalist entrepreneur who acted according to choices about what was and what was not profitable, in order to accumulate capital. This is perhaps one of the original traits, as well as one of the historical limitations, of this type of capitalist: they tend to accentuate pre-capitalist social relations of production, which in this case I still do not consider feudal, semi-feudal, or neo-feudal.

75   Based on La Mesa, Oficina de Registro. The location of these hacienda was as follows: 21 in Viotá, 12 in El Colegio, 4 in La Mesa, and 3 in San Antonio.

76   This account is based on the following deeds: ANC, Notarías de Bogo of 1875, 2119 of 1878, 38 of 1882, 74 of 1883, 234 of 1886, 710 of 1887 1373 of 1888, 564 of 1895, 631 of 1895, and 1158 of 1907 (Notaría Segunda); 3040 of 1925 (Notaría Primera); 247 of 1931, 430 of 1931 (Notaría Segunda); 863 of 1931 (Notaría Cuarta); and finally 1991 of 1931 2435 of 1931 and 577 of 1932 (Notaría Segunda).

77   For an account of the problems which arose between this British firm and Colombian businessmen, see *D.O.*, 21 November 1871, 20 December 1872, 24 July 1872, 20 January 1874, 2 January 1879.

78   Archivo Ospina, S. Ospina to Pedro N. Ospina, Medellín, November 1892: 'Nos gustan mucho las noticias que nos dan sobre la empresa de Ceilán, la mejor quizá de la República.'

79   Among the 'widow entrepreneurs' who should be mentioned are Lucía Gómez de Santamaría (La Rambla), Mercedes Obregón de Sáenz (Misiones and Liberia), Concepción Narváez de Iregui (La Argentina), Justina Cuellar de Iregui (California), María T. Hortíz de Nariño (Los Olivos), Ana M. Londoño de Sáenz (Ingenio San Antonio) (La Mesa, Oficina de Registro, and ANC, Notarías de Bogotá).

80   ANC, Notarías de Bogotá, escritura 707 of 1881 (Notaría Primera); 1192 of 1898 (Notaría Segunda).

81   *Estatutos del Banco de Exportadores* (Bogotá, 1897).

82   A brief biographical note regarding Nicolás Sáenz appeared in *R.N.A.* (written by his successor in the Banco de Exportadores, Laureano García Ortíz), 3 April 1936. See also La Mesa, Oficina de Registro, bk 1, ff. 1909 et seq., and escritura 852 of 1918, Notaría Primera de Bogotá. On the mortgage with the Bank of England see PRO, FO 371/7209.

83   Archivo Ospina, S. Ospina to Pedro N. Ospina, Medellín, 15 January 1888.

Chapter 3

1   M. Rivas, *Obras: segunda parte* (2 vols., Bogotá, 1885), vol. 1, p. 23.

2   'Informe del Prefecto de la Provincia de Tequendama', *Gaceta de Cundinamarca*, nos. 307–11 (May 1889); Samper, *La miseria*, pp. 221–2; Camacho, *Notas*, p. 29.

3   Camacho, *Escritos*, vol. 2, pp. 578–80.

4   ANC, Bienes desamortizados: Cundinamarca, vol. 16, ff. 305–9; ANC, Bienes nacionales, vol. 2, ff. 444–80, 626 et seq.; vol. 3, ff. 239–74, 883 et seq. See also Giraldo Jaramillo (ed.), *Relaciones de mando*, p. 217; D. Mendoza, *Expedición botánica de José Celestino Mutis al Nuevo Reino de Granada* (Madrid, 1909). On the quality of the *quinas* of Sumapaz and Tequendama there was a lengthy argument. See among others A. Vargas Reyes, *Memoria sobre las quinas de la Nueva Granada* (Bogotá, 1850), pp. 21–3.

5   See pp. 193–4.

6   This interpretation differs from the view generally accepted by nineteenth-century Liberal publicists and supported by such authorities as Nieto Arteta and Hernandez Rodríguez. It is, however, largely corroborated by research carried out by Glenn Curry for his doctoral thesis at Vanderbilt University of Tennessee, on material found in the notarial and judicial archives in Chía, Funza, and Zipaquirá relating to the period 1820–70 approximately. In 1974 I was fortunate enough to be present at a private seminar held on this subject. By this time the research had been largely completed and a general conclusion drawn was that the changing of hands of land from the *indios* to the *vecinos* and then to the Bogotá business groups was in fact a relatively gradual process.

7   The Tibacuy reservation provides a good example. See the question of land titles on the El Chocho estate after 1608 in *Gaceta de Cundinamarc* 8 July 1937.

8   Samper, *La miseria*, p. 71.

The clearly urban character of Church property is apparent in the section entitled 'Bienes desamortizados' in the Archivo Nacional. Several summarized lists were published, but the most comprehensive is to be foun in the *Boletín de Crédito Nacional 1863* (Bogotá, 1863), pp. 195–200. With regard to properties auctioned in the province of Pasto, see G. S. Guerrero, *Remembranzas políticas* (Pasto, 1921), in which the writer concludes that at least two-thirds of the land sold was situated within the town of Pasto. With regard to the smaller amounts of such property sold in Santander, see M. A. Estrada, *Historia documentada de los primeros cuatro años de vida del Estado de Santander, 1857–1861* (Maracaibo, 1896), pp. 198–9. M. A. Caro wrote a detailed legal account at the end of the century: *De censos redimidos pertenecientes a capellanías* (Bogotá, 1890), based on a lawsuit concerning the cattle and sugar-cane Hacienda Peñalisa in the Girardot–Jerusalem region. Among contemporary historian I. Liévano Aguirre has probably done most to lend respectability to the exaggerated and erroneous belief that one-third of all cultivable land belong to the Church in the middle of the last century. See his *El proceso de Mosquera ante el Senado* (Bogotá, 1966), p. 49. However, if we ignore this misrepresentation in the essay 'Las manos muertas', this work is possibly still one of the most perceptive to have been written on the subject. Perhaps the urban nature of these properties in their various forms suggests a need to re-examine some of the arguments put forward by G. Colmenares in his article 'Censos y capellanías: formas de crédito en una economía agrícola', *Cuadernos Colombianos*, no. 2 (1974). Particular attention should be given to the view implicit in this work, that credit was of an agricultural, self-limiting nature, whereas credit could, in fact, have been commercial although obtained at very low interest rates. Some though should also be given to the importance of the part played by the ownership of land as a security against loans from businessmen, and, by extension the tendency common to these groups to purchase land as financial backing for mortgages necessary for investment in their business operations On Boyacá, see the recently published F. Díaz Díaz, *La desamortización de bienes eclesiásticos en Boyacá* (Tunja, 1977), pp. 70–113. According to Díaz, some 80% of the Church property was in the rural sector and amount to 20,554 hectares, which I think was a very low percentage of the cultivated land in Boyacá at the time.

9   ANC, Bienes desamortizados: Cundinamarca, vol. 6, f. 711; vol. 15, f. 937; vol. 20, ff. 46–53.

10   Ibid. vol. 6, ff. 146–97, 711.

11   Ibid. vol. 16, ff. 112–36.

12   Ibid. vol. 19, ff. 482 et seq.

13   ANC, Bienes desamortizados: Medellín, vol. 2, ff. 159 et seq.; vols. 3 and 4.

14   Camacho, *Escritos*, vol. 2, p. 149.

15   M. Uribe Angel, *Geografía general y compendio histórico del Estado*

de Antioquia (Paris, 1885); J. Gaviria Toro, *Antioquia: monografías: Caldas–Fredonia* (Medellín, 1923).

16   ANC, Bienes desamortizados: Cundinamarca, vol. 15, ff. 708 et seq.; vol. 19, ff. 329–31, 406–20; vol. 23, ff. 323–7, 725–43.

17   Rivas, *Obras*, vol. 1, pp. 9, 11.

18   Ibid. vol. 1, pp. 6–7.

19   Samper, *La miseria*, p. 219.

20   Comisión Corográfica, *Geografía*, vol. 4, p. 466.

21   From the time of Humboldt until the mid nineteenth century the high density of the population and the intensity of cultivation on the *sabana* was a matter of comment. So was the gradual or sudden – little agreement here – conversion of agricultural land to cattle-pasture after the Liberal reforms, cattle-pasture being in large holdings. The present landscape of the *sabana* suggests this sort of latifundio. The *vallados*, long ditches forming the boundaries of pastures before the introduction of barbed wire, still exist, and there is at the same time little surviving evidence of *rancho* ruins that would indicate a denser population. Many new latifundia were certainly formed by the break-up of the older ones of the eighteenth century, as is documented by C. Pardo Umaña, *Haciendas de la Sabana: su historia, sus leyendas y tradiciones* (Bogotá, 1946). According to the British Consul in Bogotá, 'An idea seems to prevail [on the plain of Bogotá] that an increased production would only tend to lower the prices, and would be of no advantage to the landowner' (Dickson, *Report on the Agricultural Conditions of Colombia*, P.P. 1888, vol. 100, p. 641).

22   See *Catastro de la propiedad inmueble del Estado de Cundinamarca formado por la Comisión de Revisión* (Bogotá, 1879). The commissioners noted a transitory tendency for land prices to fall. The cadastral value amounted to 30 million pesos in 1863 and 41.3 million in 1878. Comparing this survey with that of 1888, one clearly sees the increase in land values, particularly in the most *latifundista* municipalities mentioned in the text. The cadastral survey of 1888 was published in various issues of the *Gaceta de Cundinamarca*, February–March 1889.

23   For example, while the 1879 survey shows no property in Viotá worth more than 20,000 pesos, in 1888 there were six. By comparing the two surveys it can be calculated that properties in the Tequendama region tripled their value in these ten years. This does not only refer to the land, but includes capitalized improvements. For Viotá in 1888, see *Gaceta de Cundinamarca*, 27 March 1889.

24   Archivo Histórico de Antioquia, Notarías de Medellín: Jonás, escrituras 1794 of 1891 and 569 of 1894 (Notaría Primera); San Pedro, escritura 488 of 1902 (Notaría Primera), and escritura 1085 of 1921 (Notaría Tercera). For La Granja, see Jonás Escrituras; for Cerrotusa (now La Loma, Venecia), escritura 657 of 1876 (Notaría de Fredonia); for Gualanday, escritura 53 of 1892 (Notaría de Fredonia).

25   J. Sabogal, *Fusagasugá: historia y geografía* (Bogotá, 1919), p. 25.

26   The history of San Miguel de Amanta is intimately linked to the administrative development of Viotá. See ANC, Bienes desamortizados: Cundinamarca, vol. 23, and Curas y obispos de la república, vol. 7, f. 798. The legal history of San Miguel can partially be traced in ANC, Notarías de Bogotá, escritura 554 of 1914 (Notaría Tercera). For the claims of the *hacendado* Pedro A. Forero of these lands see escritura 979 of 1897 (Notar Primera).

27   The best known research in this field is that carried out by O. Fals Borda, *Campesinos de los Andes: estudio sociológico de Saucío*, 2nd edn (Bogotá, 1961), and *El hombre y la tierra en Boyacá*, 2nd edn (Bogotá, 1973).

28   According to the *Catastro de Cundinamarca* quoted above, the majori of the *municipios* in the east of the *departamento* were almost exclusively family holdings and minifundia. For an account of central Boyacá, see among others R. Gutierrez, *Monografías* (2 vols., Bogotá, 1920–1), vol. 1, pp. 225–49, and F. J. Vergara y Velasco, *Nueva geografía de Colombia*, 2nd edn (3 vols., Bogotá, 1974), vol. 2, p. 708. On Antioquia, see Brew, 'Economic Development', p. 77.

29   See F. López, *Evolución de la tenencia de la tierra en una zona minifundista* (Bogotá, 1975; mimeographed), pp. 16–21. On the formation of the latifundio and minifundio in the seventeenth century, see Colmenares, *Historia*, pp. 139–81.

30   These observations are also based on various archival sources from haciendas and commercial enterprises which can be consulted in Bogotá, Medellín, and Fredonia and on material gained from interviews held with *hacendados* in Bogotá and Antioquia, in particular with Luis Ospina Vásquez in Medellín and at La Loma (Venecia) during December 1975 and January 1976; Dolcey Garcés Molina in Bogotá and at Valparaiso (Melgar) in April 1975; and Jaime de Narváez Vargas in Bogotá in February and March 1976. The 'peasant version' of the migratory process in the late nineteenth and early twentieth centuries was very vividly described by Benigno Galindo in a number of interviews held in Viotá in October and November 1975.

31   Carrasquilla, *Segundo Informe*, p. 42.

32   López, *Evolución*, pp. 22–4.

33   Interviews with Dolcey Garcés and Bernardo Sánchez, Valparaiso (Melgar), April 1975.

34   Rivas, *Obras*, vol. 1, p. 13.

35   E. Cortés, *Escritos varios* (Paris, 1896), p. 305. The same attitude among the Radical elite is found in the state of Santander. See Johnson, 'Social and Economic Changes', p. 7.

36   Sierra, *El tabaco*, pp. 140–1, 144–6. See also Safford, 'Commerce', pp. 252–3.

37   Vergara y Velasco, *Nueva geografía*, vol. 3, p. 666. This author virtual copies J. M. Samper, *Ensayo sobre las revoluciones políticas* (Paris, 1861), pp. 88–9, who distinguishes two basic types of 'Indians', *pastusos* and *boyacenses*. Vergara was a conservative, and Samper, at the time of writing his *Ensayo*, was still a Liberal. 'Boyacá' is here more a social than a geographical description. According to the expression of the *sabana hacendado* T. Rueda Vargas, Boyacá begins in Chía 'where already you get served two soups'. Another such *hacendado* wrote in 1946 that the Indians were 'hypocritical, taciturn, malicious' and 'their descendants have always been the best Colombian politicians' (Pardo, *Haciendas*, pp. 18–19).

38   C. Calderón, *La cuestión monetaria en Colombia* (Madrid, 1905), p. 54.
39   L. Cuervo Márquez, *Geografía médica y patológica de Colombia* (Bogotá, 1915), pp. 65–7.
40   See L. Belmonte Román, *Tesis existentes en la biblioteca de la Facultad de Medicina, Universidad Nacional* (Bogotá, 1964; mimeographed).
41   F. U. Calderón, *Fiebre amarilla en la Provincia de Cúcuta* (Bogotá, 1897), pp. 15, 22–3, 30–1, 37 et seq.
42   J. Martínez Santamaría, *Contribución al estudio de la anemia tropical en Colombia* (Bogotá, 1909), pp. i–cvi. It is odd that in some contemporary intellectual circles not only does this theme fail to arouse interest, but it is assumed that 'coffee lands have a relatively healthy climate. The coffee regions therefore offered the attraction of a better temperature [sic] and better health conditions' (Bustamante, 'Efectos económicos', p. 618, discussing migration to the coffee zone of Cundinamarca, which he wrongly believes comes from the depressed hot-country tobacco and indigo areas).
43   L. Chevelier, *Classes laborieuses et classes dangereuses à Paris pendant la première moitié du XIXe siècle* (Paris, 1958), esp. pp. iii and iv of the General Introduction.
44   See *Gaceta de Cundinamarca*, 1 July 1890; *D.O.*, 10 May 1891, 11 June 1893; Ospina, *Industria*, p. 453; Dickson, *Report on the Agricultural Conditions*, p. 651.
45   Camacho, *Escritos*, vol. 1, pp. 560–84; F. C. Aguilar, *Un paseo en verano a Peñalisa y Girardot* (Bogatá, 1886). A first-hand description of the region during the pre-coffee era is provided by J. de D. Restrepo: see Emiro Kastos, *Artículos escogidos*, 2nd edn (Bogotá, 1972), pp. 319–28.
46   See pp. 112 et seq.
47   Rivas, *Los trabajadores*, p. 46; Camacho, *Escritos*, vol. 2, p. 574. For the late-eighteenth-century troubles see La Mesa, Oficina de Registro, Libro de Registro no. 1, 1862.
48   Basic traits of the '*indio boyacense*', according to Cortés, *Escritos*, p. 356.

Chapter 4

1   For general descriptions of the types of contracts most frequent in Santander, see among others Felipe Serrano M., 'La industria del café en Santander', *Revista Cafetera de Colombia*, nos. 38–9 (May–June 1932), pp. 1477–8, and M. Galán Gómez, *Geografía económica de Colombia: Santander* (Bucaramanga, 1947), pp. 269–70, 347–54.
2   Archivo Herrera, F. Zapata to R. Herrera, Chinácota, 6 July 1897.
3   On roads and transportation, see pp. 3–5, 149–51.
4   A common theme of Colombian historiography – particularly that of Liberal inspiration – is the exclusion of the Liberal coffee bourgeoisie from political power.
5   Description and definition of the *gamonal* come from the educated oligarchy. See M. Deas, 'Algunas notas sobre la historia del caciquismo en Colombia', *Revista de Occidente*, no. 127 (October 1973), pp. 118–40.

6   Conclusions based on archival evidence, interviews, and references quoted in this chapter.

7   The consumer–worker ratio is the relation that exists in each peasant family between the number of consumers and the number of workers. This relation changes gradually with the years of a family's existence. In the first phase (10–12 years) of the family's life the ratio will be high, thereafter descending as the children change from consumers to workers and finally leave home. See A. V. Chayanov, *The Theory of Peasant Economy*, 2nd edn (Homewood, Ill., 1959), pp. 59–60.

8   Archivo Jonás, Planillas, 1905.

9   Ibid., Planillas, 1897, 1899.

10   Archivo Herrera, L. Blanco to R. Herrera, Chaparral, 15 December 1895.

11   Archivo Ospina, T. Ospina to S. Gonzalez, Medellín, 17 August 1887.

12   Archivo Herrera, C. Rubio to R. Herrera, Sasaima, 1 March 1895.

13   See T. Rueda Vargas, *La sabana de Bogotá* (Bogotá, 1919), on *orejón*.

14   G. Guzmán Campos et al., *La violencia en Colombia* (2 vols., Bogotá, 1962–4), vol. 1, p. 162.

15   Archivo de La Amalia, I. de Márquez to U. Angel, Medellín, 9 March 1900.

16   Ibid., I. de Márquez to U. Upegui, Medellín, 8 June 1898.

17   Ibid., I. de Márquez to G. Velez, Medellín, 21 October 1899.

18   Archivo Herrera, R. Gonzalez Valencia to R. Herrera, Chinácota, 31 August 1897.

19   Ibid., C. Rubio to R. Herrera, Sasaima, 11 October 1898.

20   A great deal has been written on this period. Good bibliographies are provided by C. Bergquist, 'Coffee and Conflict in Colombia, 1886–1904: Origins and Outcome of the War of the Thousand Days', unpublished Ph.D. thesis, Stanford University, 1973, and by L. Martínez Delgado in Academia Colombiana de Historia, *Historia extensa de Colombia* (30 vols., Bogotá, 1964–), vol. 10 (2 pts, 1970), pt 1: *1885–1895*; pt 2: *1895–1910*. As a result of Caro's election to the Vice-Presidency (which amounted in fact to the position of President, since Núñez had retired to Cartagena) the division among the Conservatives between the *'Históricos'* and the *'Nacionalistas'* became considerably sharpened. The former group joined forces with the anti-Núñista to form an opposition party. After Núñez's death in 1894, the importance of the Nuñista Liberals or *'Independientes'* declined considerably. Then the Liberal party was obliged to face a particularly fierce campaign of repression by the government, while internal divisions within the party led to pressure being placed on the more moderate faction captained by men such as Miguel Samper, Aquileo Parra, and Santiago Pérez (who was living in exile) and also on the *santandereano* group led by Paulo Villar. This latter group had some considerable influence on political factions in Bogotá marshalled by Rafael Uribe Uribe, and gradually moulded itself into the Liberal faction which took the view that armed struggle provided the only political alternative for Liberalism. In spite of this tendency towards factionalism, the aggressive attitude taken by President Marroquín had the effect of uniting the parties which were to

fight together in the longest of Colombian civil wars, which lasted from October 1899 until the end of 1902.

Among the memoirs of the period, see in particular *Historia de mi vida* by J. H. Palacio (Bogotá, 1942) and *Memorias* by J. M. Quijano Wallis (Rome, 1919), which both provide intelligent and perceptive accounts of the social, economic, and political climate of the time.

21   Archivo de La Amalia, I. de Márquez to G. García, Medellín, 17 August 1900.

22   Ibid., I. de Márquez to G. Vélez, Medellín, 28 May 1899.

23   Ibid., I. de Márquez to G. Vélez, Medellín, 24 March 1899.

24   Archivo Herrera, C. Rubio to R. Herrera, Sasaima, 15 March 1895.

25   Archivo de La Amalia, I. de Márquez to G. Vélez, Medellín, 7 July 1899 and 14 June 1901.

26   Archivo Jonás, instructions from M. Ospina Vásquez, July 1911.

27   *R.N.A.*, no. 3 (15 May 1906), pp. 7–8.

28   Archivo de La Amalia, I. de Marquez to G. Vélez, 20 January 1900 and 20 July 1901.

29   Ibid., I. de Márquez to G. Vélez, Medellín, 6 October 1899.

30   Ibid., I. de Márquez to G. García, Medellín, 20 February 1903.

31   Archivo Herrera, C. Rubio to R. Herrera, Sasaima, 7 February 1895.

32   Archivo de La Amalia, I. de Márquez to G. Vélez, Medellín, 30 October 1899.

33   Archivo Herrera, C. Rubio to R. Herrera, Sasaima, 25 September 1897.

34   Archivo de La Amalia, I. de Márquez to G. Vélez, Medellín, 27 October 1899.

35   Ibid., I. de Márquez to G. Vélez, Medellín, 10 October 1902.

36   For details of the botanical and agricultural aspects of the coffee tree, see F. L. Wellman, *Coffee: Botany, Cultivation and Utilization* (London, 1961). See also FNCC, *Manual del cafetero colombiano* (Bogotá, 1932 and numerous subsequent editions). For details of agronomic and ecological conditions in Colombia, there are a number of specialized publications based on the research of the Centro Nacional de Investigaciones de Café (Chinchiná, Caldas), CENICAFE, a technical branch of the FNCC. A good general description of geographical conditions is provided by E. Guhl, *Colombia: bosquejo de su geografía tropical* (Rio de Janeiro, 1967). There is a mass of technical literature dealing with coffee diseases in Colombia published by CENICAFE. For descriptions of haciendas in Cundinamarca and Antioquia around 1910 see O. Führmann and E. Mayor, *Voyage d'exploration scientifique en Colombie* (2 vols., Neuchâtel, 1914), vol. 2. Extracts from this work were published in various numbers of *R.N.A.*, nos. 5–6 (30 November 1910) and no. 7 (30 December 1910).

37   *Informe del Gobernador del Departamento del Magdalena* (Santa Marta, 1890), pp. 194–8; R. Thompson, *Informe sobre una excurción a la Sierra Nevada de Santa Marta para investigar sus capacidades agrícolas* (Barranquilla, 1895), p. 14; O. L. Flye, 'Mis impresiones de la Sierra Nevada de Santa Marta', *Revista Pan*, no. 3 (October 1935), pp. 27 et seq. Flye gives an account of his experience as a founder of coffee-growing in this region at the end of the century. In 1933 he owned Cincinnati, one of the largest coffee haciendas of the country.

38   The problems of a high *arrendatario* turnover rate are quite apparent in the correspondence between C. Rubio and R. Herrera in Archivo Herrera.
39   T. H. Holloway, 'The Coffee Colono of São Paulo, Brazil: Migration and Mobility, 1880–1930', in K. Duncan and I. Rutledge (eds.), *Land and Labour in Latin America* (Cambridge, 1977), pp. 308–12. Bergquist in 'Coffee and Conflict', p. 43, mentions some cases in which *cafetales* were established by paying for a fixed number of trees to be planted, which were bought by the landowner when they were 3 or 4 years old. I found no evidence myself of this sort of contract in the Tequendama or Fredonia regions. On the other hand, I found many cases of purchase of coffee trees bought as *mejoras* (improvements) made by the *arrendatarios* or *colonos* – some confusion here – between 1900 and 1920. This suggests that many *hacendados* were 'clearing out' their haciendas to avoid possible lawsuits from small cultivators. In any case the purchase of *mejoras* implied counting the trees sown.
40   These proportions are still the same and do not vary regionally. The improvement of the processing machinery, particularly in depulpers, results in a better quality of the bean.
41   Archivo Jonás, instruction from M. Ospina Vásquez, July 1911.
42   Beyer, 'Colombian Coffee', p. 162.
43   See for example *El Agricultor*, no. 6 (1891), no. 11 (May 1892, October 1892), no. 1 (1900).
44   M. Palacios, 'Las condiciones de la oferta de café (1870–1930): una crítica sociohistórica al modelo empleado por W. P. McGreevey', in L. Ospina et al., *Historia económica de Colombia*.

Chapter 5

1   ECLA/FAO, *Coffee in Latin America: Productivity Problems and Future Prospects*, vol. 1: *Colombia and El Salvador* (E/CN 12/490, 1958); Caja Agraria, *Manual de costos* (Bogotá, 1967); Instituto Colombiano de la Reforma Agraria, *Información sobre costos de producción* (Bogotá, 1968; mimeographed).
2   D. G. Johnson, 'Resource Allocation under Share Contracts', *Journal of Political Economy*, 58, 2 (1950), pp. 111–23; R. Schickele, 'Effect of Tenure Systems on Agricultural Efficiency', *Journal of Farm Economics*, 23 (1941), pp. 185–207; S. N. S. Cheung, 'Private Property Rights and Sharecropping', *Journal of Political Economy*, (1968), pp. 1107–22; D. W. Adams and N. Rask, 'Economics of Cost-Share Leases in Less-Developed Countries', *American Journal of Agricultural Economics*, 50 (1968), pp. 935–42.
3   I refer to the concept developed by Rafael Baraona (*asedio interno/ asedio externo*) concerning the haciendas of highland Ecuador. It is evident that the commercial estates analysed in this chapter do not conform to the types described by Baraona and I use 'besieged within' in the sense of internal pressure exerted by the resident population, rather than in the precise sense used by Baraona to describe the characteristics of a traditional hacienda in the process of disintegration. See R. Baraona, 'Una

tipología de haciendas en la sierra ecuatoriana', in O. Delgado (ed.), *Reformas agrarias en la América Latina* (Mexico City, 1965).

4   See esp. M. Urrutia, 'Estadísticas de salarios en Bogotá, 1863– 1933' and A. Berry and M. Urrutia, 'Salarios reales en la industria manufacturera y en el sector gobierno, 1915–1963' in M. Urrutia and M. Arrubla (eds.), *Compendio de estadísticas históricas de Colombia* (Bogotá, 1970), pp. 31–82.

5   A. St John, *Report on the Trade of Colombia*, P.P., vol. 83 (1886), pp. 601–11.

6   Ibid. p. 607.

7   U.S. Consular Reports, *Labour in Foreign Countries*, vol. 3 (Washington, 1884), pp. 177–81.

8   Archivo de La Amalia, I. de Márquez to G. García, Medellín, 5 July 1901.

9   Ibid., I. de Márquez to G. García, Medellín, 8 March 1903.

10   Ibid., I. de Márquez to G. Vélez, Medellín, 3 April 1901.

11   Kastos, *Artículos escogidos*, p. 402.

12   These figures relating to food rations are based on the accounts of the Jonás estate and are in fact an average which includes all men and women, both adult and adolescent. The food ration for the adult peon was likely to have been higher than this average. According to Cisneros, the daily food ration for the *antioqueño* peon in 1878 consisted of 750 g of corn, 125 g of kidney beans, 375 g of *panela*, 30 g of chocolate, 125 g of rice, 250 g of meat, 15 g of lard, 10 g of salt (José Cisneros, *Report on the Construction of a Railway from Puerto Berrío to Barbosa State of Antioquia* (New York, 1878), p. 98. There was a scarcity of salt in the coffee zones. Rice and chocolate were usually reserved for the hacienda administrator and his family.

13   Notaría de La Mesa, escritura 29 of 1931. See also escritura 1360 of 1928, ANC, Notarías de Bogotá, Notaría Cuarta.

14   Notaría de Tocaima, escritura 22 of 1934.

15   Archivo del Ministerio de Trabajo, Convenciones colectivas, 'Pacto celebrado entre la Organización Campesina de Quipile y los hacendados del mismo municipio', 2 December 1934.

16   Ibid., Collective meeting between trade union representatives of the following estates: Java, Argentina, California, Costa Rica, Olivos, Argelia, Ceilán, Arabia, Florencia, Calandaima, and Buenavista, and owners' representatives, Bogotá, 25 March 1946.

17   Archivo Municipal de Viotá, Correspondencia 1919: telegrams from the Mayor of Viotá to the Governor of Cundinamarca, 7 March 1919. J. Abondano and M. Lartignan, the owners of the Glasgow and Arabia estates, made an official complaint about the violent behaviour of the excisemen (Guardas de Aduanas). See also the reports of violent incidents on El Chocho, Subia, and Los Olivos estates in *El Espectador*, 22 March 1919. For details of efforts to stamp out the smuggling of *aguardiente* in the coffee regions and the consequences of this campaign, as well as for a general description of the political and social environment in southwest Cundinamarca, see the excellent report written by A. Forero Bena-

vides, *Informe del Secretario de Gobierno al Gobernador de Cundinamarca, 1937* (Bogotá, 1937), pp. 58 et seq.

18   The lecture by Jesús del Corral, President of the SAC, provides a good example: 'Por los siervos de la gleba', *R.N.A.*, no. 120 (June 1914). The moralizing tone is quite evident, but del Corral also attempts to find concrete solutions before what he terms the 'levelling revolt' (*revuelta niveladora*) is unleashed against the 'bosses' (*los patrones*) (pp. 9–10). A more recent example of moralizing is provided by H. Tovar, *El movimiento campesino en Colombia* (Bogotá, 1975). With complete disregard for either the historical facts or the social context, the author invents an ideal type of coffee hacienda to prove the trivial, i.e. the peasants are exploited, the peasant life is harder than the *hacendado* life; or to conclude the improbable, i.e. that peasants and *jornaleros* were united from the beginning, and so on.

19   *El Bolchevique*, 24 March 1935, p. 4. For the question of the agrarian policies of the Communist party in those years, see *El Bolchevique*, 1933–5 'Memorial del Partido Communista en el cual expresa sus puntos de vista sobre el problema agrario', *Anales de la Cámara de Representantes*, 26 October 1933, and Comité Central del Partido Comunista, *Treinta años de lucha del Partido Comunista* (Bogotá, 1960).

20   *Claridad*, 15 May 1934, p. 3.

21   *Acción Liberal*, 23 August 1935, pp. 1029–30.

22   For an overview of agrarian conflicts in the region see P. Gilhòdes, *Las luchas agrarias en Colombia* (Bogotá, 1972).

23   See among others *Anales de la Cámara de Representantes*, 3 November 1932, p. 701; 4 November 1932, p. 711; 6 November 1935 and 11 Novemb 1937, p. 767.

24   V. J. Merchán, 'Datos para la historia social, económica y del movimiento agrario de Viotá y el Tequendama: testimonio', *Estudios Marxistas*, nos. 9 and 10 (1975), 105–16, 117–19.

25   ANC, Notarías de Bogotá, escritura 1360 of 1928 (Notaría Cuarta); Notaría de La Mesa, escritura 29 of 1931; and Notaría de Tocaima, escritura 22 of 1934.

26   Based on documents quoted in previous footnote and in *Anales de la Cámara*, 27 September 1932, pp. 453–6.

27   This 'pro-*arrendatario*' attitude in vogue in 1932 was abandoned in 1933–4 in preference of a more Stalinist view of the social situation on the haciendas which saw the *jornalero* in conflict with the 'kulak'. By 1935, a 'pro-kulak' stance had once more found favour.

28   See C. Lleras Restrepo, *Informe del Secretario de Gobierno al Gobernador de Cundinamarca, 1934* (Bogotá, 1934). A most interesting chapter is devoted to the 'social agrarian problem'. For Viotá, see pp. 4–14. Lleras was responsible for the Ordenanza 35 of 1933 concerned with the dividing up of the large haciendas as well as for labour regulations relating to the coffee haciendas. See *Gaceta de Cundinamarca*, 1933, pp. 1093–4.

29   Lleras, *Informe del Secretario*, p. 14.

30   For an account of Gaitanism in these regions, the book by his daughte provides an admirable and sometimes original analysis if we ignore the obvious digressions produced, presumably, by filial affection (G. Gaitán,

Colombia: la lucha por la tierra en la década del treinta (Bogotá, 1976), based on her B.A. thesis, Universidad de los Andes, Bogotá, 1970).

31   *Boletín de la Oficina Nacional de Trabajo*, July–September 1933, p. 1410; *Memoria de Industrias 1932* (Bogotá, 1933), p. 109.

32   *Anales de la Cámara*, 20 December 1935, p. 1841.

33   Caja Agraria, Archivo de Parcelaciones, 'Informe al Ministro de Economía Nacional sobre visitas practicadas a las haciendas "Ceilán" y "Liberia" en Viotá y "El Chocho" en Fusagasugá', 17 November 1948 (typed copy, n.d.).

34   See *Boletín de la Oficina Nacional de Trabajo*, October–December 1933.

35   In a message dated 6 September 1934 sent by President López to the *hacendados* in the south-west region of Cundinamarca and Sumapaz, the President defined his policy thus: 'The last thing this government wishes to do is stifle all hopes and attempts at economic improvement by brutally enforcing those laws which condone the abuse of landowners who let their lands lie uncultivated, or laws which on occasion authorize land expropriation without compensation in the cases of *colonos* and *arrendatarios*' (*La política oficial* (5 vols., Bogotá, 1935), vol. 1, p. 71).

36   Archivo del Ministerio de Trabajo, 'Convención colectiva of 29 March 1946'.

37   Ibid.

38   J. Martínez-Alier, *Haciendas, Plantations and Collective Farms* (London, 1977), pp. 40–6.

Chapter 6

1   Ospina, *Industria*, pp. 276–92; Liévano, *Núñez*, pp. 268–313; Nieto, *Economía*, pp. 388–405; Jaramillo, *El pensamiento*, pp. 288–313. There is a general agreement that Núñez's Regeneration program was neo-Liberal, but that in the hands of Caro, a dogmatic and uncompromising personality, it assumed an anti-Liberal form. Among the many biographies and histories of Núñez, Caro, and the Regeneration, that of Bergquist ('Coffee and Conflict') is the first to provide a systematic focus of the relations between party struggle, faction, and the social and economic interests of the different oligarchic groups.

2   See above, nn. 53 and 54 to ch. 1.

3   On the subject of paper money there was an uninterrupted polemic running approximately from 1880 to 1905. The principal protagonists were perhaps Miguel Samper, a Liberal banker and importer, Santiago Pérez, the radical President, and the Presidents of the Regeneration, Rafael Núñez and Miguel A. Caro. See R. Núñez, *La reforma política en Colombia*, 2nd edn (7 vols., Bogotá, 1944–50), esp. vol. 2, pp. 280 et seq., vol. 5, pp. 71, 78–96, vol. 7, pp. 69 et seq.; M. Samper, *Escritos político–económicos* (4 vols., Bogotá, 1925–6), esp. vol. 3; M. A. Caro, *Apuntes sobre crédito, deuda pública y papel moneda* (Bogotá, 1892). The book *Crisis monetaria: artículos aparecidos en 'El Relator'* (Bogotá, 1892) collects the essential arguments of the Radicals and of some moderate Liberals on the matter, notably of Don Santiago Pérez. See also J. Camacho, *Estudios*

económicos (Bogotá, 1903), and C. Calderón, *La cuestión monetaria.*
4 *R.N.A.*, July 1909, pp. 132–3, and ser. 6, nos. 2–3 (September 1910); F. L. Petre, *The Republic of Colombia* (London, 1906), p. 265, and S. Dickson, *Report on the Present State of the Coffee Trade*, P.P., vol. 96 (1904).
5 For problems in the seventies arising from Venezuelan civil war in the frontier areas see *D.O.*, 17 and 30 March 1874, 9 and 20 April 1874, 10 June 1874. References to these Colombo-Venezuelan problems in the twentieth century are found in PRO, Strong to Grey, 10 February 1909, FO 371/236; Strong to Grey, 1 January 1909, FO 371/437; Hackin to Grey, 24 January 1910, FO 371/875; Strong to Grey, 18 February 1911, FO 371/1100; and Young to Grey, 15 January 1912, FO 371/1350.
6 I am discussing here the conclusions of two important analyses which have appeared recently: Urrutia, 'El sector externo', and Bustamante, 'Efectos económicos'. A distant precursor of these approaches is F. Garavito Armero, 'Conferencias', published in *D.O.*, 9, 10, 15, 16, 18, and 20 June 1903.
7 See also Eder, *El Fundador*, p. 448.
8 Urrutia, 'El sector externo', p. 14. I am quoting from the offprint.
9 The negotiations between the state of Cundinamarca and the national government regarding the expenses of the civil wars of 1860 and 1885 give a clear idea of this legalistic conception. See *D.O.*, 12 March 1870, and *Gaceta de Cundinamarca*, 18 September 1888. See also *Informe del Presidente del Estado Soberano de Santander, 1878*, pp. 28–9, on 'Reclamación del empréstito hecho por el estado á la nación para gastos de guerra'.
10 R. Núñez, *Mensaje, 1882* (Bogotá, 1882), p. 4.
11 Ibid. p. 3.
12 R. Núñez, *Mensaje, 1888* (Bogotá, 1888), p. 5.
13 Ibid. pp. 5–6.
14 Ibid. pp. 6–7.
15 G. Torres García, *Historia de la moneda en Colombia* (Bogotá, 1945), pp. 254–62, and C. Holguín, *Aclaraciones al Congreso Nacional de 1894* (Bogotá, 1894).
16 On the external borrowing at the time see the various accounts of Colombia published by the Council of Foreign Bondholders from 1868 on, and the reflections that make up most of J. Holguín, *Desde cerca: asuntos colombianos* (Paris, 1907).
17 For a synthesis of the Conservative divisions over Vice-Presidential elections (both factions supported the Presidential candidacy of Núñez) in 1892 see Palacio, *Historia*, pp. 49–50, and J. Holguín Arboleda, *Mucho en serio*, pp. 88 et seq.
18 C. Furtado, *Formación económica del Brazil* (Mexico City, 1962), pp. 168–74.
19 Uribe Uribe, *Discursos parlamentarios*, 2nd edn, pp. 211–14. In the account books of R. Herrera there is an entry for a payment of 10 pesos gold on 30 November 1894, which says 'voluntary contribution for the defence of the coffee interest'. It probably concerned his quota towards

the payment of the professional fees of Uribe Uribe, who had written the 'Memorial al Congreso'.

20   The representative in the Chamber for Antioquia, A. Moreno, calculated in 1896 that the merchants had bought coffee in Medellín paying in advance between 7 and 8 pesos per *arroba*, while the price by the end of the year had fallen to 4.5–5 pesos per *arroba* (*Anales de la Cámara de Representantes*, 3 November 1896).

21   'Proyecto de ley referente al Impuesto del Café', *Anales de la Cámara*, 3 November 1896.

22   *Anales de la Cámara*, 21 November 1896.

23   Ibid. 23 November 1896. Coffee in Cauca had been firmly established near Popayán since the late eighteenth century. See E. Delgado, *Memoria sobre el cultivo del café en el municipio de Popayán* (Popayán, 1867), pp. 7–8.

24;   *Anales de la Cámara*, 23 November 1896.

25   Ibid. 25 November 1896.

26   Ibid. 20 November 1896.

27   It could be that the conservative atmosphere which prevailed in Antioquia contributed to the greater prominence and political belligerence of local Liberals such as Camilo J. Echeverry, Juan de Díos Uribe, and Rafael Uribe Uribe, to cite three outstanding examples. But it should be noted that Antioquian Conservatism was the political ideology of merchants and entrepreneurs, and not of landowners as ultramontane as some of those of Boyacá or Cauca. Perhaps the term 'gradualism' expresses better than any other the political and social attitude of the *antioqueño* oligarchy. We see it captured in this excerpt from the *Mensaje* of Mariano Ospina Rodríguez to the Antioquian legislature in 1875: 'A wilderness which is transformed into cultivated fields; land which grows in value; a multiplying of capital; the lowering of the interest rate from 12% per year to 6% per year; we are climbing the ladder of civilization. For progress to be secure, it must be gradual.' According to Ospina, progress also demanded improvements in education and in communications. See *D.O.*, 5 February 1875.

28   Latorre Cabal, *Mi novela*, p. 174.

29   A full study of the personality, ideology, and political impact of Uribe Uribe remains to be made. But it seems to me that in the light of the foregoing discussion the interpretation proposed by Molina in *Las ideas*, vol. 1, fails to recognize the organic and permanent links between Uribe Uribe and the big coffee bourgeoisie, of which he was one of the first 'interest group' leaders. His moderation in political and military defeat, his sympathy with the viewpoints of Reyes and of representatives of the *antioqueño* oligarchy like Carlos E. Restrepo and Pedro N. Ospina should be borne in mind when analysing his equally significant connections with the Liberal artisans of Bogotá and Medellín.

30   Uribe Uribe, *Discursos*, pp. 211–14.

31   Ibid. p. 190.

32   Ibid. p. 191.

33   Ibid.

34   Ibid. p. 195.

35   Ibid. pp. 198–9, 201–2.
36   Ibid. pp. 207, 213.
37   Ibid. p. 205.
38   Ibid. p. 207.
39   Ibid. pp. 220–1. In *Anales de la Cámara*, 7 December 1896, there is inserted Uribe's speech in reply to the articles of Foreign Minister Jorge Holguín which appeared in *El Correo* and *La Epoca*, 30 October 1896.
40   Uribe Uribe, *Discursos*, p. 223.

Chapter 7

1   Eder, *El Fundador*, p. 251.
2   A detailed and favourable account of the period is found in B. Sanín Cano, *Administración Reyes, 1904–1909* (Lausanne, 1909). See also E. Lemaitre, *Rafael Reyes: biografía de un gran colombiano* (Bogotá, 1967), and by the same author, *Panamá y su separación de Colombia* (Bogotá, 1972).
3   See for example the enthusiastic support of the merchants in the capital for Reyes in *D.O.*, 3 and 12 September 1904. With Reyes came the renewal of permanent contacts between the private sector and the government for the planning of economic policies and regulations. This was a tradition which went back to the founding of the banks and the Cámaras de Comercio in the seventies, and which continues today, but which had lost its vigour during the Regeneration.
4   Furtado, *Formación*, pp. 183–6.
5   V. D. Wickizer, *The World Coffee Economy, with Special Reference to Control Schemes* (Stanford, 1943), pp. 137–65.
6   Uribe Uribe, *Por la América del Sur* (2 vols., Bogotá, 1908), vol. 2, p. 25. According to Uribe Uribe, valorization meant that 'in this country [Brazil] and in Argentina they have taken up almost entirely the socialist view of the functions of the state' (p. 10). It is curious that his various professions of socialist faith should have led many to confuse them with an enthusiasm for socialist revolution or for socialism as it is understood in Europe, as social democracy. Years before, Núñez for example had written: 'So-called state socialism is nothing more than the protection of the weak; the extension of political rights weakens in practice the privileges of the strong' (*La reforma política*, vol. 2, p. 55). Perhaps the socialist leanings of Uribe would be better compared to some aspects of the programme of Bismarck!
7   Uribe Uribe, *Estudios sobre café* (Bogotá, 1952), pp. 33, 142–50.
8   Ibid. pp. 26, 80.
9   Ibid. pp. 99–101.
10   Ibid. pp. 100–1.
11   Archivo de La Amalia, I de Márquez to E. de Márquez, Medellín, 28 November 1902; the peace was signed on 21 November 1902.
12   'Where the army is prices are high; when prices rise the wealth of the people is exhausted. When wealth is exhausted the peasantry will be afflicted with urgent exactions. Where troops are gathered the price of every commodity goes up because everyone covets the extraordinary profits to

be made' (Sun Tzu, *The Art of War*, trans. and with an introduction by
S. B. Griffith (London, 1963), p. 74).
13   F. Garavito A., 'Conferencias', *D.O.*, 9, 10, 15, 16, 18 and 20 June
1903; Torres García, *Historia de la moneda*, p. 275.
14   Holguín A., *Mucho en serio*, p. 203.
15   The speculative fever which came with the war can be followed
closely in the correspondence of Ignacio de Márquez; it was principally
concerned with bills of exchange. A very common procedure was to
perform a series of fictitious operations of sale and purchase of bills,
increasing the premium considerably with each successive 'transaction'.
Rumours regarding military successes or reverses, whether true or false,
provided the initial stimulus for these speculations. See also Eder, *Colombia*,
p. 75, Petre, *The Republic of Colombia*, p. 304, and S. Dickson, *Report
on the Trade of Colombia*, P.P., vol. 97 (1904), p. 609.
16   Ospina, *Industria*, p. 341; Brew, 'Economic Development', p. 75.
17   *D.O.*, 3 and 12 September 1904.
18   From the Jonás accounts, it is clear that until 1920 the hacienda
paid in the old paper money. For Cundinamarca, see *R.N.A.*, 15 (1906), p.
344: 'Before the last war many of the haciendas had their own bills in
small denominations, or nickel or tin coinage, in order to carry on internal
transactions; these were exchanged for national currency.' These were
banned during the War of the Thousand Days, to avoid falsification, but
immediately afterwards 'resort to such practices would be extremely useful, as it is almost impossible to get hold of money, even for short terms,
and paying fabulous rates of interest'. The problem was especially acute
during the three months of the harvest.
19   The monetary history of the period 1903–23 is still obscure. The
most important source is Torres, *Historia de la moneda*; see also *D.O.*,
28 October 1903, 20 January 1904, 26 July 1904, 5 September 1904,
3 December 1904, 9 February 1905, 18 March 1905; and P.R.O., F.O.
371/43 (1906), for an account of the Banco Central and the French
banks which attempted to control it. A confused panorama led to Reyes's
final resignation in 1909 and his semi-clandestine flight on board a United
Fruit Co. boat; see P.R.O., F.O. 371/234; F.O. 231/235; F.O. 371/437;
F.O. 371/644. For the economic and fiscal situation see *El Nuevo Tiempo*,
12 March 1908; *Gaceta Republicana*, 31 July 1909; *La Joven Colombia*,
1 August 1909. It is also useful to bear in mind the view of the Banco
Central as a 'nest of speculators' which was prevalent among some other
groups of speculators: B. Jaramillo Sierra, *Pepe Sierra: el método de un
campesino millonario* (Medellín, 1947), pp. 120 et seq. See also *D.O.*, 21
October 1904, 17 November 1904, 3 December 1904, 4 February 1905,
for the central aspects of Reyes's economic policy; also Santiago Pérez
Triana, *Eslabones sueltos* (London, 1907).
20   *R.N.A.*, 6 July 1906 (editorial).
21   Ibid. ser. 6, nos. 2–3 (1 September 1910) (editorial). There is a
play of words here which cannot be translated; the word *turma* means
'potato' among the peasants of the *tierra fría* in Cundinamarca and Boyacá,
and Turmequé is a municipality of Boyacá.

22   *R.N.A.*, 5 and 10 June 1909 (editorials).
23   Ibid. 1 September 1910, p. 7.
24   Ibid. no. 6 (July 1906); the impact of the three years' war on the despatching of coffee is shown clearly in the statistics for exports from Barranquilla: 1894, 254,000 bags; 1899, 86,000 bags; 1904, 574,000 bags. See Petre, *Republic*, p. 269.
25   McGreevey, *An Economic History*, p. 254.
26   *R.N.A.*, no. 5, 10 June 1909.
27   Ibid. ser. 6, nos. 2–3 (1 September 1910), p. 7.
28   Ibid. no. 4, 1 March 1906, p. 7.
29   Transport costs calculated on the basis of the accounts of Vásquez, Correa & Co. in Archivo Ospina.
30   *R.N.A.*, no. 1 (3 April 1906), p. 4.
31   Ibid. no. 12 (1 April 1908); no. 7 (20 September 1909); no. 5 (10 July 1909), p. 138; no. 13 (November 1906), p. 258; and T. E. Nichols *Tres puertos de Colombia* (Bogotá, 1972), pp. 188–9. In fact there was around 1890 and again in 1903 and 1906 very fierce competition between the river-transport companies, and the rates fell, but it must have been a transitory phenomenon. On this see also *R.N.A.*, ser. 5, nos. 3–4 (23 April 1909), and U.S. National Archives, Despatches from U.S. Consuls in Bogotá (microfilm T 116, roll 3), Beaupres to Loomis, Bogotá, 25 July 1903, and Synder to Loomis, Bogotá, 17 March 1905. See also S. Dickson, *Report on Colombia*, P.P., vol. 88 (1907).
32   *R.N.A.*, nos. 14–16 (1906).
33   Ibid. year 1, no. 14 (n.d.), pp. 312–17; no. 18 (15 January 1907).
34   Ibid. no. 15 (December 1906), pp. 334–5; no. 18 (15 January 1907); no. 21 (1 March 1907), p. 537; no. 23 (1 April 1907).
35   Ibid. no. 122 (August 1914), pp. 74–5.
36   Ibid. no. 4 (8 October 1910).
37   Ibid. no. 3 (September 1913).
38   Ibid. no. 195 (September 1920), pp. 67–8; and *El Tiempo*, 28 July 1920, p. 5; 29 July 1920, p. 1; 30 July 1920, p. 1; 26 August 1920, p. 1; 27 August 1920, p. 1; 28 August 1920, p. 5; 29 August 1920, p. 5; 31 August 1920, p. 5. The only detailed study I know on the activities of the United Fruit Company in Colombia from their origins until the conflicts at the end of the 1920s is that of J. White, 'The United Fruit Company in the Santa Marta Banana Zone, Colombia: Conflicts of the 20's', unpublishe B.Phil. thesis, Oxford University, 1971.
39   Lleras Camargo, *Mi gente*, p. 125; Palacio, *Historia de mi vida*, p. 44.
40   ANC, Notarías de Bogota, escritura 1176 of 1912 (Notaría Segunda). The properties acquired by Holguín were: Haciendas Calandaima, Batavia, Mejoras Escuelas de Tibacuy, Balaúnda, Capita and La Vuelta, and six more grazing ranches and properties, all in Nilo and Tibacuy. From then until his death in 1929 Holguín went on to create a family business and export his own coffee, averaging annual amounts of 5,000–5,500 bags. See Commercial Bank of Spanish America, Letterbooks, Bogotá to London 20 November 1921, in BOLSA Archive, University College, London.
41   D. Monsalve, *Colombia cafetera* (Barcelona, 1927), pp. 419–23.

42   Archivo Jonás, Inventarios.
43   Ospina, *Industria*, p. 311.
44   Brew, 'Economic Development', pp. 319–24.
45   *R.N.A.*, no. 152 (February 1917), pp. 1380 et seq.
46   J. Ancízar, 'La industria del café en Colombia', *R.N.A.*, nos. 239–40 (May–June 1924), pp. 235–6.
47   R. C. Beyer, 'The Marketing History of Colombian Coffee', *Agricultural History*, 23 (1949).
48   P.R.O., F.O. 371/22741, Manuel Mejía to Jose Medina, New York, 20 May 1939. It should be noted, nevertheless, that in the 1930s Colombian coffees were successfully penetrating the German market.
49   Unless otherwise attributed, all references in this section to Vásquez, Correa & Co. and the Negocio X and Y are based on the commercial correspondence of Vasquez, Correa & Co. in Archivo Ospina.
50   Negocio X and Y, circular, 16 March 1911.
51   When Pedro A. López later formed the Banco López, in 1918, it was rapidly controlled by foreign banks. Thus when, during the crisis of 1920, the clients of the bank suddenly withdrew 78% of deposits on 27 November, the following banks had to come to its aid: Banco Mercantil de las Américas, U.S. $100,000; London and River Plate, U.S. $60,000 and an additional £10,000; National City Bank, U.S. $10,000; Commercial Bank of Spanish America, £50,000. From then until its bankruptcy in 1923 the Banco López was a puppet whose strings were pulled in London and New York. See P.R.O., F.O. 371/4479, British Legation (Commercial Secretary) to Curzon, 31 December 1920. On the bankruptcy of the Banco López see F.O. 371/8445. See also E. Zuleta Angel, *El Presidente López* (Bogotá, 1966), ch. 3.
52   A. López and J. Rodríguez, *Estadísticas de Antioquia* (Medellín, 1914), pp. 148–9.
53   Ospina, *Industria*, p. 321. The cottage industries did not succeed in supplying the market's needs, so sacks had to be imported, principally from England.
54   Negocio X and Y, circular, 12 November 1908.
55   Ibid. 7 December 1908.
56   *El Tiempo*, 11 January 1919, p. 3; 7 June 1920, p. 5; 14 June 1920, p. 3. In April 1920 *El Socialista* (Bogotá) opened a campaign against the speculations of the Banco Mercantil de las Américas, 'well received even by other competitors in the internal coffee market, which awoke national interest, and inspired in popular sectors the sensation of a struggle against Yankee imperialism' (I. Torres Giraldo, *Los inconformes* (5 vols., Bogotá, 1973–4), vol. 3, pp. 141–2).
57   See esp. the correspondence of April and June 1913 of Vásquez, Correa & Co. with the commission houses of New York.
58   According to the British Vice-Consul in Medellín, the financial crisis in Antioquia in 1913 was in part caused by Vásquez, Correa & Co. establishing themselves in New York, which lost them their credit there. This forced them to raise their demands on a money supply simultaneously much reduced by the withdrawal of £400,000 from Medellín by the Junta

de Conversión, after the prohibition of paper-money holdings in the banks.
At the same time the Banco Sucre's issue of £50,000 in mortgage bonds wa
disallowed (Vice-Consul Bowle, *Report on Antioquia*, P.P., vol. 71 (1914–1

Chapter 8

1   The classic work remains Parsons, *Antioqueño Colonization*. See also
L. Arango C., *Recuerdos de la guaquería en el Quindío* (Bogotá, 1920);
Fray P. Fabo, *Historia de la ciudad de Manizales* (Manizales, 1926); A.
García, *Geografía económica de Caldas* (Bogotá, 1937); O. Morales Benítez,
Testimonio de un pueblo (Bogotá, 1951); E. Santa, *Arrieros y fundadores*
(Bogotá, 1961); J. Jaramillo Uribe, 'Historia de Pereira, 1863–1963', in
L. Duque Gómez and J. Jaramillo U., *Historia de Pereira* (Pereira, 1963);
A. Lopez Toro, *Migración y cambio social en Antioquia durante el siglo
diecinueve* (Bogotá, 1970); J. F. Ocampo, *Dominio de clase en la ciudad
colombiana* (Medellín, 1972); Brew, 'Economic Development', pp. 155–81
K. H. Christie, 'Oligarchy and Society in Caldas – Colombia', unpublished
D.Phil. thesis, Oxford University, 1974; F. R. Safford, 'Significado de los
antioqueños en el desarrollo económico colombiano: un examen crítico
de las tesis de Everett Hagen', *Anuario Colombiano de Historia Social y
de la Cultura*, no. 3 (1965), pp. 49–69.
2   A. Valencia Zapata, *Quindío histórico: monografía de Armenia* (Armenia, 1955), pp. 37–41, 59–90.
3   J. Arocha, '"La Violencia" in Monteverde, Colombia: Environmental
and Economic Determinants of Homicide in a Coffee-Growing Municipio',
unpublished Ph.D. thesis, Columbia University, 1975, pp. 246 et seq. (the
municipality studied is Córdova in the department of Quindío); Christie,
'Oligarchy and Society', pp. 225–63. For Tolima, in a different sociopolitical milieu, see D. Fajardo, 'La violencia y las estructuras agrarias en
tres municipios cafeteros del Tolima, 1933–1970', in F. Leal et al., *El
agro en el desarrollo histórico colombiano* (Bogotá, 1977), pp. 265–300.
A careful quantitative analysis of *la violencia* is that of P. Oquist, 'Violence,
Conflict and Politics in Colombia', unpublished Ph.D. thesis, University
of California at Berkeley, 1976, esp. pp. 404 et seq.
4   Parsons, *Antioqueño Colonization*, pp. 98–9 and 83, 101.
5   L. E. Nieto Arteta, *El café en la sociedad colombiana*, 2nd edn (Bogotá
1971), pp. 37–40. L. Ospina Vásquez has argued that this work is better
than his larger one, *Economía y cultura* (Ospina, 'Perspectiva histórica de
la economía colombiana', *Ciencias Económicas*, Medellín, no. 16 (n.d.),
p. 16). I do not share this opinion. Clearly both suffer from errors of fact
and naive and chancy interpretations – the common faults of a generation
that had little to build on. But in the short work the ideological bias
appears in all its nakedness: historical and social reality is distorted for the
immediate official ends of asserting that 'coffee makes the economy',
'coffee brings democracy', 'coffee makes us serious', etc., etc. The final
pages are particularly confused. For M. Ospina Pérez, see his much-cited
'Carta del Doctor Mariano Ospina Pérez al Doctor Alfonso López', in
FNCC, *Informe del Gerente al Congreso Cafetero, 1934*, pp. 56–8.

6   Carr, *Spain*, pp. 66–72; A. Domínguez Ortíz, *Sociedad y Estado en el siglo XVIII español* (Barcelona, 1976), pp. 401–53, and see n. 13 below.
7   See for instance J. M. Samper, *Ensayo sobre las revoluciones*, pp. 6–13.
8   Carrasquilla, *Segundo Informe*, p. 103.
9   D. Mendoza, 'Ensayo sobre la evolución de la propiedad en Colombia', *Repertorio Colombiano*, 1892, p. 7. Camacho Roldán was convinced at the end of the century that the legislation of the Republic had managed to abate the tendency towards latifundist concentration: 'what remains of the past (latifundia) is that which cannot be touched without shaking the foundations of social order, and what is more, it will disappear naturally in the course of two or three generations' (*El Agricultor*, no. 5 (October 1884), p. 201).
10   A. Galindo, *Estudios económicos y fiscales* (Bogotá, 1880), pp. 263 et seq. and *D.O.*, 15 July 1874.
11   I am referring to the Código Fiscal of 1873, arts. 868–949, and the additional dispositions of Law 61 of 1874, and to the Ley de Tierras of 1936. For the evolution of the law, see *Recopilación de disposiciones vigentes sobre tierras baldías* (Bogotá, 1884) and *Memorias del Ministro de Industrias* (5 vols., Bogotá, 1931), esp. vol. 3.
12   See pp. 58–9.
13   Among the best-known compilations and juridical commentaries concerning the legislation regarding public lands, see G. Amaya Ramírez, *Curso sintético de legislación agraria* (Bogotá, 1939; mimeographed); M. A. Martínez, *Régimen de tierras en Colombia* (2 vols., Bogotá, 1939); M. Salazar, *Proceso histórico de la propiedad en Colombia* (Bogotá, 1948), with a prologue by Mariano Ospina Pérez. As is almost always the case, the pleas of lawyers in the courts, when they are good, clarify the law much more than the legal texts themselves; a case in point is that of Anibal Galindo, representing the Compañía Minera Liberia against the colonist Heliodoro Cataño, who gave a brief and clear review of Law 48 of 1882 and Law 71 of 1874, the pillars, according to him, of the 'agrarian question' (*D.O.*, 2 May 1891).
14   Ospina, *Industria*, pp. 352–4.
15   Bushnell, *El régimen de Santander*, pp. 169–71, 175–6. In 1853 the President sought authorization from Congress to concede 50,000 hectares more to the soldiers of the Independence campaign (*Mensaje, 1853* (Bogotá, 1853), p. 29).
16   Thus for example in the 1840s Jorge Child bought title deeds conceded by the Secretary of War to Thomas Murray for 1,077 hectares, to José Buenaventura Rangel for 628 hectares, and to Marcelo Calvera for 108 hectares. In 1854 Child sold the title deeds for these 1,813 hectares, already assigned to him in the Cunday region, to Schloss & Co. In the same year Lorenzana & Montoya acquired 5,128 hectares in the Montepío Militar, and 653 hectares from soldiers of lower rank in the same area. The Schloss and Lorenzana & Montoya holdings, totalling 7,594 hectares, were contiguous, but their boundaries had not been settled. In 1893 the companies sought to have the boundaries established, both to forestall possible conflicts with

established small colonists, whose legal rights they had already recognized, and to protect themselves in view of the concession of lands to Mariano Tanco, holder of the concession for the Ibagué railway. ANC, Bienes baldíos: Correspondencia, 1894–5. Regarding the concession to Tanco, see *D.O.*, 7 June 1893.

17   Galindo's complete report appears in *D.O.*, 15 July 1874. Among other mistaken readings of the report, see F. Posada, *Colombia: violencia y subdesarrollo* (Bogotá, 1969), p. 30, and A. Tirado Mejía, who reproduces it in his *Introducción a la historia económica de Colombia* (Bogotá, 1971), p. 169. This error does not invalidate in any way the analytical and pedagogical value of the work of these authors. I wish simply to show that the latifundia based on these public land bonds were only *potential* at this stage, as their holders had not even gone through the administrative procedures, nor paid for the surveying necessary to convert them into demarcated land with due title. The point is an important one, as it reveals the apathy of foreign capital regarding Colombian public lands and immigration and also the difficulties which backwardness and geography imposed on Colombian merchants who sought to invest in tropical agriculture at the time.

18   If it is true that the difference between *concesionarios* and *adjudicatar* was essentially a legal one, I emphasize it and distinguish between the two so as to avoid confusions. Reading the *Diario Oficial* clarifies the legal and administrative problems regarding the concession, adjudication, and issuing of title to public lands, problems which were created by the obscurity, casuistry, and anti-technical nature of the different legal dispositions. See 'Reglamentación de concesiones', *D.O.*, 27 January 1870; 'Derechos de compañías colonizadoras en Magdalena, Guajira y Sierra Nevada', *D.O.*, 7 July 1870; 'Plazos para levantar los planos de la concesión', *D.O.*, 9 and 21 July 1871 and 15 May 1872; 'Limitación del área en Santander y Valle del Cauca', *D.O.*, 21 May 1873; 'Fomento a la colonización en Casanare y San Martín', *D.O.*, 30 April 1874; 'Formalidades de los expedientes', *D.O.*, 2 August 1879; 'Problemas de mensura de los baldíos concedidos ó adjudicados', *D.O.*, 20 December 1899; 'Registro de baldíos ya concedidos', *D.O.*, 16 December 1904. It should be recalled that until 1886 the federal states could concede public lands which the nation had granted them since 1821, and that the centralized administration of public lands could pass very easily from one Ministry to another: from the Treasury to Public Works, then to Agriculture, from there to Industry, and then back to Agriculture again.

19   Galindo in *D.O.*, 15 July 1874.

20   See *Diario de Avisos*, 30 March, 28 April, 26 May, 21 July 1855; *Boletín de la Agencia de Comisionistas de Productos Nacionales*, May 1864–June 1865; *El Comercio*, 1858–63.

21   Parsons, *Antiqueño Colonization*, p. 98.

22   E. Restrepo E., *Una excurción al territorio de San Martín*, 2nd edn (Bogotá, 1957), pp. 110–11. This work, written in 1869, describes the establishment of several large haciendas that prospered for a time with coffee (pp. 114–38). Forty years later only the shadow could be seen; see M. Triana, *Al Meta* (Bogotá, 1913), pp. 94–7.

23   Camacho Roldán, *Escritos*, vol. 2, pp. 532–58.

24   Ospina, *Industria*, p. 241.

25   Based on table 27, p. 176.

26   See Law 61 of 1874, Law 48 of 1882, Law 56 of 1905, Law 110 of 1912, Law 45 of 1917, Law 85 of 1920, and Law 47 of 1926, all clearly legislative antecedents of the famous Law 200 of 1936. The latter did not break with juridical tradition as both Liberals and Conservatives, from their different ideological positions, would have us believe; its impact was in fact very limited.

27   This disposition (art. 4 of Law 61 of 1874) partially contradicts the foregoing, which simply allows the duplication of the extent put under permanent cultivation. It is an example of how technically bad much of this legislation was. For McGreevey's view, see his *Economic History*, p. 131.

28   *Memoria de Hacienda, 1869–70* (Bogotá, 1871), p. lxxxi.

29   Ibid. p. lii. See also *Memoria del Ministro de Hacienda, 1870* (Bogotá, 1870), pp. liii–liv and its anexo, pp. 143 et seq.

30   *D.O.*, 10 May 1905.

31   *D.O.*, 27 June 1907.

32   *Mensaje, 1916* (Bogotá, 1916), p. 41.

33   *D.O.*, 27 November 1917.

34   *D.O.*, 1 December 1926.

35   Geographers, particularly Agustín Codazzi, Felipe Pérez, and Francisco Javier Vergana y Velasco, gave estimates of the extent of public lands. Cruz Lopera Berrío made his own calculation on the basis of their work in *Colombia agraria* (Manizales, 1920). The different *Anuarios de Estadística* have published statistics regarding adjudications, etc. At the moment of writing I do not know of any recent estimate regarding such concessions. My calculations are based on the *Memorias del Ministro de Industrias* (1931), and should be used with caution.

36   Unless I specifically state the contrary, I always refer to the old department of Caldas, created in 1905 and dismembered in the sixties, creating three new departments, Caldas, Risaralda, and Quindío.

37   See p. 185.

38   Brew, 'Economic Development', pp. 173–5.

39   ANC, Bienes baldíos: Correspondencia, 1892, Pbro. C. Pérez to President of the Republic, Yolombó, 15 October 1892.

40   Archivo Ospina, Medellín, 4 October 1892. But the nominal price of land bonds remained depressed. Thus in 1894 Ospina Hermanos valued bonds for 8,100 hectares at 42 centavos (Colombian paper money) a hectare.

Chapter 9

1   Parsons, *Antioqueño Colonization*, p. 103.

2   *Censos de población*, 1870 and 1905.

3   Taken from a report of 1850 published in *Archivo Historial de Manizales*, no. 36 (November 1923), p. 355.

4   *Archivo Historial de Manizales*, no. 38 (December 1924).

5   Ibid. nos. 8–9 (March–April 1919), pp. 362–5.

6   T. Arbeláez, *Impresiones de viaje por las regiones del Quindío y An-serma* (Manizales, 1912), p. 6.

7   Arbeláez, *Impresiones*, p. 10; the vertiginous growth of Armenia was anticipated twenty years before it occurred, but it was expected that it would come from the development of mining (H. Peña, *Geografía e historia de la Provincia del Quindío* (Popayán, 1892)). See also Ministerio de Guerra, 'Informe relativo a la topografía general de la Provincia del Quindío', *D.O.*, 24 August 1896.

8   Arbeláez, *Impresiones*, pp. 18, 22.

9   'Informe del Prefecto de Pereira, 1913', in *Informe del Secretario General al Gobernador de Caldas* (Manizales, 1913).

10   N. Arango V., 'Para la historia de Armenia', *Archivo Historial de Manizales*, no. 36 (November 1923), p. 348.

11   Arbeláez, *Impresiones*, p. 45; Peña, *Geografía*, p. 60; Jaramillo, 'Historia de Pereira', p. 387.

12   Ortega, *Ferrocarriles: resumen*, esp. vol. 1. More specific references are found in Beyer, 'Colombian Coffee', pp. 390–1, and A. S. Pearse, *Colombia with Special Reference to Cotton* (London, 1926), p. 55.

13   Parsons, *Antioqueño Colonization*, pp. 72–4; Ocampo, *Dominio de clase*, p. 53; Christie, 'Oligarchy and Society', pp. 18–19.

14   R. Gutierrez, *Monografías* vol. 2, pp. 19–20; 'Documentos relativos á la distribución de tierras en Salamina, Neira y Manizales', *Repertorio Histórico*, Medellín, July 1942.

15   This description, in some ways different from that of Parsons, is based entirely upon the documents and correspondence contained in ANC, Bienes baldíos: Correspondencia, 1853–71 and Correspondencia, 1856–1900, and in *D.O.*, 28 September 1860. Much of the material used in these two chapters is based on the correspondence on public lands in the ANC. I have not given the page references, but each volume has an alphabetical index. My attention was drawn to this source, which is not the same as the archive on *baldíos* in the hands of the Instituto Colombiano de Reforma Agraria, Bogotá, by Terry Horgan and Katy LeGrand.

16   Padre Fabo argues exactly the opposite in the matter of names (*Historia de la ciudad*, p. 69).

17   Eder, *El Fundador*, pp. 411–12; Christie, 'Oligarchy and Society', pp. 50–7.

18   *Informe del Gerente de la Empresa 'Burila' a la Junta General de Accionistas* (Manizales, 1890).

19   Ibid. p. 3.

20   Christie, 'Oligarchy and Society', p. 54.

21   Personero of Calarcá to Minister of Public Works, Calarcá, 31 July 1905, and Concejo Municipal of Calarcá to same, 23 December 1905, in ANC, Bienes baldíos: Correspondencia, 1904–5.

22   *Memorial* of 180 *colonos* to Minister of Public Works, Calarcá, 12 August 1905, in ibid.

23   Ministerio de Industrias, *Boletín de la Oficina General de Trabajo*, March 1930.

24   Joaquín Buenaventura was one of the best-known of rural surveyors in the area of Tolima colonization, and was the butt of many accusations of 'favouritism'. In 1905 he obtained for himself a concession of 400 hectares in the fertile area of Salento (Quindío); see *D.O.*, 16 August 1905. Ricardo Arana, another well-known surveyor of the Caldas region, began his career alongside the colonists of Villamaría in their suit against the elite of Manizales in 1860, and ended up defending the latifundists of the Valle del Río de la Vieja. These are two typical careers among many such.

25   A. M. Jimenez, 'Orígenes de Armenia', *Archivo Historial de Manizales*, nos. 27–8 (April 1921), pp. 94–5, and 'Fundación de Armenia', ibid. no. 36 (November 1923), pp. 385–6.

26   ANC, Bienes baldíos: Correspondencia, 1856–1900. (I should mention that these volumes are not in any chronological order. The reference here is to a single volume.)

27   Valencia, *Quindío histórico*, pp. 128–9.

28   Ibid. p. 92.

29   'Solicitud al señor Gobernador del Departamento de Caldas', Belalcazar, 2 June 1906, in ANC, Bienes baldíos: Correspondencia, 1906.

30   Ibid.

31   Arocha, '"La Violencia" in Monteverde', p. 93.

32   'Vecinos de Manzanares al Presidente de la Unión', 8 July 1879 in ANC, Bienes baldíos: Correspondencia, 1878–80.

33   'Vecinos de Manzanares al Presidente de la Unión', 27 January 1880, in ibid.

34   *Dos palabras* (Fresno, 1892). It is important to emphasize that the *fundadores* were often not the first to arrive. The example of Líbano is typical; when Isidro Parra arrived with his group at the future settlement there were already, as in the case of Fresno, colonists who had been established there for some time, but without legal protection or, more precisely, without their existence having been officially recognized. See Santa, *Arrieros*, pp. 34–9.

35   *Dos palabras*, p. 6.

36   Concejo of Calarcá to Minister of Public Works, 29 October 1909, ANC, Bienes baldíos: Correspondencia, 1909.

37   Telegrams of Personero and Cura Parroco of Calarcá to Minister of Public Works, 29 October 1909, in ibid.

38   ANC, Bienes baldíos: Correspondencia, 1912. The reply of the Ministry in Bogotá is for the second time a categorical no. As the Jaramillo brothers were in possession of the lands and enjoyed the support of local authorities and of the police, it is probable that they later acquired legal title, alleging *usucapio* (usucaption). This term in the Colombian civil law has the same meaning as defined in the *Concise Oxford Dictionary*: 'Acquisition of the title or right to property by uninterrupted and undisputed possession for prescribed term', which in Colombia is ten years (*Código Civil*, art. 2529).

39   Pedro Henao to Minister of Public Works, Calarcá, 28 October 1907, in ANC, Bienes baldíos: Correspondencia, 1901–31. Henao appears to have been a very active *colono* leader in 1906–7. The *colonos* of Belalcazar mentioned above complain in their petition of his lack of understanding and failure to support them.

40   'Circular del Gobernador de Caldas', Manizales, 2 November 1905, in ANC, Bienes baldíos: Correspondencia, 1904–5.

41   Ibid. 1908–11. Letters and telegrams along the same lines came from Armenia, Calarcá, Salento, Belalcazar, Filandia, etc.
42   These names are very common among the *fundadores* of Armenia and Calarcá.
43   In reply the central government ordered the Personero of Filandia to collect four testimonies from 'respectable people' in the settlement stating whether there were established colonists or mines (ANC, Bienes baldíos: Correspondencia, 1887).
44   Ibid. 1889–90. On 10 November 1889 the Personero of Salento sent a letter to the Treasury Minister denouncing the fact that Lisandro Caicedo (the owner of Burila) 'wants to extend the boundaries of the hacienda La Paila, giving the name "Sierra de Pijao" to the "Los Andes" range, which would give him a further 100,000 hectares, at the expense of the nation and the colonists . . . the confusion in this case is caused by the change of names; by clearing up this point the nation will easily get back the public lands which these people want to take from it'. Undoubtedly on many occasions the poor colonists used similar tricks, and as often, too, but their tricks involved expanses of land at least five hundred times smaller.
45   Antonio M. Hoyos to Minister of Hacienda, Salento, 28 April 1891, in ANC, Bienes baldíos: Correspondencia, 1891.
46   Ibid. 1912. The central government decided 'to call the attention of the Personero of Pereira to the terms of Law 48 of 1882'.
47   ANC, Bienes baldíos: Correspondencia, 1913–14.
48   Ibid. 1894.
49   A. López, *Problemas colombianos* (Paris, 1927), pp. 45–63.
50   ANC, Bienes baldíos: Correspondencia, 1894.
51   *Tierras baldías ubicadas en el Municipio de Pandi* (Bogotá, 1914), pp. 17–18. Carlos Liévano, himself a concessionary of public lands in his capacity as a contractor for public works in Cundinamarca, accused General Antonio B. Cuervo and the Compañía Agrícola e Industrial de Rionegro of illegitimately gaining control of 30,000 hectares of public lands by adjusting boundaries. They were also accused of taking advantage of the fact that a number of poor colonists were detained on the orders of the Criminal Court of Guaduas by initiating police action and expelling them from their plots. See C. Liévano, *Tierras baldías de La Ceiba, Guásimo y Rionegro* (Bogotá, 1894).
52   E. Röthlisberger, *El Dorado: estampas de viaje y cultura de la Colombia suramericana*, 2nd edn (Bogotá, 1963); F. von Schenk, *Viajes por Antioquia en el año 1880*, 2nd edn (Bogotá, 1952); J. Brisson, *Viajes por Colombia en los años 1891 a 1897* (Bogotá, 1899); M. Pombo, 'Viaje entre Medellín y Bogotá en 1851 a lomo de buey', *Obras inéditas* (Bogotá, 1914). Certain characteristics of *antioqueño* society and of *antioqueño* entrepreneurs of peasant origins at the turn of the century are described in Jaramillo, *Pepe Sierra*, and M. Restrepo, *El rey de la leña* (Buenos Aires, 1958). The first emigrated to Bogotá, and the second escaped to Ecuador, where he became one of the largest landowners, providing an example that was both anti-Velasquista and 'anti-*huasipunguero*'.
53   ECLA/FAO, *Coffee in Latin America: Productivity Problems and*

Future Prospects, vol. 1: *Colombia and El Salvador* (E/CN 12/490) (1958), pp. 78–9.
54   ANC, Bienes baldíos: Correspondencia, 1929.
55   *Informe relativo al año 1925 del Secretario de Gobierno al Gobernador de Caldas* (Manizales, 1926), pp. 89–91; García, *Geografía económica*, pp. 208–23; E. Guhl et al., *Caldas: memoria explicativa del 'Atlas' socioeconómico del Departamento* (2 vols., Bogotá, 1956–7), vol. 1, pp. 179–87.
56   *Informe relativo al año 1925*, p. 94. The river ports of the Magdalena were also *foci* of this type of disease, principally Girardot, La Dorada, Puerto Berrío, and Barrancabermeja.
57   *Informe Anual del Gobernador de Caldas, 1922* (Manizales, n.d.), pp. 16, 49, 52, 61, 75, 99.
58   García, *Geografía económica*, pp. 391–2.
59   See pp. 205–6.
60   Guhl et al., *Caldas*, vol. 1, p. 101.
61   *Informe relativo al año 1925*, p. 25.
62   *Informe del Gobernador del Departamento de Caldas, 1925* (Manizales, n.d.), p. 43.
63   *Mensaje del Gobernador a la Asamblea, 1928* (Manizales, n.d.), pp. 4–7. It is all the same a year of euphoria: the foundation-stone of the cathedral was laid (pp. 40–1). *Mensaje del Gobernador de Caldas a la Asamblea en sus sesiones extraordinarias de 1928* (Manizales, n.d.), pp. 5–12. It should be borne in mind that Aquilino Villegas, a prominent Conservative of the Manizales elite, was Minister of Public Works between 1922 and 1926.
64   García, *Geografía económica*, pp. 545–9.
65   Although I do not share the work's optimism about such processes, the expansion of exports from an economy with a peasant base and abundant land and labour described in H. Myint, *The Economics of Developing Countries* (London, 1964), pp. 44–50, seems in its description of peasant self-financing to fit the Colombian case very well. The similarity between the 1920s coffee boom and the tobacco boom of the preceding century is an additional element in the criticism of McGreevey's view, which I develop further below. See also my contribution, 'Las condiciones de la oferta', in Ospina Vásquez et al, *Historia económica*.

Chapter 10

1   The growth rates have been calculated from the formula

$$r = \left(\sqrt[m]{\frac{Xn}{Xt}} - 1 \right) 100$$

where r is growth rate, Xn is the value for the last period, Xt is the value for the first period, and m is the difference in years between the two periods.
2   Though in historical interpretations of Latin America, several comparative models are being debated, this view has not been favoured by Colombian historians, in spite of its clear advantages in terms of Latin

American analysis taken as a whole. The view I hold is developed in F. H.
Cardoso and E. Faletto, *Desarrollo y dependencia en América Latina*
(Mexico City, 1969), esp. pp. 22–38, 42–8, 57–81, 109–15. Another
analytical view with similar content is W. P. Glade in *The Latin American
Economies: A Study of the Institutional Evolution* (New York, 1969),
pp. 376 et seq., which he calls the 'orthodox approach to development'.
For Colombia, I know of only one study in which, with several reservations
the analytical view of Cardoso and Faletto is used: the work by D. Pecaut,
Política y sindicalismo en Colombia (Bogotá, 1973), esp. pp. 9–67. Pecaut'
analysis is much more complex than the one I offer here, especially
in regard to industrial entrepreneurs; I differ on many specific points of
information or interpretation.

3   McGreevey, *An Economic History*, pp. 228 et seq.

4   ECLA, *Analyses and Projections of Economic Development*, vol. 3:
The Economic Development of Colombia (E/CN 12/365/Rev. 1) (1957),
pp. 152 et seq.

5   D. S. C. Chu, *The Great Depression and Industrialization in Colombia*,
Rand Paper Series (Santa Monica, Calif., 1977; mimeographed); ECLA,
The Economic Development, pp. 220–8.

6   U.S. Department of Commerce, *U.S. Investments in Foreign Countries*
(Washington, 1960), pp. 58–9, 92; ECLA, *The Economic Development*,
p. 20, on the 'Share of Public Investments in Industry (1925–53)'.

7   A mere summary of the problems in these distinctions would require
pages. In his impressive *mea culpa*, Regis Debray discusses some of the
problems of the 'classification of Latin America'. See especially his statements on the 'economism' of the bourgeois and neo-Marxist point of view
of the theory of unequal exchange, as well as his penetrating analysis of
the misuse in Marxist vocabulary of terms such as 'colonial', 'semi-colonial',
and 'neo-colonial' (*La crítica de las armas* (2 vols., Mexico City, 1975),
vol. 1, pp. 27–50). A good summary of the ECLA line of thought can
be found in O. Rodríguez, 'On the Conception of the Centre–Periphery
System', *CEPAL Review* (Santiago, 1977), pp. 195–239. On the formulations of dependent capitalism in the above-mentioned work by Cardoso
and Faletto must be added F. H. Cardoso, 'Dependency and Development
in Latin America', *New Left Review*, no. 74 (July–August 1972), pp. 83–
95, and F. Fernandes, 'Problemas de conceptualización de las clases sociales
en América Latina', in Fernandes et al., *Las clases sociales en América
Latina* (Mexico City, 1973), pp. 195–257.

8   Naturally, the political implications of the return to *laissez-faire* under
the Conservative Republic are notable. Ospina Vásquez summarizes them
in a good turn of phrase: the Conservatives inverted the formula of the
Radicals: 'it is not that liberty brings us progress, but rather that progress
brings us liberty' (*Industria*, p. 327).

9   Ibid. p. 325. Some economists tend to accept this point of view *in
toto*: Urrutia, 'El sector externo', p. 14; McGreevey, *An Economic History*,
pp. 199–200; H. López, 'La inflación en Colombia en la década de los
veintes', *Cuadernos Colombianos*, no. 5 (1975), pp. 53–5.

10   Ospina, *Industria*, p. 358.

11   Ibid. p. 359.

12   Ibid. pp. 361–3.

13   Ibid. pp. 365–9.

14   This matter, which is already common in the economic literature, does not seem to be much appreciated by Colombian historians. The rate of exchange, the monetary standard, the internal transport costs, the idiosyncrasies of the market, the systems of commercial finance are all combined in the phenomenon of protection, of course in addition to the native ability to industrialize: internal demand, entrepreneurial experience, resources, etc. The well-known case of the inefficiency of tariffs as industrial protection, and their purely fiscal function in Latin America, is documented in D. C. M. Platt, *Latin America and British Trade, 1806–1914* (London, 1972).

15   Between 1919 and 1921, the Colombian *peso oro*, which had been quoted at U.S. $1.07, fell to $0.85, but from 1922 it was revalued, and it continued to oscillate between U.S. $0.96 and $0.99 until 1932. See Urrutia and Arrubla (eds.), *Compendio de estadísticas*, p. 138.

16   A concise compilation of statistics, based on the *Revista del Banco de la República* and the *Anuario de Comercio Exterior*, among other documents, can be found in J. Diot, 'Colombia económica, 1923–29', DANE, *Boletín Mensual de Estadística*, no. 300 (July 1976), pp. 120 et seq.

17   P. L. Bell, *Colombia: A Commercial and Industrial Handbook* (Washington, 1921), p. 60.

18   In this Colombia differs from the 'Brazilian model' as described by C. Furtado in *Development and Underdevelopment* (Berkeley, 1964), pp. 127–40.

19   ECLA, *The Economic Development*, p. 9.

20   McGreevey, *An Economic History*, p. 110 (table 15).

21   Bell, *Colombia*, pp. 181, 225–35, 252–5, 319–22, 362, 366–7; *Memoria del Ministro de Hacienda, 1916* (Bogotá, 1916); Diot, 'Colombia económica', pp. 143, 219.

22   Chu, 'The Great Depression', p. 13 (table 5).

23   The Kemmerer Mission has not received the attention it deserves in the economic history of Colombia. See, among others, Mision Kemmerer, *Proyecto de Ley de la Comisión de Consejeros Financieros sobre Establecimientos Bancarios, Banco de la República y Presupuesto Nacional* (Bogotá, 1930); R. Seidel, 'American Reformers Abroad: The Kemmerer Mission in South America, 1923–1931', *Journal of Economic History*, 32, 2 (1972), pp. 520–45; R. Triffin, 'La moneda y las instituciones bancarias en Colombia', *Revista del Banco de la República*, no. 202, supp. (August 1944); Ospina, *Industria*, pp. 366–7. A clear description of the functioning of the Banco de la República during the 1920s, of the conflicts between bankers, industrial businessmen, and importers and between the Banco and the debt policy of the government is found in J. A. Andrade, *El Banco de la República: glosas y comentarios* (Bogotá, 1929).

24   All coffee price quotations in this chapter are based on the Banco de la República's *XLII y XLIII Informe Anual*, vol. 2, p. 190. They are quotations for Manizales coffee in New York. For the purpose of showing price movement, the quotations are sufficient. Naturally, for economic analysis it is most suitable to work on the basis of effective prices.

25   An account is found in Bell, *Colombia*, pp. 55–65. See also *El
Tiempo*, 29 October 1920, p. 3, and 4 December 1920, pp. 1, 4; Torres
García, *Historia de la moneda*, pp. 324–33; Harvey to Curzon, Bogotá,
15 January 1919, PRO, FO 871/3704.
26   Harvey to Curzon, Bogotá, 26 February 1921, PRO, FO 371/5561.
27   Ibid. 28 March 1922, FO 371/7210.
28   In the liquidation process Pedro N. Ospina intervened; after 1923,
M. Ospina Pérez also became involved and was designated as liquidator.
Public political criticism was very insistent in Medellín. A good example
is *La República*, 27 August 1921.
29   BOLSA Archive, University College, London. See esp. Commercial
Bank of Spanish America, Ltd, Letterbooks 1920–6; Anglo-South America
Bank, Letterbooks 1931–3. On the American banks, see the typescript
in the Biblioteca Nacional de Bogotá by W. L. Sisson, 'Informe sobre los
Recursos de la República de Colombia' (Bogotá, 1920–1). On the Banco
Mercantil de las Américas, see E. Zuleta Angel, *El Presidente López*, 2nd
edn (Bogotá, 1968), pp. 33–49.
30   On the relationship between Huth and Pinzón & Co. there is a
dossier in PRO, FO 371/11132.
31   Archivo Ospina, Vásquez, Correa & Co., Correspondencia Comercial,
November 1918.
32   *El Tiempo*, 22 April 1927, p. 9.
33   'There is a new coffee organization which is not precisely Colombian,
which does not cultivate coffee, but which has practically established a
monopoly over purchases, with a control over prices in the interior and
abroad, and over fluctuations in the exchange rate, which presents a great
danger for our economy' (*R.N.A.*, no. 372 (June 1935), p. 334).
34   A very complete account is found in I. Torres Giraldo, *Los inconform*
(5 vols., Bogotá, 1973–4), vols. 3–5. See also Urrutia, *Historia del sindicalismo*, pp. 115–36; White, 'The United Fruit Company', and Pecaut,
Política, pp. 89–99.
35   H. López, 'La inflación', pp. 89 (table 9), 92 (table 10), 99 (table 12)
121 (table 16), 123 (table 17), 124 (table 18).
36   J. H. Dunning, 'Capital Movements in the Twentieth Century', in
Dunning (ed.), *International Investment* (London, 1972), pp. 59–64.
37   The best-known account of American investments and activities in
Colombia in the 1920s is J. E. Rippy, *Capitalists and Colombia* (New York
1931); the reports of the British Ministers in Bogotá are extremely amusing
on the inexperience of the Colombian governments in regard to debt and
alleged corrupt practices by many lenders and North American contractors
See PRO, FO 371/13479, 'Report for the Year ending June 1928', pp.
8–10.
38   The law of 3 August 1926, called the 'emergency law', about which
there was national debate, very drastically lowered the tariff for food
agriculture, traditionally protected since colonial times. A combination of
drought, an increase in urban demand and problems of rigidity in producti
and marketing created problems of supply. The freed products were rice,
sugar, wheat, wheat flour, corn, beans, cereals, pork fat, salted meat, and
potatoes. The law was issued after an agreement between the government

and the SAC, but was only executed in June 1927. It was abolished in
the package of economic measures of 1931.
39   The fiscal deficit in 1930 was 30 million pesos. The initial measures,
before the arrival of the Kemmerer Mission, were as follows: drastically
reducing expenditure, ending public credit, incurring a short-term dollar
debt with an association of American and European bankers, and placing
6 million pesos in IOUs in the national Treasury (*Mensaje 1931* (Bogotá,
1931), pp. 28–31).
40   C. Abel, *Conservative Politics in Twentieth-Century Antioquia
(1910–1953)*, Oxford University Latin American Centre Occasional
Papers (1974; mimeographed).
41   *R.N.A.*, no. 161 (May 1920), no. 195 (September 1920), pp. 67–8.
42   The 'Leviathans' was the name given by their enemies to a close-
knit circle of *antioqueño* interests linked to the government and composed
of Esteban Jaramillo, Mariano Ospina Pérez and José M. Marulanda (Abel,
Conservative Politics, p. 17).
43   Monson to Chamberlain, Bogotá, 12 April 1929, PRO, FO 371/13479.
44   Ibid. A. Gaitán, *Porqué cayó el Partido Conservador* (Bogotá, 1935);
A. Arguedas, 'La danza de las sombras', in his *Obras completas* (2 vols.,
Madrid, 1959), vol. 1, pp. 720–885.
45   Monson to Chamberlain, Bogotá, 12 April 1929, PRO, FO 371/13479.
46   PRO, FO 371/15832, 16570, 16571, and 17510.
47   *El Tiempo*, 10 October 1935, pp. 1, 8. On the commercial treaty
with the U.S.A., see Parks, *Colombia and the United States*, ch. 28. On
the negotiations for a new commercial treaty with Great Britain, see PRO,
FO 371/21439 and 21443.
48   McGreevey, *An Economic History*, p. 110 (table 15), and Diot,
'Colombia económica', p. 128.
49   ECLA, *The Economic Development*, pp. 220–8.
50   FNCC, *Boletín de Información y Estadística*, 1, 4 (October 1932),
pp. 110–11.
51   *Mensaje del Presidente, 1931*, pp. 27–48; C. Lleras Restrepo, *Borradores
para una historia de la República Liberal* (Bogotá, 1975), pp. 40–2; *Revista
del Banco de la República*, no. 41 (March 1931), pp. 89–90; PRO, FO
371/15083, 15087, and 15803.
52   Parks, *Colombia and the United States*, pp. 473–80; PRO, FO 371/
16750.
53   *Revista del Banco de la República*, no. 52 (February 1932), pp. 45–8,
no. 66 (April 1933), pp. 128–9, no. 78 (April 1934), p. 116; PRO, FO 371/
16750.
54   *D.O.*, 9 January and 11 February 1931. See also the 'Report on the
U.S. Activities in Colombia' (1934) in PRO, FO 371/17511. The full text
of the Colombo-American commercial treaty was published in *El Tiempo*,
10 October 1935.
55   ECLA, *The Economic Development*, pp. 118, 153 et seq.; *Mensaje
1937* (Bogotá, 1937), p. 37; *Mensaje 1941* (Bogotá, 1941), pp. 36–9.
56   Chu, 'The Great Depression', pp. 33–40.
57   *La Razón*, Liberal opposition newspaper, was the mouthpiece of the
industrialists promoting great debates about the tax reform, governmental

participation in trade unionism, and the possibility that foreign firms
would invest in protected areas such as manufacture of cigarettes. Its
tone could not have been more conservative, including its tone on sub-
jects of agricultural legislation.

58   ECLA, *The Economic Development*, pp. 96, 107–10.
59   *Mensaje 1936* (Bogotá, 1936), pp. 30–1.
60   Ibid. pp. 27–30.
61   *Mensaje 1937* (Bogotá, 1937), pp. 77–82.
62   Chu, 'The Great Depression', p. 21; M. Urrutia and A. Berry, *La
distribución del ingreso en Colombia* (Medellín, 1975), pp. 110–23;
M. Urrutia, 'Nota sobre los cambios históricos en la participación del
ingreso nacional de los grupos más acaudalados en Colombia', *Revista
del Banco de la República*, no. 516 (October 1970), pp. 1457–60.
63   *Mensaje 1937*, p. 37.
64   See B. E. Koffman, 'The National Federation of Coffee-Growers of
Colombia', unpublished Ph.D. thesis, University of Virginia, 1969. Koffman considers that the FNCC, despite being a self-perpetuating bureaucrac
has the characteristics of a real 'association of interests'. The departmental
committees of the FNCC are more similar to pressure groups, and the FNC
is a kind of intermediary between them and the central government.
P. Gilhòdes in *La question agraire en Colombie* (Paris, 1974), pp. 180–216
classifies it among the pressure groups of a reformist nature, in a rapid and
general gloss.
65   FNCC, *Economía Cafetera*, 7, 6 (November 1977), p. 1.
66   Though an 'ethnographic' study of the group running the FNCC, or
of the Banco de la República, would yield important evidence on the
reciprocal determinations of the 'traditional' and the 'modern', I think it
is more urgent to understand the role of this group in the constitution of
power, and more specifically of state power.
67   *El Tiempo*, 18 April 1911, p. 1, 25 April 1911, p. 1, 26 April 1911,
p. 1, 30 July 1920, p. 1, 27 August 1920, p. 3; *Revista Cafetera de Colomb
no. 1 (November 1928), pp. 20–1.
68   *El Tiempo*, 22 April 1927, p. 9, 22 June 1927, p. 1, 22 July 1927,
pp. 4, 12, 1 August 1927, pp. 5–6.
69   *El Tiempo*, 10 February 1929, p. 1, 17 February 1929, p. 7, 3 March
1929, pp. 1, 5, 28 November 1929, p. 12, 13 December 1929, pp. 1, 3,
25 June 1930, p. 4. See also *Compilación Cafetera 1920–1939*, 2nd
edn (Bogotá, 1958), pp. 101–57, and *El Tiempo*, issues of December 193C
and 1 January 1931, p. 12, 26 May 1931, p. 1, 19 July 1931, pp. 1, 13,
and 6 August 1931, pp. 1, 4.
70   For this decisive period in the reorganization of the FNCC, see esp.
the *Informes* of Mariano Ospina Pérez to the Congresos Cafeteros of 1932,
1934, and 1935 in *Revista Cafetera de Colombia*, nos. 58–62 (January–
March 1934), pp. 1815 et seq., nos. 73–9 (November 1935), pp. 1951–9;
and *R.N.A.*, no. 368 (May 1935), pp. 266–8.
71   *Compilación Cafetera 1920–1939*, pp. 207–9, 275–6.
72   See *El Tiempo*, issues of April 1954.
73   *El Tiempo*, 22 November 1930, pp. 4, 10.
74   *Compilación Cafetera 1920–1939*, pp. 112, 251, 323–6, 354–5,

361–92. The *Prenda agraria* is a contract similar to a mortgage, except that the debtor does not give the land as guarantee, but generally what it produces, in this case coffee. It was created in 1921 and ten years later the FNCC applied pressure for its greater diffusion among small and medium cultivators.

75   *Compilación Cafetera 1920–1939*, pp. 393–416.

76   Ibid. pp. 449–77.

77   The conflicts between debtors and the national and foreign banks can be seen in FNCC, *Informe del Gerente, 1934* (Bogotá, 1935), pp. 76–81, and PRO, FO 371/16571.

78   *Compilación Cafetera 1920–1939*, pp. 116, 228, 354.

79   By 1935 it was clear that the coffee group in the FNCC were better able to understand and act in the international market than the changing Ministers of the Exchequer.

80   This logic is what complicates the international producers' agreements and production strategies in regard to the policy of restrictions on world supply.

81   V. D. Wickizer, *Coffee, Tea and Cocoa* (Stanford, Calif., 1951), p. 79.

82   Ibid. pp. 82 et seq.

83   An impartial account of these conflicts is found in the *Informe* of Agustín A. Moran and Alfonso Rocha C., sent by the government of El Salvador to study the coffee policies of Brazil and Colombia. See *El Café*, ser. A, no. 2 (January 1938) and no. 4 (September 1938). See also *El Tiempo*, esp. the issues of December 1937.

84   See pp. 224–6.

85   FNCC, *Boletín de Información y Estadística*, 3, 15 (July 1937), p. 161, and PRO, FO 371/18673.

86   *Revista del Banco de la República*, no. 151 (May 1940), pp. 181–2. See also the economic justification of the measure in C. Lleras Restrepo, *Política fiscal y económica del gobierno, 1941* (Bogotá, 1941), pp. 6–10, 38–40. It is interesting to note that the basis for Lleras's argument is that the fall in price drastically limited the internal market based on the small cultivators; this statement is the heart of the official ideology on the role of coffee in the Colombian economy.

87   Wickizer, *Coffee*, pp. 91–152.

88   S. D. Krasner, 'Business–Government Relations: The Case of the International Coffee Agreement', *International Organization*, no. 4 (1973), p. 502; J. W. Rowe, *The World's Coffee* (London, 1963), pp. 190–1.

89   FNCC, *Informe del Gerente, 1954* (Bogotá, 1954), p. 12.

90   *Compilación Cafetera 1939–1951* (Bogotá, 1951), pp. 203–13.

91   Wickizer, *Coffee*, pp. 130–1.

92   FNCC, *Informe del Gerente, 1954*, pp. 6–20.

93   FAO, *The World Coffee Economy*, Commodity Bulletin Series, 33 (Rome, 1961); FNCC, *Boletín de Información y Estadística*, no. 43 (1969), p. 5.

94   FNCC, *Boletín de Información y Estadística*, no. 44 (1970), pp. 10–11.

95   T. Geer, *An Oligopoly: The World Coffee Economy and Stabilization Schemes* (New York, 1971), p. 21 (table 1).

96   Glade, *The Latin American Economies*, chs. 11, 12; International Bank for Reconstruction and Development, *The Basis of a Development Program for Colombia* (Washington, 1950).

Chapter 11

1   See *Anuario de Estadística de Colombia 1875* (Bogotá, 1875), p. 137; *Boletín de Estadística de Cundinamarca*, October 1923, pp. 20–3 (gives coffee statistics for 1918/19); López and Rodríguez, *Estadísticas de Antioquia*, pp. 135–7; M. Monsalve, *Economía y estadística* (Medellín, 1929), pp. 55–6; J. Ancízar, 'La industria del café en Colombia', pp. 287–92; D. Monsalve, *Colombia cafetera*, pp. 205–615. Monsalve's figures highlight clearly a number of inconsistencies between the 1932 census and the regional censuses carried out in the 1920s. This work is of enormous value to the scholar for the information it contains relating to the names of estates and their owners. These are of particular help to anyone wishing to carry out investigations in the notarial archives. The statistical data are, however, rather more doubtful.
2   For example, if the investigator should wish to assess the specific weight of each of the different groupings of small coffee producers, then the 1970 coffee census will prove a great disappointment. Some of the tables refer to 'producers of less than 120 *arrobas* per annum' while others refer to areas under coffee cultivation according to size (e.g. less than 0.5 hectares, etc.), or to total surface area of the *fincas*. It is not possible, for example, to determine how many *fincas* produce less than 60 *arrobas* from the above figure of 120 *arrobas*, nor is it possible to calculate how much land is given to coffee cultivation out of the total surface area mentioned. On the other hand, it has also been claimed that all the producer countries tend to hold secret stocks and that they, on occasion, distort the figures relating to the annual harvest. In Colombia, there are three different sources for such statistics: the FNCC, the Banco de la República, and the Contraloria General of the Republic.
3   See FNCC, *Informe del Gerente, 1965* (Bogotá, 1965; mimeographed). This lays out the aims of the Programa de Desarrollo y Diversificación de las Zonas Cafeteras and its concentration in Viejo Caldas and Valle. Its principal features were credit, a rural training programme, new methods of cultivation, technical assistance, marketing, and co-operatives.
4   The role of risk and uncertainty in the economic decisions of the small coffee-planter rarely appears in the literature. A notable exception is the complete study of a community of coffee-growers carried out by S. de Ortíz, *Uncertainties in Peasant Farming: A Colombian Case* (London, 1973).
5   See FNCC, *Revista Cafetera de Colombia*, nos. 80–7 (July 1936): 'the coffee plantations in Norte de Santander, which so much resemble dense forest, give me the impression that in all Colombia this is the *Departamento* which most closely reproduces the conditions found in Abyssinia, the original home of the coffee tree' (pp. 2020–1). See also FNCC, *Revista Cafetera de Colombia*, January–February 1932, pp. 1292–5, 1301–2, and January 1958, pp. 15–18.

Glade, *The Latin American Economies*, p. 369.

See P. Streeten and D. Elsan, *Diversification and Development: The use of Coffee* (New York, 1971).

FNCC, *Plan Nacional de Política Cafetera* (Bogotá, 1969; mimeographed).

ECLA/FAO, *Coffee in Latin America*, vol. 1.

Ibid. pp. 46–50.

The ranking of productivity according to size is similar for the five g producers and the marginals:

Finca (ha)	Five	Marginals
		(kg per ha)
Over 100	663.9	437.2
50–99.9	633.2	385.1
20–49.9	586.6	388.3
Less than 1	585.3	395.9
10 to 19.9	582.8	391.7
6 to 9.99	571.3	389.1
1 to 5.99	553.1	381.0
Average	599.4	395.2

urce: FNCC, *Censo Cafetero de 1970.*

he coefficient of variation is very low: 5.8% for the five and 4.4% for the arginals.

2   The best economic analysis I know on this subject is that of Urrutia d Berry: *La distribución del ingreso*, pp. 69–105.

3   ECLA/FAO, *Coffee in Latin America*, vol. 1, pp. 52 et seq.

4   R. Junguito, *Objetivos de la política cafetera colombiana* (Bogotá, 974; mimeographed).

5   Interview with Germán Valenzuela S. (Gerente Técnico of the FNCC), ogotá, 13 March 1975. See FNCC, *Plan Quinquenal de Desarrollo y Diversicación para las Zonas Cafeteras Colombianas* (2 vols., Bogotá, 1973; imeographed).

6   Interview with Valenzuela cited above.

7   FNCC, *Boletín de Información y Estadística*, no. 44 (1970), pp. 35–7.

8   Ibid. no. 5 (February 1933), and *Censo Cafetero de 1970.* In this ntext *minifundistas* can be considered as the peasants' lower strata.

9   In T. Shanin (ed.), *Peasants and Peasant Societies* (London, 1971), 15.

0   R. Weitz, *From Peasant to Farmer: A Revolutionary Strategy for evelopment* (New York, 1971), p. 20.

1   It must be borne in mind that the average number of coffee trees r the range of producers having between 5,000 and 20,000 trees was in 932 only 7,521, according to the census of that year.

2   In general, economists find this hypothesis credible, but very difficult prove empirically. See among others Urrutia and Berry, *La distribución*, . 88 et seq.; K. Griffin, *The Political Economy of Agrarian Change* ondon, 1974), p. 31.

23   I think that the use of the Censo Agropecuario in comparison with the inquiry of the ECLA/FAO previously cited caused L. Currie to conclu that the growth in active population on the coffee farms reached the un- believable inter-annual rate of 11.2% (*La industria cafetera en la agri- cultura colombiana* (Bogotá, 1962), pp. 44–51).

24   Oficina Internacional del Trabajo, *Hacia el pleno empleo* (trans. fro English) (Bogotá, 1970), pp. 37, 125.

25   Since roughly 1930, various specialists have emphasized the dangers of aggravating soil erosion in the coffee zones due in part to methods of cultivation in use on the higher slopes. Far from improving, the problem shows signs of getting worse. One has only to look at the *Atlas de Econo- mía Colombiana: Primera Entrega* of the Banco de la República (Bogotá, 1959), Cartograma no. 10 and its Complemento, to see how 'severe erosic has affected, in particular, the coffee zones of the Santanderes, Cundin- amarca, Tolima, Caldas, etc. In general, the shade trees provided protectic for the topsoil on the coffee plantations. Methods of planting without shade (*á pleno sol*) have led to leaching, particularly on the higher slopes, and this process has not been successfully counteracted by the extensive use of fertilizers. An interesting personal comment has been made by Lui Ospina Vásquez, who claimed that the cultivation of the *caturra* without shade amounted 'not to agriculture but to mining'. For details of a concre case, see Instituto Geográfico Agustín Codazzi, *Levantamiento agrológico de la región cafetera central de Antioquia* (Bogotá, 1959). See also FNCC *Revista Cafetera de Colombia*, nos. 80–7 (July 1936), pp. 2052–3.

26   See FEDESARROLLO, *Las industrias azucarera y panelera en Colo* (Bogotá, 1976).

27   In general, Latin American Marxists tend to severely limit their angl of analysis, accepting almost exclusively the formulations derived from th classical analyses of Kautsky on (*a*) the superiority of the capitalist units *vis-à-vis* the peasants and (*b*) on the processes of social differentiation in the peasantry. Chayanov, for example, has been until now practically unknown in Colombia. An interesting revisionist analysis of the Kautskia thesis, and one which integrates certain Marxist postulates with the Chayanov analysis is found in S. Amin and K. Vergopoulos, *La question paysanne et le capitalisme* (Paris, 1974). For an analysis of the 'social differentiation' in the Russian peasantry, see T. Shanin, *The Awkward Class* (Oxford, 1972).

28   A general analysis is found in A. Hirschmann, *Journeys toward Prog* (New York, 1963), pp. 96–141. A brief analysis of the effects of the law of 1961 was made by R. W. Findley, 'Ten Years of Land Reform in Col- ombia', *Wisconsin Law Review*, no. 3 (1972), pp. 880–923. Naturally, th Colombian legal, economic, and sociological literature is enormous. Some titles appear in the bibliography at the end of this book.

29   Salomón Kalmanovitz is one of the few Colombian Marxist economi who have argued against the postulate of extraction of the agricultural surplus by means of the unequal exchange between agriculture and indust See his *La agricultura en Colombia, 1950–72*, DANE, *Boletín Mensual de Estadística*, nos. 276–8 (offprint, 1974), pp. 71–107.

30   See among others, H. Agudelo Villa, *Cuatro etapas de la inflación en*

olombia (Bogotá, 1967); C. Sáenz de Santamaría, *Una época difícil*
Bogotá,1965), esp. pp. 237–97; *Informe Semanal de Economía*,
(March 1965). See also L. Currie, *La industria cafetera*, pp. 66–7,
nd L. Zuleta, 'El sector cafetero y los fenómenos inflacionarios',
uadernos Colombianos, no. 7 (1975), pp. 431–524.

1   R. M. Bird, 'Coffee Tax Policy in Colombia', *Inter-American Econ-
mic Affairs*, 22, 1 (1968), pp. 75–86.

2   The 1969 'sharing agreement' between the national government and
he FNCC stipulated that the increases in the international price of coffee
bove 57 U.S. cents per pound should be distributed as follows: 35% to
roducers via adjustment of the internal support price; 30% to the Fondo
Nacional del Café, and 35% to the Comités Departamentales of the FNCC
arrying out electrification, health, education, and housing programmes
1 the coffee zones. In 1972 the limit was lowered to 54 U.S. cents.

3   E. R. Walker, 'Beyond the Market', in K. W. Rothschild (ed.), *Power
1 Economics* (London, 1971) pp. 36–55; H. Melo and I. López Botero,
l imperio clandestino del café (Bogotá, 1976). See also the series of
rticles by D. Samper Pizano appearing in *El Tiempo* under the suggestive
itle of 'Café amargo' ('Bitter Coffee') in the editions of 3, 4, 5, 6, 7, 8,
nd 9 October 1974, all on p. 4–A.

4   International Coffee Organization, *Quarterly Statistical Bulletin on
'offee*, 1, 4 (October–December 1977), table III–8.

Bibliography

(A) MANUSCRIPT SOURCES

Bogotá   ARCHIVO NACIONAL DE COLOMBIA
(*a*) Bienes desamortizados: Cundinamarca, vols. XIV—XXXIII
Medellín, vols. II—III
(*b*) Consulados: Correspondencia consular de Colombia: Consulado de Londres, vols. II, IV, VI, IX; Consulado de Liverpool, vols. IV, VI, VIII, IX; Consulado de Maracaibo, vols.
II, IV; Consulado de New York, vols. XX—XXIII
(*c*) Bienes baldíos: Correspondencia, vols. from 1865 to 1929
(*d*) Notarías de Bogotá (Notaría Primera, 1865—1935; Notaría
Segunda, 1865—1919; Notaría Tercera, 1865—1925; Notaría
Cuarta, 1865—1910; Notaría Quinta, 1865 to 1911). *Note*:
Notaría papers are in the National Archive for the dates
named here; papers for later dates are to be found in the
Notaría in question.
(*e*) Bienes nacionales, vols. II—III
(*f*) Curas y obispos de la República, vol. VII
(*g*) Fondo E. Ortega Ricaurte, box 38

ARCHIVO DEL MINISTERIO DE TRABAJO
Convenciones colectivas, 1930—50

ARCHIVO DE LA CAJA DE CREDITO AGRARIO
INDUSTRIAL Y MINERO
Parcelaciones del Banco Agrícola Hipotecario y otras, 1926—6

ARCHIVO DEL SR ROBERTO HERRERA RESTR
Letterbooks and account books, 1879—1903. 64 vols.

Fredonia   OFICINA DE REGISTRO DE INSTRUMENTOS
PUBLICOS Y PRIVADOS
Libros de registro de compraventas, hipotecas y sucesiones,
1870—1960

NOTARIA PRIMERA
Escrituras, 1870—1905

ARCHIVO DE LA HACIENDA JONAS
Accounts, 1896—1920. 120 vols.

La Mesa   OFICINA DE REGISTRO DE INSTRUMENTOS
PUBLICOS Y PRIVADOS
Libros de registro de compraventas, hipotecas y sucesiones,
1860–1950

NOTARIA DE LA MESA
Escrituras, 1870–1938

London   PUBLIC RECORD OFFICE
Foreign Office, Series 371: Colombia, 1906–46

BANK OF LONDON AND SOUTH AMERICA
ARCHIVES (BOLSA), UNIVERSITY COLLEGE
(*a*) Letterbooks of the Commercial Bank of Spanish America
Ltd, 1920–7
(*b*) Letterbooks of the Anglo South American Bank, 1931–3

Medellín   ARCHIVO DE LA FUNDACION ANTIOQUENA
PARA LOS ESTUDIOS SOCIALES (cited as Archivo
Ospina)
(*a*) Ospina Hermanos: Commercial letterbooks, 1880–1905.
32 vols.
(*b*) Vásquez, Correa & Co.: Accounts and letterbooks, 1908–23
(*c*) Haciendas La Loma and La Carolina: Payrolls, 1930–50
(some years)

ARCHIVO DE LA HACIENDA LA AMALIA
Letterbooks, 1898–1904. 4 vols.

ARCHIVO HISTORICO DE ANTIOQUIA
Notarías de Medellín (Notaría Primera, 1885–1940; Notaría
Segunda, 1885–99; Notaría Tercera, 1897–1959)

Oxford   BODLEIAN LIBRARY
United States National Archives (microfilms): Despatches from
U.S. Consuls in Bogota, 1850–1905

Tocaima   NOTARIA DE TOCAIMA
Escrituras, 1928 and 1934

Viotá   Cartas y telegramas del Alcalde de Viotá al Gobernador de
Cundinamarca, 1919–20 and 1934–37. 2 vols. (in possession
of Sr Benigno Galindo)

(B) PRINTED SOURCES

(1) Primary sources

(*a*) PERIODICALS

Acción Liberal (Bogotá, 1935)

Anales de la Cámara de Representantes (Bogotá, 1894–8, 1932–6)
Anales de la Junta del Camino de Occidente (Bogotá, vols. 1–3, 1870)
Archivo Historial de Manizales (Manizales, 1918–25)
Boletín de Estadística de Cundinamarca (Bogotá, 1923)
Boletín de la Agencia de Comisionistas de Productos Nacionales (Bogotá, 1864–5)
Boletín de la Oficina General del Trabajo (Bogotá, 1927–35)
Boletín Industrial (Bogotá, 1868–75)
Claridad (Bogotá, 1934)
Diario de Avisos (Bogotá, 1865)
Diario Oficial (Bogotá, 1870–1910)
El Agricultor (Bogotá, 1875–95)
El Bolchevique (Bogotá, 1933–5)
El Comercio (Bogotá, 1858–63)
El Tiempo (Bogotá, 1911–70; from 3 July 1955 until 1 June 1957 *El Intermedio*)
Federación Nacional de Cafeteros de Colombia
    Boletín de Información y Estadística del Café (Bogotá, 1932–77)
    Revista Cafetera de Colombia (Bogotá, 1928–77)
Gaceta de Cundinamarca (Bogotá, 1870–1940)
Informe Semanal de Economía (Bogotá, vol. 1, March 1964–March 1965)
Revista del Banco de la República (Bogotá, 1927–77)
Revista Nacional de Agricultura (Bogotá, 1906–36)

(*b*)OFFICIAL REPORTS
Ordenanzas espedidas por la Lejislatura Provincial de Santander, 1850, Socorro, n.d.
Ordenanzas de la Cámara Provincial del Socorro espedidas en 1850, Socorro, 1850.
Ordenanzas de la Cámara Provincial del Socorro, 1852, Socorro, 1852.
Constitución Municipal i Ordenanzas espedidas por la Lejislatura Provincial de Santander en sus sesiones de 1853, Socorro, 1854.
Memoria del Gobernador de Cundinamarca, 1858, Bogotá, n.d.
Los doce códigos del Estado de Cundinamarca, 3 vols., Bogotá, 1859.
Boletín de Crédito Nacional, 1863, Bogotá, 1863.
Informe del Secretario de Hacienda del Estado Soberano de Cundinamarca á la Asamblea, 1865, Bogotá, n.d.
Mensaje del Gobernador de Cundinamarca á la Asamblea Lejislativa, 1870, Bogotá, 1870.
Informe del Presidente del Estado de Santander, 1874, Socorro, n.d.
Informe del Presidente del Estado de Santander, 1875, Socorro, n.d.
Memoria que el Secretario General dirije al Gobernador de Cundinamarca para la Asamblea Lejislativa, 1877, Bogotá, 1877.
Informe del Gobernador de Cundinamarca, 1877, Bogotá, 1877.
Informe del Presidente del Estado Soberano de Santander, 1878, Socorro, n.d.
[Carrasquilla, J. de D.], *Segundo Informe Anual que presenta el Comisario de la Agricultura Nacional al Poder Ejecutivo para conocimiento del Congreso: año 1880*, Bogotá, 1880.

*atastro de la Propiedad Inmueble del Estado de Cundinamarca formado
     por la Comisión de Revisión, 1879*, Bogotá, 1879.
J.S. Consular Reports, *Labour in Foreign Countries* (4 vols., Washington,
     1884), vol. 3.
ecopilación de disposiciones vigentes sobre tierras baldías, Bogotá, 1884.
Iemoria que el Gobernador de Cundinamarca dirige a la Asamblea, 1888,
     Bogotá, n.d.
nforme del Presidente de la Junta Administradora del Camino de Occidente,
     Bogotá, March 1888.
Catastro de la Propiedad Inmueble del Estado de Cundinamarca', *Gaceta
     de Cundinamarca*, February–April 1889.
nforme del Gobernador del Departamento del Magdalena, Santa Marta,
     1890.
nforme del Gerente de la Empresa 'Burila' a la Junta General de accionistas,
     Manizales, 1890.
nforme del Gobernador de Santander, Bucaramanga, 1891.
Liévano, Carlos] , *Alegato del apoderado de la Empresa del Ferrocarril
     del Nordeste y Camino de Herradura de Villeta al Río Magdalena*,
     Bogotá, 1892.
*nforme que presenta el subsecretario encargado del Ministerio de Gobierno
     de Colombia al Congreso Constitucional de 1894*, Bogotá, 1894.
Liévano, Carlos] , *Tierras baldías de La Ceiba, Guásimo y Rionegro*,
     Bogotá, 1894.
Holguín, Carlos] , *Aclaraciones al Congreso Constitucional de 1894*, Bogotá,
     1894.
nforme del Gobernador de Cundinamarca á la Asamblea, 1896, Bogotá,
     1896.
Informe relativo a la topografía general de la Provincia del Quindío', *Diario
     Oficial*, 24 August 1896.
*isita del Gobernador de Cundinamarca a las Provincias de Sumapaz, Girar-
     dot y Tequendama*, Facatativá, 1906.
nforme del Secretario General al Gobernador de Caldas, Manizales, 1913.
ierras baldías ubicadas en el Municipio de Pandi, Bogotá, 1914.
nforme Anual del Gobernador de Caldas, 1922, Manizales, n.d.
*nforme relativo al año 1925 del Secretario de Gobierno al Gobernador
     de Caldas*, Manizales, 1926.
nforme del Gobernador del Departamento de Caldas, 1925, Manizales,
     n.d.
nforme del Gobernador de Caldas, 1928, Manizales, n.d.
*Iansaje del Gobernador de Caldas á la Asamblea en sus sesiones extra-
     ordinarias de 1928*, Manizales, n.d.
Misión Kemmerer] , *Proyecto de Ley de la Comisión de Consejeros
     Financieros sobre Establecimentos Bancarios, Banco de la República
     y Presupuesto Nacional*, Bogotá, 1930.
Lleras Restrepo, C.] , *Informe del Secretario de Gobierno al Gobernador
     de Cundinamarca, 1934*, Bogotá, 1934.
a Política Oficial, 5 vols., Bogotá, 1935.
nforme del Secretario de Gobierno al Gobernador de Cundinamarca, 1937,
     Bogotá, 1937.

G. Giraldo Jaramillo (ed.), *Relaciones de mando de los virreyes de la Nueva Granada*, Bogotá, 1954.

Mensaje del Presidente de la República al Congreso for 1853, 1882, 1888, 1894, 1904, 1916, 1930, 1931, 1933, 1934, 1936, 1937, 1938, 1940, 1941.

Memoria del Ministro de Hacienda for 1869–71, 1912, 1914, 1916, 1920, 1921, 1930, 1931, 1941.

Memorias del Ministro de Industrias, 5 vols., Bogotá, 1931.

Ministerio de Hacienda, *Medidas tomadas por el Gobierno Nacional con motivo de la crisis del café*, Bogotá, 1938.

Federación Nacional de Cafeteros de Colombia, *Informe del Gerente al Congreso Cafetero* for 1929, 1930, 1932, 1934, 1935, 1937, 1938, 1943, 1944, 1945, 1947, 1948, 1954, 1957, 1961, 1962, 1963, 1965, 1967, 1970.

  Manual del cafetero colombiana, Bogotá, 1932 and subsequent editions.

  Compilación Cafetera 1920–1939, Bogotá, 1958.

  Compilación Cafetera 1939–1951, Bogotá, 1951.

  Plan Nacional de Política Cafetera, Bogotá, 1969 (mimeographed).

  Plan Quinquenal de Desarrollo y Diversificación para las Zonas Cafeteras Colombianas, 2 vols., Bogotá, 1973 (mimeographed).

International Coffee Organization, *Coffee in Colombia*, London, 1971 (mimeographed).

Parliamentary Papers, Consular Reports from Colombia, London, 1870– 1913.

U.S. Department of Commerce, *U.S. Investments in Foreign Countries*, Washington, 1960.

(*c*) STATISTICS

Estadística de Colombia: año fiscal de 1874 á 1875: segunda parte, Bogotá, 1876.

Anuario estadístico de Colombia 1875, Bogotá, 1875.

Anuario estadístico de Colombia 1882, Bogotá, n.d.

Arboleda C., H., *Estadística general de la República de Colombia*, Bogotá, 1905.

López, A. and Rodríguez, *Estadísticas de Antioquia*, Medellín, 1914.

Ministerio de Gobierno, *Censo General de la República levantado el 5 de marzo de 1912*, Bogotá, 1912.

Dirección General de Estadística, *Censo de la población de la República de Colombia levantado el 14 de octubre de 1918*, Bogotá, 1923.

Censo General de la Población: 5 de julio de 1938, 8 vols., Bogotá, 1940–

Departamento Administrativo Nacional de Estadística (DANE), *Censo de población del 9 de mayo de 1951*, Bogotá, 1954.

  Muestra Agropecuaria Nacional 1954, Bogotá, 1954.

  Directorio Nacional de explotaciones agropecuarias 1960, 2 vols., Bogotá, 1964.

  XIII Censo Nacional de Poblacion 1964, Bogotá, 1967.

  Censo Nacional de la Población 1970 (preliminares), Bogotá, 1974 (mimeographed).

[Diot, J.], 'Colombia económica 1923–1929', *Boletín Mensual de Estadística*, no. 300 (July 1976).
[Kalmanovitz, S.], *La agricultura en Colombia, 1950–1972*, offprint from *Boletín Mensual de Estadística*, Bogotá, 1974.
Federación Nacional de Cafeteros de Colombia, *Censo Cafetero de 1970*, 2 vols., Bogotá, 1973 (mimeographed).

(2) **Secondary sources**

(*a*) BOOKS AND ARTICLES
Abel, C., *Conservative Politics in Twentieth-Century Antioquia*, Latin American Centre Occasional Papers, Oxford, 1974 (mimeographed).
Academia Colombiana de Historia, *Historia extensa de Colombia* (30 vols., 1964–), vol. 10, L. Martínez Delgado (2 pts, Bogotá, 1970), pt 1: *1885–1895*; pt 2: *1895–1910*.
Adams, D. W. and N. Rask, 'Economics of Cost-Share Leases in Less Developed Countries', *American Journal of Agricultural Economics*, 50 (1968).
Agudelo Villa, H., *Cuatro etapas de la inflación en Colombia*, Bogotá, 1967.
Aguilar, F. C., *Colombia en presencia de las repúblicas americanas*, Bogotá, 1884.
    Un paseo en verano á Peñalisa y Girardot, Bogotá, 1886.
    Excurción de tres días a La Pradera, Bogotá, 1886.
Amaya Ramírez, G., *Curso sintético de legislación agraria*, Bogotá, 1939 (mimeographed).
Ancízar, J., 'La industria del café en Colombia', *Revista Nacional de Agricultura*, nos. 239–40 (May–June 1924).
Ancízar, M., *Peregrinación del Alpha*, 2nd edn, 2 vols., Bogotá, 1970.
Andrade, J. A., *El Banco de la República: glosas y comentarios*, Bogotá, 1929.
Arango, M., *Café è industria, 1850–1930*, Bogotá, 1977.
Arango Cano, L., *Recuerdos de la guaquería en el Quindío*, Bogotá, 1920.
Arbeláez, T., *Impresiones de viaje por las regiones del Quindío y Anserma*, Manizales, 1912.
Arguedas, A., 'La danza de las sombras', *Obras completas* (2 vols., Madrid, 1959), vol. 1, pp. 720–885.
Banco Agrícola Hipotecario, *La parcelación de tierras en Colombia*, Bogotá, 1937.
Banco Comercial Antioqueño, *Banco Comercial Antioqueño: bodas de oro, 1912–1962*, Medellín, 1962.
Banco de Bogotá, *Trayectoria de una empresa de servicio, 1870–1960*, Bogotá, 1960.
Banco de Colombia, *Cuadro que indica el premio que han tenido en Bogotá los giros sobre Londres por moneda corriente colombiana, 1874–1906*, Bogotá, n.d.
Banco de Exportadores, *Estatutos*, Bogotá, 1897.

320   *Bibliography*

Banco de la República, *Atlas de economía colombiana*, 4 vols., Bogotá,
     1959–64.
  XLII y XLIII Informe Anual del Gerente á la Junta Directiva, 2 vols.,
     Bogotá, 1965–6.
Baraona, R., 'Una tipología de haciendas en la sierra ecuatoriana', in O.
     Delgado (ed.), *Reformas agrarias en la América Latina*, Mexico City,
     1965.
Baraya, R., *Fotografías políticas*, Bogotá, 1898.
Bejarano, J. A., 'El fín de la economía exportadora y los orígines del
     problema agrario', *Cuadernos Colombianos,* nos. 6, 7, 8 (1975).
Bell, P. L., *Colombia: A Commercial and Industrial Handbook*, Washington,
     1921.
Belmonte Román, L., *Tesis existentes en la biblioteca de la Facultad de
     Medicina, Universidad Nacional*, Bogotá, 1964 (mimeographed).
Beyer, R. C., 'The Marketing History of Colombian Coffee', *Agricultural
     History*, 23 (1949).
  'Transportation and the Coffee Industry in Colombia', *Inter-American
     Economic Affairs*, 2 (1948).
Bird, R., *Taxation and Development: Lessons from Colombia*, Cambridge,
     Mass., 1970.
Bolívar, S., *Obras completas*, ed. V. Lecuna (3 vols., Havana, 1950), vol. 2.
Bravo Betancur, J. M., *Monografía sobre el Ferrocarril de Antioquia*,
     Medellín, 1974.
Brisson, J., *Viajes por Colombia en los años 1891 a 1897*, Bogotá, 1899.
Buenaventura, N., 'Proletariado agrícola: trabajo temporero', *Estudios
     Marxistas*, Bogotá, 8–9 (1975).
Bureau of the American Republics, *Colombia*, Washington, 1892.
  'Coffee in America', *Bulletin*, 1 (1893).
Bushnell, D., *The Santander Regime in Gran Colombia*, Newark, N. J.,
     1954; Spanish trans. *El régimen de Santander*, Bogotá, 1966.
  'Two Stages in Colombian Tariff Policy: The Radical Era and the
     Return to Protection, 1861–1885', *Inter-American Economic Affairs*,
     9 (1956).
Bustamante, D., 'Efectos económicos del papel moneda durante la Regen-
     eración', *Cuadernos Colombianos*, no. 4 (1974).
Caballero, L., *Memoria de la Guerra de los Mil Días*, Bogotá, 1939.
Caja Agraria, *Manual de costos*, Bogotá, 1939.
Calderón, C., *La cuestión monetaria en Colombia*, Madrid, 1905.
Calderón, C. and E. Britton, *Colombia, 1893*, New York, 1893.
Calderón, F. U., *Fiebre amarilla en la Provincia de Cúcuta*, Bogotá, 1897.
Camacho, J., *Estudios económicos*, Bogotá, 1903.
Camacho Roldán, S., *Escritos varios*, 2 vols., Bogotá, 1892.
  Memorias, 2 vols., Bogotá, 1923; 2nd edn, 2 vols., 1946.
  Notas de viaje, Bogotá, 1890.
Cardoso, F. H., 'Dependency and Development in Latin America', *New
     Left Review*, 74 (July–August 1972), 83–95.
Cardoso, F. H. and E. Faletto, *Desarrollo y dependencia en América
     Latina*, Mexico City, 1969.
Caro, M. A., *Apuntes sobre crédito, deuda pública y papel moneda*, Bogotá,
     1892.
  El Centenario de 'El Tradicionista', ed. C. Andrade Valderrama, Bogotá,

De censos redimidos pertenecientes a capellanías, Bogotá, 1890.

Carr, R., *Spain, 1808–1939*, Oxford, 1966.

Carriazo, M., *Llanos Orientales*, Bogotá, 1910.

Chayanov, A. V., *The Theory of Peasant Economy*, Homewood, Ill., 1966.

Cheung, S. N. S., 'Private Property Rights and Sharecropping', *Journal of Political Economy*, 76 (1968).

Chevelier L., *Classes laborieuses et classes dangereuses à Paris pendant la première moitié du XIXe siècle*, Paris, 1958.

Chu, D. S. C., *The Great Depression and Industrialization in Colombia*, Rand Paper Series, Santa Monica, Calif., 1977 (mimeographed).

Cisneros, F. J., *Report on the Construction of a Railway from Puerto Berrío to Barbosa (State of Antioquia)*, New York, 1878.

Colmenares, G., 'Censos y capellanías: formas de crédito en una economía agrícola', *Cuadernos Colombianos*, no. 2 (1974).

Historia económica y social de Colombia, 1537–1719, Cali, 1973.

Colombia: relación geográfica, topográfica, agrícola, comercial y política de este país, 2nd edn, 2 vols., Bogotá, 1974.

Comisión Corográfica, *Geografía física y política de las provincias de la Nueva Granada*, 2nd edn, 4 vols., Bogotá, 1957–9.

Comité Central del Partido Comunista, *Treinta años de lucha del Partido Comunista*, Bogotá, 1960.

Conrad, A. H. and J. R. Meyer, 'The Economics of Slavery in the Antebellum South', *Journal of Political Economy*, 66 (1958), 95–130.

Cordovez Moure, J. M., *Reminiscencias de Sante Fé y Bogotá*, Madrid, 1957.

Correa, R., *Estudios sobre notariato y registro*, Bogotá, 1929.

Cortés, E., *Escritos varios*, Paris, 1896.

Crisis monetaria: artículos aparecidos en 'El Relator', Bogotá, 1892.

Cuervo, A., *Cómo se evapora un ejército*, Paris, 1900.

Cuervo Márquez, L., *Geografía médica y patológica de Colombia*, Bogotá, 1915.

Currie, L., *La industria cafetera en la agricultura colombiana*, Bogotá, 1962.

Deas, M., 'A Colombian Coffee Estate: Santa Bárbara, Cundinamarca, 1870–1912', in K. Duncan and I. Rutledge (eds.), *Land and Labour in Latin America* (Cambridge, 1977), pp. 269–98.

'Algunas notas sobre la historia del caciquismo en Colombia', *Revista de Occidente*, no. 127 (1973), 118–40.

'Poverty, Civil War and Politics: Ricardo Gaitán Obeso and his Magdalena River Campaign in Colombia, 1885' (forthcoming).

Debray, R., *La crítica de las armas*, 2 vols., Mexico City, 1975.

Delgado, E., *Memoria sobre el cultivo del café en el municipio de Popayán*, Popayán, 1867.

Díaz Díaz, F., *La desamortización de bienes eclesiásticos en Boyacá*, Tunja, 1977.

Dix, R. H., *Colombia: The Political Dimensions of Change*, New Haven, Conn., 1967.

Domínguez Ortíz, A., *Sociedad y Estado en el siglo XVIII español*, Barcelona, 1976.

Dos Palabras, Fresno, 1892.

Dunning, J. H., 'Capital Movements in the Twentieth Century', in Dunning (ed.), *International Investment*, London, 1972.

Dupuy, J. J., *Estudio sobre organización y defensa de la industria cafetera en Colombia*, Bogotá, 1929.

Duque Gómez, L. and J. Jaramillo Uribe, *Historia de Pereira*, Pereira, 1963.

Echavarría, E., *Crónicas de la industria bancaria de Antioquia*, Medellín, 1946.

ECLA, *Analyses and Projections of Economic Development*, vol. 3: *The Economic Development of Colombia*, 1957 (E/CN 12/365 Rev. 1).

ECLA/FAO, *Coffee in Latin America: Productivity Problems and Future Prospects*, vol. 1: *Colombia and El Salvador*, 1958 (E/CN 12/490).

Eder, J. P., *Colombia*, London, 1913.

El Fundador, Bogotá, 1959.

Escritos de dos economistas coloniales: don Antonio de Narváez y la Torre y don José I. de Pombo, 2nd edn, Bogotá, 1965.

Estrada, M. A., *Historia documentada de los primeros cuatro años de vida del Estado de Santander, 1857–1861*, Maracaibo, 1896.

Fabo, Padre Fr., *Historia de la ciudad de Manizales*, Manizales, 1926.

Fajardo, D., 'La violencia y las estructuras agrarias en tres municipios cefeteros del Tolima, 1933–1970', in F. Leal et al., *El agro en el desarrollo histórico colombiano*, Bogotá, 1977.

Fals Borda, O., *Campesinos de los Andes: estudio sociológico de Saucío*, 2nd edn, Bogotá, 1961.

El hombre y la tierra en Boyacá, 2nd edn, Bogotá, 1973.

Febres Cordero, L., *Del antiguo Cúcuta*, 2nd edn, Bogotá, 1975.

FEDESARROLLO, *Las industrias azucarera y panelera en Colombia*, Bogotá, 1976.

Fernandes, F. et al., *Las clases sociales en América Latina*, Mexico City, 1973.

Findley, R. W., 'Ten Years of Land Reform in Colombia', *Wisconsin Law Review*, no. 3 (1972).

Florescano, E. (ed.), *Haciendas plantaciones y latifundios en América Latina*, Mexico City, 1975.

Fluharty, V. L., *Dance of Millions: Military Rule and the Social Revolution in Colombia, 1930–1956*, Pittsburgh, Pa., 1957.

Flye, O. L., 'Mis impresiones de la Sierra Nevada de Santa Marta', *Revista Pan*, no. 3 (1935).

Fogel, R. W., 'The Specification Problem in Economic History', *Journal of Economic History*, 27 (1967), 283–308.

Food and Agriculture Organization (FAO), *The World's Coffee*, Rome, 1947.

The World Coffee Economy, Commodity Bulletin Series, 33, Rome, 1961.

Friede, J., *El indio en la lucha por la tierra*, Bogotá, 1944.

Führmann, O. and E. Mayor, *Voyage d'exploration scientifique en Colombie*, 2 vols., Neuchâtel, 1914.

Furtado, C., *Development and Underdevelopment*, Berkeley, Calif., 1964.

Formación económica del Brasil, Mexico City, 1962.

Gaitán, A., *Porqué cayó el Partido Conservador*, Bogotá, 1935.

Gaitán, G., *Colombia: la lucha por la tierra en la década del treinta*, Bogotá, 1976.

Galán Gómez, M., *Geografía económica de Colombia: Santander*, Bucaramanga, 1947.

Galindo, A., *Estudios económicos y fiscales*, Bogotá, 1880.

Historia económica i estadística de la hacienda nacional, desde la Colonia hasta nuestros días, Bogotá, 1874.

Recuerdos históricos, 1840–1895, Bogotá, 1900.

Garavito Armero, F., 'Conferencias', *Diario Oficial*, 9–20 June 1903.

García, A., *Gaitan y problema de la revolución colombiana*, Bogotá, 1955.

Geografía económica de Caldas, Bogotá, 1937.

Pasado y presente del indio, Bogotá, 1939.

García, J. H., *En la tierra de Robledo*, Caracas, 1908.

García, J. J., *Crónicas de Bucaramanga*, Bogotá, 1896.

Gaviria Toro, J., *Antioquia: monografías: Caldas–Fredonia*, Medellín, 1923.

Geer, T., *An Oligopoly: The World Coffee Economy and Stabilization Schemes*, New York, 1971.

Gilhòdes, P., 'Agrarian Struggles in Colombia', in R. Stavenhagen (ed.), *Agrarian Problems and Peasant Movements in Latin America*, New York, 1970.

La question agraire en Colombie, Paris, 1974.

Gilmore, R. L. and J. P. Harrison, 'Juan Bernardo Elbers and the Introduction of Steam Navigation on the Magdalena River', *Hispanic American Historical Review*, 28 (August 1948).

Glade, W. P., *The Latin American Economies: A Study of the Institutional Evolution*, New York, 1969.

Gómez Barrientos, E., *Don Mariano Ospina y su época*, 2 vols., Medellín, 1913–15.

Griffin, K., *The Political Economy of Agrarian Change*, London, 1974.

Guerrero, G. S., *Remembranzas políticas*, Pasto, 1921.

Guhl, E., *Colombia: bosquejo de su geografía tropical*, Rio de Janeiro, 1967.

'El aspecto económico–social del cultivo del café en Antioquia', *Revista Colombiana de Antropología*, no. 1 (1953).

Guhl, E. et al., *Caldas: memoria explicativa del 'Atlas' socio-económico del Departamento*, 2 vols., Bogotá, 1956–7.

Gutierrez, R., *Monografías*, 2 vols., Bogotá, 1920–1.

Gutierrez de Pineda, V., *Familia y cultura en Colombia*, 2nd edn, Bogotá, 1975.

Guzmán Campos, G. et al., *La violencia en Colombia*, 2 vols., Bogotá, 1962–4.

Hall, C., *El café y el desarrollo histórico–geográfico de Costa Rica*, San José, 1976.

Havens, E. and W. C. Flinn, *Internal Colonialism and Structural Change in Colombia*, New York, 1970.

Helguera, J. L., 'Antecedentes sociales de la Revolución de 1851 en el sur de Colombia (1848–1849)', *Anuario Colombiano de Historia Social y de la Cultura*, no. 5 (1970).

Hernandez Rodríguez, G., *De los Chibchas á la Colonia y á la República*, Bogotá, 1949.

Hinsley, F. H. (ed.), *The New Cambridge Modern History*, vol. 11: *Material Progress and World-Wide Problems, 1870–98*, Cambridge, 1962.

Hirschmann, A., *Journeys toward progress*, New York, 1963.

Hobsbawm, E., *The Age of Capital*, London, 1976.

Holguín, J., *Desde cerca: asuntos colombianos*, Paris, 1908.

Holguín Arboleda, J., *Mucho en serio y algo en broma*, Bogotá, 1959.
    21 años de vida colombiana, Bogotá, 1967.

Holloway, T. H., 'The Coffee *Colono* of São Paulo, Brazil: Migration and Mobility, 1880–1930', in K. Duncan and I. Rutledge (eds.), *Land and Labour in Latin America* (Cambridge, 1977), pp. 301–21.

Humboldt, A., *Viaje a las regiones equinocciales del nuevo continente*, Paris, 1826.

Instituto Colombiano de la Reforma Agraria, *Información sobre costos de producción*, Bogotá, 1968 (mimeographed).

International Bank for Reconstruction and Development, *The Basis of a Development Program for Colombia*, Washington, 1950.
    Economic Growth of Colombia: Problems and Prospects, Baltimore and London, 1972.

International Coffee Organization, *Coffee in Colombia* (document JAP/cp/mh), London, 30 July 1973 (mimeographed).

Jacob, H. E., *Coffee: The Epic of a Commodity*, New York, 1935.

Jaramillo Sierra, B., *Pepe Sierra: el método de un campesino millonario*, Medellín, 1947.

Jaramillo Uribe, J., *El pensamiento colombiano en el siglo XIX*, Bogotá, 1964.
    'Historia de Pereira, 1863–1963', in L. Duque Gómez and J. Jaramillo Uribe, *Historia de Pereira*, Pereira, 1963.

Johnson, D. G., 'Resource Allocation under Share Contracts', *Journal of Political Economy*, 58, 2 (1950).

Joslin, D., *A Century of Banking in Latin America*, Oxford, 1963.

Junguito, R., *Objetivos de la política cafetera colombiana*, Bogota, 1974 (mimeographed).

Kastos, E. [J. de D. Restrepo], *Artículos escogidos*, 2nd edn, Bogotá, 1972

Krasner, S. D., 'Business–Government Relations: The Case of the International Coffee Agreement', *International Organization*, no. 4 (1973

Kula, W., *La théorie économique du système féodal*, Paris, 1970.

Latorre Cabal, H., *Mi novela: apuntes autobiográficos de Alfonso López*, Bogotá, 1961.

Lemaitre, E., *Panamá y su separación de Colombia*, Bogotá, 1972.
    Rafael Reyes: biografía de un gran colombiano, Bogotá, 1967.

Lewis, W. A. (ed.), *Tropical Development, 1880–1913*, London, 1970.

Liberalismo en el gobierno, 1930–1946, 2 vols., Bogotá, n.d.

Liévano Aguirre, I., *El proceso de Mosquera ante el Senado*, Bogotá, 1966.

  Rafael Núñez, 2nd edn, Bogotá, 1958.

Lleras Camargo, A., *Mi gente*, Bogotá, 1975.

Lleras Restrepo, C., *Borradores para una historia de la República Liberal*, Bogotá, 1975.

  ~~Política~~ *fiscal y económica del gobierno, 1941*, Bogotá, 1941.

  nd J. A. Hanson, 'The First Venezuelan Coffee Cycle,

  Agricultural History, 44, 4 (October 1970).

  , Colombia agraria, Manizales, 1920.

López, A., *El café: desde el cultivador al consumidor*, London, 1929.

  El desarme y la usura, London, 1933.

  Problemas colombianos, Paris, 1927.

López, F., *Evolución de la tenencia de la tierra en una zona minifundista*, Bogotá, 1975 (mimeographed).

López, H., 'La inflación en Colombia en la década de los veintes', *Cuadernos Colombianos*, no. 5 (1975).

López Michelsen, A., *Cuestiones colombianas*, Mexico City, 1955.

López Toro, A., *Migración y cambio social en Antioquia durante el siglo diecinueve*, Bogotá, 1970.

McGreevey, W. P., *An Economic History of Colombia, 1845–1930*, Cambridge, 1971.

Machado, C. A., *El café: de la aparcería al capitalismo*, Bogotá, 1977.

Manuelita: una industria centenaria, 1864–1964, Bogotá, 1964.

Martínez, E., *Memoria sobre el café*, Mexico City, 1875.

Martínez, M. A., *Régimen de tierras en Colombia*, 2 vols., Bogotá, 1939.

Martínez-Alier, J., *Haciendas, Plantations and Collective Farms*, London, 1977.

  La estabilidad del latifundismo, Paris, 1968.

Martínez Santamaría, J., *Contribución al estudio de la anemia tropical en Colombia*, Bogotá, 1909.

Martínez Silva, C., *Capítulos de historia política de Colombia*, 2nd edn, 3 vols., 1973.

Maya, R., 'Mi José Asunción Silva', in J. A. Silva, *Obras completas*, Bogotá, 1955.

Melo, H. and I. López Botero, *El imperio clandestino del café*, Bogotá, 1976.

Mendoza, D., 'Ensayo sobre la evolución de la propiedad en Colombia', *Repertorio Colombiano*, 1892.

  Expedición botánica de José Celestino Mutis al Nuevo Reino de Granada, Madrid, 1909.

Merchan, V. J., 'Datos para la historia social, económica y del movimiento agrario de Viotá y El Tequendama: testimonio', *Estudios Marxistas*, nos. 9 and 10 (1975).

Miramón, A., *José A. Silva*, 2nd edn, Bogotá, 1957.

Molina, G., *Las ideas liberales en Colombia*, vol. 1: *1849–1914*, Bogotá, 1970, 2nd edn, 1971; vol. 2: *1914–1934*, Bogotá, 1974.

326   *Bibliography*

Monbeig, P., *Novos estudios de geografía humana brasileira*, São Paulo, 1957.

Pionniers et planteurs de São Paulo, Paris, 1952.

Monsalve, D., *Colombia cafetera*, Barcelona, 1927.

Monsalve, M., *Economía y estadística*, Medellín, 1929.

Montaña, F. et al., *Prescriptibilidad de los baldíos en Colombia*, Bogotá, n.d.

Montaña Cuellar, D., *Colombia: País formal, país real*, Buenos Aires, 1963.

Morales Benítez, O., *Testimonio de un pueblo*, Bogotá, 1951.

Mörner, M., *Race Mixture in the History of Latin America*, Boston, 1967.

Mosk, S. A., 'The Coffee Economy of Guatemala, 1850–1918: Development and Signs of Instability', *Inter-American Economic Affairs*, 11 (1955).

Myint, H., *The Economics of Developing Countries*, London, 1964.

Naranjo, E., *Monografía del Río Magdalena*, Bogotá, 1916.

Nelson, R., T. Schultz and R. Slighton, *Structural Change in a Developing Economy: Colombia's Problems and Prospects*, Princeton, N.J., 1971.

Nichols, T. E., *Tres puertos de Colombia*, Bogotá, 1972.

Nieto Arteta, L. E., *Economía y cultura en la historia de Colombia*, Bogotá, 1942.

El café en la sociedad colombiana, 2nd edn, Bogotá, 1971.

Núñez, R., *La reforma política en Colombia*, 2nd edn, 7 vols., Bogotá, 1944–50.

Ocampo, J. F., *Dominio de clase en la ciudad colombiana*, Medellín, 1972.

Organización Internacional del Trabajo, *Hacia el pleno empleo*, Bogotá, 1970 (trans. from English).

Ortega, A., *Ferrocarriles colombianos: resumen histórico*, 2 vols., Bogotá, 1920.

Ferrocarriles colombianos: la última experiencia ferroviaria del país, 1920–1930, Bogotá, 1932.

Ortíz, S. de, *Uncertainties in Peasant Farming: A Colombian Case*, London, 1973.

Ospina Vásquez, L., *Industria y protección en Colombia, 1810–1930*, Medellín, 1955.

'Perspectiva histórica de la economía colombiana', *Ciencias Económicas*, no. 16 (n.d.).

Ospina Vásquez, L. et al., *Historia económica de Colombia: un debate en marcha*, Bogotá (forthcoming).

Ossa, V. P., 'Terrenos baldíos en Colombia', *Boletín de la Sociedad Geográfica de Colombia*, 2 (1935).

Oviedo, B. V. de, *Cualidades y riquezas del Nuevo Reino de Granada*, 2nd edn, Bogotá, 1930.

Palacio, J. H., *Historia de mi vida*, Bogotá, 1942.

Palacios, M., 'Las condiciones de la oferta de café (1870–1930): una crítica sociohistórica al modelo empleado por W. P. McGreevey', in L. Ospina Vásquez et al., *Historia económica de Colombia: un debate en marcha*, Bogotá (forthcoming).

Pardo Umaña, C., *Haciendas de la Sabana: su historia, sus leyendas y tradiciones*, Bogotá, 1946.

París Lozano, G., *Geografía económica del Tolima*, Bogotá, 1946.

Parks, E. T., *Colombia and the United States, 1765–1934*, Newark, N.J., 1935; 2nd edn, New York, 1970.

Parra, A., *Memorias de Aquileo Parra, Presidente de Colombia de 1876 á 1878*, Bogotá, 1912.

Parsons, J. J., *The Antioqueño Colonization in Western Colombia*, 2nd edn, Berkeley, Calif., 1968.

Pearse, A. S., *Colombia with Special Reference to Cotton*, London, 1926.

Pecaut, D., *Política y sindicalismo en Colombia*, Bogotá, 1973.

Peláez, C. M., *Essays on Coffee and Economic Development*, Rio de Janeiro, 1973.

Peña, H., *Geografía é historia de la Provincia del Quindío*, Popayán, 1892.

Pérez, F., *Jeografía física i política del Estado de Santander*, 3rd edn, 2 vols., Bogotá, 1863.

Pérez Triana, S., *Eslabones sueltos*, London, 1907.

Petre, F. L., *The Republic of Colombia*, London, 1906.

Pizano, M. A., *Navegación del Magdalena*, Bogotá, 1886.

Platt, D. C. M., *Latin America and British Trade, 1806–1914*, London, 1972.

Pombo, M., 'Viaje entre Medellín y Bogotá en 1851 á lomo de buey', *Obras inéditas*, Bogotá, 1914.

Posada, F., *Colombia: violencia y subdesarrollo*, Bogotá, 1969.

Poveda Ramos, G., *Antioquia y el Ferrocaril de Antioquia*, Medellín, 1974.

Prado, C., jun., *Historia económica do Brasil*, 2nd edn, São Paulo, 1969.

Quijano Wallis, J. M., *Memorias autobiográficas, historico–políticas y de carácter social*, Rome, 1919.

Quimbaya, Anteo, *El problema de la tierra en Colombia*, Bogotá, 1967.

Quiñones Neira, R., *Manuel Murillo Toro*, Bogotá, 1936.

Ramirez Hoyos, J. L., *La industria cafetera*, Bogotá, 1937.

Ramos, A., *O café no Brasil e no estrangeiro*, Rio de Janeiro, 1923.

Reichel-Dolmatoff, Alicia and Gerardo, *The Aritama People*, London, 1961.

Restrepo, J. M. et al., *Memorias sobre el cultivo del café*, Bogotá, 1952.

Restrepo, M., *El rey de la leña*, Buenos Aires, 1958.

Restrepo Echavarría, E., *Una excurción al territorio de San Martín*, 2nd edn, Bogotá, 1957.

Rippy, J. F., *Capitalists and Colombia*, New York, 1931.

    'Dawn of the Railway Era in Colombia', *Hispanic American Historical Review*, 23 (August 1943).

Rivadeneira, A. J., *Don Santiago Pérez: Biografía de un carácter*, Bogotá, 1967.

Rivas, M., *Los trabajadores de tierra caliente*, 2nd edn, Bogotá, 1972.

    Obras: segunda parte, 2 vols., Bogotá, 1885.

Rodríguez, O., 'On the Conception of the Centre–Periphery System', *CEPAL Review*, 1977.

Rodríguez Maldonado, C., *Hacienda Tena, 1543–1943*, Bogotá, 1944.

Rodríguez Piñeres, E., Diez años de política liberal, 1892–1902, Bogotá, 1952.

El olimpo radical, Bogotá, 1950.

Rodríguez Plata, H., La inmigración alemana al Estado Soberano de Santander en el siglo XIX, Bogotá, 1968.

Romero, M., Cultivo del café en la costa meridional de Chiapas, Mexico City, 1875.

Röthlisberger, E., El Dorado: estampas de viaje y cultura de la Colombia suramericana, 2nd edn, Bogotá, 1963.

Rowe, J. W., The World's Coffee, London, 1963.

Rueda Vargas, T., La sabana de Bogotá, Bogotá, 1919.

Sabogal, J., Fusagasugá: historia y geografía, Bogotá, 1919.

Safford, F. R., The Ideal of the Practical, Austin, Texas, 1976.

'Empresarios nacionales y extranjeros en Colombia durante el siglo XIX', Anuario Colombiano de Historia Social y de la Cultura, no. 4 (1969).

'Significado de los antioqueños en el desarrollo económico colombiano: un examen crítico de las tesis de Everett Hagen', Anuario Colombiano de Historia Social y de la Cultura, no. 3 (1965), 49–69.

Salazar, M., Proceso histórico de la propiedad en Colombia, Bogotá, 1948.

Samper, A., Importancia del café en el comercio exterior de Colombia, Bogotá, 1948.

Samper, J. M., Derecho público interno de Colombia, 2nd edn, 2 vols., Bogotá, 1974.

Ensayo sobre las revoluciones políticas, Paris, 1861.

Samper, M., Escritos politico–económicos, 4 vols., Bogotá, 1925–6.

La miseria en Bogotá y otros escritos, 2nd edn, Bogotá, 1969.

Sanín Cano, B., Administración Reyes, 1904–1909, Lausanne, 1909.

Santa, E., Arrieros y fundadores, Bogotá, 1961.

Rafael Uribe Uribe, Bogotá, 1968.

Santamaría, E., Conversaciones familiares, Le Havre, 1871.

Sanz de Santamaría, C., Una época difícil, Bogotá, 1965.

Schenk, F. von, Viajes por Antioquia en el año 1880, 2nd edn, Bogotá, 1952.

Schickele, R., 'Effect of Tenure Systems on Agricultural Efficiency', Journal of Farm Economics, 23 (1941).

Schurmann, F., Ideology and Organization in Communist China, 2nd edn, Berkeley, Calif., 1968.

Seidel, R., 'American Reformers Abroad: The Kemmerer Mission in South America, 1923–1931', Journal of Economic History, 32, 3 (1972).

Serrano, F., 'La industria del café en Santander', FNCC, Revista Cafetera de Colombia, nos. 38–9 (May–June 1932).

Shanin, T., The Awkward Class, Oxford, 1972

Shanin, T. (ed.), Peasants and Peasant Societies, London, 1971.

Sierra, L. F., El tabaco en la economía colombiana del siglo XIX, Bogotá, 1971.

Silva, J. A., Obras completas, Bogotá, 1955.

Silvestre, F., Descripción del Reino de Santa Fé de Bogotá, 2nd edn, Bogot 1968.

Smith, T. L., *Colombia: Social Structure and the Process of Development*, Gainesville, Fla., 1967.

Springett, L. E., *Quality Coffee*, New York, 1935.

Stein, S., *Vassouras: A Brazilian Coffee County, 1850–1900*, Cambridge, Mass., 1957.

Streeten, P. and D. Elsan, *Diversification and Development: The Case of Coffee*, New York, 1971.

Suárez, M. F., *Obras*, vol. 2, Bogotá, 1966.

Thompson, R., *Informe sobre una excurción á la Sierra Nevada de Santa Marta para investigar sus capacidades agrícolas*, Barranquilla, 1895.

Thuber, F. B., *Coffee: From Plantation to Cup*, New York, 1885.

Tirado Mejía, A., *Introducción a la historia económica de Colombia*, Bogotá, 1971.

Tirado Mejía, A. (ed.), *Aspectos sociales de las guerras civiles*, Bogotá, 1976.

Torres, E., *Geografía del Departamentos del Tolima*, Ibagué, 1923.

Torres García, G., *Historia de la moneda en Colombia*, Bogotá, 1945.

Torres Giraldo, I., *Los inconformes*, 5 vols., Bogotá, 1973–4.

Triana, M., *Al Meta*, Bogotá, 1913.

Tovar, H., *El movimiento campesino en Colombia*, Bogotá, 1975.

Triffin, R., 'La moneda y las instituciones bancarias en Colombia', *Revista del Banco de la República*, no. 202, supp. (August 1944).

Ukers, W., *All about coffee*, New York, 1935.

Coffee Merchandising, New York, 1924.

Uribe Angel, M., *Geografía general y compendio histórico del Estado de Antioquia*, Paris, 1885.

Uribe Uribe, R., *Discursos parlamentarios*, Bogotá, 1896; 2nd edn, 1897.

Por la América del Sur, 2 vols., Bogotá, 1908.

Estudios sobre café, Bogotá, 1952.

Urrutia, M., *Historia del sindicalismo en Colombia*, Bogotá, 1969.

'El sector externo y la distribución de ingresos en Colombia en el siglo XIX', *Revista del Banco de la República*, no. 541 (November 1972).

'Nota sobre los cambios históricos en la participación del ingreso nacional de los grupos más acaudalados en Colombia', *Revista del Banco de la República*, no. 516 (1970).

Urrutia, M. and M. Arrubla (eds.), *Compendio de estadísticas históricas de Colombia*, Bogotá, 1970.

Urrutia, M. and A. Berry, *La distribución del ingreso en Colombia*, Medellín, 1975.

Valderrama Andrade, C. (ed.), M. A. Caro, *El Centenario de 'El Tradicionista'*, Bogotá, 1972.

Valencia Zapata, A., *Quindío histórico: monografía de Armenia*, Armenia, 1955.

Van Delden Laërne, C. F., *Brazil and Java: Report on Coffee-Culture in America, Asia and Africa*, London, 1885.

Vargas Reyes, A., *Memoria sobre las quinas de la Nueva Granada*, Bogotá, 1850.

Vergara y Velasco, F. J., *Nueva geografía de Colombia*, 2nd edn, 3 vols., Bogotá, 1974.

Vergopoulos, K., 'Capitalisme difforme (le cas de l'agriculture dans le capitalisme)', in S. Amin and K. Vergopoulos, *La question paysanne et le capitalisme*, 2nd edn, Paris, 1977.
Vilar, P., *Crecimiento y desarrollo*, Barcelona, 1964.
Walker, E. R., 'Beyond the Market', in K. W. Rothschild (ed.), *Power in Economics* (London, 1971), pp. 36–55.
Weitz, R., *From Peasant to Farmer: A Revolutionary Strategy for Development*, New York, 1971.
Wellman, F. L., *Coffee: Botany, Cultivation and Utilization*, London, 1961
Wickizer, V. D., *Coffee, Tea and Cocoa*, Stanford, Calif., 1951.
  The World Coffee Economy, with Special Reference to Control Schemes Stanford, Calif., 1943.
Zuleta, L. A., 'El sector cafetero y los fenómenos inflacionarios', *Cuadernos Colombianos*, no. 7 (1975), 431–524.
Zuleta Angel, E., *El Presidente López*, Bogotá, 1966; 2nd edn, 1968.

(*b*) UNPUBLISHED THESES
Abel, C., 'Conservative Party in Colombia, 1930–1953', D. Phil. thesis, Oxford University, 1974.
Arocha, J., '"La Violencia" in Monteverde, Colombia: Environmental and Economic Determinants of Homicide in a Coffee-Growing Municipio' Ph.D. thesis, Columbia University, 1975.
Bergquist, C., 'Coffee and Conflict in Colombia, 1886–1904: Origins and Outcome of the War of the Thousand Days', Ph.D. thesis, Stanford University, 1973.
Beyer, R. C., 'The Colombian Coffee Industry: Origins and Major Trends, 1740–1940', Ph.D. thesis, University of Minnesota, 1947.
Brew, R. J., 'The Economic Development of Antioquia from 1850 to 1920' D.Phil. thesis, Oxford University, 1973.
Christie, K. H., 'Oligarchy and Society in Caldas–Colombia', D.Phil. thesis, Oxford University, 1974.
Gaitán, G., 'Causas de la presencia de los movimientos agrarios en el occidente de Cundinamarca y el oriente del Tolima y su incidencia en el cambio de la tenencia de la tierra', B.A. thesis, Universidad de los Andes, 1970.
Johnson, D. C., 'Social and Economic Change in Nineteenth Century Santander, Colombia', Ph.D. thesis, University of California at Berkeley, 1975.
Koffman, B. E., 'The National Federation of Coffee-Growers of Colombia', Ph.D. thesis, University of Virginia, 1969.
Lleras de la Fuente, F., 'El café: antecedentes generales y expansión hasta 1914', B.A. thesis, Universidad de los Andes, 1970.
Oquist, P., 'Violence, Conflict and Politics in Colombia', Ph.D. thesis, University of California at Berkeley, 1976.
Palacios, M., 'Coffee in Colombia: Its Economic, Social and Political History, 1870–1970', D.Phil. thesis, Oxford University, 1977.
Safford, F. R., 'Commerce and Enterprise in Central Colombia, 1821–1870', Ph.D. thesis, Columbia University, 1965.
White, J., 'The United Fruit Company in the Santa Marta Banana Zone, Colombia: Conflicts of the 20's', B.Phil. thesis, Oxford University, 1971.

Index

Acerías Paz del Río, 225
accompanying products, 18
adjudicatarios, 175–8
African coffee, 224–5
Agrarian Commission, 187
agrarian policies, 247–8
agraristas, 247–8
agregados, 82–3
agricultural congresses, 218
agricultural machinery, 152
agricultural modernization, 225
agricultural production, 209
agricultural structure, 12
agriculture: capitalist and peasant sectors, 243–6
agronomy, 285 n.36
aguardiente: entrepreneurs, 31; smuggling, 112, 287–8 n.17
alcoholism in coffee zones, 112
Almacenes Generales de Depósito, 220, 224
American Civil War, 7
American Coffee Co., 205
Amsinck, 40, 42, 205
Anglo-South American Bank, 205
Antilles, 15, 229
Antioquia: agrarian ideologies, 13–14; bourgeois values, 136; colonization, 13–14, 161–97, 228, 233, 235; Conservatives, 2, 129; depulpers, 153; financial conditions, 41–2; financial crisis, 295–6 n.28; FNCC, 219; foundries, 152; monopsonies, 154–60; pioneering haciendas, 41–2; population, 180; public lands, 175–9; social conflict, 178–9; types of coffee hacienda, 78–80, 82; workers on haciendas, 102
Aranda, 166
Arboleda, J., 2, 27
archbishop primate, 210–11
Armenia colonization, 180–1, 186–8, 190–1
arrendamiento, 13, 81–2, 115–17
arrendatarios, 98–9; conflicts, 114–19; deflation, 117–18; discontent, 117;

economic functions, 113; as employers, 116–18; 'feudalism', 114–15; income, 112–13, 116–17; *jornaleros*, 114–16; kulaks, 113–14; land rents, 116–17; restrictions, 113–14; status, 112; strikes, 119; turnover, 286 n.38
Asociación Nacional de Industriales, 250

balance of payments, 200, 215, 225
Balmaceda, F. J., 167
bananas, 147
Banco Central, 147, 293 n.19
Banco de Bogotá, 28, 51
Banco de Colombia, 28–9
Banco de Exportadores, 54
Banco de la República, 146, 207, 221–3, 251, 305 n.23
Banco del Tequendama, 277 n.53
Banco Francés e Italiano, 51–2
Banco Hipotecario del Estado de Cundinamarca, 277 n.53
Banco López, 204, 295 n.51
Banco Mercantil de las Américas, 205, 295 nn.51, 56
Banco Nacional, 10, 123, 126, 142, 147
Banco Ruíz, 204
Banco Sucre, 160, 204
bankruptcies, 8, 203–4
banks, 28–9, 121, 126, 211, 306 n.29, 309 n.77; London and River Plate, 295 n.51; National City, 205, 295 n.51; *see also individual banks*
Belalcazar colonization, 188–9
Beyer, R. C., 130
Bogotá, 4, 17–18, 28, 30, 53, 170–1, 208, 219, 273–4 n.7
Bolívar, S., 15
botany, 91–2, 285 n.36
Botero, Luis M. & Sons, 154
Bourbons, 16, 166
bourgeoisie, 31–3, 129; and the state, 125, 211
Boyacá, 69–70
Brazil, 15; coffee expansion, 129–30; coffee policies, 220–1, 224, 230;

331

internal split, 284 n.20; land policies, 56–9; 'minorities law', 142; moderation, 29; 'new class', 26–7; in opposition, 127–8, (1936) 307–8 n.57; peasant agitations, 117–19; populism, 211; public lands, 184; 'Republic', 216–17; Santander, 269 n.8; socialism, 71–2; state, 201; youth, 10
Llanos de San Martín, 168
Lleras Camargo, A., 151
Lleras Restrepo, C., 117, 288 n.28, 309 n.86
López, Alejandro, 220–2
López, Pedro A., 137, 274 n.7; & Co., 155, 204
López Pumarejo, A., 14, 119, 205, 216–17, 219–22, 289 n.35
Lorenzana & Montoya, 297 n.16

McGreevey, W. P., 44–5, 130, 173, 269 n.4
Magdalena, 285 n.37
Magdalena river navigation, 4
malaria, 73–4
Manizales: cableway, 195; coffee, 196, (brands) 220–1; colonization, 182–5; elite, 183–4; money, 203; population, 180; social problems, 195–6; transport, 195
Manzanares colonization, 188–9
Maracaibo, Lake, 15
'Maracaibo' brand, 19
marginal productivity, 228
marijuana, 258
marketing, 143, 148, 153, 155, 206, 219–20, 222
markets for coffee, 123, 141, 154, 212
Márquez, Ignacio de, 145
Marroquín, J. M., 27, 145, 284 n.20
Marshall Plan, 224
Marxism, 1, 211, 217, 242–3, 304 n.7, 312 nn.27, 29
Mejía, Manuel, 295 n.48
mejoras, 90, 117–18, 186, 286 n.39
Mendoza, Diego, 167
Meta, 298 n.22
Mexico, 15, 29
Mexico Agreement, 1958, 252
middle classes, 211
milds, 18, 220–1
Minas Gerais, 143
minifundista crisis in central highlands, 68–71

mining legislation, 147
Ministry of Agriculture, 217
modernization, 210; 'modern' techniques, 235
monetarists, 203
money wages, 105–6
monopsonies, 141, 153, 249; American, 203, 205; control, 202; freights, 149; as intermediaries, 160; risks, 154–5; organization, 154–60
Monsalve, Diego, 310 n.1
Montoya y Sáenz, 8, 203
moralist interpretation of *arrendatario*'s status, 288 n.18
Moreno & Walker, 183
mortgage risks, 38, 49–53
Mory Velarde, 13
Mosquera, T. C., 27, 183, 274 n.11
municipal committees of FNCC, 219
municipalities, 74–6
municipal patriotism, 172, 186
Murillo, T. M., 26, 270 n.8
Murray, Thomas, 297 n.16

national debt, 129, 201, 204, 215, 306 n.37
National Front, 249–50
national integration, 135, 209
nationalism, 144
nation state, 9–11, 257
natural fertility, 92, 235, 236–8
navigation, 4, 149, 225, 294 n.31
Negocio X and Y, 155–60, 206, 255
neo-colonial capitalism, 200
Nieto Arteta, L. E., 166, 296 n.5
Norte de Santander, 14–23, 310 n.5
Núñez, R., 9–10, 18, 125–6, 135–6, 142, 147, 284 n.20, 289 nn.1, 3, 292 n.6

Obando, J. M., 2
occupational structure, 213
Olavide, 166
Olaya Herrera, E., 14
old families, 67
oligarchy: corruption, 151; economic rationality, 30–1; formation, 25–42; local and national, 131, 209–11
Ospina, Pedro N., 33, 291 n.29, 306 n.28
Ospina family, 205
Ospina Hermanos, 30–3, 41–2, 54, 275 n.26, 277 n.60, 299 n.40
Ospina Pérez, M., 166, 216, 221–2,

CAMBRIDGE LATIN AMERICAN STUDIES

General editor: Malcolm Deas

Advisory Committee: Werner Baer, Marvin Bernstein, Al Stepan and Bryan Roberts